McGraw-Hill Education
CONQUERING
ACT
English, Reading, and Writing

THIRD EDITION | Steven W. Dulan

New York   Chicago   San Francisco   Athens   London   Madrid   Mexico City
Milan   New Delhi   Singapore   Sydney   Toronto

1 2 3 4 5 6 7 8 9 RHR 21 20 19 18 17 16

ISBN: 978-1-259-83733-3
MHID: 1-259-83733-5

e-ISBN: 978-1-259-83734-0
e-MHID: 1-259-83734-3

Library of Congress Control Number: 2011928666

McGraw-Hill Education books are available at special quantity discounts to use as premiums and sales promotions or for use in corporate training programs. To contact a representative, please visit the Contact Us pages at www.mhprofessional.com.

ACT is a registered trademark of ACT, Inc., which was not involved in the production of, and does not endorse, this product.

CONTENTS

ABOUT THE AUTHOR

Steven W. Dulan, J.D., has been involved with ACT preparation since 1989, when, as a former U.S. Army Infantry Sergeant, and undergraduate student at Michigan State University, Steve became an ACT instructor. He has been helping students to prepare for success on the ACT, PSAT, SAT, and other standardized exams ever since. Steve scored in the 99th percentile on every standardized test he has ever taken.

After graduating from Michigan State University, Steve attended The Thomas M. Cooley Law School on a full Honors Scholarship. While attending law school, Steve continued to teach standardized test prep classes (including ACT, SAT, PSAT, GRE, GMAT, and LSAT) an average of 30 hours each week, and tutored some of his fellow law students in a variety of subjects and in essay exam writing techniques. Steve has also served as an instructor at Baker University, Cleary University, Lansing Community College, The Ohio State University–Real Estate Institute, and The Thomas M. Cooley Law School. Guest lecturer credits include Michigan State University, University of Michigan, Detroit College of Law, Marquette University, Texas Technical University, University of Miami, and Wright State University.

Thousands of students have benefited from Steve's instruction, coaching, and admissions consulting, and have secured entry to the colleges and universities of their choice. Steve's students have gained admission to some of the most prestigious institutions of higher learning in the world, and have received numerous scholarships of their own. Since 1997, Steve has served as the president of Advantage Education® (www.AdvantageEd.com), a company dedicated to providing effective and affordable test prep education in a variety of settings, including one-on-one tutoring via the Internet worldwide using its Personal Distance Learning® system. The information and techniques included in this book are the result of Steve's experiences with test preparation students at all levels over many years.

ACKNOWLEDGMENTS

I would like to acknowledge the outstanding contribution of the faculty and staff of Advantage Education. Your hard work and dedication have made this endeavor a success. You are not only the smartest, but also the best.

Special thanks must be given to the following Advantage Education faculty and staff members: Aishah Ali, Lisa DiLiberti, Amy Dulan, Ryan Particka, Andrew Sanford, Alexander Savinov, and Amanda Thatcher.

INTRODUCTION

ABOUT THE ACT

The ACT is the fastest-growing and most widely accepted college entrance exam in the United States. It is designed to assess high school students' general educational development and their ability to complete college-level work. The authors of the ACT insist that the ACT is an achievement test, not a direct measure of abilities. It is not an IQ test, nor is it a measure of your worth as a human being. It is not even a perfect measure of how well you will do in college. Theoretically, each of us has a specific potential to learn and acquire skills. The ACT doesn't measure your natural, inborn ability. If it did, we wouldn't be as successful as we are at raising students' scores on ACT exams.

The ACT actually measures a certain knowledge base and skill set. It is "trainable," meaning that you can do better on your ACT if you work on learning the knowledge and gaining the skills that are tested.

STRUCTURE OF THE ACT

The ACT is broken up into four multiple-choice tests for a total of 215 questions, with one optional essay. The multiple-choice tests are called English, Mathematics, Reading, and Science. They are always given in the same order, with the optional essay coming after the four multiple-choice tests. There is a lot of predictability when it comes to the ACT. In fact, the current exam still has very much in common with ACT exams from past years. This means that we basically know what is going to be on your ACT in terms of question types and content.

Following is a table showing a breakdown of the question types, number of each question type, and time allotted for each section of the ACT:

ACT Structure

ENGLISH	
75 Questions 45 Minutes	
Content/Skills	**Number of Questions**
Usage/Mechanics	**40**
Punctuation	10
Grammar/Usage	12
Sentence Structure	18
Rhetorical Skills	**35**
Strategy	12
Organization	11
Style	12

MATHEMATICS	
60 Questions 60 Minutes	
Content	**Number of Questions**
Pre-Algebra and Elementary Algebra	24
Intermediate Algebra and Coordinate Geometry	18
Plane Geometry	14
Trigonometry	4

READING	
40 Questions 35 Minutes	
Passage Type	**Number of Questions**
Prose Fiction	10
Social Science	10
Humanities	10
Natural Science	10

SCIENCE	
40 Questions 35 Minutes	
Format	**Number of Questions**
Data Representation	15
Research Summaries	18
Conflicting Viewpoints	7
Content Areas: Biology, Physical Sciences, Chemistry, Physics	

Note: There are 7 passages in this section, and the order is not always as shown above. You will generally see 3 Data Representation passages, 3 Research Summaries passages, and 1 Conflicting Viewpoints passage.

WRITING TEST
ACT offers an optional 40-minute Writing Test.

Chapters 1, 8, and 15 include more information about the format and scoring of the ACT English, Reading, and Writing Tests respectively.

Scoring the ACT

Each of the multiple-choice sections of the ACT (English Test, Mathematics Test, Reading Test, Science Test) is given a score on a scale of 1 to 36. These four "scaled scores" are then averaged and rounded according to normal rounding rules to yield a Composite Score. It is this Composite Score that is most often meant when someone refers to your ACT score.

You don't have to be perfect to get a good score on the ACT. The truth is that you can miss a pretty fair number of questions and still get a score that places you in the top 1 percent of all test takers. In fact, this test is so hard and the time limit is so unrealistic for most test takers that you can get a score that is at the national average (about a 21) even if you get almost half of the questions wrong.

The practice tests in this book are simulations created by experts to replicate the question types, difficulty level, and content areas that you will find on your real ACT. The scoring worksheets provided for each test are guides to computing approximate scores. Actual ACT exams are scored from tables that are unique to each test. The actual scaled scores depend on a number of factors: the number of students who take the test, the difficulty level of the items (questions and answer choices), and the performance of all of the students who take the test. Do not get too hung up on your test scores while you practice; the idea is to learn something from each practice experience and to get used to the "look and feel" of the ACT English, Reading, and Writing tests.

Who Writes the ACT?

There is a company called ACT, Inc. that decides exactly what is going to be on your ACT exam. The experts at ACT, Inc. consult with classroom teachers at the high school and college level. They look at high school and college curricula, and they employ educators and specialized psychologists called "psychometricians" (measurers of the mind), who know a lot about the human brain and how it operates under various conditions. Later in this book, we'll lay out the details of how you will be tested so that you can get yourself ready for the "contest" on test day.

Why Do ACT Exams Exist?

Colleges use the ACT for admissions decisions and sometimes for advanced placement into certain college courses. The test is also used to make scholarship decisions. Because there are variations in grading standards and requirements among high schools around the country, the admissions departments at colleges use the ACT, in part, to help provide a standard for comparison. There are studies that reveal a fair amount of "grade inflation" at some schools; therefore, colleges cannot simply rely upon grade-point averages when evaluating academic performance.

How Do I Register for the ACT?

You should register for the ACT in advance. You do not just show up on test day with a Number 2 pencil and dive right in. The best source of information for all things ACT is, not surprisingly, the ACT web site: www.act.org. There is also a very good chance that a guidance counselor and/or pre-college counselor at your school has an ACT Registration Book, which includes all of the information that you need for your test registration.

▓▓▓ HOW TO USE THIS BOOK

This book contains general information about the ACT and chapters on English grammar, speed reading, verbal exercises, and in-format English Test and Reading Test practice questions. There is also a chapter on the optional ACT Writing Test.

In a perfect situation, you will be reading this book at least several weeks before you take your ACT exam. If that is not the case, you can still benefit from this book. You should look at the section in this chapter on General Test-Taking Strategies first, and then take the Diagnostic Tests in Chapter 2 (English), Chapter 9 (Reading), and Chapter 16 (Writing). These tests will help you to pinpoint areas of strength and weakness in your knowledge base and skill set. Even just a few hours of study and practice can have a beneficial impact on your ACT score.

If you are reading this only days before your ACT exam, it is important to mention that you should not preorder any ACT score reports. As of the writing of this book, ACT, Inc. allows you to pick and choose which scores you send out to colleges. So, you should only send scores after you have a chance to review them yourself. If your score is not acceptable, you can always retake the ACT and only send the scores from your best testing day to your schools of choice. This is especially important if you are unsure of how you will score and if you are going in with only minimum preparation.

As you work with the practice material in this book, you should be aware that it is simulated to match actual ACT verbal items. If you work through all of the material provided, you can rest assured that there won't be any surprises on test day. Be aware, though, that ACT exams are sensitive to factors such as fatigue and stress. The time of day that you take the practice tests, your surroundings, and other things going on in your life can have an impact on your scores. Don't get worried if you see some variations due to an off day or because the practice test exposed a weakness in your knowledge base or skill set. Just use the information that you gather as a tool to help you improve.

In our experience, the students who see the largest increase in their scores are the ones who put in consistent effort over time. Try to keep your frustration to a minimum if you struggle with the practice tests and aren't doing as well as you had hoped. Similarly, try to keep yourself from becoming overconfident when you have a great practice-testing day.

There is an explanation for each of the practice questions in this book. You will probably not need to read all of them. Sometimes, you can tell right away why you answered a particular question incorrectly. We have seen countless students smack themselves on the forehead and say "stupid mistake." We try to refer to these errors as "concentration errors." Everyone makes them from time to time, and you should not worry when they occur. There is a good chance that your focus will be a little better on the real test as long as you train yourself properly with the aid of this book. You should distinguish between concentration errors and any holes in your knowledge base or understanding. If you have the time, it is worth reading the explanations for any of the questions that were at all challenging for you. Sometimes, students get questions correct for the wrong reason, or because they guessed correctly. While you are practicing,

---

Study Tip

Your score will improve with practice! Decide when you are going to take the ACT and allow for sufficient practice time leading up to the test. We recommend 6–8 weeks of preparation before the test.

you should mark any questions that you want to revisit and be sure to read the explanations for them.

■■■ GENERAL TEST-TAKING INFORMATION AND STRATEGIES

Now it's time to take a look at some general test-taking information and strategies that should help you approach the ACT with confidence. We'll start by discussing the importance of acquiring the skills necessary to maximize your ACT scores, and finish with some tips on how to handle stress, before, during, and after the test. Additional chapters in the book include strategies and techniques specific to each of the ACT verbal sections.

KSA (Knowledge, Skills, Abilities)

Cognitive psychologists who study learning and thinking use the letters KSA to refer to the basic components of human performance in all human activities, from academics to athletics, playing music to playing games. The letters stand for Knowledge, Skills, and Abilities. As mentioned previously, the ACT measures a specific set of skills that can be improved through study and practice. You probably already understand this since you are reading this book. In fact, many thousands of students over the years have successfully raised their ACT scores through study and practice.

Learning Facts vs. Acquiring Skills

The human brain stores and retrieves factual knowledge a little differently from the way it acquires and executes skills. Knowledge can generally be learned quickly and is fairly durable, even when you are under stress. You learn factual information by studying, and you acquire skills through practice. There is some overlap between these actions; you will learn while you practice, and vice versa. In fact, research shows that repetition is important for both information storage and skills acquisition.

As we just mentioned, repetition is necessary to acquire and improve skills: knowing *about* a skill, or understanding how the skill should be executed, is not the same as actually *having* that skill. For instance, you might be told *about* a skill such as driving a car with a standard transmission, playing the piano, or typing on a computer keyboard. You might have a great teacher, have wonderful learning tools, and pay attention very carefully. You might *understand* everything perfectly. But, the first few times that you actually attempt the skill, you will probably make some mistakes. In fact, you will probably experience some frustration because of the gap between your understanding of the skill and your actual ability to perform the skill. Perfecting skills takes practice. When skills are repeated so many times that they can't be further improved, psychologists use the term *perfectly internalized skills*, which means that the skills are executed automatically, without any conscious thought. You need repetition to create the pathways in your brain that control your skills. Therefore, you shouldn't be satisfied with simply reading this book and then saying to yourself, "I get it." You will not reach your full ACT scoring potential unless you put in sufficient time practicing in addition to understanding and learning.

Practicing to Internalize Skills

We hope that you will internalize the skills you need for top performance on the ACT so that you don't have to spend time and energy figuring out what to do during the introduction to the exam. We are hoping that you will be well into each section while some of your less-prepared classmates are still reading the directions and trying to figure out exactly what they are supposed to be doing. We suggest that you practice sufficiently so that you develop your test-taking skills, and, specifically, good ACT-taking skills. While you practice, you should distinguish between practice that is meant to serve as a learning experience and practice that is meant to be a realistic simulation of what will happen on your actual ACT.

During practice that is meant for learning, it is okay to "cheat." You should feel free to disregard the time limits and just think about how the questions are put together; you can stop to look at the explanations included in this book. It is even okay to talk to others about what you are learning during your "learning practice." However, you also need to do some simulated testing practice, where you time yourself carefully and try to control as many variables in your environment as you can. Some research shows that you will have an easier time executing your skills and remembering information when the environment that you are testing in is similar to the environment where you studied and practiced.

There is a psychological term, *cognitive endurance*, which refers to your ability to perform difficult mental tasks over an extended period of time. Just as with your physical endurance, you can build up your cognitive endurance through training. As you prepare yourself for the ACT, you should start off with shorter practice sessions and work up to the point where you can easily do a 45-minute ACT English Test and a 35-minute Reading Test with no noticeable fatigue.

Now, let's explore the skills and strategies important to ensuring your success on the ACT.

Do the Easy Stuff First

First, you should get familiar with the format of each section of the ACT so that you can recognize passages and questions that are likely to give you trouble. The formats are covered in Chapter 1 (English), Chapter 8 (Reading), and Chapter 15 (Writing).

All of the questions on an ACT test are weighted exactly equally to one another. When you are taking the test, we suggest that you "bypass pockets of resistance." Don't get sucked into a battle with a hard question while there are still other, probably less difficult, questions waiting for you later in the section. It is a much better use of your time and energy to pick up all of the correct answers that you can early on, and then go back and work on the tougher questions.

There will be some time-consuming questions that show up early in each section that are meant to lure you into wasting time that would be better spent answering some more reasonable questions later. Don't get caught up in these. Move on and come back to them later. By the time you take the test, you will have learned to recognize the question types that are likely to give you trouble. When you see them, don't be surprised. Just recognize them and work on the easier material first. If time permits, you can always come back and work on the challenging problems in the final minutes before the proctor calls, "Time!"

This book contains specific suggestions for which question types you should probably skip. You'll also develop "likes and dislikes" while practicing, meaning you will know that certain question types are always going to be tough for you. By test day you will have done enough timed practice to develop a "feel" for how

Study Tip

It is important to note that you should not attempt any timed practice tests when you are mentally or physically exhausted. This will add unwanted stress to an already stressful situation. You must be realistic about how you spend your time and energy during the preparation process.

Study Tip

Because what is easy for some is not necessarily easy for others, do enough practice to quickly recognize the question types that will be easy for *you*. Answer those questions first, then go back to work on the more difficult questions if time allows.

long you should be spending on each question. Be flexible. Even if a question is of a type that you can usually answer easily, do not spend more time than you should on it. There is usually time to come back if you leave a question too soon. However, once you waste a second of time, you cannot get it back.

Stay "On Point"

Most *incorrect* ACT answers are incorrect because they are irrelevant. That is, they are beyond the scope of the English and Reading Test passages. If you get very good at spotting and eliminating answer choices that are too general or too specific, for example, you'll go a long way toward improving your score.

This process can be difficult because some of the irrelevant answer choices will contain terms and ideas from either the question stem or the passage itself. A good way to check for relevance is to ask yourself "so what?" and "does this have anything to do with the passage?" when evaluating the answer choices.

When your training is complete, you will be able to do this type of analysis on most of the questions and answer choices that you encounter on your ACT exam. You will quickly and efficiently eliminate all of the answer choices that are irrelevant or "not on point."

Manage the Answer Sheet

Be certain to avoid the common mistake of marking the answer to each question on your answer document (bubble sheet) as you finish the question. In other words, you should NOT go to your answer sheet after each question. This is dangerous and wastes time. It is dangerous because you run an increased risk of marking your answer sheet incorrectly and perhaps not catching your error on time. It wastes time because you have to find your place on the answer sheet and then find your place back in the test booklet over and over again. The amount of time that is "wasted" is not large as you mark each question. But, it adds up over the course of an entire test section and could cost you the amount of time you need to answer a few more questions correctly.

Instead, you should mark your answers in the test booklet and transfer your answers from the test booklet to the answer sheet in groups. On any of the sections, filling in circles (bubbles) on your answer sheet can be a good activity to keep you busy when you simply need a break to clear your head. Be sure to practice this technique until you are comfortable with it.

Use the Test Booklet

The ACT test booklets are meant to be used by one test taker only. You will not have any scratch paper on test day! (except for the Writing test). You are expected to do all note-taking on the booklet itself. Generally, no one ever bothers to look at the test booklet because you cannot receive credit for anything that is written there. Your score comes only from the answers that you mark on the answer sheet. Therefore, you should feel comfortable in marking up the passages, crossing off incorrect answer choices, and so on, to help you to stay focused on relevant information. More on this later in the book!

Guess Wisely

Because there is no added scoring penalty for incorrect answers on the ACT, you should never leave a bubble blank on your answer sheet. We counted all

Study Tip

The answers
are distributed
fairly evenly
across the posi-
tions, so
you should
always guess
the same
position if you
are guessing
at random. Of
course, if you
can eliminate a
choice or two,
or if you have a
hunch, then
this advice
doesn't apply.

of the correct answers on three recently released ACT exams and found that the distribution of answers by position on the answer sheet was almost exactly even. This means that there is no position that is more likely to be correct than any other. We use the term *position* when referring to the answer sheet because the letter assigned to the positions changes depending on whether you are working on an odd or even question. The odd-numbered questions have answer choices labeled A through D, and the even-numbered questions have answer choices that are labeled F through J on both the English and Reading Tests.

Make educated guesses by eliminating answer choices. It's a good idea to add a symbol or two to the common repertoire to help distinguish between the answer choices that you eliminate and those that could be correct. For example, when you eliminate an answer choice, make a mark through the letter so that you no longer consider it a viable choice, as shown here:

(A̶)
(B)
(C̶)
(D̶)
(E)

The step shown above is fairly common. If you think that an answer choice *may* be correct, but want to consider the remaining choices before you make your final decision, underline the answer choice, as shown below. This might be a new step in your standard process:

(A̶)
(B)␣␣␣␣
(C̶)
(D̶)
(E)

Once you've decided on your final answer, circle it for later transfer to the answer sheet, as follows:

(A̶)
(B)␣␣␣␣
(C̶)
(D̶)
Ⓔ

If you have eliminated one or more of the answer choices and still don't feel comfortable guessing among those that remain, place a large **X** next to the question, leave the circle empty on your answer sheet, and come back to the question later if you have time. Try to budget your time so that you have at least a minute or two left at the end of each section to locate the questions you've marked with an **X**; because you will be making an educated guess, select one of the answer choices that you did not already eliminate and fill in the corresponding circle on your answer sheet.

You also need to find out whether you are an answer-changer; if you change an answer, are you more likely to change it *to* the correct answer, or *from* the correct answer? You can only learn this about yourself by doing practice exams and paying attention to your tendencies.

Some students worry if they notice strings of the same answers on their answer sheets. This does not necessarily indicate a problem. While analyzing actual, released ACT exams, we counted strings of up to five questions long, all marked in the same answer column on the answer sheet, and all correct. You should not be concerned even if you find a string of five answer choices that are all in the same column.

Manage Stress

In college, stress arises from sources such as family expectations, fear of failure, heavy workload, competition, and difficult subjects. The ACT is designed to create similar stresses. The psychometricians we mentioned earlier who contribute to the design of standardized tests use artificial stressors to test how you will respond to the stress of college. In other words, they are actually trying to create a certain level of stress in you.

The main stressor is the time limit. The time limits are set on the ACT so that most students cannot finish all of the questions in the time allowed. Use the specific strategies mentioned in Chapters 4, 11, and 17 to help you select as many correct answers as possible in the time allowed.

Another stressor is the element of surprise that is present for many test takers, as they don't know what to expect on test day. Remember, if you practice enough, there should be no surprises!

Relax to Succeed

Probably the worst thing that can happen to a test taker is to panic. When you panic, you can usually identify a specific set of easily recognizable symptoms: sweating, shortness of breath, muscle tension, increased pulse rate, tunnel vision, nausea, lightheadedness, and, in rare cases, even loss of consciousness. These symptoms are the results of chemical changes in the brain brought on by some stimulus. The stimulus does not have to be external. Therefore, we can panic ourselves just by thinking about certain things. The stress chemical in your body called epinephrine, more commonly known as adrenaline, brings on these symptoms. Adrenaline changes the priorities in your brain activity. It moves blood and electrical energy away from some parts of the brain and to others. Specifically, it increases brain activity in the areas that control your body and decreases blood flow to the parts of your brain that are involved in complex thinking. Therefore, panic makes a person stronger and faster—and also less able to perform the type of critical thinking that is important on the ACT. It is not a bad thing to have a small amount of adrenaline in your bloodstream due to a healthy amount of excitement about your exam. But, you should be careful not to panic before or during your test.

You can control your adrenaline levels by minimizing the unknown factors in the testing process. The biggest stress-inducing questions are: "What do the test writers expect?"; "Am I ready?"; and "How will I do on test day?"

The goals of your preparation should be to learn about the test, acquire the skills that are being measured by the test, and learn about yourself and how you respond to the different parts of the test. You should also consider which question types you will try to answer on test day and which ones you will give an educated guess on. You need to be familiar with the material that is tested on each section of your test. As you work through this book, make an assessment of the best use of your time and energy. Concentrate on the areas

Study Tip

If you spend your time and energy studying and practicing under realistic conditions before test day, you will have a much better chance of controlling your adrenaline levels and handling the exam with no panic.

that will give you the highest score in the amount of time that you have until you take the ACT. This will give you a feeling of confidence on test day even when you are facing very challenging questions.

Relaxation Techniques

The following are suggestions to help you feel as relaxed and confident as possible on test day.

Be Prepared

The more prepared you feel, the less likely it is that you'll be stressed on test day. Study and practice consistently during the time between now and your test day. Be organized. Have your supplies and lucky testing clothes ready in advance. Make a practice trip to the test center before your test day.

Know Yourself

Get to know your strengths and weaknesses on the ACT and the things that help you to relax. Some test takers like to have a slightly anxious feeling to help them focus. Other folks do best when they are so relaxed that they are almost asleep. You will learn about yourself through practice.

Have a Plan of Attack

Know how you are going to work through each part of the exam. There is no time to create a plan of attack on test day. Practice enough that you internalize the skills you need to do your best on each section, and you won't have to stop to think about what to do next.

Breathe

If you feel yourself tensing up, slow down and take deeper breaths. This will relax you and get more oxygen to your brain so that you can think more clearly.

Take Breaks

You cannot stay sharply focused on your ACT for the whole time in the testing center. You are certainly going to have distracting thoughts, or moments when you just can't process all the information. When this happens, close your eyes, clear your mind, and then start back on your test. This process should take only a minute or so. You could pray, meditate, or just visualize a place or person that helps you relax. Try thinking of something fun that you have planned to do after your test.

Be Aware of Time

Time yourself on test day. You should have timed yourself on some of your practice exams, so you will have a sense of how long each section should take you. We suggest that you use an analog (dial face) watch. You can turn the hands on your watch back from noon to allow enough time for the section on which you are working. For example, set your watch to 11:15 for the 45-minute English Test and 11:25 for the 35-minute Reading Test.

Clear Your Head

Remember, all that matters during the test is your test. All of life's other issues will have to be dealt with after your test is finished. You might find this attitude easier to attain if you lose track of what time it is in the "outside world"—another benefit of resetting your watch.

Eat Right

Sugar is bad for stress and brain function in general. Consuming refined sugar creates biological stress that has an impact on your brain chemistry. Keep it to a minimum for several days before your test. If you are actually addicted to caffeine (you can tell that you are if you get headaches when you skip a day), get your normal amount. Don't forget to eat regularly while you're preparing for the ACT. It's not a good idea to skip meals simply because you are experiencing some additional stress.

A Note on Music

Some types of music increase measured brain stress and interfere with clear thinking. Specifically, some Rock, Hip-Hop, and Dance rhythms, while great for certain occasions, can have detrimental effects on certain types of brain waves that have been measured in labs. Other music seems to help to organize brain waves and create a relaxed state that is conducive to learning and skills acquisition.

The Impact of Mozart

There is a great debate raging among scientists and educators about a study that was done some years ago, which seemed to show that listening to Mozart made students temporarily more intelligent. While not everyone agrees that it helps, no one has ever seriously argued that it hurts. So, get yourself a Mozart CD and listen to it before practice and before your real test. It might help. In the worst-case scenario, you will have listened to some good music and maybe broadened your horizons a bit. You cannot listen to music *during* your ACT, so do not listen to it during your practice tests.

WHAT TO DO ON TEST DAY

If you work through the material in this book and do some additional practice on released ACT items (visit www.act.org), you should be more than adequately prepared for the test. Use the following tips to help the entire testing process go smoothly.

Do a Dry Run

Make sure that you know how long it will take to get to the testing center, where you will park, alternative routes, and so on. If you are testing in a place that is new to you, try to get into the building between now and test day so that you can absorb the sounds and smells, find out where the bathrooms and snack machines are, and so on.

Rest Up and Wake Up Early

You generally have to be at the testing center by 8:00 A.M. Set two alarms if you have to. Leave yourself plenty of time to get fully awake before you have to run out the door. Be sure to get enough rest the night before the test. The better rested you are, the better things seem. When you are fatigued, you are more likely to look on the dark side of things and worry more, which hurts your test scores.

Dress for Success

Wear loose, comfortable clothes in layers so that you can adjust to the temperature. Remember your watch. There might not be a clock in your testing room. (See page 10 for more information on timing!)

Fuel Up

It is important to eat something before you take the test. An empty stomach might be distracting and uncomfortable on test day. Foods without too much sugar are probably best. Get your normal dose of caffeine, if any. (Test day is not the time to "try coffee" for the first time!)

Bring Supplies

Bring your driver's license (or passport), your admission ticket, several sharpened Number 2 pencils, erasers, a timepiece, and your approved calculator. If you need them, bring your glasses or contact lenses. You won't be able to eat or drink while the test is in progress, but you can bring a snack for the breaktime.

Warm Up Your Brain

Read a newspaper or something similar, or review some practice material so that the ACT isn't the first thing you read on test day. If you review ACT material, make sure that it is something that you have worked through before and focus on the part of the test that you tend to be best at. This is certainly the time to accentuate the positive!

Plan a Mini-Vacation

Most students find it easier to concentrate on their test preparation and on their ACT if they have a plan for some fun right after the test. Plan something that you can look forward to as a reward for all the hard work and energy that you're putting into preparing for and taking the test.

■■■■   WHAT'S NEXT?

The remaining chapters in this book include more detailed information about the format and scoring of the ACT verbal sections, diagnostic tests to evaluate your current readiness for the ACT verbal sections, strategies specific to each ACT verbal section, exercises to hone your verbal skills, and practice questions in format.

For additional practice on full-length, simulated ACT exams, choose *McGraw-Hill's 10 ACT Practice Tests*.

Good luck!

PART I

THE ACT ENGLISH TEST

CHAPTER 1

FORMAT AND SCORING

As explained in the Introduction, the ACT includes four multiple-choice tests (English, Mathematics, Reading, and Science) and an optional essay. This chapter will provide more information on the format of the ACT English Test and briefly discuss how this test is scored.

The ACT English Test is designed to measure your ability to understand and interpret Standard Written English, and it includes questions that measure certain elements of effective writing, including grammar and usage, punctuation, sentence structure, and essay strategy, organization, and style. Each English Test includes 5 passages (essays) with 15 questions each, for a total of 75 multiple-choice questions. The passages cover a variety of subjects, ranging from historical discussions to personal narratives. The questions are divided into two main categories: Usage/Mechanics questions and Rhetorical Skills questions. Usage/Mechanics questions test your basic English and grammar skills, while Rhetorical Skills questions test your ability to express an idea clearly and concisely. You are given 45 minutes to complete the English Test.

Here is a brief description of the types of questions in each category, including the approximate percentage of the test devoted to the different elements of effective writing:

- Usage/Mechanics

    ○ Grammar and Usage (16 percent): These questions test your understanding of basic grammatical concepts such as subject/verb agreement, verb formation, pronouns and their antecedents, comparative and superlative forms of adjectives and adverbs, and idiom.
    ○ Punctuation (13 percent): These questions test your knowledge of standard conventions of punctuation, including the relationship of punctuation to sentence structure and meaning.
    ○ Sentence Structure (24 percent): These questions test your understanding of parallel construction, the relationships between clauses, and the correct placement of modifiers.

- Rhetorical Skills

    ○ Strategy (16 percent): These questions test your ability to evaluate the essay's audience and purpose, and to add, revise, or delete material based on relevance.
    ○ Organization (15 percent): These questions measure your understanding of effective introductory and concluding ideas, as well as the appropriate use of transitions.

○ Style (16 percent): These questions test precise and appropriate word choice, your ability to maintain a consistent style and tone throughout the essay, and your ability to avoid ambiguity, wordiness, and redundancy.

Subsequent chapters in this book will provide a grammar review and further discussion of the content area and question types on the ACT English Test.

ANATOMY OF AN ACT ENGLISH QUESTION

As mentioned in the Introduction, each multiple-choice English question includes four answer choices (A, B, C, and D for odd-numbered questions or F, G, H, and J for even-numbered questions). The answer choices correspond to the circles (bubbles) on your answer sheet.

Here is the basic structure of an ACT English question:

Employees began cleaning up their workspaces and gathering their belongings to go home.

The security guard performed his daily duty of locking one of two 9th-floor exits as a measure to

prevent theft. All seemed normal until someone on the 8th floor cry, "Fire!" [2]
$$\overline{1}$$

1. **A.** NO CHANGE
   B. cries
   C. crying
   D. cried

2. At this point, the author is considering adding the following sentence:
   Factories typically have large quantities of a variety of flammable materials.
   Should the author add this sentence?
   F. Yes, because it adds interesting information about the fire warning system in the building.
   G. Yes, because this sentence is necessary to the reader's understanding of the moments that led up to the fire.
   H. No, because the information is already implied in the paragraph.
   J. No, because the sentence doesn't add to the development of the paragraph.

Note that most ACT English questions (approximately 53 percent) are comprised only of answer choices (like # 1 above) from which you must select the best alternative to the underlined portion in the passage. The questions that refer to a number in a box generally ask you about the style and structure of the passage. As you practice, you will become more familiar with the question types and learn which (if any) to skip on your first pass through each passage.

THE ACT ENGLISH TEST SCORE

Each of the ACT multiple-choice tests is given a score on a scale of 1–36. In 2014, the average ACT English Test score in the United States was 20.3. Your score will be rounded to the nearest whole number before it is reported. The schools that you select to receive score reports will get three ACT English Test scores: your total score based on all 75 questions, a subscore based on the Usage/Mechanics questions, and a subscore based on the Rhetorical Skills questions. Because most colleges and universities focus only on the total score, we have not included specific information on calculating subscores. Check with the admissions departments at your schools of choice to find out how (or if) they use English Test subscores.

Your ACT English Test score will be used along with the scores from the other multiple-choice tests to calculate your composite score. Refer to the Scoring Worksheets provided with the explanations for the English Practice Tests in this book to calculate your approximate scaled score (1–36) on each test.

◼ WHAT'S NEXT?

Chapter 2 includes an ACT English Diagnostic Test, which you should use to determine your current readiness for the real ACT English Test. Then read Chapters 3 through 5 to learn the best approach to answering the questions on the simulated tests included in this book (Chapters 6 and 7), and on your actual ACT.

CHAPTER 2

ACT ENGLISH DIAGNOSTIC TEST

The following Diagnostic Test will help you to evaluate your current readiness for the ACT English Test. Make an honest effort to answer each question, then review the explanations that follow. Don't worry if you are unable to answer many or most of the questions at this point. Chapter 3, "Grammar Review," Chapter 4, "Strategies and Techniques," and Chapter 5, "Applying Strategies, Building Skills," contain information and resources to help you maximize your ACT English scores. Once you have identified your areas of strength and weakness, you should review those particular chapters in the book.

■■■ ANSWER SHEET

ACT ENGLISH DIAGNOSTIC TEST
Answer Sheet

ENGLISH

1 (A) (B) (C) (D)
2 (F) (G) (H) (J)
3 (A) (B) (C) (D)
4 (F) (G) (H) (J)
5 (A) (B) (C) (D)
6 (F) (G) (H) (J)
7 (A) (B) (C) (D)
8 (F) (G) (H) (J)
9 (A) (B) (C) (D)
10 (F) (G) (H) (J)
11 (A) (B) (C) (D)
12 (F) (G) (H) (J)
13 (A) (B) (C) (D)
14 (F) (G) (H) (J)
15 (A) (B) (C) (D)
16 (F) (G) (H) (J)
17 (A) (B) (C) (D)
18 (F) (G) (H) (J)
19 (A) (B) (C) (D)
20 (F) (G) (H) (J)

21 (A) (B) (C) (D)
22 (F) (G) (H) (J)
23 (A) (B) (C) (D)
24 (F) (G) (H) (J)
25 (A) (B) (C) (D)
26 (F) (G) (H) (J)
27 (A) (B) (C) (D)
28 (F) (G) (H) (J)
29 (A) (B) (C) (D)
30 (F) (G) (H) (J)
31 (A) (B) (C) (D)
32 (F) (G) (H) (J)
33 (A) (B) (C) (D)
34 (F) (G) (H) (J)
35 (A) (B) (C) (D)
36 (F) (G) (H) (J)
37 (A) (B) (C) (D)
38 (F) (G) (H) (J)
39 (A) (B) (C) (D)
40 (F) (G) (H) (J)

41 (A) (B) (C) (D)
42 (F) (G) (H) (J)
43 (A) (B) (C) (D)
44 (F) (G) (H) (J)
45 (A) (B) (C) (D)
46 (F) (G) (H) (J)
47 (A) (B) (C) (D)
48 (F) (G) (H) (J)
49 (A) (B) (C) (D)
50 (F) (G) (H) (J)
51 (A) (B) (C) (D)
52 (F) (G) (H) (J)
53 (A) (B) (C) (D)
54 (F) (G) (H) (J)
55 (A) (B) (C) (D)
56 (F) (G) (H) (J)
57 (A) (B) (C) (D)
58 (F) (G) (H) (J)
59 (A) (B) (C) (D)
60 (F) (G) (H) (J)

61 (A) (B) (C) (D)
62 (F) (G) (H) (J)
63 (A) (B) (C) (D)
64 (F) (G) (H) (J)
65 (A) (B) (C) (D)
66 (F) (G) (H) (J)
67 (A) (B) (C) (D)
68 (F) (G) (H) (J)
69 (A) (B) (C) (D)
70 (F) (G) (H) (J)
71 (A) (B) (C) (D)
72 (F) (G) (H) (J)
73 (A) (B) (C) (D)
74 (F) (G) (H) (J)
75 (A) (B) (C) (D)

ENGLISH TEST

45 Minutes—75 Questions

DIRECTIONS: In the passages that follow, some words and phrases are underlined and numbered. In the answer column, you will find alternatives for the words and phrases that are underlined. Choose the alternative that you think is best, and fill in the corresponding bubble on your answer sheet. If you think that the original version is best, choose "NO CHANGE," which will always be either answer choice A or F. You will also find questions about a particular section of the passage, or about the entire passage. These questions will be identified by either an underlined portion or by a number in a box. Look for the answer that clearly expresses the idea, is consistent with the style and tone of the passage, and makes the correct use of standard written English. Read the passage through once before answering the questions. For some questions, you should read beyond the indicated portion before you answer.

PASSAGE I

Swing to the Beat

Before there was rap and hip-hop, Americans tapped their toes to swing, a music style centered on a steady beat, rich sounds, and classy musicians. Swing music emerged in the early 1900s but gained popularity during the war years as soldiers employed it as an escape from the reality of the conflict at hand. As swing music became increasingly popular; toe tapping evolved into a more organized dance
_____
1

style known as swing dancing. From the late 1910s through the 1940s, teenagers and adults alike filled their local dance halls to lunge, dip, and spin the night away. ②

Although, Swing dancing is often lumped into
_____
3

one category, there are (it's true) more than
_____
4

ten different styles of swing dancing.

1. **A.** NO CHANGE
    B. popular toe
    C. popular, toe
    D. popular. Toe

2. The author is considering adding the following sentence:
    > Swing dancing is great exercise for young people.

    Should the writer make this addition?
    F. Yes, because it demonstrates the enjoyment swing dancing brought Americans during the difficult war years.
    G. Yes, because without this sentence, the reader wouldn't know that Americans enjoyed swing dancing.
    H. No, because swing dancing is not a physically active form of recreation.
    J. No, because the paragraph is about swing dancing as entertainment and not as exercise.

3. **A.** NO CHANGE
    B. Although swing
    C. Although—swing
    D. Although; swing

4. **F.** NO CHANGE
    G. it's true,
    H. it's true—
    J. DELETE the underlined portion.

GO ON TO THE NEXT PAGE.

Included among these styles are. The Lindy Hop, the
5
Charleston, the Foxtrot, and the Carolina shag. Another
style, East Coast Swing, is perhaps the most widely
recognized style in the United States. It involves a six-count
dance step, which is repeated throughout the dance. Once
dancers have mastered this step, they can be incorporated
6
into a variety of moves, which are then combined and
repeated over the course of a song. East Coast Swing is both
fast-paced and smooth when performed correctly, and thus
7
can be paired with a variety of styles.
8

Unfortunately, interest, in swing dancing has fallen
9
significantly since the 1940s because of new music and
dance styles, as well as the increasing ages and shrinking
numbers of the original "swingers." Aside from the
10
occasional grandparent or special group focused on
11
being dedicated to keeping the tradition alive, most swing
11
dancing is limited to the competitive dancing realm. [12]

Despite this decrease in interest, swing era enthusiasts
13

5. A. NO CHANGE
   B. are the,
   C. is the
   D. are the

6. F. NO CHANGE
   G. it can be incorporated
   H. there is then the ability to incorporate it
   J. the dancers will find it easy to incorporate the step

7. A. NO CHANGE
   B. correctly—and
   C. correctly. And
   D. correctly; and

8. F. NO CHANGE
   G. various
   H. varied
   J. variation of

9. A. NO CHANGE
   B. interest, in swing dancing,
   C. interest in swing dancing
   D. interest in swing dancing,

10. Which of the following alternatives to the underlined portion is LEAST acceptable?
    F. Except for
    G. Apart from
    H. Besides
    J. Without

11. A. NO CHANGE
    B. focused on the dedication
    C. dedicated
    D. being dedicated to the focus of

12. The writer is considering adding the following sentence:
    Competitive swing dancing requires years of instruction and practice.

    Should the writer make this addition?
    F. Yes, because it gives a needed detail about the competitive realm of swing dancing.
    G. Yes, because it helps readers understand why swing dancing is generally restricted to the competitive dancing realm.
    H. No, because it adds unnecessary information that only draws the reader away from the essay's main topic.
    J. No, because it misleads the reader regarding the work that goes into competitive swing dancing.

13. A. NO CHANGE
    B. In addition to
    C. Excluding
    D. Due to

GO ON TO THE NEXT PAGE.

continue to cross their fingers, hoping that swing dancing and
<u>it's music</u> will make a comeback.
₁

14. **F.** NO CHANGE
    G. its' music
    H. their music
    J. its music

> Question 15 asks about the preceding passage as a whole.

15. Suppose the author intended to write an essay that illustrates the role that swing music has played in the lives of American soldiers over the years. Does this essay fulfill that goal?
    A. Yes, because the essay describes how swing music affected the experiences of all American soldiers.
    B. Yes, because the author explains that swing music grew in general popularity as more and more soldiers listened to it.
    C. No, because this essay only discusses swing dancing, and does not mention swing music.
    D. No, because the author doesn't give enough detail about how swing music has affected American soldiers.

PASSAGE II

Playing Waitress

Nearly every kid has a favorite hobby. Some kids love

playing with dolls, some kids love playing with trucks, and

some kids love playing teacher. While all of these hobbies are

fun, my favorite hobby as a <u>child, without a doubt</u> was playing
₁₆

waitress.

　　<u>Which it</u> seems like a strange pastime, right? I mean,
　　₁₇

I now know a lot of people <u>that</u> don't enjoy "playing
₁₈

waitress" in reality, so why was I so fond of playing it in a

make-believe world? At the time, my special game gave me

a sense of responsibility that only a child could find so

<u>satisfying</u>.
₁₉

16. **F.** NO CHANGE
    G. child without a doubt
    H. child, without a doubt,
    J. child without a doubt,

17. **A.** NO CHANGE
    B. This
    C. While it
    D. So it

18. **F.** NO CHANGE
    G. whom
    H. they
    J. who

19. If the author replaced the underlined portion with "useful," what would the paragraph lose?
    A. The paragraph wouldn't lose anything.
    B. The paragraph wouldn't convey the lack of fun that the author experienced in other activities.
    C. The paragraph wouldn't convey the ultimate fulfillment the author found while playing waitress.
    D. The paragraph wouldn't convey to the reader that the author enjoyed playing waitress as an adult.

GO ON TO THE NEXT PAGE.

My favorite place to play was at my grandparents house.
                                            ——————
                                              20

They had an in-ground pool in their backyard, and that pool
                                      ———————————————
                                             21
was my restaurant.

As I said, ones childhood idea of playing waitress was
           ————
            22
not your average role playing. However, the game held a
postive appeal. Probably the best part about my pool
restaurant was its multitude of invisible customers who
never criticized and did not care Some entrée they were
                                  ————
                                   23
served. It didn't matter if the daily special was fried
       ——
                            24
octopus with a side of cow tongue; no matter how
——
                      24
unappetizing my restaurant's food may have been
——
                      24
my customers never complained.
——————————————————————————
            24

Not only were my customers easy to serve, the food
                                           ————————
                                              25
was easy to serve as well. All I had to do was dip
——————————————
      25
a bowl plate cup, or dessert tray into the swimming pool,
—————————————————————————————————
              26
and dinner was served. Buon appetito!

Than came clean up. This, too, I might add, was a simple
————
 27
process. All I had to do was dump my customer's "dinners"
                                    ——————————
                                        28
back into the swimming pool. Everything was clean within
two minutes! I wish cleaning was still that easy.

20. F. NO CHANGE
    G. grandparent's
    H. grandparents'
    J. their

21. Which of the following would NOT be an appropriate
    alternative to the underlined portion?
    A. backyard. That
    B. backyard that
    C. backyard; that
    D. backyard. The

22. F. NO CHANGE
    G. their
    H. my
    J. some

23. A. NO CHANGE
    B. such
    C. that
    D. which

24. The author is considering deleting the underlined portion.
    What would the paragraph lose if the author deletes this?
    F. It wouldn't lose anything.
    G. It would lose an indication of the pleasure of working
       in a restaurant.
    H. It would lose a descriptive detail about the positive
       appeal of make-believe.
    J. It would lose a description of the food served at an
       actual restaurant.

25. A. NO CHANGE
    B. the serving of food was easy
    C. the food serving was easy
    D. the food serving was done with ease

26. F. NO CHANGE
    G. a bowl, plate, cup, or dessert tray
    H. a bowl plate cup or dessert tray
    J. a bowl plate, cup or dessert tray

27. A. NO CHANGE
    B. Than,
    C. Then
    D. Then:

28. F. NO CHANGE
    G. customer
    H. customers
    J. customers'

GO ON TO THE NEXT PAGE.

[1] I'll never know why playing waitress was my favorite hobby. [2] However, despite my current attitude, I will always cherish my times as a member of the swimming pool restaurant staff. [3] Nowadays, waiting tables is the last job that I'd ever want. [4] Experience has shown me that waitressing is very hard work, and not child's play. [29]

29. Which of the following sequences of sentences makes the most sense?
   A. NO CHANGE
   B. 3, 1, 2, 4
   C. 4, 3, 1, 2
   D. 1, 3, 4, 2

Question 30 asks about the preceding passage as a whole.

30. Suppose the writer had decided to write an essay discussing one way in which she amused herself as a child. Would this essay successfully fulfill the writer's goal?
   F. Yes, because the essay explains how the author played make-believe "waitress" as a child.
   G. Yes, because the essay does not discuss how other chidren played make-believe.
   H. No, because the author does not identify the girl in the essay, so the reader has no basis for determining that it is the author.
   J. No, because the essay limits itself to describing the author's work in a restaurant.

PASSAGE III

Dancing through the Water

Have you ever done a handstand, somersault, or pirouette in a swimming pool? Chances are that you have, and even if you hadn't, it is likely that you've seen someone else attempt such a feat. For synchronized swimmers, performing handstands, somersaults, and pirouettes is just one aspect of this demanding sport.

   A hybrid of swimming, ballet, and gymnastics, synchronized swimming is a sport and often goes unappreciated. Whenever most people have a hard time figuring out how to dive into a pool without getting water up their noses, synchronized swimmers manage to spin and kick for the timely duration of their routine, all while they are upside down underwater. These athletes exhibit an

31. A. NO CHANGE
    B. haven't
    C. won't
    D. didn't

32. F. NO CHANGE
    G. were
    H. are
    J. was

33. A. NO CHANGE
    B. in which
    C. that
    D. it

34. F. NO CHANGE
    G. But
    H. If
    J. Whereas

35. A. NO CHANGE
    B. during
    C. during the times of
    D. in the time and duration of

GO ON TO THE NEXT PAGE.

impressive display of endurance, flexibility, strength,

grace, and, agility .
— 36

Unlike many other team sports, synchronized swimming
— 37

involves no physical contact with competitors. Instead,

several teams perform their routines before a panel of judges

that critiques each team individually, rather then by how
— 38

they perform in physical contact against their competitors.

The teams are scored on an incremental scale of one to ten,
— 39

with points awarded for both technical merit and artistic

expression. Technical merit includes the correctness of the

figures presented and the synchronization of the piece, while

artistic expression includes the choreography, music,

involvement of the swimmer, and presentation. The team

with the highest score wins.
— 40

[1] Although they can be found among varying age
— 41

groups, synchronized swimming still lags behind many
— 42

other sports in the race for acknowledgment and respect. [2]

Perhaps if more people were aware, of the dedication and
— 43

talent required for success in the sport, it would be taken

more seriously. [3] Synchronized swimming teams are

formed at the elementary, secondary, collegiate, and

Olympic levels. 44

36. F. NO CHANGE
  G. grace and agility
  H. grace, and agility
  J. grace and, agility

37. A. NO CHANGE
  B. sports synchronized
  C. sports; synchronized
  D. sports. Synchronized

38. F. NO CHANGE
  G. than
  H. if
  J. for

39. A. NO CHANGE
  B. On an incremental scale of one to ten the teams are scored,
  C. The teams performing are incrementally scored by the judges on a scale of one to ten,
  D. Scored on an incremental scale of one to ten are the teams,

40. F. NO CHANGE
  G. most highest
  H. higher
  J. highly

41. A. NO CHANGE
  B. it
  C. some
  D. DELETE the underlined portion.

42. Which of the following alternatives to the underlined portion would be LEAST acceptable?
  F. falls
  G. ends
  H. trails
  J. follows

43. A. NO CHANGE
  B. aware of
  C. aware by
  D. aware, of,

44. Which of the following sentence sequences will make the preceding paragraph more logical?
  F. NO CHANGE
  G. 3,2,1
  H. 2,3,1
  J. 3,1,2

GO ON TO THE NEXT PAGE.

Question 45 asks about the preceding passage as a whole.

45. Suppose the writer's goal was to describe the difficulties experienced by athletes participating in under-recognized sports. Does the essay meet this goal?
  A. Yes, because the essay highlights how synchronized swimming is under-recognized.
  B. Yes, because the essay explains how people don't take synchronized swimming seriously.
  C. No, because the essay shows support for only one under-recognized sport.
  D. No, because the essay doesn't identify synchronized swimming as an under-recognized sport.

PASSAGE IV

Sandra Day O'Connor: Supreme Court Trendsetter

As the saying goes there is a first time for everything. In
                        ‾‾‾‾‾‾‾‾
                           46

September of 1981, America experienced a monumental

first, with the appointment of a female Supreme Court
‾‾‾‾‾‾‾‾
   47

Justice. Sandra Day O'Connor took her seat on the Supreme

Court bench following her appointment by President Reagan

two months earlier. The Senate confirmed Justice O'Connor

with 91 votes, which pushed and moved Justice O'Connor
              ‾‾‾‾‾‾‾‾‾‾‾‾‾‾‾‾‾‾‾‾
                       48

and the United States into uncharted territory.

Unprepared for the scrutiny that came with being the first

woman on the bench, Justice O'Connor received thousands

of critical letters during her first year on the job. Whether
                                                    ‾‾‾‾‾‾‾
                                                      49

Justice O'Connor was caught off guard by this

overwhelming response from the American public, she
‾‾‾‾‾‾‾‾‾‾‾
   50

didn't let it hold her back.

Justice O'Connor enjoyed her position as a judge.
‾‾‾
                     51

She made it her duty to give rulings that were fair and

46. F. NO CHANGE
  G. goes there,
  H. goes, there
  J. goes, there,

47. A. NO CHANGE
  B. first, by
  C. first, because
  D. first, when

48. F. NO CHANGE
  G. pushing and moving
  H. which pushed, and moved
  J. pushing

49. A. NO CHANGE
  B. Subsequently
  C. Although
  D. Whereby

50. Which of the following alternatives to the underlined portion would be the LEAST acceptable?
  F. impassioned
  G. expected
  H. intense
  J. strong

51. Given that all choices are true, which one would best introduce this paragraph?
  A. NO CHANGE
  B. Justice O'Connor had many legal goals as a judge.
  C. Justice O'Connor saw her loyalties lying with both the American people and the legal system.
  D. Justice O'Connor saw the law as the least important aspect of her job.

GO ON TO THE NEXT PAGE.

that preserved the integrity of the law. Justice O'Connor
       ――――
        52
made sure that the public understood the high court's
commitment to the law. She emphasized that the
Supreme Courts role was to interpret the law, not create it.
――――――――
      53

     Given Justice O'Connor's appointment by a famously
conservative president, the public was often taken aback
                                 ―――
                                  54

by her politically independent. Justice O'Connor often
       ――――――――――――――
               55

cast the "swing vote," or the vote that decided the case when
――――
 56
the remaining eight justices were split down the middle on
a ruling. As a result, many people considered Justice
O'Connor the most powerful woman in the United States.
     After 25 years on the Supreme Court Bench, Justice
O'Connor retired. While her influence in judicial matters is
most certainly notable, it is her status as a woman
that she most remembers; Justice O'Connor helped
――――――――――――――
        57

to pave the way for future generations of women. As in the
―――――
  58

very words of Justice O'Connor herself, "The power I exert
――――
 59
on the Court depends on the power of my arguments, not on
my gender."

---

52. F. NO CHANGE
    G. preservation
    H. preservative
    J. preservative of

53. A. NO CHANGE
    B. Supreme Court
    C. Supreme Court's
    D. Supreme Courts'

54. F. NO CHANGE
    G. are
    H. would have been
    J. will be

55. A. NO CHANGE
    B. political independent
    C. politics independence
    D. political independence

56. F. NO CHANGE
    G. was casting
    H. casted
    J. casting

57. A. NO CHANGE
    B. in which she is most remembered for
    C. for which she is most remembered
    D. that she is most remembered

58. F. NO CHANGE
    G. paving
    H. the paving
    J. with the paving

59. A. NO CHANGE
    B. exact
    C. distinct
    D. DELETE the underlined portion.

Question 60 asks about the preceding passage as a
whole.

60. Suppose the writer's goal was to write an essay describing the struggles of American women. Does this essay fulfill that goal?
    F. Yes, because it highlights the struggles endured by Sandra Day O'Connor, an American women.
    G. Yes, because it exemplifies the struggles that an American woman can face.
    H. No, because it only highlights the struggle of one American woman in one profession.
    J. No, because it does not include information about female justices working in other levels of the American court system.

GO ON TO THE NEXT PAGE.

PASSAGE V

The Faces of Mount Rushmore

During the summer before my senior year in high school, my family took a vacation out <u>west. To</u> experience
₆₁

magnificent Yellowstone National Park. <u>Although</u>
₆₂
Yellowstone itself was absolutely amazing, I was most enthralled by the numerous unique landmarks my family was able to visit on the cross-country journey. Perhaps the most memorable of these side trips <u>was</u> to Mt. Rushmore.
₆₃

Mt. Rushmore allows millions of people to stand <u>face to face</u> four of the greatest presidents in American
₆₄
history. Year after year, the faces of George Washington, Thomas Jefferson, Abraham Lincoln, and Theodore Roosevelt leave many visitors <u>feeling emotions of</u>
₆₅
<u>inspiration.</u> <u>What they symbolize is what each president</u>
₆₅   ₆₆
<u>was chosen for</u> George Washington for his commitment to
₆₆
independence; Thomas Jefferson for his idea of democracy; Abraham Lincoln for his dedication to equality and unity among the states; and Theodore Roosevelt for his hand in developing the <u>United State's</u> role in twentieth-century
₆₇

world affairs. By <u>storing</u> the memory of these men in stone,
₆₈
Mt. Rushmore also upholds the ideas represented.

[1] Perhaps as interesting as the faces in the mountain <u>are</u>
₆₉
how they were put there in the first place. Sculptor Gutzon Borglum and his crew began work in 1927 on <u>which</u> would
₇₀
be a 5,700-foot tall sculpture. [2] As the crew neared

61. A. NO CHANGE
B. west; to
C. west: to
D. west to

62. Which of the following alternatives to the underlined portion would be LEAST acceptable?
F. NO CHANGE
G. Even though
H. While
J. Because

63. A. NO CHANGE
B. is
C. are
D. were

64. F. NO CHANGE
G. face-to-face against
H. face-to-face with
J. face-to-face near

65. A. NO CHANGE
B. emotional with inspiration
C. inspirational feeling
D. feeling inspired

66. F. NO CHANGE
G. Symbols are what each president was chosen for characteristically:
H. Symbolically each president was chosen for his characteristic:
J. Each president was chosen for the characteristic he best symbolized:

67. A. NO CHANGE
B. United States'
C. United States
D. United States's

68. Which of the following would be the best alternative to the underlined portion?
F. NO CHANGE
G. retrieving
H. infusing
J. preserving

69. A. NO CHANGE
B. were
C. is
D. had been

70. F. NO CHANGE
G. what
H. that what
J. that which

GO ON TO THE NEXT PAGE.

completion in 1938, Borglum had a revolutionary idea.

[3] <u>Wanted</u> to be sure that no future generation was left
         71

unaware of the great American tradition, Borglum <u>begun</u>
                                                    72

carving a vault into the canyon wall located directly behind
Mount Rushmore. [4] Unfortunately, Borglum's death
marked the end of work on Mt. Rushmore, and the vault
remained unfinished. [5] His goal was to fill the vault with
records of the memorial's <u>construction and</u> records
                                      73

of Western civilization and freedom. ☐74

   Mt. Rushmore now serves more than 2 million visitors
annually. Not only is it the largest sculpture in the world, it
also celebrates some of the biggest ideas ever formulated in
the United States. Mt. Rushmore is one of the great
American traditions that <u>you</u> should go without
                           75
experiencing.

71. A. NO CHANGE
B. Wanting
C. He wanted
D. He was wanting

72. F. NO CHANGE
G. begins
H. began
J. beginning

73. A. NO CHANGE
B. construction
C. construction and as
D. construction; and

74. For the sake of logic, Sentence 4 should be placed where
in the paragraph?
F. NO CHANGE
G. After Sentence 2.
H. Before Sentence 1.
J. After Sentence 5.

75. A. NO CHANGE
B. everyone
C. anyone
D. no one

END OF THE ENGLISH TEST
STOP! IF YOU HAVE TIME LEFT OVER, CHECK YOUR WORK ON THIS SECTION ONLY.

◼◼ ANSWERS AND EXPLANATIONS

1. **The best answer is C.** Use a comma to separate introductory phrases and clauses from the main clause in a sentence. The main clause begins with its subject, "toe tapping."

2. **The best answer is J.** The paragraph indicates that swing dancing became popular with soldiers "as an escape." In addition, the last sentence of the paragraph suggests that swing dancing was primarily a social activity. No mention of swing dancing as exercise is made in the paragraph, so the addition would not be relevant.

3. **The best answer is B.** Do not use any punctuation to separate an initial subordinating conjunction like "Although" from the subject of a subordinate clause, which in this case is "swing dancing."

4. **The best answer is J.** As a reader of nonfiction such as this passage, you expect the writer to tell the truth. The parenthetical clause "(it's true)" is unnecessary. Furthermore, the claim that swing dancing includes 10 different styles is sufficiently believable, so as not to warrant the author's reinforcement of his or her credibility.

5. **The best answer is D.** The underlined portion as written creates an incomplete sentence. Answer choice B contains an extraneous comma after "the"; answer choice C incorrectly includes a singular verb.

6. **The best answer is G.** The underlined portion refers to a single step to be mastered, so the singular pronoun "it" is correct. Answer choice G is the most succinct answer, so it is best.

7. **The best answer is A.** As written, the clause following the comma in the sentence does not have its own subject. The verb "can be" links to the subject of the first clause, "East Coast Swing." Therefore, the two clauses cannot be separated with a period (answer choice C) or a semicolon (answer choice D). The dash used in answer choice B gives special emphasis to clauses and phrases, but that emphasis is not called for here.

8. **The best answer is F.** The singular indefinite article "a" before the underlined portion means that the underlined portion should take a singular noun. Answer choices G and H create suitable noun phrases ("various music styles" and "varied music styles"); however, these noun phrases are plural, and thus cannot take the singular indefinite article "a." Answer choice F ("variety") is singular, and is the appropriate adjective.

9. **The best answer is C.** The noun phrase "interest in swing dancing" constitutes the subject of the sentence and must not be divided by any comma. Remember that you can determine subjects and objects in a sentence by the pronoun test: "interest in swing dancing" can become "it," making the sentence, "Unfortunately, it has fallen significantly since the 1940s … ."

10. **The best answer is J.** The adverbs "aside from," "except for," "apart from," and "besides" have nearly the same meaning ("with the exception of"). There is some ambiguity whether answer choice J, "without," would mean "as there is not" or "if there were not" in this case. This ambiguity means that "without" is the least acceptable among the answer choices.

11. **The best answer is C.** The single verb "dedicated" conveys the intended meaning in the simplest way and avoids redundancy.

12. **The best answer is H.** The paragraph is about the general loss of interest in swing dancing and not about competitive swing dancing in particular, so the addition would not be relevant.

13. **The best answer is A.** The sentence as written conveys the correct meaning. "Despite" is used with circumstances like "this decrease in interest" that are adverse or contrary to the main clause.

14. **The best answer is J.** The proper form is the possessive adjective "its." The form "it's," as written in the sentence, is the contraction of "it is," which does not make sense here. Answer choice G can be eliminated. "It" is a singular pronoun and cannot, therefore, take a plural possessive form. This is a fairly common trap on the ACT English Test, and should always be avoided! Answer choice H incorrectly uses the plural pronoun "their."

15. **The best answer is D.** The essay explains the origin, steps, and current state of swing dancing. It does not address the role swing dancing played in the lives of soldiers.

16. **The best answer is H.** The words "without a doubt" constitute a nonrestrictive phrase, which must be separated from the sentence using commas. The first comma appears in the correct place in the sentence, but a second comma is necessary after "doubt."

17. **The best answer is B.** The pronoun "this" correctly refers to the specific pastime of playing waitress. Answer choices A, C, and D create awkward and grammatically incorrect sentences.

18. **The best answer is J.** The appropriate relative pronoun to use with people (and in many cases pets, ships, countries, and other things humans personify) is "who." Because the pronoun replaces the subject, "people," it is appropriate to use "who" instead of "whom."

19. **The best answer is C.** The word "satisfying" emphasizes the degree to which the author, as a child, enjoyed playing waitress, a sentiment not shared by most adults. The word "useful" does not convey this sense of fulfillment.

20. **The best answer is H.** A possessive form is necessary to modify the noun "house." The next sentence begins with "their," so you know there is more than one grandparent. Therefore, a plural form is needed. Answer choice G is singular, so eliminate it. Answer choice F is not possessive, so eliminate it. Answer choices H and J are correct grammatically; however, answer choice J must be eliminated because there is not an antecedent to which it would clearly refer.

21. **The best answer is B.** This sentence contains two independent clauses that must either be joined by a comma plus a conjunction like "and," or punctuation like a period or semicolon.

22. **The best answer is H.** The passage is presented as a narrative, so the correct pronoun is "my" because it refers directly to the narrator. The other answer choices are not specific enough to the context of the passage.

23. **The best answer is D.** The author chose which dishes she served her imaginary customers. This idea is best conveyed using the interrogative adjective "which" before the noun "entrée." The other answer choices are not appropriate.

24. **The best answer is H.** The author mentions a specific pretend dish ("fried octopus with a side of cow tongue") that she served her pretend customers. Such a vivid image is used to enhance the description of the author's table-waiting make-believe, and would probably not describe a meal served in an actual restaurant!

25. **The best answer is A.** This question requires you to analyze a sentence for parallel structure. The form of the verb "serve" in the underlined portion should have the same form as "serve" in the first clause.

26. **The best answer is G.** Commas must be used to separate every item in a series of more than two items.

27. **The best answer is C.** The appropriate word is the adverb of time "then" used without punctuation.

The word "than" can serve as a conjunction or a preposition used in comparative constructions, for example "more difficult than I thought it would be" or "prettier than Sue."

28. **The best answer is J.** The passage refers to more than one customer, so the plural possessive form "customers'" should be used.

29. **The best answer is D.** Sentence 1 is a good statement of the main idea of the short paragraph. Only answer choice D places Sentence 1 in the first position, so it must be the correct choice. Indeed, Sentences 3 and 4 offer support for Sentence 1, and Sentence 2 is a sound concluding sentence for the passage.

30. **The best answer is F.** The entire passage explains how the author amused herself as a child. Therefore, eliminate answer choices H and J. Answer choice G must be eliminated because how other children played is irrelevant to the question, and is only mentioned briefly in the essay.

31. **The best answer is B.** This verb should be parallel to the previous instance of "have." Only answer choice B has the correct verb in the correct, present tense.

32. **The best answer is F.** The present tense matches the other sentences in the passage. The singular form is necessary to match with its singular subject, "performing," and the phrase "one aspect."

33. **The best answer is C.** The relative pronoun "that" is the appropriate choice here and serves as the subject of the verb "goes." Answer choices A, B, and D do not make sense in place of the underlined portion.

34. **The best answer is J.** Using the conjunctive adverb "whereas" appropriately sets the first clause in contrast to the second clause. Answer choice G, "but," indicates an exception and answer choice H, "if," indicates a condition, neither of which is appropriate here. Likewise, answer choice F does not fit context structure.

35. **The best answer is B.** The single preposition "during" is the best choice because it conveys the correct meaning concisely. The other answer choices are awkward and redundant.

36. **The best answer is H.** Commas should be used to separate the elements in this list. Between the second-to-last and last elements is the conjunction "and." The comma falls between the second-to-last element and the conjunction.

37. **The best answer is A.** The prepositional phrase "unlike many other team sports," when beginning

the sentence, must be separated from the subject, "synchronized swimming", by a comma. Answer choice B leaves out this necessary comma, and answer choices C (semicolon) and D (period) are inappropriate because the introductory phrase is not a fully formed clause (it lacks a verb).

38. **The best answer is G.** The word "than" shows contrast.

39. **The best answer is A.** The sentence is clearest and most concise as written. The other answer choices are wordy and awkward.

40. **The best answer is F.** The superlative of an adjective is generally formed by adding "-est" and is used to compare more than two things. Since the number of teams is not identified, the superlative "highest" is correct here. Answer choice G is incorrect because it uses a double comparison by including "most."

41. **The best answer is B.** This pronoun should refer to "synchronized swimming," which is singular. The pronoun "it" is the only singular choice.

42. **The best answer is G.** The verb "ends" does not make sense in the sentence. All the other answer choices are verbs indicating that synchronized swimming is losing the metaphorical "race" mentioned in the sentence.

43. **The best answer is B.** To indicate the object of the people's awareness, the preposition "of" is appropriate, for example in, "I am aware of the problem." In addition, no comma should separate the adjective "aware" from the prepositional phrase that modifies it, "of the dedication and talent required for success in the sport."

44. **The best answer is J.** Sentence 1 clearly ties the information from Sentence 3 to the information from Sentence 2. Therefore, only answer choice J is possible, because it places Sentence 3 in the first position and Sentence 1 in the second position.

45. **The best answer is C.** The question asks about "under-recognized sports" (plural), which indicates more than one such sport or all such sports. The passage only addresses synchronized swimming and is therefore too specific to fulfill the writer's goal.

46. **The best answer is H.** The verb "goes" is part of the dependent clause that begins the sentence, "As the saying goes … ." A comma must separate this clause from the next one, "there is a first time for everything."

47. **The best answer is A.** The prepositional phrase "with the appointment of a female Supreme Court Justice" defines the noun phrase "a monumental first." The prepositions "by," "because," and "when" are not idiomatically appropriate.

48. **The best answer is J.** In this case "push" and "move" have nearly the same meaning. Answer choice J eliminates the redundancy by using only one of the two verbs.

49. **The best answer is C.** The conjunctive adverb "although" correctly introduces the dependent clause, which describes a circumstance ("this overwhelming response") in opposition to the main clause ("she didn't let it hold her back").

50. **The best answer is G.** The "critical letters" that Justice O'Connor received cannot be construed as "expected" because that doesn't make sense based on the context. By comparison, the other answer choices more accurately describe the receipt of the critical letters, since she was "caught off guard."

51. **The best answer is C.** The paragraph discusses Justice O'Connor's duty as a Supreme Court justice and that she "made sure that the public understood the high court's commitment to the law." This best supports answer choice C.

52. **The best answer is F.** The relative pronoun "that" is parallel to "that" in the clause "that were both fair." Just as with "were" in the first construction, the underlined portion should be a verb in the simple past tense. Both "preservation" and "preservative" generally serve as nouns, which is not appropriate here.

53. **The best answer is C.** The Supreme Court is a singular noun, so the appropriate possessive form is "Supreme Court's." This is appropriate to modify the noun "role" that follows.

54. **The best answer is F.** The events took place in the past and the noun phrase "the public" is singular so the singular past-tense verb "was" is correct.

55. **The best answer is D.** The possessive determiner "her" indicates that the underlined portion should be a noun phrase. Answer choice A is an adjective phrase, so it can be eliminated. Answer choice B contains two adjectives that modify nothing, so it can be eliminated. Answer choice C is an awkward compound of two nouns, so it can be eliminated. Only answer choice D is a well-formed noun phrase using an adjective (political) and a noun (independence).

56. **The best answer is F.** The simple past form "cast" is appropriate here to parallel the past tense of the entire passage. Recall that "cast" has irregular past forms: "cast" not "casted."

57. The best answer is C. The sentence as written does not convey the correct meaning. O'Connor doesn't remember most "her status as a woman"; the public does. Of the remaining answer choices, only answer choice C makes sense.

58. The best answer is F. The verb phrase "to pave" clearly indicates the action that Justice O'Connor was able to achieve for future generations of women. The "-ing" form of the word is not correct here.

59. The best answer is D. This question requires you to carefully analyze the entire sentence, not just the underlined word, for redundancy. The word "herself" before the quotation gives the same emphasis that "very," "exact," or "distinct" would give as a modifier to "words." Therefore, it is best to omit the redundancy created by using any additional modifiers.

60. The best answer is H. The question indicates "the struggles of American women." Although the passage details some struggles of one particular American woman, it does not address the issue of women's struggles in any broader context.

61. The best answer is D. As written, the sentence beginning with "To" is a fragment. Therefore, answer choices A and B are not appropriate. Answer choice C is not a proper use of the colon. The sentences are joined most effectively without punctuation.

62. The best answer is J. The author is contrasting her enjoyment of Yellowstone with her enjoyment of sights seen along the way. Answer choice J is not appropriate because the author's enjoyment of Yellowstone was not the reason she enjoyed other landmarks, which use of the word "because" indicates.

63. The best answer is A. The noun phrase "the most memorable of these side trips" is singular. Be careful not to interpret the plural noun "trips" as controlling the grammatical number (singular vs. plural) of the greater phrase. Because the "side trip" took place in the past, the singular past-tense form "was" is appropriate.

64. The best answer is H. The only preposition appropriate to use with the adverb "face-to-face" is "with." The remaining answer choices are not idiomatic.

65. The best answer is D. This is the most concise answer choice and makes sense in context. It is also in the preferred active voice. Answer choice C, while concise, uses "inspirational" incorrectly.

Someone feeling inspired is not inspirational. Whatever or whoever made the person feel inspired is inspirational.

66. The best answer is J. This answer choice is clear and concise, and correctly conveys the intended meaning. Answer choice F has awkward word order. Answer choices G and H use the word-root "symbol" incorrectly.

67. The best answer is B. "United States" has the form of a plural noun phrase ending in "s." Therefore, to make it possessive, an apostrophe is added to the end without an additional "s." Use the possessive form because "United States' " modifies the noun "role."

68. The best answer is J. The idea of "preserving" something suggests that it will last a long time. In the case of Mt. Rushmore, the memory of the four presidents will be preserved indefinitely. The meanings of the other answer choices do not suit the sentence.

69. The best answer is C. This sentence has inverted structure: predicate, verb, subject. Therefore, it is essential to identify the person and number of the subject to select the correct verb form. In this sentence, the subject is "how they were put there in the first place." Consider the sentence put in standard order: "How they were put there in the first place *is* perhaps as interesting as the faces in the mountain." A clause acting as a subject is singular; therefore, the singular present-tense verb "is" is appropriate.

70. The best answer is G. The correct pronoun is "what," which can be used to head fused relative clauses, which act as nouns. The clause "what would be a 5,700-foot tall sculpture" passes the pronoun test (substitute "it" for the entire clause), so it acts as a noun.

71. The best answer is B. The underlined portion begins a long introductory phrase that modifies the main clause, which begins with the subject "Borglum." Therefore, the only choice that would not create a comma splice (run-on) is the gerund form "wanting" without the subject pronoun "he."

72. The best answer is H. As in the rest of the passage, the simple past form of "begin" ("began") is appropriate here. ("Begun" is the past participle of "begin" and should be used with a helping verb such as "had.")

73. The best answer is A. The simple coordinating conjuction "and" is appropriate to join the clauses in this sentence.

74. **The best answer is J.** Sentence 4 describes the conclusion of the vault project; therefore, it is best suited at the end of the paragraph.

75. **The best answer is D.** The appropriate pronoun is the negative indefinite pronoun "no one." It properly refers to people (who would visit the monument). The negative pronoun is necessary to negate "go without experiencing." The author is using this double negative to suggest that every person should visit Mt. Rushmore.

■■■   SCORING WORKSHEET

On each ACT multiple-choice test (English, Mathematics, Reading, and Science) you will receive a SCALED SCORE on a scale of 1 to 36. Use the following guidelines to determine your approximate SCALED SCORE on the ACT English Diagnostic Test that you just completed.

Step 1   Determine your RAW SCORE.

Your RAW SCORE is the number of questions that you answered correctly. Because there are 75 questions on the ACT English Test, the highest possible RAW SCORE is 75.

Step 2   Determine your SCALED SCORE using the following Scoring Worksheet

English   ——————— × 36 = ——————— ÷ 75 = ———————
             RAW SCORE   − 2   (*correction factor)
                                                        ———————
                                                        SCALED SCORE

*The correction factor is an approximation based on the average from several recent ACT tests. It is most valid for scores in the middle 50 percent (approximately 16–24 scaled composite score) of the scoring range. The scores are all approximate. Actual ACT scoring scales vary from one administration to the next based upon several factors.

Your SCALED SCORE should be rounded to the nearest number according to normal rules. For example, $31.2 \approx 31$ and $31.5 \approx 32$. If you answered 61 questions correctly on the English Test, for example, your SCALED SCORE would be 29.

CHAPTER 3
GRAMMAR REVIEW

The Usage and Mechanics questions on the ACT English Test address punctuation, grammar and usage, and sentence structure. The 40 Usage/Mechanics questions on the actual ACT ask you to apply the rules of standard written English to specific sections of the passage, which are usually underlined. This chapter provides a review of the grammar that is often tested on the ACT English Test.

PUNCTUATION RULES

A properly punctuated sentence helps the reader understand the organization of the writer's ideas. The ACT English Test includes questions that address punctuation usage. You should be able to identify and correct errors involving the following punctuation marks:

- Commas [,]
- Apostrophes [']
- Colons [:] and Semicolons [;]
- Parentheses [( )] and Dashes [—]
- Periods [.], Question Marks [?], and Exclamation Points [!]

Commas

A comma is used to indicate a separation of ideas or of elements within a sentence.

Use a comma with a coordinating conjunction to separate independent clauses within a sentence.

There are seven basic coordinating conjunctions in English:

1. Jenny sings in the choir, **and** she plays the guitar in a rock band.
2. Amanda enjoys her job, **but** she is looking forward to her vacation.
3. I will either study mathematics, **or** I will study chemistry.
4. His mother doesn't eat meat, **nor** does she eat dairy products.
5. Jordan will be playing football this year, **for** he made the team.
6. Frank earned a promotion, **so** we decided to celebrate.
7. I just completed my workout, **yet** I'm not tired.

Use a comma to separate elements that introduce and modify a sentence.

1. **Yesterday,** I painted the entire garage.
2. **Before deciding on a major at college,** Rana discussed her options with her parents.

Use commas before and after a parenthetical expression.

A parenthetical expression is a phrase that is inserted into the writer's train of thought. Parenthetical expressions are most often set off using commas.

1. Stephanie's decision, **in my opinion,** was not in her best interest.
2. The new park, **of course,** is a popular tourist destination.

Use a comma to separate an appositive from a clause.

An appositive is a noun or phrase that renames the noun that precedes it.

1. My brother, **a well-respected scientist,** made an important discovery.
2. Mr. Smith, **the fifth-grade math teacher,** was a favorite among the students.

Use commas to set off interjections.

1. **Well,** it's about time that you got here.
2. **Say,** did you pass your history test?

Use commas to separate coordinate adjectives.

If two adjectives modify a noun in the same way, they are called coordinate adjectives. Coordinate adjectives can also be joined with the coordinating conjunction *and* instead of a comma.

1. We walked the **long, dusty** road to the abandoned farm.
   OR: We walked the **long and dusty** road to the abandoned farm.
2. Cows are **gentle, friendly** creatures.
   OR: Cows are **gentle and friendly** creatures.

Use commas to set off nonrestrictive phrases and clauses.

A nonrestrictive phrase can be omitted from a clause without changing the meaning of the clause. Nonrestrictive clauses are useful because they can modify the nouns that they follow.

1. My sister's dog, **a brown and white terrier,** barks at me whenever I visit.
2. Katie celebrated her birthday, **which was in June,** with a party and a chocolate cake.

Use a comma to separate elements in a list or series.

1. Jill decided to purchase a **leash, a collar, and a water dish** for her dog.
2. Skippy **packed his suitcase, put on his jacket, and left the house**.
3. Please bring the following items to camp: **pillow, blanket, toothbrush, and other personal hygiene products**.

Use commas in dates, addresses, place names, numbers, and quotations.

1. Mary is leaving for Jamaica on **Monday, February 21, 2011**.
2. The Library of Congress is located at **101 Independence Avenue, Washington, D.C., U.S.A.**
3. Forecasted annual earnings are currently **$42,521,000**.
4. **"My sister is a nurse,"** Becky said proudly.

5. John replied, **"So where are we exactly?"**
6 **"You'll soon regret this,"** Luc cautioned under his breath, **"for things are not as they seem."**

---

*Do **NOT** use a comma:*

-to separate a subject from a verb.

My cousin Mary walked down to the corner.
NOT – My cousin **Mary, walked** down to the corner.

-to separate an adjective from the word it modifies.

The pretty girl sat in front of me on the bus.
NOT – The **pretty, girl** sat in front of me on the bus.

-before a coordinate conjunction that is NOT joining independent clauses

Before he goes to bed, Jeff likes to relax on his couch and listen to music.
NOT – Before he goes to bed, Jeff likes to relax on his **couch, and** listen to music.

In this sentence, the coordinating conjunction *and* is joining the verb phrases "relax on his couch" and "listen to music." These are not independent clauses because they lack a subject.

-to separate two independent clauses; this is known as a comma-splice.

1. I plan to attend a liberal arts college. My parents want me to get a well-rounded education.
   NOT – I plan to attend a liberal arts **college, my** parents want me to get a well-rounded education.

This sentence could be fixed by adding a conjunction, for example: "I plan to attend a liberal arts college, *as* my parents want me to get a well-rounded education." A semicolon would also be appropriate in place of the period in the first sentence.

Apostrophes

An apostrophe is used to form the possessive in nouns, to show the omission of letters in contractions, and to indicate plurals of letters and (as a matter of preference) numerals.

*Use an apostrophe with **s** to form the possessive of singular nouns, plural nouns that do not end in **s**, or indefinite pronouns that do not end in **s**.*

1. My **friend's** house is at the end of the street.
2. The **Women's** Society meets every Thursday at the high school.
3. **Someone's** bicycle is leaning against the building.

*Use an apostrophe to form the possessive of plural nouns ending in **s**.*

1. The **horses'** stalls were filled with straw.
2. I did not enjoy the **brothers'** rendition of my favorite song.

Use an apostrophe with the last noun in a series to indicate joint possession.

1. Frank and **Ruth's** anniversary is in September.
2. Roger, Clark, and **Mike's** proposal will certainly beat any other trio's (proposal).

Add an apostrophe to all nouns to indicate individual possession.

> **Brian's, Jason's, and Michael's** computers were stolen.

Add an apostrophe to indicate contractions.

1. **It's** raining outside again. (It's = It is)
2. **We're** running against each other in the election. (We're = We are)
3. If **you're** going to the movie with me, we should leave now. (you're = you are)
4. My cousin **should've** taken the bus. (should've = should have)
5. **Didn't** Kevin know that classes had begun? (Didn't = Did not)
6. Regrettably, I **won't** be able to attend the party. (won't = will not)
7. **That'll** break his heart! (That'll = That will)

Add an apostrophe to form the plural of letters and numbers.

1. Did you dot your *i***'s** and cross your *t***'s**?
2. There are a total of four **7's** in my phone number.

Do __NOT__ use apostrophes with possessive pronouns.

1. The car with the flat tire is ours.
   NOT – The car with the flat tire is **our's**.
2. Yours is the dog that barks all night.
   NOT – **Your's** is the dog that barks all night.

Colons and semicolons

A colon is used before a list or after an independent clause that is followed by information that directly modifies or adds to the clause. An independent clause can stand alone as a complete sentence. A semicolon is used to join closely related independent clauses when a coordinate conjunction is not used, with conjunctive adverbs to join main clauses, to separate items in a series that contains commas, and to separate coordinate clauses when they are joined by transitional words or phrases.

Use a colon before a list.

> We are required to bring the following items to camp**:** a sleeping bag, a pillow, an alarm clock, clothes, and personal care items.

Use a colon after an independent clause that is followed by information that directly modifies or adds to the clause.

1. Jennifer encountered a problem that she had not anticipated**:** a power outage.
2. My sister suggested a great location**:** the park down the street from our house.

Colons can be used before direct quotations, after salutations in business correspondence, and between titles and subtitles.

1. Captain John Paul Jones said**:** "I have not yet begun to fight."
2. Dear Mr. Smith**:**
3. *Blaze: A Story of Courage*

Use a semicolon to join closely related independent clauses when a coordinate conjunction is not used.

1. Jane starts a new job today**;** she is very excited.
2. I don't understand the directions**;** my teacher must explain them to me.

Use a semicolon with conjunctive adverbs to join independent clauses.

1. Martha is interested in taking the class**; however,** it does not suit her schedule.
2. My brother is very tall**; in fact,** he is the tallest person in our family.

Use semicolons in a series to separate elements containing commas.

1. The art museum contained some fragile, old oil paintings**;** bronze, plaster, and marble statues**;** and recently completed modern art pieces.
2. My first meal at college consisted of cold, dry toast**;** runny, undercooked eggs**;** and very strong, acidic coffee.

Use a semicolon to separate coordinate clauses when they are joined by transitional words or phrases.

When a sentence contains more than one clause, each of which is considered to be equally as important as the other, the clauses are called coordinate clauses. They are typically joined by a coordinating conjunction. When the coordinating conjunction is not used, a semicolon should be.

1. My sister and I enjoyed the play**; afterwards,** we stopped for an ice cream cone.
   OR: My sister and I enjoyed the play, **and afterwards,** we stopped for an ice cream cone.
2. Betty often misplaces her keys**; perhaps** she should get a key locator.
   OR: Betty often misplaces her keys, **so perhaps** she should get a key locator.

Parentheses and dashes

Parentheses are used to enclose supplemental information that is not essential to the meaning of the sentence. Dashes are used to place special emphasis on a word or phrase within a sentence.

Use parentheses to enclose explanatory or secondary supporting details.

1. In addition to serving as Class Treasurer **(a challenging job)**, she was also a National Merit Scholar.
2. Alan visited the Football Hall of Fame **(after years of begging his parents)** during his summer vacation.

Study Tip

The ACT English Test will never include a combination of one parenthesis and one dash in a correct answer.

Use dashes in place of parentheses to place special emphasis on certain words or phrases.

1. Dr. Evans—**a noted scientist and educator**—spoke at our commencement ceremony.
2. The homecoming float—**a cobbled mess of wire and nails**—meandered dangerously down the street.

Periods, question marks, and exclamation points

Periods, question marks, and exclamation points are considered end punctuation, which means that they should be used at the end of a sentence.

Use a period to end most sentences.

1. Scott enrolled in classes at the university**.**
2. Mary wanted to know what John made for dinner**.**

Use a question mark to end a direct question.

1. Do you think it will rain today**?**
2. What is the shortest route to the stadium**?**

Use an exclamation point to end an emphatic statement.

1. Please don't leave your vehicle unattended**!**
2. Wow**!** What a huge trout**!**

GRAMMAR RULES

The ACT English Test includes questions that will test your ability to identify and correct poorly written sentences. You should have a firm grasp of the following concepts:

- Subject/Verb Agreement
- Nouns and Pronouns
- Verbs and Verb Forms

Subject/verb agreement

A well-constructed sentence contains a subject and a verb and expresses a complete thought. The *subject* is who or what the sentence is about. The *verb* tells you what is happening with the subject or the state of the subject. Subjects and verbs are linked and must agree; they must match in form according to person (first, second, or third) and number (singular or plural). Some complex sentences on the ACT try to conceal the subject, making identification of proper subject/verb agreement more of a challenge.

Person—A main verb must agree with the subject in person:

1. *First Person* – **I am** eating lunch. **We left** the movie early.
2. *Second Person* – **You are** eating lunch.
3. *Third Person* – **She is** eating lunch. **He mowed** the lawn Tuesday. **It snows** often here in winter. **Someone is** paying for this mistake.

Number—A singular subject requires a singular verb.

1. The **earth is** round.
2. **One** of the boys **has** a dog.
3. **Everyone thinks** that I will win.

A plural subject requires a plural verb.

1. The **girls are** waiting for the bus.
2. **Patricia and Janet enjoy** suspense novels.
3. Do **football players like** classical music?

Voice—*Voice* defines whether the subject performs the action of the verb or receives the action of the verb. The active voice is usually the preferred mode of writing. *Active voice* means that the subject is acting, as in the following sentence:

1. The **dog licked** my brother.

Passive voice means that the subject is being acted upon, as in the following sentence:

2. My **brother was licked** by the dog.

Passive voice often appears as a present or past form of *be* (*am, are is, was, were*) + past participle (*shot, laughed [at], interviewed, impressed*).

Tense—Verb *tense* provides you with information about when the action took place. Actions take place in the present, in the past, or in the future, as shown below:

1. *Simple present*—the action takes place continuously or regularly (this tense has the sense that the action has taken place in the past and will continue taking place in the future): Robin **works** at the mall after school.
2. *Present perfect*—the action began in the past and is ongoing: Robin **has worked** at the mall for the last two years.
3. *Present progressive*—the action is ongoing *or* the action will take place in the near future: Robin **is working** today until 6 o'clock. Robin **is working** for her father this summer.
4. *Simple past*—the action happened in the past: Robin **worked** at the mall last year.
5. *Past perfect*—the action took place before another specified action: Robin **had worked** at the mall before taking a job at the theater.
6. *Past progressive*—the action was ongoing in the past (and was interrupted): Robin **was working** when the tornado hit.
7. *Future tense*—the action will take place in the future: Robin **will work** Tuesdays and Thursdays next semester.
8. *Future perfect*—the action takes place in the past relative to a time in the future: Robin **will have worked** at the mall for two years as of next week.
9. *Future progressive*—the action is ongoing relative to a time in the future: Robin **will be working** 40 hours per week by the end of the summer.

Nouns and pronouns

English nouns can be categorized as *proper nouns*, which name specific people, places, objects, or ideas, or *common nouns*, which name nonspecific people, places, objects, or ideas. Proper nouns begin with an uppercase letter, and common nouns do not.

Examples of proper nouns:

- Lieutenant Commander Bobby Hernandez (people and their titles)
- Fido (pets)
- R.M.S. *Titanic* (boats—note also that boat names are italicized or underlined when written)

- The Louvre (buildings)
- Toronto, Ontario, Canada (cities, provinces/states/territories, countries)
- Japanese (languages and nationalities)
- *Of Mice and Men* (novels—note also that only significant words in titles are capitalized, and the whole title is italicized when typed or underlined when written)
- Market Street Bistro (businesses)
- Death Valley (specific geographic features)
- Thursday, January 4, 2018 (days of the week and months)
- The Middle Ages (historical periods)
- The Protestant Reformation (political, social, and philosophical ideas and movements)
- New Year's Eve (holidays)

Though not proper nouns, acronyms and the first-person singular subject pronoun are capitalized:

- CPR, NASA, NAFTA, OPEC, DNA
- You will like how I make my chili.

Be careful with family members:

- Lowercase: "I went sailing with my mom and dad last year."
- Capitalized: "I went sailing with Mom and Dad last year."

In the first sentence, *mom* and *dad* are used like an occupation, since they are preceded by the possessive determiner *my*. In the second sentence, *Mom* and *Dad* are used like their proper names.

Pronouns take the place of either a proper or a common noun. Generally, a pronoun begins with an uppercase letter only if the pronoun begins a sentence. (The exception is *I*, which is always capitalized.) You should be able to determine and correctly apply pronoun case, as follows:

Nominative Case (renames the noun)—*I*, *you*, *he*, *she*, *it*, *they*, *we*

Mandy recently graduated from college; **she** now has a degree in nursing.

Possessive Case (shows possession)—*mine*, *ours*, *yours*, *his/hers*, *theirs*

That one is John's plane ticket, and this one is **mine**.

Objective Case (acts as direct or indirect object)—*me*, *us*, *you*, *him*, *her*, *it*, *them*

The monkey made faces at **him** through the bars of the cage.

English possessive determiners (*my*, *our*, *your*, *his/her/its*, *their*—sometimes called possessive adjectives) must match the person and number of the possessor and not the noun phrase to which they are linked:

Richard likes **his** hot dogs with lots of relish. (*his* is third-person singular to match with Richard, NOT third-person plural [*their*] to match with hot dogs.)

Use the *nominative* case of a personal pronoun with a compound subject.

If the subject consists of one or more nouns it is a compound subject.

1. Alan and **I** worked together on the project.
2. **She** and Pamela have been friends for a long time.

Use the *nominative* case for pronouns that are the subject of an incomplete clause.

Completing the clause will lead you to the correct pronoun case.

1. No one in the classroom was as surprised as **I** (was).
2. He worked longer today than **she** (worked).

Use a *possessive* determiner before a gerund.

A *gerund is* a verb ending in *-ing*, which can function as a noun.

1. **Her** singing has often been admired.
2. The class was shocked by **his** studying for the exam.

Use the *objective* case when the pronoun is the object of a verb.

1. A large dog chased **me** down the road. (What/who was chased? Me.)
2. The teacher gave **them** passing grades. (To what/whom did the teacher give passing grades? To them.)

Use the *objective* case when the pronoun is the object of a preposition.

A *preposition* is a word such as *from* or *before* that establishes a relationship between an object and some other part of the sentence, often expressing a location in place or time.

1. Matt received the greatest support from **you** and **me**.
2. The paper fluttered to the ground before **him**.

Relative pronouns—used to identify people, places, and objects in general. The relative pronouns **who**, **whom**, and **whose** refer to people. The relative pronouns **which**, **what**, **that**, and **whose** refer to places and objects.

Indefinite pronouns—used to represent an indefinite number of persons, places, or things. Indefinite pronouns are treated as singular pronouns. Following are some examples of indefinite pronouns:

1. **Everyone** gather around the campfire!
2. There will be a prize for **each** of the children.
3. **One** of my sisters always volunteers to drive me to school.
4. **Some** are friendlier than others.

Be sure to maintain consistency in pronoun person and number. It is not grammatically correct to use the plural pronoun *their* to represent neutral gender. This is an example of a major difference between Standard Written English and the English that we ordinarily use when speaking.

A small child should always be with **his or her** parent or guardian.
NOT: A small child should always be with **their** parent or guardian.

Misleading and ambiguous pronoun usage

A pronoun should be placed so that it clearly refers to a specific noun, called its *antecedent*. One of the errors that the ACT commonly tests is usage of a pronoun with a missing or unclear antecedent. Following are examples of misleading or ambiguous pronouns, along with corrected sentences:

1. *Misleading pronoun*—Despite the controversy surrounding the candidates, the committee made **their** decision very quickly.
   In this sentence, the plural pronoun **their** incorrectly refers to the singular noun **committee**. To correct this sentence, replace **their** with **its**.

Study Tip

The ACT English Test often requires you to select the correct pronoun; be aware of to whom or what the pronoun refers!

2. *Misleading pronoun*—**Several** of the group elected to return home following the decision.

   In this sentence the plural pronoun **several** refers to the singular noun **group**. To correct this sentence, add the plural noun **members** after the plural pronoun **several**.

In addition, a pronoun should be placed so that it clearly refers to a specific noun. If it does not, it is known as an *ambiguous pronoun*. See the following examples:

1. *Ambiguous pronoun*—Matt and Phil left rehearsal early to get **his** guitar repaired.

   In this sentence, it is unclear whose guitar is getting repaired.

   Correct sentence—Matt and Phil left rehearsal early to get **Phil's** guitar repaired.

2. *Ambiguous pronoun*—Some foods are dangerous for your pets, so **they** should be placed out of reach.

   In this sentence, it is unclear what should be placed out of reach: the potentially dangerous foods or your pets.

   Correct sentence—Some foods are dangerous for your pets; **these foods** should be placed out of reach.

Verbs and verb forms

A *verb* describes the action that is taking place in the sentence. All verbs have five principle forms:

> *Bare form*—I like to **write**. (In this sentence, tense is carried on "like.")
> *Simple present*—I **write**.
> *Simple past*—I **wrote**.
> *Gerund*—I am **writing**. (In this sentence, tense is carried on "am.")
> *Past participle*—I have **written**. (In this sentence, tense is carried on "have.")

Simple Past vs. Past Participle—The *simple past* and *past participle* forms of verbs can sometimes be confusing. Most past participles are formed by adding *-ed* to the word, as shown in the examples below:

1. *Simple present tense*—We **move** often.
2. *Past perfect tense*—We have **moved** again this year.

Remember that there are many irregular past participles in English, such as *written*, *eaten*, *come*, *gone*, and so on.

Some verbs have irregular simple past-tense forms, as shown in the examples below:

1. *Simple present tense*—I **see** my best friend every day.
2. *Simple past tense*—I **saw** my best friend yesterday.
3. *Simple present tense*—My little sister **eats** her breakfast quickly.
4. *Simple past tense*—My little sister **ate** her breakfast quickly.

Remember that the perfect and progressive tenses include so-called helping or *auxiliary* verbs, as shown in the examples below:

1. *Present perfect*—They **have** already **passed** Calculus II.
2. *Past perfect*—I **had seen** my best friend the day before.

3. *Present progressive*—My little sister **is eating** her breakfast quickly.
4. *Past progressive*—The winds **were howling** loudly as the vinyl siding began flying off the house.

Parallel construction

Parallel construction, or *parallelism*, allows a writer to show order and clarity in a sentence or a paragraph by putting grammatical elements that have the same function in the same form. Parallelism creates a recognizable pattern within a sentence and adds unity, force, clarity, and balance to writing. All words, phrases, and clauses used in parallel construction must share the same grammatical form. We have included some examples of sentences that include faulty parallelism, followed by revised versions of each sentence:

1. *Non-parallel construction*—Patricia enjoyed **running** and **to ride** her bike.

    In this sentence, the verb forms do not match. The first of the two verbs is a gerund (*running*), and the second verb is in the infinitive form (*to ride*), which is composed of the participle *to* and the bare form of the verb.

    Correct Sentence—Patricia enjoyed **running** and **riding** her bike.

2. *Non-parallel construction*—**The distance** from Los Angeles to Detroit is greater than Detroit to New York City.

    In this sentence, "The distance" only links with the first portion of the comparative construction: "from Los Angeles to Detroit."

    Correct Sentence—**The distance** from Los Angeles to Detroit is greater than **the distance** from Detroit to New York City.

Run-on sentences

A *run-on sentence* is a sentence that is composed of more than one main idea, and does not use proper punctuation or connectors. Following are examples of run-on sentences along with suggested corrections:

1. *Run-on sentence*—Janet is an actress **she** often appears in major network television shows.
   Correct sentence—Janet is an actress **who** often appears in major network television shows.

2. *Run-on sentence*—My nephew loves to play **football, you** can find him on the practice field almost every day.
   Correct Sentence—My nephew loves to play **football. You** can find him on the practice field almost every day.

Run-on sentences are often created by substituting a comma for a semicolon or a period, as shown in the incorrect sentence discussing football. Remember that this is called a *comma splice*, and it is incorrect.

Sentence fragments/incomplete sentences

A *sentence fragment* has end punctuation (so it appears as a sentence) but lacks one or more crucial features of a sentence (subject, verb, or predicate). Following are examples of sentence fragments along with suggested corrections:

1. *Sentence fragment*—My car is difficult to start in the **winter. Because** of the cold weather.
   Correct sentence—My car is difficult to start in the **winter because** of the cold weather.

2. *Sentence fragment*—John is a heavy **eater. Two** hot dogs for lunch and four for dinner.

Correct sentence—John is a heavy **eater; he normally eats two** hot dogs for lunch and four for dinner.

Sentence fragments may lack a verb, as shown in the examples below:

1. *Incomplete sentence*—Yesterday, the **winning** float in the parade.

   The sentence as it is written is incomplete; there is no main verb. The sentence should be revised so that the **winning float** either performs an action or has an action performed upon it.

   Revised sentence—Yesterday, the **winning float** in the parade **received** its prize.

2. *Incomplete sentence*—**Releasing** personal information by many school districts to third parties.

   The sentence as it is written is incomplete; the gerund **releasing** is being used as a noun in this sentence. Add a verb with tense.

   Revised sentence—Many school districts **prohibit releasing** personal information to third parties.

Misplaced modifiers

A sentence must contain at least one main clause. A complex sentence may contain more than one main clause, as well as one or more *relative clauses*. *Relative clauses* follow the nouns that they modify. In order to maintain clarity within a sentence, it is important to place a relative clause near the object that it modifies. A *modifier* is a word, phrase, or clause that modifies, or changes, the meaning of another word or part of the sentence. Often, a modifier helps explain or describe who, when, where, why, how, and to what extent. Misplaced modifiers can inadvertently change the meaning of the sentence. We have included some examples of sentences that contain misplaced modifiers, followed by revised versions of each sentence:

1. *Misplaced modifier*—Cassie had trouble deciding which college to attend **at first**.

   The meaning of this sentence is obscured by the placement of the modifying clause **at first**. It is unlikely that the writer intended to suggest that Cassie was considering attending more than one college.

   Correct sentence—**At first,** Cassie had trouble deciding which college to attend.

2. *Misplaced modifier*—**As a teacher,** the school board hired Mrs. Smith to coach our team.

   This sentence as it is written suggests that the school board, and not Mrs. Smith, is a teacher.

   Correct sentence—The school board hired Mrs. Smith, **a teacher,** to coach our team.

Idiom

Idiom refers to the common or everyday usage of a word or phrase. Idiom is part of standard written English and must be considered when making corrections to or improving sentences on the ACT. The following is a short list of common idiomatic phrases as they might be used in a sentence:

1. Mary thought that the test was a **piece of cake**.
   The phrase **piece of cake** typically signifies the relative ease of a task.
2. During our winter break, my friends and I **hit the slopes**.
   The phrase **hit the slopes** is generally used to indicate snow-skiing.
3. My father insisted that I put my **nose to the grindstone** next semester.
   The phrase **nose to the grindstone** is used to suggest that one is working hard.
4. Throughout the summer I lived a **stone's throw** from a popular beach.
   The phrase **stone's throw** generally indicates a short distance.
5. Sandy is often too **bogged down** with her studies to spend time with her friends.
   The phrase **bogged down** is most often used to mean overwhelmed.

Additionally, on the ACT English Test, idiom is tested less conspicuously. For example, you might be asked to identify the correct preposition to use in a sentence:

1. I often sit across **from** my sister on the bus.
   NOT: with, by, to
2. Ryan's professor casually glanced **at** him.
   NOT: to, upon

In each of the example sentences above, the preposition is used idiomatically: that is, in the way that has come to be accepted through common usage. When you see this question type on the ACT English Test, don't overanalyze it! Simply select the answer choice that makes the most sense to you.

Rhetoric

Rhetoric refers to the effective and persuasive use of language. Rhetorical skills, then, refer to your ability to make choices about the effectiveness and clarity of a word, phrase, sentence, or paragraph. Good writing involves effective word choice as well as clear and unambiguous expression. The best-written sentences will be relevant based on the context of the paragraph, will avoid redundancy, and will clearly and simply express the intended idea. The ACT Rhetorical Skills questions will evaluate your ability to clearly and effectively use Standard Written English. The exercises in Chapter 5 will help you to clearly and simply express an idea, a skill that the ACT English and Writing Tests reward.

Commonly misused words

Although there are thousands of different word-usage errors that could appear on the ACT, the test repeatedly includes commonly misused words. We've included a list of some of these words here, along with definitions and examples of the proper use of each word.

Accept, Except

Accept is a verb that means "to agree to receive something."
Example: I could not pay for my purchases with a credit card because the store would only **accept** cash.
Except is either a preposition that means "other than," or "but," or a verb meaning "to omit or leave out."
Example: **Except** for a B+ in history, Andrea received all A's on her report card.

Affect, Effect

Affect is usually a verb meaning "to influence."
Example: Fortunately, Sam's sore ankle did not **affect** her performance in the game.
Effect is usually a noun used to "indicate or achieve a result." Effect is also sometimes used as a transitive verb meaning "to bring into existence," but it is generally not used in this way on the ACT.
Example: Studies have shown that too much exercise can have a negative **effect** on a person's health.

Among, Between

Among is used with more than two items.
Example: Jackie's performance last night was the best
among all of the performances in the play.
Between is usually used with two items.
Example: Simon could not decide **between** the two puppies at the pound, so he adopted them both.

Assure, Ensure, Insure

Assure means "to convince" or "to guarantee" and usually takes a direct object.
Example: If we leave two hours early, I **assure** you that we will arrive at the concert on time.
Ensure means "to make certain."
Example: Our company goes to great lengths to **ensure** that every product that leaves the warehouse is of the highest quality.
Insure means "to guard against loss."
Example: Before he could leave for his trip, Steve had to **insure** his car against theft.

Compare to, Compare with

Compare to means "assert a likeness."
Example: The only way to describe her eyes is to **compare** them **to** the color of the sky.
Compare with means "analyze for similarities and differences."
Example: For her final project, Susan had to **compare** bike riding **with** other aerobic activities and report her findings.

Complement, Compliment

Complement implies "something that completes or adds to" something else.
Example: My favorite place to dine is on the terrace; the breathtaking views are the ideal **complement** to a romantic dinner.
A **compliment** is "flattery or praise."
Example: Larry was thrilled when the award-winning author **complimented** him on his writing style.

Farther, Further

Farther refers to distance.
Example: At baseball camp, Jackson learned that with the correct stance and technique, he could throw the ball **farther** this year than he could last year.
Further indicates "additional degree, time, or quantity."
Example: I enjoyed the book to a certain degree, but I felt that the author should have provided **further** details about the characters.

Fewer, Less

Fewer refers to units or individuals that can be counted.
Example: Trish received all the credit, even though she worked **fewer** hours on the project than did the other members of the group.
Less refers to mass or bulk that can't be counted.
Example: When it comes to reading, Mike is **less** inclined to read for pleasure than is Cassie.

Imply, Infer

Imply means "to suggest."
Example: His sister did not mean to **imply** that he was incorrect.
Infer means "to deduce," "to guess," or "to conclude."
Example: The professor's **inference** was correct concerning the identity of the student.

Its, It's

Its is the possessive form of "it."
Example: In the summer, my family enjoys drinking white tea for **its** refreshing, light flavor.
It's is the contraction of "it is."
Example: Fortunately for the runners, **it's** a sunny day.

The ACT will regularly include **its'** as an answer choice. This is never correct, as "it" is a singular pronoun and cannot show plural possession.

Lay, Lie

Lay means "to put" or "to place," and requires a direct object to complete its meaning.
Example: To protect your floor or carpet, you should always **lay** newspaper or a sheet on the ground before you begin to paint a room.

Lie means "to recline, rest, or stay," or "to take a position of rest." This verb cannot take a direct object. The past tense of **lie** is *lay*, so use extra caution if you see these words on the ACT.

Example: On sunny days, our lazy cat will **lie** on the porch and bask in the warmth of the sunlight.

Example: Yesterday, our lazy cat **lay** in the sun for most of the afternoon.

Like, Such As

Like should be used to indicate similarity.

Example: Andrea and Carol were very close, **like** two peas in a pod.

Such as should be used to indicate an example or examples.

Example: Composers **such as** Mozart and Bach are among my favorites.

Number, Amount

Number should be used when the items can be counted.

Example: The **number** of students enrolled at Hill College has increased during the last five years.

Amount should be used to denote quantity.

Example: A small **amount** of rain has fallen so far this year.

Precede, Proceed

Precede means "to go before."

Example: When I go to an expensive restaurant, I expect a salad course to **precede** the main course.

Proceed means "to move forward."

Example: As a result of failed negotiations, the labor union announced its plan to **proceed** with a nationwide strike.

Principal, Principle

Principal is a noun meaning "the head of a school or an organization."

Example: A high school **principal** is responsible not only for the educational progress of his students, but also for their emotional well-being.

Principal can also mean "a sum of money."

Example: I hope to see a 30 percent return on my **principal** investment within the first two years.

Principal can also be used as an adjective to mean "first" or "leading."

Example: Our **principal** concern is the welfare of our customers, not the generation of profits.

Principle is a noun meaning "a basic truth or law."

Example: A study of basic physics will include Newton's **principle** that every action has an opposite and equal reaction.

Set, Sit

The verb **set** takes an object.

Example: I **set** the bowl of pretzels in the middle of the table so that everyone could reach it.

The verb **sit** does not take an object.

Example: When I dine alone, I always **sit** by the window so that I can watch all the people who pass by the restaurant.

Than, Then

Than is a conjunction used in comparison.
Example: Roberta made fewer mistakes during her presentation **than** she thought she would make.
Then is an adverb denoting time.
Example: Mandy updated her resume, **then** applied for the job.

That, Which

That is used to introduce an essential clause in a sentence. Commas are not required before the word **that**.
Example: I usually take the long route because the main highway **that** runs through town is always so busy.
Which is best used to introduce a clause containing nonessential and descriptive information. Commas are required before the word **which** if it is used in this way. **Which** can also be used to introduce an essential clause in order to avoid repeating the word **that** in the sentence.
Example: The purpose of the Civil Rights Act of 1991, **which** amended the original Civil Rights Act of 1964, was to strengthen and improve Federal civil rights laws.
Example: I gave Michael that book **which** I thought he might like.

There, Their, They're

There is an adverb specifying location.
Example: Many people love to visit a big city, but few of them could ever live **there**.
Their is a possessive pronoun.
Example: More employers are offering new benefits to **their** employees, such as daycare services and flexible scheduling.
They're is a contraction of "they are."
Example: **They're** hoping to reach a decision by the end of the day.

To, Too, Two

To has many different uses in the English language, including the indication of direction and comparison. It is also used as an infinitive in verb phrases.
Example: Mary is driving **to** the beach tomorrow.
Example: Janet's painting is superior **to** Alan's painting.
Example: I try **to** run three miles every day.
Too generally means "in addition," or "more than enough."
Example: It is important that we consider Kevin's opinion **too**.
Example: Yesterday, I ran **too** far and injured my foot.
Two is the number 2.
Example: **Two** cats is too many for one apartment.

Whether, If

Whether should be used when listing alternatives.
Example: Traci could not decide **whether** to order the fish or the chicken.
If should be used when referring to a future possibility.
Example: **If** Traci orders the fish, she will be served more quickly.

Your, You're

Your is a possessive pronoun.
Example: Sunscreen protects **your** skin from sun damage.
You're is a contraction of "you are."
Example: When **you're** at the beach, always remember to wear sunscreen.

▬▬▬ WHAT'S NEXT?

Chapter 4 includes a review of the strategies that will help you to maximize your ACT English Test score. These strategies will show you how to use your time wisely and approach each question with confidence. Chapter 5 includes exercises designed to help you perfect your English grammar skills. You should refer back to Chapter 3 as needed while you work through the simulated English Tests and explanations found in Chapters 6 and 7. In addition, apply the rules in this chapter when you write your practice essays based on the ACT Writing Test prompts found in Chapters 16, 19, and 20.

CHAPTER 4

STRATEGIES AND TECHNIQUES

As you write more in high school and college, the ability to recognize your mistakes will become very important. Good writers can express ideas clearly by correctly applying the rules of grammar and selecting the most appropriate words and phrases.

As mentioned in Chapter 1, "Format and Scoring," the ACT English Test includes seventy-five multiple-choice questions that test your basic English and grammar skills. These questions also assess your ability to make choices about the effectiveness and clarity of a word, phrase, sentence, or paragraph. In this chapter, we'll give you useful strategies and techniques for effectively answering ACT English questions.

Follow these general strategies to select the best answers on the ACT English Test.

SKIM THE PASSAGE

Most of the ACT English Test questions are presented as underlined portions of the passages. It is helpful to read the passage through once quickly before you answer the questions. If you have a general sense of the structure and overall meaning of the passage, you will be more likely to choose the correct answers on questions that ask about a specific part of the passage. The ACT English Test passages are relatively short essays that you should be able to skim fairly quickly.

Take a look at this example. Skim the excerpt and answer the question that follows:

> Like most college students, I usually needed extra cash. However, I was a bit too discriminating in how I earned that money. Since my parents were paying my tuition, I couldn't very well get a job that interfered with my classes, nor did I want to give up any of my extracurricular activities. Babysitting often fit within these parameters, but it usually didn't pay very well. I scoured the campus papers, but the good jobs were always taken by the time I called to get more information. And then, one day, I found it—the perfect part-time job.

> As I left my sociology class one day, I saw a flyer posted near the door: "Help wanted for Psychology Dissertation Research—Acting Experience Requested." Normally, I avoided psychology research because it generally involved some form of pain or deprivation for a very small stipend—in the range of $20 to $50. Nevertheless, I was intrigued by the request for "acting experience," and since most of my extracurricular time was spent on stage, I decided this job posting warranted a phone call.

> **Question:** Suppose that the editor of a magazine had assigned the writer to depict a firsthand account of an undergraduate majoring in Sociology. Does the essay successfully fulfill this assignment?
> **A.** Yes, because the essay describes what happens when the writer is leaving a sociology class.
> **B.** Yes, because sociology and psychology are closely linked.
> **C.** No, because the essay describes a part-time job working on a psychology dissertation research project.
> **D.** No, because the essay's tone is too formal and too personal for such an assignment.

Study Tip

You will generally not be required to infer anything about the people or places mentioned in these passages. Inference questions are reserved for the ACT Reading Test, which we will discuss in Chapters 8–14.

The best answer is C. This question relies on identifying the main idea of the essay. The main idea is stated at the end of the first paragraph: "a description of the perfect part-time job." The author's perfect job is in psychology, not sociology. In fact, there is no indication that the author is even a sociology major, only that the author is taking a sociology class. Therefore, the essay would not be appropriate for the magazine article because its content is off-topic.

This type of question usually appears at the end of the set of questions following an English passage.

▮▮▮ REVIEW THE UNDERLINED PORTION

The portion of the sentence that is underlined might need to be revised, replaced, or omitted. When reading the sentence, pay attention to the underlined portion. If the underlined portion makes the sentence awkward, or contains errors in standard written English, it will need to be revised or omitted. Many errors are obvious, and if you can spot them right away, you will be able to move quickly through this section.

Look for common problems, such as redundancy, misplaced modifiers, faulty parallelism, ambiguous pronouns, and disagreement between the subject and the verb. Be sure that the answer choice you select does not contain any of these errors, which were discussed in Chapter 3, "Grammar Review."

If the underlined portion seems correct within the sentence as it is, mark either A or F on your answer sheet. The test is designed to assess your ability to improve sentences, which also includes recognizing when a sentence is best as it is written. Consider the following examples:

Chinese calligraphy <u>dates back</u> nearly 5,000 years. Around 200 B.C., a 3,000-character
                       1
index was established <u>for use of</u> Chinese scholars.
                       2

Underlined Portion 1:   **A**. NO CHANGE
                                 B. date back from
                                   C. date back
                                   D. were dated back

Underlined Portion 2:   **F.** NO CHANGE
                                   G. for to be used by
                                   H. for the use with
                                   J. for use by

1. **The best answer is A.** To maintain parallelism in this sentence, the subject must match the verb. Since the subject, "Chinese calligraphy," is singular, the correct verb form is "dates back," answer choice A.

2. **The best answer is J.** The Chinese scholars used the index; therefore, the index was established "for use by" the Chinese scholars. This is an example of both verb choice and idom.

▮▮▮ PREDICT AN ANSWER

If the underlined portion does not seem correct, try to predict the correct answer. If an answer choice matches your predicted answer, it is most likely correct. If you can recognize a paraphrase of your predicted answer, choose it. Mark the question in your test booklet if you are unsure. Use a mark that will be easy to spot when you are looking back through the test, as discussed in the Introduction. Whatever symbol you decide to use, be consistent so that the mark means the same thing every time you use it. Remember that you can always come back to the question later if there is time.

If your predicted answer does not match any of the answer choices, determine which of the selections is the most clear and simple. Read the sentence again, replacing the underlined portion with the answer choices in order. Remember that answer choice A or F ("NO CHANGE") will always be a repeat of the original underlined portion. Consider the following example:

According to health experts, over the past 30 years the childhood obesity rate in the United States has more than tripled for <u>some of them</u> aged 6–11, and has doubled for
1
younger children and adolescents.

Underlined Portion 1:   **A.** NO CHANGE
B. them
C. children
D. those of them

1. **The best answer is C.** The pronoun "them" is rather ambiguous. Be sure that all pronouns have a clear antecedent. In this case, based on the context of the sentence you might have predicted "children," the correct answer, because it eliminates the ambiguity.

■■■ TRUST WHAT YOU KNOW

Subvocalize (read "aloud silently" to yourself) to allow your brain to "hear" the sentence with each of the answer choices inserted. Your brain might automatically make the necessary improvement, or recognize the best version of the sentence.

You can usually trust your impulses when answering many of the questions on the English Test. In other words, if it sounds right to you, it probably is. You will recognize when and how to apply basic rules of grammar, even if you don't recall what the specific rule is. You can tap into the part of your brain that controls speech and hearing as you read. That part of your brain "knows" how English is supposed to sound. Let that part of your brain work for you. Remember, the ACT English Test does NOT require you to state a specific rule, only to apply it correctly. Consider the following example:

No sooner had Michael arrived on campus <u>so his mother began</u> calling him repeatedly.
1

Underlined Portion 1:   **A.** NO CHANGE
B. than his mother began
C. but his mother had began
D. then he was called by his mother

1. **The best answer is B.** The context of the sentence indicates that first one thing happened, and then another thing happened. To best express this chronology of events, the comparative word "than" should be used. The other answer choices are awkward and grammatically incorrect.

■■■ USE THE PROCESS OF ELIMINATION

Elimination is the process that most test takers use for all the questions that they answer. It is reliable, but slow. Use it as a backup strategy on questions for which either you cannot predict an answer, or your prediction is not listed as a choice. Consider the following example:

Despite <u>it's popularity</u>, the play closed after only two weeks.
1

Underlined Portion 1:   **A.** NO CHANGE
B. their popularity
C. it's being popular
D. its popularity

Study Tip

Since there can only be one correct answer for each question, you can eliminate any two choices that mean the same. If you find that two of the choices are synonyms, eliminate them both.

1. The best answer is D. Your first step should be to decide whether "it's" is correct in this sentence. Because "it's" is the contraction of "it is," you would not use "it's" in this sentence. Therefore, you can eliminate answer choices A and C. Next, because there is only one play, you can eliminate answer choice B, which includes the plural possessive pronoun "their." You are now left with the correct answer.

TAKE DELETE SERIOUSLY

You will sometimes see the answer choice "DELETE the underlined portion." Selecting this option will remove the underlined portion from the sentence or paragraph. "DELETE" is a viable answer choice when it eliminates redundant or irrelevant statements. When DELETE is given as an answer choice on the ACT, it is correct about half of the time. Consider the following example:

The first sign that our remodeling project might have its ups and downs was when the contractor announced his bottom-line price to cover all our wondrous plans; it became immediately clear right away that a scale-back was necessary.

1

Underlined Portion 1: **A.** NO CHANGE
 B. at the onset
 C. instantly
 D. DELETE the underlined portion.

1. The best answer is D. Because the sentence already includes the word "immediately," it is not necessary to include language such as "right away," "at the onset," or "instantly," which all have essentially the same meaning. This is a good example of eliminating redundancy.

FEAR CHANGE (SOMETIMES!)

On the ACT English Test, the first answer choice for almost every question is "NO CHANGE." This answer choice should come up about as often as the others do on your answer sheet. Just because a portion of the passage is underlined doesn't mean that there is something wrong with it. Consider the following example:

Amanda took voice lessons last year, and she has been singing in the choir ever since.

1

Underlined Portion 1: **A.** NO CHANGE
 B. and in the choir she has been singing ever since.
 C. so singing in the choir she has been ever since
 D. ever since then she has been singing in the choir

1. The best answer is A. The sentence is clear and concise as written. Answer choices B and C are awkward, so they would not be the best choice. Answer choice D is incorrect because it creates a comma splice.

GO WITH THE FLOW

The ACT English Test includes *rhetorical skills* questions, which address writing strategy, organization, and style. These questions test your ability to express an idea clearly and concisely. They also assess whether you can identify a well-constructed essay. Make sure that you understand what's going on in the passage/essay, and pay attention to introductory and transitional words and phrases that might suggest a continuation, contrast, or comparison.

Following are tables of commonly used introductory and transitional words and transitional words and phrases:

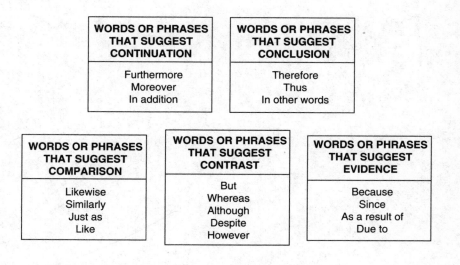

PRACTICE, PRACTICE, PRACTICE

Remember from the Introduction that the best way to internalize a skill is to practice it. Use the practice material in this book to hone your skills so that you can attack the ACT English Test with confidence.

You might also want to purchase some additional practice tests; we recommend the following:

> *McGraw-Hill's 10 ACT Practice Tests*. This book includes, not surprisingly, 10 full-length simulated practice ACT tests, written by the faculty of Advantage Education. Each test is followed by explanations for every question.

> *The Real ACT Prep Guide*. Written by the makers of the ACT, this book includes three full-length practice ACT tests along with explanations.

Both of the above titles can be purchased online at www.AdvantageEd.com/ACTBooks.htm. They are also available in major bookstores around the country.

WHAT'S NEXT?

Chapter 5 includes exercises designed to help you master the ACT English Test questions. Focus on those areas that give you the most trouble, and be sure to review the explanations. The exercises in Chapter 5 will also help you to become a better writer, so be sure to apply what you learn to the essay-writing tasks in Chapters 15–20.

CHAPTER 5

APPLYING STRATEGIES, BUILDING SKILLS

This chapter contains exercises designed to help you apply the concepts generally tested on the ACT English Test—namely, grammar and rhetorical skills.

These exercises will help you to become familiar with the following content areas:

- Grammatical Voice
- Modifying Clauses
- Verb Tense
- Irregular Past Verbs
- Subject/Verb Agreement
- Adjectives and Adverbs
- Pronouns
- Idiom
- Redundancy
- Punctuation

GRAMMATICAL VOICE

The ACT English Test generally prefers active voice. The only exceptions are where the passive voice is significantly clearer or more concise than any active voice revision, or where the active voice revision(s) would violate some other grammar rule.

Exercises

In the following sentences, choose the best revision for the underlined portion. If the sentence is best as written, select "NO CHANGE." Read the explanations at the end of the chapter for each question that you missed.

1. The sun was setting quickly behind the leftfield bleachers, and the infield continued to be muddied by the steady downpour.
   A. NO CHANGE
   B. the infield, by the steady downpour, continued to be muddied
   C. the steady downpour, muddying the infield, continued
   D. the steady downpour continued to muddy the infield

2. <u>It being our home, the ninety-year-old cottage is</u> miles from civilization.
   F. NO CHANGE
   G. Our home is a ninety-year-old cottage
   H. Being our home, it is a ninety-year-old cottage
   J. Our home, it being a ninety-year-old cottage, is

3. <u>The hurricane destroyed the municipal pier</u>, although it caused only minor damage to coastal homes.
   A. NO CHANGE
   B. The hurricane was the destroyer of the municipal pier
   C. The municipal pier was destroyed by the hurricane
   D. The destruction of the municipal pier was caused by the hurricane

4. Having little evidence to support her client's statements, <u>the plea agreement was accepted by the attorney</u>.
   F. NO CHANGE
   G. the attorney accepted the plea agreement
   H. the plea agreement in being accepted by the attorney
   J. the attorney the plea agreement accepted

5. It was a banner night for the concert planners: the band rocked, <u>many shirts and CDs were sold by vendors</u>, and security reported no problems.
   A. NO CHANGE
   B. vendors, having sold many shirts and CDs
   C. vendors sold many shirts and CDs
   D. shirts and CDs, many being sold by venders

6. <u>Jenny's friends Sue, Raquel, and Melinda were invited by Jenny to the party</u>.
   F. NO CHANGE
   G. Jenny invited her friends Sue, Raquel, and Melinda to the party.
   H. Sue, Raquel, and Melinda, Jenny's friends, were invited by Jenny to the party.
   J. The invitation to the party of her friends Sue, Raquel, and Melinda was made by Jenny.

7. <u>Attending school six days a week and taking as many as nine courses each term, most Japanese students are</u>.
   A. NO CHANGE
   B. Most Japanese students, attending school six days a week and taking as many as nine courses each term.
   C. Most Japanese students attend school six days a week and take as many as nine courses each term.
   D. By attending school six days a week and taking as many as nine courses are most Japanese students.

8. <u>Water towers are used by cities</u> to ensure adequate water supply during peak-usage times of day, such as early morning and late evening.
   F. NO CHANGE
   G. Used by cities are water towers
   H. Water towers get used by cities
   J. Cities use water towers

9. Young cows are called calves, whereas <u>young pigs are called piglets</u>.
   A. NO CHANGE
   B. piglets are known as young pigs
   C. young pigs being called piglets
   D. called piglets are young pigs

10. <u>City fire officials take great pains to give</u> smoke detectors to all residents whose homes lack them.
   F. NO CHANGE
   G. Great pains are taken by city fire officials to give
   H. By city fire officials, great pains are taken to give
   J. Taking great pains, city fire officials give

■ MODIFYING CLAUSES

In order to maintain clarity within a sentence, it is important to place a modifier—a word, phrase, or clause that modifies, or changes, the meaning of another word or part of the sentence—near the object that it modifies. Often, a modifier helps explain or describe who, when, where, why, how, and to what extent. Misplaced modifiers can inadvertently change the meaning of the sentence.

Exercises

In the following sentences, choose the best revision for the underlined portion. If the sentence is best as written, choose "NO CHANGE." Read the explanations at the end of the chapter for each question that you missed.

1. The potter took the assorted greenware down to the kiln, <u>it is a brick structure</u> designed to bake pottery to a hardness that drying alone cannot produce.
   A. NO CHANGE
   B. the brick structure is
   C. a brick structure
   D. brick

2. The magician, for one of his many tricks, <u>mysteriously pulled a rabbit from his hat</u>.
   F. NO CHANGE
   G. with great mystery from his hat pulled a rabbit
   H. pulled from mysteriously his hat a rabbit
   J. mysterious from his hat pulled a rabbit

3. The paddler pulls one end <u>through the water</u> of the paddle on alternating sides of the boat.

   The best placement for the underlined portion would be:
   A. where it is now.
   B. after the word *paddler*.
   C. after the word *pulls*.
   D. after the word *paddle*.

4. New developments extend the time that scientists can work <u>greatly</u> in space.

   The best placement for the underlined portion would be:
   F. where it is now.
   G. after the word *developments*.
   H. after the word *time*.
   J. after the word *scientists*.

5. Bolted to a 300 ton platform sixty-six feet below sea level, <u>scientists at this research outpost are offered</u> a unique opportunity to study the impact of temperature change on fish species.
   A. NO CHANGE
   B. this research outpost offers scientists
   C. scientists researching at this outpost are offered
   D. research scientists at this outpost are offered

6. My grandmother looked at me sadly <u>at the age of seventeen</u> and said that I was abandoning our traditions by leaving home.

   The best placement for the underlined portion would be:
   F. where it is now.
   G. after the word *said*.
   H. after the word *abandoning*.
   J. after the word *home* (ending the sentence with a period).

7. Last weekend, Luke saw seventy-three dogs <u>driving around town</u>.

   The best placement for the underlined portion would be:
   A. where it is now.
   B. after the phrase *seventy-three*.
   C. after the word *saw*.
   D. before the word *last* (capitalize the word *driving*).

8. When Michelle got back to the campground, her boyfriend was <u>cleaning the fish he had just caught with his pocketknife</u>.
   F. NO CHANGE
   G. cleaning the fish with his pocketknife that he had just caught
   H. using his pocketknife to clean the fish he had just caught
   J. catching the fish he had just cleaned with his pocketknife

9. <u>Our manager overheard that we were planning her a birthday party, on the way to her car.</u>
   A. NO CHANGE
   B. On the way to her car, our manager overheard that we were planning her a birthday party.
   C. Our manager on the way to her car overheard that we were planning her a birthday party.
   D. Our manager overheard that we were on the way to her car planning her a birthday party.

10. <u>Crumpled in the corner of her room</u>, Miranda noticed Christopher's love letter.

    The best placement for the underlined portion would be:
    F. where it is now.
    G. after *Miranda*.
    H. after the word *noticed*.
    J. after the word *letter* (ending the sentence with a period).

███ **VERB TENSE**

A verb describes the action that is taking place in the sentence. The ACT English Test will often test your ability to select the correct verb tense.

Irregular Past Forms of Verbs

Grammatical *past* is expressed in both the simple past form and the past participle of a verb. Remember that the simple past form can be used alone as the main verb in a clause, whereas the past participle can be used as an adjective or as the main verb in a clause when paired with a form of the auxiliary verb "have" (as in the perfect tenses) or "be" (as in passive-voice).

Exercises

In the following sentences, choose the best revision for the underlined portion. If the sentence is best as written, choose "NO CHANGE." Read the explanations at the end of the chapter for each question that you missed.

1. Amanda must <u>have heard</u> us talking, because she began to walk toward us.
   A. NO CHANGE
   B. have heard of
   C. of heard about
   D. of heard

2. Danielle, it turns out, is a Siamese cat that my grandfather had <u>started raising</u> over twenty years ago.

   Which of the following alternatives to the underlined portion would NOT be acceptable?
   F. begun to raise
   G. started to raise
   H. started up raising
   J. begun raising

3. My aunt said that she <u>would have checked</u> with my parents, who had each agreed that if I wanted to take responsibility for the puppy, I could take him home with me.
   A. NO CHANGE
   B. had checked
   C. would check
   D. will be checking

4. The clock <u>keeps</u> precise time for the last seventy years.
   F. NO CHANGE
   G. has kept
   H. keeping
   J. still keeps

5. Some mammals sleep in ancient caverns, waking after months to feed and <u>to be bred</u>.
   A. NO CHANGE
   B. for breeding
   C. breed
   D. breeding

6. Heat-loving bacteria <u>by flourishing</u> in temperatures over 150 degrees Celsius.
   F. NO CHANGE
   G. were flourishing
   H. having flourished
   J. flourish

7. I just feel better <u>to have known</u> a pencil is handy.
   A. NO CHANGE
   B. to knew that
   C. known that
   D. knowing

8. It takes a great degree of focus <u>to hit</u> a golf ball cleanly on your first swing.
   F. NO CHANGE
   G. for hitting
   H. to hitting
   J. that hit

9. Norm Bruce is best remembered for making it possible for generations of baseball players taking batting practice <u>concentrated</u> on their swings without worrying about wild pitches.
   A. NO CHANGE
   B. concentrating
   C. concentrate
   D. to concentrate

10. Sidestepped by progress and <u>frozen</u> in time, Mackinaw City is now a living historical museum.
    F. NO CHANGE
    G. froze
    H. freezed
    J. frozed

■ SUBJECT/VERB AGREEMENT

In a well-constructed sentence, subjects and verbs are linked and must agree; they must match in form, according to person (first, second, or third) and number (singular or plural). Some complex sentences on the ACT try to conceal the subject, making identification of proper subject/verb agreement more of a challenge.

Exercises

In the following sentences, choose the best revision for the underlined portion. If the sentence is best as written, choose "NO CHANGE." Read the explanations at the end of the chapter for each question that you missed.

1. When one of the European Union's twenty official languages <u>are used</u> at a meeting, translation services must be available for all of the other languages.
   A. NO CHANGE
   B. is used
   C. are being used
   D. are in use

2. The equipment for both types of boats <u>are</u> similar, and fairly simple.
   F. NO CHANGE
   G. is
   H. were
   J. being

3. At the end of the day, most of my clothes <u>will have been covering</u> with paint splotches from careless brush strokes.
   A. NO CHANGE
   B. had been covered
   C. are covering
   D. are covered

4. The glasses constructed according to his designs fit so well and so comfortably that the satisfaction of his patients <u>are being</u> measurably improved.
   F. NO CHANGE
   G. was
   H. are
   J. were

5. What was once hidden away behind the mountains <u>are</u> now out in the open for everyone to observe.
   A. NO CHANGE
   B. is
   C. were
   D. have been

6. The test on mathematics <u>are</u> tomorrow during third period, so we are having a review session at Lindsay's house tonight.
   F. NO CHANGE
   G. was
   H. is
   J. were

7. With four brothers and three sisters, your family <u>have</u> never been able to agree on anything.
   A. NO CHANGE
   B. would
   C. will
   D. has

8. According to the city charter, the mayor may only adjourn the meeting after the committee <u>set</u> the agenda for the following month.
   F. NO CHANGE
   G. sat
   H. setting
   J. sets

9. The Prime Minister, accompanied by several of his Ministers, <u>is</u> expected to travel to the United States next week.
   A. NO CHANGE
   B. will have been
   C. are
   D. were

10. Based on the performance evaluations from his department, it is clear that it's the courses he teaches, not Mr. Kennedy himself, that <u>has</u> received poor reviews.
- **F.** NO CHANGE
- **G.** having
- **H.** have
- **J.** will have

ADJECTIVES AND ADVERBS

Adjectives modify nouns or pronouns, whereas adverbs modify verbs, adjectives, or other adverbs. Some items on the ACT English Test will require you to recognize correct usage of adjectives and adverbs based on context. The ACT English Test does NOT require you to form correct comparatives and superlatives; however, it does require you to understand their usage in sentences.

Exercises

In the following sentences, choose the best revision for the underlined portion. If the sentence is best as written, choose "NO CHANGE." Read the explanations at the end of the chapter for each question that you missed.

1. The campers glimpsed the <u>arresting beautiful</u> sunset from the top of the hill.
- **A.** NO CHANGE
- **B.** arrestingly beautiful
- **C.** arresting beautifully
- **D.** arrestingly beautifully

2. The judges will choose <u>the best singer</u> from among the fifty contestants.
- **F.** NO CHANGE
- **G.** a better singer
- **H.** the better singer
- **J.** the bestest singer

3. Riverbank erosion is a <u>continue</u> source of anxiety for state environmental officials.
- **A.** NO CHANGE
- **B.** continual
- **C.** continuously
- **D.** continually

4. For years, cargo vessels were <u>unwitting introduction</u> many exotic species to the St. Lawrence Seaway by discharging ballast water the ships had taken from faraway seas.
- **F.** NO CHANGE
- **G.** unwitting introducing
- **H.** unwittingly introduction
- **J.** unwittingly introducing

5. Although the warning light comes on often, it does not <u>usually signal</u> a major problem.
- **A.** NO CHANGE
- **B.** usual signal
- **C.** usually signaling
- **D.** usual signaling

6. Watching hockey is best experienced with the <u>frightening closeness</u> of first-row seats.
   F. NO CHANGE
   G. frighteningly close
   H. closely frightening
   J. closely frighten

7. We ultimately decided that waiting out the traffic jam would be <u>the best</u> course of action than exiting the Interstate to take a detour.
   A. NO CHANGE
   B. the most better
   C. a better
   D. a best

8. <u>The speaker sincerely thanked</u> the audience members for their steadfast attention and thoughtful questions.

   Which of the choices would NOT be acceptable?
   F. With sincerity the speaker thanked
   G. The speaker sincere thanked
   H. Sincerely the speaker thanked
   J. The speaker thanked with sincerity

9. Raspberries are expensive, in part because they must be <u>harvest careful</u>.
   A. NO CHANGE
   B. careful harvest
   C. harvested careful
   D. carefully harvested

10. Kindergarten teachers are always prepared for the <u>occasionally</u> spill of classroom liquids such as water, juice, and glue.
    F. NO CHANGE
    G. occasion
    H. occasional
    J. on occasion

▆▆▆ PRONOUNS

Pronouns take the place of either a proper or a common noun, known as the antecedent. Generally, a pronoun begins with an uppercase letter only if the pronoun begins a sentence. (The exception is *I*, which is always capitalized.) You should be able to determine and correctly apply pronoun case.

Exercises

In the following sentences, choose the best revision for the underlined portion. If the sentence is best as written, choose "NO CHANGE." Read the explanations at the end of the chapter for each question that you missed.

1. He had dismantled a clockwork mouse borrowed from a master craftsman, made detailed drawings of <u>it's</u> components, and returned it—fully functioning—to the craftsman.
   A. NO CHANGE
   B. its'
   C. its
   D. their

2. The physicist quickly became engrossed in his studies and began to calculate the paths of the Sun, Moon, and other celestial bodies. Using <u>them,</u> he predicted a solar eclipse that occurred four years later.
   F. NO CHANGE
   G. these calculations,
   H. those,
   J. these things,

3. I usually carry a handful of pens in my backpack; who knows when <u>they</u> will run dry.
   A. NO CHANGE
   B. the one I am using
   C. something
   D. either one

4. My exercise habit is not without <u>it's</u> negative consequences.
   F. NO CHANGE
   G. they're
   H. their
   J. its

5. Both fields and forests were dear to me and important to the development of <u>one's</u> interactions with the world.
   A. NO CHANGE
   B. their
   C. your
   D. my

6. Mrs. Kervin rewarded Jake and <u>he</u> for their contributions to the research project.
   F. NO CHANGE
   G. him
   H. you
   J. they

7. Several of <u>we</u> theatre majors went out for coffee after our performance last weekend.
   A. NO CHANGE
   B. you
   C. those
   D. us

8. Although Ashley and <u>me</u> thought we were fluent in Spanish, it was very difficult to understand many of the people in northern Spain.
   F. NO CHANGE
   G. I
   H. us
   J. them

9. My younger sister recently finished a book on dog grooming, and now she wants to learn everything she can about <u>them.</u>
   A. NO CHANGE
   B. it
   C. him
   D. those

10. If people want to live by themselves in a dormitory, <u>you</u> must pay twice the usual room rate, unless those people become resident assistants.
    F. NO CHANGE
    G. we
    H. one
    J. they

▍ IDIOM

Idiom refers to the commonly accepted usage of a word or phrase. The ACT English Test will often test your ability to recognize idiomatic prepositional phrases.

Exercises

In the following sentences, choose the best revision for the underlined portion. If the sentence is best as written, choose "NO CHANGE." Read the explanations at the end of the chapter for each question that you missed.

1. Each time more wood is added to the fire, smoke swirls <u>from the chimney into</u> the night sky.

    Which of the following alternatives to the underlined portion would NOT be acceptable?
    A. at the chimney in
    B. up the chimney toward
    C. through the chimney into
    D. out the chimney into

2. The doctor focused his imagination and intelligence <u>to</u> devising a way to solve the problem.
    F. NO CHANGE
    G. at
    H. on
    J. for

3. <u>By</u> the Park Service's stewardship, the city's park system flourished.
    A. NO CHANGE
    B. As
    C. In
    D. Under

4. The college professor had a method <u>about</u> calculating grades.
    F. NO CHANGE
    G. with
    H. by
    J. for

5. My father did not understand that information is communicated <u>different from</u> other cultures.
    A. NO CHANGE
    B. different than
    C. differently in
    D. differently than

6. Steven should have known that Angela's comment was not meant <u>as</u> an insult.
   F. NO CHANGE
   G. of
   H. to
   J. for

7. The members of the Williams family <u>made their living</u> working alternately as field hands and as touring musicians.

   Which of the following alternatives to the underlined portion would NOT be acceptable?
   A. earned their living by
   B. made their living from
   C. made their living on
   D. earned their living

8. Aaron walked into the stadium with a chip <u>of</u> his shoulder; it was obvious that he wanted a rematch.
   F. NO CHANGE
   G. over
   H. off
   J. on

9. Since Matt was superstitious, his first thought was to knock <u>with</u> wood whenever someone wished him good luck.
   A. NO CHANGE
   B. by
   C. on
   D. through

10. <u>In</u> the dusk of a late summer evening, we strolled along the beach toward the lighthouse.
    F. NO CHANGE
    G. On
    H. With
    J. From

■■■ REDUNDANCY

The ACT English Test often questions your ability to recognize and eliminate redundancy in sentences and paragraphs. You will be rewarded for clearly and simply expressing the intended idea.

Exercises

In the following sentences, choose the best revision for the underlined portion. If the sentence is best as written, choose "NO CHANGE." Read the explanations at the end of the chapter for each question that you missed.

1. Over many weeks, <u>as time goes by</u>, the potter's collection slowly grows: terra cotta bowls, vases, and urns fill the studio.
   A. NO CHANGE
   B. with the passing of time,
   C. gradually
   D. DELETE the underlined portion.

2. Last week, my mother told me she had to go on a business trip in connection with her work and that I'd be staying with my aunt for three days.
   F. NO CHANGE
   G. having something to do with her job
   H. that involved traveling to another city
   J. DELETE the underlined portion.

3. He began to calculate annual tables of yearly sets of astronomical data, which became the basis for almanacs published in the 1790s.
   A. NO CHANGE
   B. covering a year's worth
   C. about twelve months
   D. DELETE the underlined portion.

4. My two views of the world provide varied and different reactions to more than just politics.
   F. NO CHANGE
   G. difference in their varying
   H. different
   J. variously different

5. Finally, her father acquiesced, when he thought about it and gave in, allowing her to pursue her dream.
   A. NO CHANGE
   B. in that he gave in,
   C. by finally agreeing,
   D. DELETE the underlined portion.

6. Underwater explorer Jacques Cousteau, exploring under the sea, predicted that one day humans would be able to work and even live underwater.
   F. NO CHANGE
   G. Cousteau—exploring under the sea—
   H. Cousteau who explored under the sea,
   J. Cousteau

7. Norm Bruce is most widely remembered today for his invention and creation of the pitching machine.
   A. NO CHANGE
   B. invention
   C. invention, that is, the creation
   D. invention, which was the creation

8. In both of these cases, Gary recognized a need and set out to find a way to fulfill it.
   F. NO CHANGE
   G. a lack of something that was needed
   H. that a need was in existence
   J. a need that was out there

9. It was a routine Sunday evening and like many others
   A. NO CHANGE
   B. evening
   C. evening, typical for us
   D. evening, just as usual

10. <u>In due course, after waiting for a while</u>, my neighbor signaled for the waitress and asked her why he still had not received his calamari.
   F.   NO CHANGE
   G.   While waiting and after a while
   H.   After waiting a while
   J.   After a due course of time while waiting

■■ PUNCTUATION

Commas

The comma is among the most frequently tested punctuation marks on the ACT English Test. It has many usages that are standard and invariable. In correct answer choices involving commas, all the commas are necessary ones. Review Chapter 3 for more detailed information on the proper use of commas.

Semicolons and Colons

The ACT English Test normally includes several items testing semicolon usage. Although it is not a commonly used punctuation mark, the semicolon can be useful. A semicolon is used to join closely related independent clauses when a coordinate conjunction is not used, with conjunctive adverbs to join main clauses, to separate items in a series that contains commas, and to separate coordinate clauses when they are joined by transitional words or phrases. A colon is used before a list or after an independent clause that is followed by information that directly modifies or adds to the clause. (An independent clause can stand alone as a complete sentence.)

Apostrophes

Apostrophe usage is frequently tested on the ACT English Test. There are only two standard usages of the apostrophe: to form possessives and to form contractions.

Parentheses and Dashes

Neither parentheses nor dashes are tested frequently on the ACT English Test. When they are tested, the parentheses are often enclosing nonessential, irrelevant, or redundant information. In many of these cases, several answer choices replace the parentheses with commas or dashes. Usually, one answer choice eliminates the parenthetical material entirely and reads, "DELETE the underlined portion." If the parenthetical material is nonessential, irrelevant, or redundant, mark this answer choice.

End Punctuation

End punctuation refers to the period, question mark, and exclamation point. On the ACT English Test, only these three punctuation marks may end sentences. The comma, semicolon, colon, dash, and all other punctuation marks may NOT end a sentence.

Exercises

In the following sentences, choose the best revision for the underlined portion. If the sentence is best as written, choose "NO CHANGE." Read the explanations at the end of the chapter for each question that you missed.

1. The following <u>night, using twigs, for kindling</u> she started a small blaze in the fire pit.
   A. NO CHANGE
   B. night, using twigs for kindling,
   C. night, using twigs for kindling;
   D. night using twigs, for kindling,

2. Shortly after I arrived, my <u>uncle said</u> he had a gift for me.
   F. NO CHANGE
   G. uncle, said
   H. uncle said,
   J. uncle said;

3. I was told that I should fence off an area in each of my <u>parents' backyards</u> to give my new pet somewhere to play.
   A. NO CHANGE
   B. parent's backyards
   C. parents backyards
   D. parents backyards,

4. Becca's father taught her <u>about nature, and she</u> attended various orienteering competitions during the summer.

   Which of the following alternatives to the underlined portion would NOT be acceptable?
   F. about nature; she
   G. about nature, and she also
   H. about nature, she
   J. about nature. She

5. The two principal types of <u>skis are;</u> alpine skis and cross-country skis.
   A. NO CHANGE
   B. skis, are
   C. skis are
   D. skis—are

6. Seabirds often use <u>thermals columns of hot air</u> to help them travel long distances with very little effort.
   F. NO CHANGE
   G. thermals; columns of hot air,
   H. thermals, columns of hot air,
   J. thermals columns of hot air,

7. In the glacial fjords of Norway, long considered too cold, <u>too windy or too isolated,</u> for humans to inhabit, many small towns now thrive.
   A. NO CHANGE
   B. too cold, too windy, or too isolated
   C. too cold, too windy, or too isolated,
   D. too cold too windy, or too isolated

8. Most of these complex organisms didn't merely inhabit new regions that had been occupied by other animals; they took control of them.

Which of the following alternatives to the underlined portion would NOT be acceptable?
F. animals; rather, they
G. animals—they
H. animals. They
J. animals, they

9. Throughout his childhood, in Africa in the 1970s Jamal was convinced that he was destined for greatness.
A. NO CHANGE
B. childhood in Africa in the 1970s,
C. childhood, in Africa in the 1970s,
D. childhood in Africa, in the 1970s

10. His mother recruited the best educators to tutor Sasha in: jazz and contemporary dance.
F. NO CHANGE
G. in, jazz
H. in jazz
J. in jazz,

11. I learned that my countrys heritage was a mixture of four distinct traditions.
A. NO CHANGE
B. countrys'
C. country's
D. countries

12. Although Marcus passed away in 2005, his finest achievement: *Le Theatre de Danse*—continues to be a beacon of artistic excellence.
F. NO CHANGE
G. achievement,
H. achievement—
J. achievement

13. More often than not, Nadia would find herself returning someone else's mail to the front desk.
A. NO CHANGE
B. elses'
C. elses
D. else

14. Remember, at a height of seven thousand feet. The air is considerably thinner than it is at the surface.
F. NO CHANGE
G. height, of seven thousand feet, the
H. height of seven thousand feet; the
J. height of seven thousand feet, the

15. Astronauts are able to leave the shuttle via a series of airlocks, unique chambers that protect the manufactured atmosphere inside the craft.
A. NO CHANGE
B. airlocks. Unique
C. airlocks; unique
D. airlocks unique

16. The duplicates made by <u>Mitchells invention</u> were virtually identical to the originals.
 F. NO CHANGE
 G. Mitchell's invention
 H. Mitchell's invention,
 J. Mitchells invention,

17. A world-champion <u>archer:</u> she is best known for her multiple gold medals.
 A. NO CHANGE
 B. archer;
 C. archer,
 D. archer

18. Professor Melville's <u>depiction of reality</u> and her unique philosophy toward thought in animals appear quite dissimilar.
 F. NO CHANGE
 G. depiction, of reality,
 H. depiction, of reality
 J. depiction of reality,

19. The charming elements of the city are difficult to <u>avoid</u> the vintage lights, the cobbled streets, and the historic buildings.
 A. NO CHANGE
 B. avoid:
 C. avoid,
 D. avoid;

20. The overhead wires used to provide electricity were replaced with underground <u>cables, they</u> made a new cityscape possible.
 F. NO CHANGE
 G. cables, which
 H. cables in which
 J. cables those

■■■ ANSWERS AND EXPLANATIONS

Grammatical Voice

1. **The best answer is D.** This choice uses the active voice to clearly indicate the subject of the clause, "the steady downpour," as the agent that performed the action— "continued to muddy the infield."
2. **The best answer is G.** This choice uses the active voice to clearly and effectively convey the intended meaning of the sentence. The other answer choices are awkward and passive.
3. **The best answer is A.** This sentence is correctly written in the active voice. The other answer choices are written in the passive voice.
4. **The best answer is G.** This choice uses the active voice to clearly indicate the subject of the clause, "the attorney," as the agent who performed the action—"accepted the plea agreement."
5. **The best answer is C.** This choice uses the active voice to clearly indicate the subject of the clause, "vendors," as the agents who performed the action—"sold many shirts and CDs."
6. **The best answer is G.** This choice uses the active voice to clearly indicate the subject, "Jenny," as the agent who performed the action—"invited her friends."
7. **The best answer is C.** This choice uses the active voice to clearly and effectively convey the intended meaning of the sentence. The original sentence is awkward and written in the passive voice. The other answer choices create incomplete sentences.
8. **The best answer is J.** This choice uses the active voice to clearly indicate the subject of the clause, "cities," as the agents that performed the action— "use water towers."
9. **The best answer is A.** This sentence is correctly written in the active voice. The other answer choices are awkward and written in the passive voice.
10. **The best answer is F.** This sentence is correctly written in the active voice. The other answer choices are written in the passive voice.

Modifying Clauses

1. **The best answer is C.** The phrase "brick structure" is a description of the "kiln." Remove the ambiguous pronoun "it" and the verb "is" to clarify this sentence.
2. **The best answer is F.** This sentence is correct as written. The adverb "mysteriously" clearly modifies the verb "pulled."
3. **The best answer is D.** This sentence requires you to clearly indicate that a "paddle" is being pulled through the water. Therefore, the modifying phrase "through the water" should be placed directly after "paddle."
4. **The best answer is G.** The adverb "greatly" modifies the verb "extend." Therefore, you should place "greatly" directly before "extend" (after "developments").
5. **The best answer is B.** The sentence as written suggests that the scientists were bolted to the platform. It makes more sense that the research outposts were bolted to the platform; only answer choice B places the subject clause directly after the modifying clause.
6. **The best answer is J.** It is unlikely that the grandmother mentioned in the sentence is seventeen. Place the phrase "at the age of seventeen"

at the end of the sentence to clearly indicate that the writer, "I," was abandoning her traditions at a specific age.

7. **The best answer is D.** As it is written, the sentence suggests that the dogs were "driving around town." Since it is more likely that Luke was driving, place the modifying phrase at the beginning of the sentence.

8. **The best answer is H.** It is unlikely that Michelle's boyfriend caught the fish with his pocketknife, as the sentence suggests. Rephrase the underlined portion, placing "pocketknife" with the act of cleaning the fish to clarify the meaning of the sentence.

9. **The best answer is B.** The birthday party was not being planned on the way to the manager's car; instead, it is likely that while walking to her car, the manager overheard the party being planned.

10. **The best answer is J.** As it is written, the sentence suggests that Miranda was "crumpled in the corner of her room." It is more likely that Miranda noticed the letter itself crumpled in the corner, so place the modifying clause at the end of the sentence.

Verb Tense

1. **The best answer is A.** It is correct to use the past perfect form of the verb "to hear," which is "heard." It is a common mistake to say "must of," because the written contraction "must've" is often assumed to mean "must of" in spoken English. However, this is never correct.

2. **The best answer is H.** All of the options except for "started up raising" are appropriate usages of the past tense with the auxiliary verb "had." This selection is awkward and not appropriate in standard written English.

3. **The best answer is B.** Since the sentence states that the speaker's parents had "agreed," you must mirror the same verb tense in the underlined portion of the sentence using the simple past tense "checked."

4. **The best answer is G.** The phrase "the last seventy years" implies that the clock started keeping precise time seventy years ago and has continued doing so since that time. Use the past perfect form "has kept."

5. **The best answer is C.** The first verb in the sentence is in the infinitive form "to feed" so the second verb must also be in the infinitive, "to breed." The "to" can be implied from the first verb, so you need not repeat it.

6. **The best answer is J.** The verb in this sentence must be in the simple present tense, as the action is currently happening. As it is written, the sentence is incomplete.

7. **The best answer is D.** The gerund form of the verb, "knowing," is most appropriate in the context of the sentence.

8. **The best answer is F.** The sentence is correct as written. It is appropriate to use the infinitive form of a verb in a sentence when the verb has previously been conjugated in the third person.

9. **The best answer is D.** The infinitive form of the verb "to concentrate" should be used in this sentence to clearly indicate the action taking place.

10. **The best answer is F.** The sentence is correct as written. The correct past-tense form of the verb "to freeze" is the irregular verb "frozen."

Subject/Verb Agreement

1. **The best answer is B.** The singular subject "one" requires the singular present-tense verb "is."

2. **The best answer is G.** The singular subject "equipment" requires the singular present-tense verb "is."

3. **The best answer is D.** This sentence requires the simple present-tense verb "are covered."

4. **The best answer is G.** The singular subject "satisfaction" requires the singular past-tense verb "was." The sentence is written in the past tense.

5. **The best answer is B.** The singular pronoun subject "what" requires the singular present-tense verb "is." The "mountains" are not out in the open; "what was once hidden" is.

6. **The best answer is H.** The singular subject "test" requires the singular verb "is."

7. **The best answer is D.** The singular subject "family" requires the singular auxiliary verb "has." The verb "been" requires an auxiliary verb, so neither answer choice A nor answer choice B is correct.

8. **The best answer is J.** The singular subject "committee" requires the singular present-tense verb "sets." There are several words in the English language that, although they may represent a body made up of many members, are singular; committee is one such word.

9. **The best answer is A.** The sentence is correct as written. The singular subject "Prime Minister" requires the singular verb "is."

10. **The best answer is H.** The plural subject "courses" requires the plural verb "have."

Adjectives and Adverbs

1. **The best answer is B.** The adjective "beautiful" is being modified; therefore you must use an adverb. Add "-ly" to create the adverb "arrestingly."

2. **The best answer is F.** The sentence is correct as it is written. Use the superlative "best" to describe one member of a group with three or more members.

3. **The best answer is B.** Use the adjective "continual" to modify the noun "source."

4. **The best answer is J.** "Introduction" is a noun, and the sentence requires the verb "introducing." Verbs must be modified by adverbs; "unwitting" needs to be changed to its adverb form, "unwittingly."

5. **The best answer is A.** The sentence is correct as written. The adverb "usually" correctly modifies the verb "signal."

6. **The best answer is F.** The sentence is correct as written. The adjective "frightening" correctly modifies the noun "closeness."

7. **The best answer is C.** The sentence offers you two courses of action: waiting out the traffic jam, or exiting the Interstate to take a detour. When choosing between two different things, use the comparative "better." "Best" is appropriate when there are three or more items, and "most better" is not grammatically correct.

8. **The best answer is G.** Each of the correct options conveys the notion that the speaker is sincere in his thanks. Within the sentence, "thanked" is acting as a verb and must be modified by an adverb. Answer choice G includes the adjective "sincere," which is incorrect.

9. **The best answer is D.** The verb "harvest" must be modified by an adverb. Add "-ly" to create the adverb "carefully." In addition, "harvested" is the correct verb form to use with "be."

10. **The best answer is H.** The noun "spill" must be modified by the adjective "occasional." "Occasionally" is the adverbial form of "occasion."

Pronouns

1. **The best answer is C.** Use the singular possessive "its" to show that the "components" belonged to the "clockwork mouse." "It's" is the contraction of "it is," and "its'" is never correct. The plural possessive pronoun "their" is incorrect because there is only one mouse.

2. **The best answer is G.** The underlined pronoun "them" is ambiguous. To make the sentence clearer, restate the antecedent.

3. **The best answer is B.** The underlined pronoun "they" is ambiguous. To make the sentence clearer, indicate precisely what is likely to run dry.

4. **The best answer is J.** Use the possessive "its" to indicate that the "exercise habit" has "negative consequences." There is only one habit, so the plural pronouns "they" and "their" are incorrect. "It's" is the contraction of "it is."

5. **The best answer is D.** Since the fields and forests were dear to the speaker, "me," use the possessive pronoun "my."

6. **The best answer is G.** This sentence contains a compound subject, Jake and someone else. Use the objective pronoun "him" to indicate the two people being rewarded.

7. **The best answer is D.** Use the objective pronoun "us" in this sentence to match the possessive pronoun "our" used later.

8. **The best answer is G.** Use the nominative case of the personal pronoun "I" with a compound subject. Completing the clause will lead you to the correct pronoun case; "Ashley thought we were fluent in Spanish" and "I thought we were fluent in Spanish."

9. **The best answer is B.** The singular pronoun "it" should take the place of the singular antecedent "dog grooming."

10. **The best answer is J.** The subject of this sentence is "people," a third-person plural noun. Use the third-person plural personal pronoun "they."

Idiom

1. **The best answer is A.** The context of this sentence indicates that the smoke is exiting the chimney and entering the "night sky." The words "up," "through," and "out" each reflect this context. It would not be appropriate to say that the smoke swirls "at" the chimney.

2. **The best answer is H.** The generally acceptable, or idiomatic, phrase is "focused…on."

3. **The best answer is D.** The generally acceptable, or idiomatic, preposition is "under." The noun "stewardship" refers to "managing or supervising" something; it makes sense to say that the parks were "under" the management or supervision of the Park Service.

4. **The best answer is J.** The generally acceptable, or idiomatic, preposition is "for."

5. **The best answer is C.** You must use the adverb "differently" to describe the verb "communicated," and it is idiomatic to use the preposition "in."

6. **The best answer is F.** The generally acceptable, or idiomatic, preposition is "as."

7. **The best answer is C.** The context of this sentence indicates that the family worked as field hands and musicians in order to "earn" or "make" a living. Both "earn" and "make" are idiomatic. Likewise, the prepositions "by" and "from" are appropriate in this context. It would not be idiomatic to say that the family earned its living "on working."

8. **The best answer is J.** The generally acceptable, or idiomatic, phrase is "chip on his shoulder."

9. **The best answer is C.** The generally acceptable, or idiomatic, phrase is "knock on wood."

10. **The best answer is F.** Within the context of the sentence, "dusk" represents a certain time of day. It is appropriate to say "in the dusk."

Redundancy

1. **The best answer is D.** You can assume that time would go by over many weeks. This makes the underlined portion of the sentence redundant, so DELETE it.

2. **The best answer is J.** You can assume that a business trip is made in connection with one's work. This makes the underlined portion of the sentence redundant, so DELETE it.

3. **The best answer is D.** The word "annual" means "yearly." This makes the underlined portion of the sentence redundant, so DELETE it.

4. **The best answer is H.** The words "varied" and "different" share essentially the same meaning. This redundancy can be easily resolved by simply getting rid of one of the two words, as in answer choice H.

5. **The best answer is D.** The word "acquiesce" means to "give in." This makes the underlined portion of the sentence redundant, so DELETE it.

6. **The best answer is J.** It is implied that an underwater explorer would explore under the sea. This redundancy is corrected by deleting the unnecessary information from the underlined portion.

7. **The best answer is B.** The words "invention" and "creation" share essentially the same meaning. This redundancy can be easily resolved by simply getting rid of one of the two words, as in answer choice B.

8. **The best answer is F.** This sentence is clear and concise, and does not contain redundancy. The other answer choices are either redundant or awkward.

9. **The best answer is B.** The word "routine" implies that the Sunday in question was "like many others." This redundancy is corrected by deleting the unnecessary information from the underlined portion.

10. **The best answer is H.** The phrases "in due course" and "waiting for a while" are very similar in meaning. The best way to resolve this redundancy is to eliminate one of the phrases, changing the underlined portion to "After waiting a while." This retains the meaning of the sentence in a clear and concise manner.

Punctuation

1. **The correct answer is B.** The phrase "using twigs for kindling" is a parenthetical phrase that should be set off from the rest of the sentence with commas.

2. **The correct answer is F.** The sentence is correct as written; there is no need to separate the indirect quotation from the rest of the sentence with any punctuation.

3. **The correct answer is B.** The sentence discusses each of the speaker's parents individually, so "parent" is a singular noun. The correct way to make a singular noun (that does not end in s) possessive is to add an ['s] to the word.

4. **The correct answer is H.** Each of the clauses in this sentence could stand alone as a separate, complete sentence. The only choice that does not correctly join these clauses is answer choice H, which creates a comma splice.

5. **The correct answer is C.** The underlined portion of this sentence does not require any punctuation. The semicolon is used to connect two related, but complete ideas—the phrase "alpine skis and cross-country skis" lacks a verb.

6. **The correct answer is H.** The phrase "columns of hot air" is an appositive that must be set off from the rest of the sentence with commas.

7. **The correct answer is B.** Each item in a series, including the one that comes directly before the conjunction (and/or), must be followed by a comma. Do not place a comma after "isolated."

8. **The correct answer is J.** Each of the clauses in this sentence could stand alone as a separate, complete sentence. The only choice that does not correctly join these clauses is answer choice J, which creates a comma splice.

9. **The correct answer is B.** The phrase "throughout his childhood in Africa in the 1970s" is an introductory clause and must be joined to the rest of the sentence with a comma. No commas are needed within the introductory clause.

10. **The correct answer is H.** The underlined portion of this sentence does not require any punctuation. Colons are typically used to introduce a list, often one punctuated by commas in a series. In this case, the structure of the sentence is such that a colon is not necessary or even appropriate.

11. **The correct answer is C.** In this sentence, the singular noun "country" is possessive. The "heritage" belongs to one country, so the standard rules for possessive punctuation apply—add 's to the end of the word.

12. **The correct answer is H.** You should use a dash before and after the parenthetical information in this sentence. Do not mix punctuation in this instance.

13. **The correct answer is A.** The sentence is correct as written. In order to make the compound noun "someone else" possessive, add an apostrophe + s to "else." The word "someone" is singular, which implies that "someone else" is also a singular noun.

14. **The correct answer is J.** The clause that contains the phrase "height of seven thousand feet" is a dependent clause. Therefore, neither a period nor a semicolon is correct. The appositive "at a height of seven thousand feet" must be set off with commas.

15. **The correct answer is A.** The sentence is correct as written. The phrase "unique chambers that protect the manufactured atmosphere inside the craft" serves as an appositive that describes the airlocks mentioned earlier in the sentence. Such phrases must be set off from the rest of the sentence with commas.

16. **The correct answer is G.** Apply the standard rules of possession (apostrophe + s) to indicate that the invention belongs to Mitchell. You should not use a comma to separate the subject clause from its verb.

17. **The correct answer is C.** This sentence requires a comma between the dependent introductory clause, "A world-champion archer" and the independent clause "she is best known for her multiple gold medals."

18. **The correct answer is F.** The underlined portion of the sentence is correct as written and requires no punctuation.

19. **The correct answer is B.** The underlined portion of the sentence needs a colon because it is an introduction to a list of the city's charming elements: vintage lights, cobbled streets, and historic buildings.

20. **The correct answer is G.** As it is written, the sentence includes a comma splice. Using "which" in the underlined portion of the sentence creates a nonrestrictive clause that provides additional information. Such clauses must be separated from the rest of the sentence by commas.

WHAT'S NEXT?

Chapters 6 and 7 present simulated ACT English Tests. Apply the strategies and techniques you learned in the previous chapters to correctly answer as many of these questions as possible in the time allowed.

CHAPTER 6

ACT ENGLISH PRACTICE TEST 1

This chapter should help you to evaluate your progress in preparing for the ACT English Test. Make an honest effort to answer each question, and then review the explanations that follow. Review Chapter 3, "Grammar Review," Chapter 4, "Strategies and Techniques," and Chapter 5, "Applying Strategies, Building Skills," if you continue to struggle with the questions on this simulated practice test.

ACT ENGLISH PRACTICE TEST 1
Answer Sheet

ENGLISH

1 Ⓐ Ⓑ Ⓒ Ⓓ	21 Ⓐ Ⓑ Ⓒ Ⓓ	41 Ⓐ Ⓑ Ⓒ Ⓓ	61 Ⓐ Ⓑ Ⓒ Ⓓ
2 Ⓕ Ⓖ Ⓗ Ⓙ	22 Ⓕ Ⓖ Ⓗ Ⓙ	42 Ⓕ Ⓖ Ⓗ Ⓙ	62 Ⓕ Ⓖ Ⓗ Ⓙ
3 Ⓐ Ⓑ Ⓒ Ⓓ	23 Ⓐ Ⓑ Ⓒ Ⓓ	43 Ⓐ Ⓑ Ⓒ Ⓓ	63 Ⓐ Ⓑ Ⓒ Ⓓ
4 Ⓕ Ⓖ Ⓗ Ⓙ	24 Ⓕ Ⓖ Ⓗ Ⓙ	44 Ⓕ Ⓖ Ⓗ Ⓙ	64 Ⓕ Ⓖ Ⓗ Ⓙ
5 Ⓐ Ⓑ Ⓒ Ⓓ	25 Ⓐ Ⓑ Ⓒ Ⓓ	45 Ⓐ Ⓑ Ⓒ Ⓓ	65 Ⓐ Ⓑ Ⓒ Ⓓ
6 Ⓕ Ⓖ Ⓗ Ⓙ	26 Ⓕ Ⓖ Ⓗ Ⓙ	46 Ⓕ Ⓖ Ⓗ Ⓙ	66 Ⓕ Ⓖ Ⓗ Ⓙ
7 Ⓐ Ⓑ Ⓒ Ⓓ	27 Ⓐ Ⓑ Ⓒ Ⓓ	47 Ⓐ Ⓑ Ⓒ Ⓓ	67 Ⓐ Ⓑ Ⓒ Ⓓ
8 Ⓕ Ⓖ Ⓗ Ⓙ	28 Ⓕ Ⓖ Ⓗ Ⓙ	48 Ⓕ Ⓖ Ⓗ Ⓙ	68 Ⓕ Ⓖ Ⓗ Ⓙ
9 Ⓐ Ⓑ Ⓒ Ⓓ	29 Ⓐ Ⓑ Ⓒ Ⓓ	49 Ⓐ Ⓑ Ⓒ Ⓓ	69 Ⓐ Ⓑ Ⓒ Ⓓ
10 Ⓕ Ⓖ Ⓗ Ⓙ	30 Ⓕ Ⓖ Ⓗ Ⓙ	50 Ⓕ Ⓖ Ⓗ Ⓙ	70 Ⓕ Ⓖ Ⓗ Ⓙ
11 Ⓐ Ⓑ Ⓒ Ⓓ	31 Ⓐ Ⓑ Ⓒ Ⓓ	51 Ⓐ Ⓑ Ⓒ Ⓓ	71 Ⓐ Ⓑ Ⓒ Ⓓ
12 Ⓕ Ⓖ Ⓗ Ⓙ	32 Ⓕ Ⓖ Ⓗ Ⓙ	52 Ⓕ Ⓖ Ⓗ Ⓙ	72 Ⓕ Ⓖ Ⓗ Ⓙ
13 Ⓐ Ⓑ Ⓒ Ⓓ	33 Ⓐ Ⓑ Ⓒ Ⓓ	53 Ⓐ Ⓑ Ⓒ Ⓓ	73 Ⓐ Ⓑ Ⓒ Ⓓ
14 Ⓕ Ⓖ Ⓗ Ⓙ	34 Ⓕ Ⓖ Ⓗ Ⓙ	54 Ⓕ Ⓖ Ⓗ Ⓙ	74 Ⓕ Ⓖ Ⓗ Ⓙ
15 Ⓐ Ⓑ Ⓒ Ⓓ	35 Ⓐ Ⓑ Ⓒ Ⓓ	55 Ⓐ Ⓑ Ⓒ Ⓓ	75 Ⓐ Ⓑ Ⓒ Ⓓ
16 Ⓕ Ⓖ Ⓗ Ⓙ	36 Ⓕ Ⓖ Ⓗ Ⓙ	56 Ⓕ Ⓖ Ⓗ Ⓙ	
17 Ⓐ Ⓑ Ⓒ Ⓓ	37 Ⓐ Ⓑ Ⓒ Ⓓ	57 Ⓐ Ⓑ Ⓒ Ⓓ	
18 Ⓕ Ⓖ Ⓗ Ⓙ	38 Ⓕ Ⓖ Ⓗ Ⓙ	58 Ⓕ Ⓖ Ⓗ Ⓙ	
19 Ⓐ Ⓑ Ⓒ Ⓓ	39 Ⓐ Ⓑ Ⓒ Ⓓ	59 Ⓐ Ⓑ Ⓒ Ⓓ	
20 Ⓕ Ⓖ Ⓗ Ⓙ	40 Ⓕ Ⓖ Ⓗ Ⓙ	60 Ⓕ Ⓖ Ⓗ Ⓙ	

ENGLISH TEST

45 Minutes—75 Questions

DIRECTIONS: In the passages that follow, some words and phrases are underlined and numbered. In the answer column, you will find alternatives for the words and phrases that are underlined. Choose the alternative that you think is best, and fill in the corresponding bubble on your answer sheet. If you think that the original version is best, choose "NO CHANGE," which will always be either answer choice A or F. You will also find questions about a particular section of the passage, or about the entire passage. These questions will be identified by either an underlined portion or by a number in a box. Look for the answer that clearly expresses the idea, is consistent with the style and tone of the passage, and makes the correct use of standard written English. Read the passage through once before answering the questions. For some questions, you should read before and beyond the indicated portion before you answer.

PASSAGE I

Tragedy at the Factory

Sometimes it takes tragedy to induce change. This was the case with the Triangle Shirtwaist Company Fire.

March 25, 1911, was a day <u>not being any different from</u>
$\overset{}{\underset{1}{}}$
the rest. Things changed, however, when the workday ended. Employees began cleaning up their workspaces and gathering their belongings to go home. The security guard performed his daily duty of locking one of two ninth-floor exits as a measure to prevent theft. All <u>is seeming</u>
$\overset{}{\underset{2}{}}$

normal until someone on the eighth floor <u>cry,</u>
$\overset{}{\underset{3}{}}$

"Fire!" ④

1. **A.** NO CHANGE
   B. without difference
   C. being no different
   (D.) no different

2. **F.** NO CHANGE
   G. seems as if
   (H.) seemed
   J. seeming

3. **A.** NO CHANGE
   B. cries
   C. crying
   (D.) cried

4. At this point, the author is considering adding the following sentence:

   > Factories typically have large quantities of a variety of flammable materials.

   Should the author add this?

   F. Yes, because it adds interesting information about the fire warning system of the early twentieth century.
   G. Yes, because this sentence is necessary to the reader's understanding of the moments that led up to the Triangle Shirtwaist Factory Fire.
   H. No, because the information is already implied in the paragraph.
   (J.) No, because the sentence doesn't add to the development of the paragraph.

GO ON TO THE NEXT PAGE.

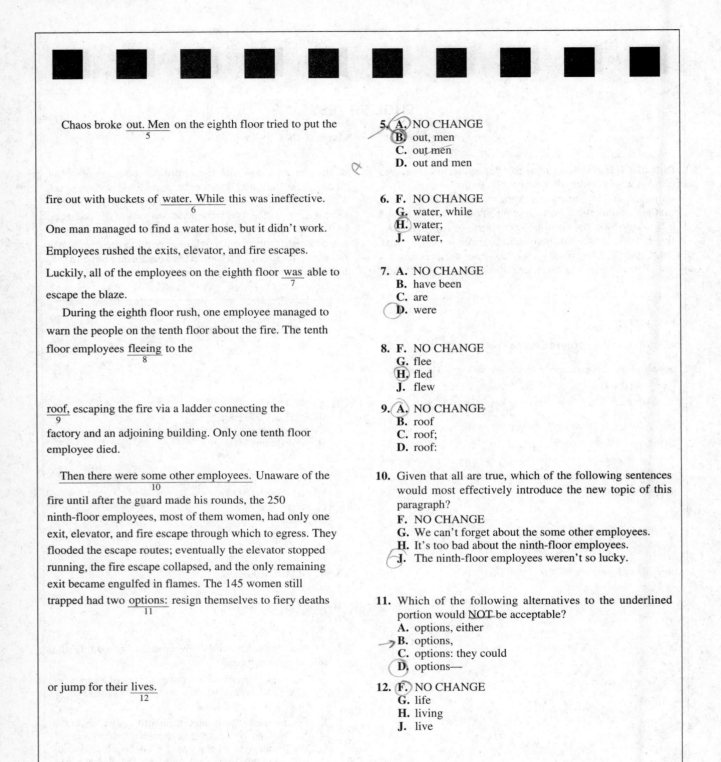

Chaos broke out. Men on the eighth floor tried to put the
$\underset{5}{}$

fire out with buckets of water. While this was ineffective.
$\underset{6}{}$

One man managed to find a water hose, but it didn't work.

Employees rushed the exits, elevator, and fire escapes.

Luckily, all of the employees on the eighth floor was able to
$\underset{7}{}$

escape the blaze.

During the eighth floor rush, one employee managed to

warn the people on the tenth floor about the fire. The tenth

floor employees fleeing to the
$\underset{8}{}$

roof, escaping the fire via a ladder connecting the
$\underset{9}{}$

factory and an adjoining building. Only one tenth floor

employee died.

Then there were some other employees. Unaware of the
$\underset{10}{}$

fire until after the guard made his rounds, the 250

ninth-floor employees, most of them women, had only one

exit, elevator, and fire escape through which to egress. They

flooded the escape routes; eventually the elevator stopped

running, the fire escape collapsed, and the only remaining

exit became engulfed in flames. The 145 women still

trapped had two options: resign themselves to fiery deaths
$\underset{11}{}$

or jump for their lives.
$\underset{12}{}$

5. A. NO CHANGE
   B. out, men
   C. out men
   D. out and men

6. F. NO CHANGE
   G. water, while
   H. water;
   J. water,

7. A. NO CHANGE
   B. have been
   C. are
   D. were

8. F. NO CHANGE
   G. flee
   H. fled
   J. flew

9. A. NO CHANGE
   B. roof
   C. roof;
   D. roof:

10. Given that all are true, which of the following sentences
    would most effectively introduce the new topic of this
    paragraph?
    F. NO CHANGE
    G. We can't forget about the some other employees.
    H. It's too bad about the ninth-floor employees.
    J. The ninth-floor employees weren't so lucky.

11. Which of the following alternatives to the underlined
    portion would NOT be acceptable?
    A. options, either
    B. options,
    C. options: they could
    D. options—

12. F. NO CHANGE
    G. life
    H. living
    J. live

GO ON TO THE NEXT PAGE.

It took just eighteen minutes for firemen to extinguish the blaze. Nevertheless, in those eighteen minutes, 146 women died, fifty-four of whom jumped from the building in vain. The Triangle Shirtwaist Company fire <u>remains to be</u> the
13
worst factory fire in New York City's history.

After the fire, the governor of New York appointed the Factory Investigating Commission to look into the disaster. <u>Then resulting</u> was the passage of the most
14
sweeping workplace labor reforms in American history. While the Triangle Shirtwaist Company Fire was tragic, it managed to awaken the American public to many problems that existed in the labor system of the early twentieth century.

13. A. NO CHANGE
    B. are
    C. remains
    D. as remains

14. F. NO CHANGE
    G. The result
    H. Resulting
    J. Then

Question 15 asks about the preceding passage as a whole.

15. Suppose the author intended to write an essay that describes the history of American labor reforms. Does this essay fulfill that goal?
    A. Yes, because the essay highlights the labor reforms that resulted from the Triangle Shirtwaist Company Fire.
    B. Yes, because the essay describes several workplace accidents that led to workplace regulatory reforms.
    C. No, because the Triangle Shirtwaist Factory Fire is not a crucial event in the history of American labor reforms.
    D. No, because the essay details only one specific incident in the history of American labor reforms.

My "Normal" Family

My family is far from ordinary. Although this analysis risks appearing <u>trite my family</u> certainly belongs in a category all
16
of <u>it's</u> own.
17

16. F. NO CHANGE
    G. trite, my family,
    H. trite, my family
    J. trite my family,

17. A. NO CHANGE
    B. its
    C. its'
    D. their

Perhaps the best way to illustrate this idea is by offering a glimpse into a "normal" evening at my house. 18 Obsessed with sports, my brother does anything and everything he can to turn even the most mundane of activities into

Olympic-caliber spectacles. 19 Take going down the steps, for example. He says that simply walking down the steps

isn't any fun. Instead, he insists on riding down the steps
                                    ___
                                    20

via a surfboard. He simply stands, sits, or belly flops onto the board, and down the stairs he goes. I guess I have to give him credit for at least attempting to make the whole ordeal safe; a huge pile of couch cushions and pillows breaks his fall at the end of his ride.

Some people, respond to my brother's tirades with, "He's
     _____
        21
a teenage boy. What do you expect?" This argument indeed has merit; however, no one can deny that the moments following my brother's stair-surfing manifest the
                                      _____
                                         22
ridiculousness of my family. See, it's not just my brother who stair-surfs. My mom also plays along. Throwing caution to the wind, she is inspired to surf down the steps into a giant heap of pillows.

The childlike silliness doesn't stop with my mom and brother. My dad and me have our own quirks, too.
                    _____
                       23

18. The writer wants to add a sentence here that would indicate her favorable opinion of her brother. Given all are true, which of the following would most effectively accomplish this?
    F. I will illustrate using my brother as an example.
    G. My brother is perhaps the strangest member of my family.
    H. My brother always seems to find curious ways to pass the time.
    J. Everyone usually follows the lead of my endearing brother.

19. At this point, the author is considering adding the following true statement:
    Our family enjoys watching the Olympics together.
    Should the writer make this addition here?
    A. Yes, because the sentence explains why the author's brother is treating everyday activities as if they were Olympic sports.
    B. Yes, because the sentence establishes that the author's brother is an exceptionally talented athlete.
    C. No, because the sentence is not supported by evidence that the author's brother has dreams of competing in the Olympics.
    D. No, because the sentence distracts from the paragraph's focus on how the author's brother amuses himself.

20. F. NO CHANGE
    G. that
    H. in
    J. DELETE the underlined portion.

21. A. NO CHANGE
    B. people respond,
    C. people, respond,
    D. people respond

22. F. NO CHANGE
    G. manifests
    H. manifested
    J. is manifest in

23. A. NO CHANGE
    B. me has
    C. I have
    D. I has

Leaving the staircase antics to my mom and brother, we prefer <u>to dance</u> in the living room. It's not even the dancing
₂₄
part that's abnormal, but rather what we're wearing.

My dad is clothed in one of his "retro" 80s <u>jumpsuits</u>
₂₅
<u>and I am</u> equally tacky in my outdated high school prom
₂₅

dress and tiara. This family picture <u>of all four of us</u> is a sight
₂₆
to be seen.

[1] In truth, I wouldn't trade this weirdness for anything. [2] I love my family, and I enjoy the fact that I can tell stories of such behaviors as <u>stair-surfing and dance parties.</u>
₂₇
[3] I want to make sure I am not sending the wrong impression about my family. [4] In my opinion, abnormality is the spice of life. [5] After all, <u>whose</u> really normal,
₂₈

anway? [29]

24. F. NO CHANGE
    G. to dancing
    H. to be dancing
    J. to have danced

25. Which of the following alternatives to the underlined portion would NOT be acceptable?
    A. jumpsuits; I am
    B. jumpsuits. I am
    C. jumpsuits, I am
    D. jumpsuits—I am

26. F. NO CHANGE
    G. with all four of us in it
    H. with my brother, dad, mom, and me
    J. DELETE the underlined portion.

27. A. NO CHANGE
    B. stair-surfing, and, dance parties
    C. stair-surfing, and dance parties
    D. stair-surfing, dance parties

28. F. NO CHANGE
    G. who's
    H. whom is
    J. that is

29. For the sake of logic and coherence, the order of the sentences in this paragraph should be:
    A. NO CHANGE
    B. 3,1,2,4,5
    C. 2,4,5,1,3
    D. 5,4,2,1,3

Question 30 asks about the preceding passage as a whole.

30. Which of the following could be one of the main points of the essay?
    F. A good family life is not necessarily a normal one.
    G. Stair-surfing is dangerous.
    H. Families should spend more time together.
    J. Extreme sports are a great way for a family to bond.

PASSAGE III

Reclaiming a National Emblem

In a country where the bald eagle is an important allegory, the U.S. general population knows very little about this majestic bird. Declared in 1782 by the Second Continental Congress as the national emblem of the

GO ON TO THE NEXT PAGE.

United States of America, the bird was <u>chose</u> because
₃₁

<u>its</u> a species unique to North America. Representing the
₃₂

spirit of freedom and excellence in the United States

<u>symbolically,</u> the bald eagle has played an important
₃₃

role in American art, music, and architecture.

    <u>While</u> the bald eagle can be found in every U.S. state
₃₄

<u>accept</u> Hawaii, few Americans have actually seen a bald
₃₅

eagle. Because bald eagles prefer nesting in tall trees and

eating fish, people have a better chance of spying the bird

<u>in a boat or along a lakeshore.</u> Unfortunately, bald eagle
₃₆

sightings are not as common as they were in the country's

formative years.

    [1] Bald eagles were once common throughout the United

States in the early 1700s, but <u>there</u> population fell
₃₇

dramatically <u>as to</u> human activity. [2] Hunting, habitat
₃₈

destruction, waterway contamination, and the use of

pesticides by humans caused the bald eagle population to

fall from 500,000 in the 1700s to <u>less than</u> 1,000 by the
₃₉

1960s. [3] In an effort to counteract this decline, the United

States government enacted strong endangered species and

environmental protection laws. [4] This increased public

awareness of environmental quality issues <u>has</u> helped the
₄₀

---

31. **A.** NO CHANGE
   B. choose
   C. chosen
   D. choosing

32. **F.** NO CHANGE
   G. they're
   H. it's
   J. of

33. **A.** NO CHANGE
   B. being symbolic
   C. as a symbol
   D. DELETE the underlined portion.

34. All of the following alternatives to the underlined portion
are appropriate EXCEPT:
   F. Even though
   G. Instead of
   H. Whereas
   J. Although

35. **A.** NO CHANGE
   B. accepts
   C. except
   D. accepting

36. The best placement for the underlined portion would be:
   F. where it is now.
   G. after the word *nesting*.
   H. after the word *eagles*.
   J. after the word *people*.

37. **A** NO CHANGE
   B. they're
   C. their
   D. its

38. Which of the following alternatives would best replace the
underlined portion?
   F. apart from
   G. as a result of
   H. contrary to
   J. despite

39. **A.** NO CHANGE
   B. fewer than
   C. less then
   D. fewer then

40. **F.** NO CHANGE
   G. have
   H. had
   J. having

GO ON TO THE NEXT PAGE.

process along. 41

Unfortunately, some practices that pollute or alter the environment continues on harassing and threaten the bald
                    ‾‾‾‾‾‾‾‾‾‾‾‾‾‾‾‾‾‾‾‾
                            42

eagle population, makes preservation efforts even more
      ‾‾‾‾‾‾‾‾‾‾‾‾‾‾‾‾
              43

important. Seeing the American spirit of freedom and excellence embodied in the bird, politicians and citizens alike continue to work towards the protecting of the bald eagle.
                 ‾‾‾‾‾‾‾‾‾‾‾‾‾‾‾‾‾‾‾‾‾‾
                          44

Maybe one day the bald eagle will be restored to its original majesty.

41. Upon reviewing this paragraph, the author notices that some information has been left out. The author composes the following sentence, incorporating the missing information:

    Private conservation organizations have also joined the effort to revive the bald eagle population, and through their efforts and those of the national government, the bald eagle population has increased to over 55,000 birds.

    For the sake of logic, this sentence should be placed after Sentence:
    A. 1.
    B. 2.
    C. 3.
    D. 4.

42. F. NO CHANGE
    G. continues harassing
    H. continue and harass
    J. continue to harass

43. A. NO CHANGE
    B. population in order to make
    C. population. This makes
    D. population—makes

44. F. NO CHANGE
    G. towards the protection of
    H. protect
    J. towards protecting

Question 45 asks about the preceding passage as a whole.

45. Suppose the writer's goal was to describe the varying habitat and diet of the bald eagle in different states. Does the essay meet this goal?
    A. Yes, because the essay addresses the preferred habitat and diet of the bald eagle.
    B. Yes, because the essay indicates that the bald eagle is present in every U.S. state except one.
    C. No, because the essay never specifically addresses variations in the habitat or diet of the bald eagle.
    D. No, because the essay lists changes to the environment by humans as the cause of fluctuations in the bald eagle population.

PASSAGE IV

Jackie Robinson: Activist and Athlete

Any discussion of the history of Major League Baseball would be incomplete without mentioning Jackie Robinson, the league's first African-American player.

GO ON TO THE NEXT PAGE.

Robinson's athletic career began long before his years in the major league. While at the University of California, Los Angeles, Robinson played football, basketball, track, and baseball. Making him the first student to letter in four
46
sports. Following college, Robinson played baseball in the Negro League. Whites and African Americans played in separate leagues because Major League Baseball was officially segregated. 47

Segregation couldn't last forever, at least according
48
to Brooklyn Dodgers' vice-president Branch Rickey, who

by choosing Jackie Robinson to help integrate major league
49

baseball. By hoping to ease the public into the change,
50
Rickey placed Robinson with the Dodgers' farm team, the Montreal Royals, in 1945. After two years in the minors, Robinson was finally given his shot on the Dodgers' roster.

Initially, many baseball fans and members of Robinson's
51
team objected to having an African American on the bench. Game-time heckling was especially common and

exceptionally cruel, as well as threats to both Robinson and
52
his family. Despite these hindrances, Robinson pushed through. During his rookie year, he hit 12 home runs and

helped assist the Dodgers win the national pennant. For his
53
triumphs on the baseball field, Robinson received the 1947 Rookie of the Year Award.

46. **F.** NO CHANGE
    G. baseball, making
    H. baseball; making
    J. baseball, and making

47. If the writer were to delete the phrase "because Major League Baseball was officially segregated" from the preceding sentence, the sentence would primarily lose:
    A. the reason why African Americans did not play in the major leagues.
    B. its lighthearted and sarcastic tone.
    C. the writer's expression of regret over the obstacles that Jackie Robinson had to overcome.
    D. details that explain an apparent contradiction.

48. **F.** NO CHANGE
    G. forever because
    H. forever;
    J. forever

49. **A.** NO CHANGE
    B. chose
    C. choose
    D. has chosen

50. **F.** NO CHANGE
    G. Hope
    H. Hoping
    J. He was hoping

51. Which of the following alternatives to the underlined portion is LEAST acceptable?
    A. Starting with,
    B. At first,
    C. In the beginning,
    D. From the outset,

52. **F.** NO CHANGE
    G. and included
    H. so too were
    J. and

53. **A.** NO CHANGE
    B. helped to assist
    C. assisted in helping
    D. helped

GO ON TO THE NEXT PAGE.

Robinson's talent for succeeding against hard odds impressed both the public and his teammates. In 1949, he is receiving the National League's Most Valuable is
$\underline{\text{54}}$

Player Award. Robinson's accolade just kept mounting.
$\overline{\text{55}}$
Over the course of his career, Robinson led the Dodgers to several pennants, as well as victory in the 1955 World Series.

Robinson retired in 1956, concluding a ten, year, long
$\overline{\text{56}}$
career. After retiring, Robinson worked for the cause of social justice. Among his most important accomplishments were the founding of Freedom National Bank in Harlem.
$\overline{\text{57}}$
Robinson knew that banks were crucial to sustaining a community, and he believed that Harlem's African Americans needed one of their own. In its heyday, Freedom National Bank was the largest black-owned and operated financial institution in New York State. Following his death in 1972, Robinson's wife established the Jackie Robinson Foundation, which continues to honor his life and struggle for social justice following his death.
$\overline{\text{58}}$

Jackie Robinson was an example of the good that comes from integrating America's wide range of social and ethnic groups not only in baseball, but also in life. His efforts helped pave the way for the success of African Americans to come. His life was perhaps best summarized when Robinson said.
$\overline{\text{59}}$
"A life is not important except in the impact it has on other lives."

54. F. NO CHANGE
    G. receives
    H. received
    J. will receive

55. Which of the following alternatives to the underlined portion would NOT be acceptable?
    A. awards
    B. honors
    C. gifts
    D. distinctions

56. F. NO CHANGE
    G. ten years, long,
    H. ten-year-long
    J. ten year-long

57. A. NO CHANGE
    B. was
    C. being
    D. DELETE the underlined portion.

58. F. NO CHANGE
    G. in his absence
    H. after his death
    J. DELETE the underlined portion.

59. Which of the following alternatives to the underlined portion would NOT be acceptable?
    A. with Robinson saying
    B. when Robinson said:
    C. by Robinson himself, who said,
    D. in Robinson's own words:

GO ON TO THE NEXT PAGE.

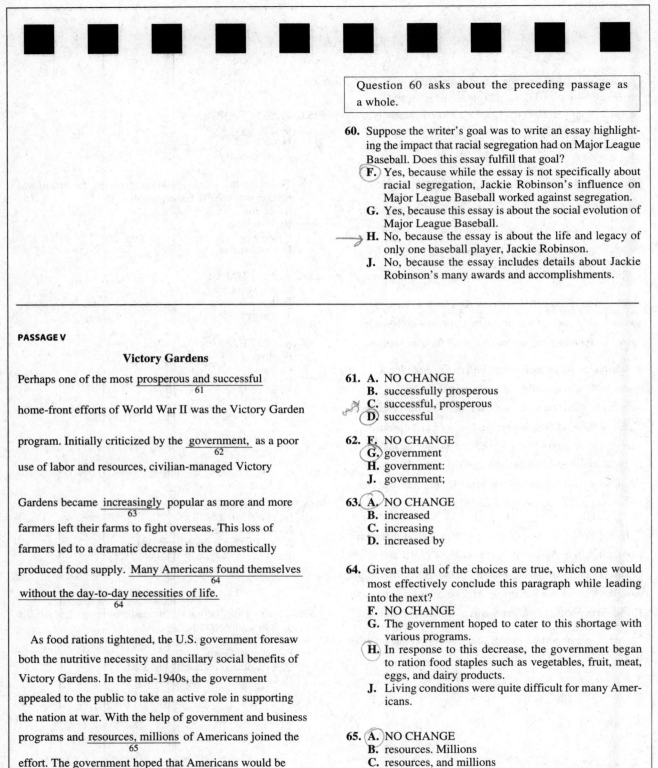

Question 60 asks about the preceding passage as a whole.

60. Suppose the writer's goal was to write an essay highlighting the impact that racial segregation had on Major League Baseball. Does this essay fulfill that goal?
   F. Yes, because while the essay is not specifically about racial segregation, Jackie Robinson's influence on Major League Baseball worked against segregation.
   G. Yes, because this essay is about the social evolution of Major League Baseball.
   → H. No, because the essay is about the life and legacy of only one baseball player, Jackie Robinson.
   J. No, because the essay includes details about Jackie Robinson's many awards and accomplishments.

PASSAGE V

Victory Gardens

Perhaps one of the most prosperous and successful
                                61

home-front efforts of World War II was the Victory Garden

program. Initially criticized by the government, as a poor
                                      62
use of labor and resources, civilian-managed Victory

Gardens became increasingly popular as more and more
                        63
farmers left their farms to fight overseas. This loss of

farmers led to a dramatic decrease in the domestically

produced food supply. Many Americans found themselves
                                    64
without the day-to-day necessities of life.
                    64

   As food rations tightened, the U.S. government foresaw

both the nutritive necessity and ancillary social benefits of

Victory Gardens. In the mid-1940s, the government

appealed to the public to take an active role in supporting

the nation at war. With the help of government and business

programs and resources, millions of Americans joined the
                    65
effort. The government hoped that Americans would be

61. A. NO CHANGE
    B. successfully prosperous
    C. successful, prosperous
    D. successful

62. F. NO CHANGE
    G. government
    H. government:
    J. government;

63. A. NO CHANGE
    B. increased
    C. increasing
    D. increased by

64. Given that all of the choices are true, which one would most effectively conclude this paragraph while leading into the next?
    F. NO CHANGE
    G. The government hoped to cater to this shortage with various programs.
    H. In response to this decrease, the government began to ration food staples such as vegetables, fruit, meat, eggs, and dairy products.
    J. Living conditions were quite difficult for many Americans.

65. A. NO CHANGE
    B. resources. Millions
    C. resources, and millions
    D. resources: millions

GO ON TO THE NEXT PAGE.

able to provide many of their own fruits and vegetables, for
$\underline{}$
66

leaving the bulk of mass-produced crops for the troops.

[1] By the end of World War II, more than 20 million

67

Americans have transformed backyards, empty lots, baseball

68

fields, schoolyards, and apartment rooftops into over

20 million Victory Gardens; which yielded between 9 and

69

10 million tons of produce. [2] It wasn't uncommon for

them to say, "My food is fighting!" [3] Distributed

70

small-scale agriculture provided sustenance to American
troops and civilians alike, the summer and fall crops eaten
fresh or dutifully canned for the winter and spring by
amateur gardeners. [4] For Americans young and old alike,

71

Victory Gardens were their way of taking the fight to the

72

enemy. 73

Victory Gardens were a resounding success. Thanks to

the millions of green-thumbed Americans that answered the

74

government's call for action, a serious domestic food crisis
was avoided. Although Victory Gardens are no longer
needed when America's armed forces are fighting, their
memory survives as a testament to the patriotism and
resourcefulness so characteristic of this nation.

66. F. NO CHANGE
    G. vegetables, and then
    H. vegetables,
    J. vegetables, but

67. A. NO CHANGE
    B. Following
    C. Concluding
    D. After completing

68. F. NO CHANGE
    G. are transforming
    H. had been transforming
    J. had transformed

69. A. NO CHANGE
    B. Gardens, and
    C. Gardens,
    D. Gardens:

70. F. NO CHANGE
    G. it
    H. those
    J. citizens

71. If the author were to delete the phrase, "For Americans young and old alike," the sentence would lose:
    A. an explanation of how Victory Gardens allowed people of all ages to work together in the war effort.
    B. an explanation of how easy it was to maintain a Victory Garden.
    C. valuable information about who was eligible to participate in the Victory Gardens program.
    D. a logical connection to "civilians" in the preceding sentence.

72. F. NO CHANGE
    G. they're
    H. there
    J. its

73. For the sake of logic and coherence, the order of the sentences in this paragraph should be:
    A. NO CHANGE
    B. 1,3,2,4
    C. 3,2,1,4
    D. 2,1,4,3

74. F. NO CHANGE
    G. whom
    H. who
    J. DELETE the underlined portion.

GO ON TO THE NEXT PAGE.

75. Suppose the writer had decided to write an essay that illustrates one way civilians actively supported the American cause during World War II. Would this essay fulfill the writer's goal?
   A. Yes, because the essay makes the point that Victory Gardens maintained by civilians were crucial for feeding both civilians and deployed armed forces personnel.
   B. Yes, because the essay indicates that many farm laborers had to leave their land to fight in the war.
   C. No, because the essay limits its focus to the Victory Garden program, only one of many that the U.S. government developed to support the war effort.
   D. No, because the essay implies that Victory Gardens were easily maintained by amateur and expert gardeners alike.

END OF THE ENGLISH TEST
STOP! IF YOU HAVE TIME LEFT OVER, CHECK YOUR WORK ON THIS SECTION ONLY.

ANSWERS AND EXPLANATIONS

1. **The best answer is D.** This question tests your ability to recognize effective word choice. Answer choice D provides the most concise and logical restatement of the ideas expressed in the underlined portion.

2. **The best answer is H.** This sentence describes events in the past, so the simple past tense is appropriate here.

3. **The best answer is D.** The passage describes a fire that occurred in the past. Therefore, the verb "to cry" must be in the simple past tense, "cried," in order to maintain parallelism.

4. **The best answer is J.** While the sentence adds information about the conditions of factories, it does not add specific information about the conditions of the Triangle Shirtwaist Company factory that contributed to the fire. Therefore, it is irrelevant.

5. **The best answer is A.** "Chaos" is the subject of the first clause, and "men" is the subject of the second clause. Therefore, answer choices B and C would create run-ons. Answer choice D can be eliminated because joining independent clauses with a coordinating conjunction also requires using a comma.

6. **The best answer is H.** The phrase "this was ineffective" is an independent clause that modifies the preceding clause; therefore, a semicolon alone is appropriate. Answer choices G and J create comma splices, while answer choice F creates an incomplete sentence.

7. **The best answer is D**. The subject ("employees") of the underlined verb is plural. Therefore, the underlined verb must also be plural. In addition, because the passage refers to a fire in the past, the verb must be in the past tense.

8. **The best answer is H.** The underlined portion should be in the simple past tense because the action occurred in the past and is completed. "Flew" is the past tense form of "to fly." In this case the best answer is the simple past tense of the verb "to flee," which is "fled."

9. **The best answer is A.** The gerund phrase beginning with "escaping" modifies the main clause of the sentence and should be set apart with a comma. The colon and semicolon have specific usages and are not possible punctuation here. Without punctuation (as in answer choice B), the gerund phrase would modify the immediately preceding noun, "roof," which does not make sense.

10. **The best answer is J.** This sentence links well to the previous paragraph by offering a contrast to the experiences of the tenth-floor workers, most of whom survived. The other answer choices are too general.

11. **The best answer is B.** Answer choice B creates a comma splice by joining two independent clauses with a comma.

12. **The best answer is F.** The underlined portion "lives" refers to those of the women stuck on the ninth floor. Because the preceding possessive determiner "their" is plural, the underlined noun must also be plural.

13. **The best answer is C.** The verb "remains" should be used alone, without "to be" or "as." Answer choice B is in plural form when the subject "the Triangle Shirtwaist Company fire" is singular.

14. **The best answer is G.** The clearest revision to the underlined portion is a noun phrase, "the result," answer choice G, because it is the subject of the sentence.

15. **The best answer is D.** While the essay does explain the significance of the Triangle Shirtwaist Company fire in relation to American labor reform, the fire constitutes only one of many events in the history of American labor reforms.

16. **The best answer is H.** Dependent clauses beginning with "although" must be set apart from the main clause with a comma. The main clause begins with the subject "my family."

17. **The best answer is B.** The underlined portion is part of the idiom "all of its own," in which "its" is a possessive determiner. Compare this to "all of my own," "all of your own," and so on. "It's" is the contraction of "it is," and "its'" is never correct in standard written English. Because "family" is a singular noun, the plural pronoun "their" is not correct.

18. **The best answer is J.** The question stem says "favorable opinion." Answer choice F says little about the writer's feelings towards her brother. Answer choice G seems to set the writer's brother in a negative light. While both answer choices H and J seem to represent the writer's brother favorably, only answer choice J has a specific word demonstrating the favorable opinion: "endearing," an adjective meaning "evoking affection."

19. The best answer is D. While the addition contains information about the writer's family, it adds little to the development of the passage. It distracts the reader from the topic of the essay, the family's idiosyncrasies, and toward an unrelated organized sporting event.

20. The best answer is F. Gerund phrases such as "riding down the steps via a surfboard" act as nouns. The verb "insist" can take a noun as its complement when the noun is headed by the pronoun "on" or "upon." The conjunction "that" can be used after "insist," but only when the complement is a well-formed clause, which it is not in this case.

21. The best answer is D. The subject of a clause must never be separated from the verb immediately following it using punctuation; therefore, answer choices A and C can be eliminated. Answer choice B can be eliminated because a comma must not separate a verb ("respond") from its complement ("to my brother's tirades …").

22. The best answer is F. The underlined verb has the complex subject "moments following my brother's stair-surfing," the simple subject of which is "moments," which is plural. Therefore, the verb "manifest" must be in plural form, as it is written. Answer choice H, the simple past tense, could be plural, too; however, the paragraph is written in the present tense.

23. The best answer is C. "Me" is an object pronoun, but in this place in the sentence, the subject pronoun "I" is necessary. In addition, the compound subject "my dad and I" is plural. Answer choice C correctly uses both a subject pronoun and a plural verb form.

24. The best answer is F. After the participle "to," the bare form "dance" is best. Combined, "to dance" is called the infinitive form, which is the correct form for many verb complements, including those of "prefer."

25. The best answer is C. As written in the underlined portion, the comma and coordinating conjunction "and" correctly connect two independent clauses: "My dad is clothed in one of his 'retro' 80s jumpsuits," and "I am equally tacky in my outdated high school prom dress and tiara." Independent clauses can be connected in this way or with a semicolon, dash, or period. Independent clauses cannot be linked with only a comma, as in answer choice C. This error is called a comma splice.

26. The best answer is J. Because the noun phrase "family picture" implies the involvement of all four members of the writer's family, the underlined portion is redundant. Therefore, it should be omitted.

27. The best answer is A. When joining elements in a series using a coordinating conjunction, commas are only needed when there are more than two elements. In this case, there are only two elements, "stair-surfing" and "dance parties," so no commas are needed. Answer choice D eliminates the coordinating conjunction by substituting a comma, which makes the sentence awkward.

28. The best answer is G. The underlined portion "whose" heads relative clauses and is not appropriate in this case. The underlined portion should be a subject and a verb, and because the sentence is a question, an interrogative pronoun such as "who" can be used. Answer choice G is the contraction "who's," representing "who is," an interrogative subject pronoun and a simple present-tense verb.

29. The best answer is B. Sentence 3 successfully shifts the focus of the passage from a description of the writer's family's unusual activities to a personal statement of the writer's opinion of the activities. Sentence 1 begins with "in truth," which indicates that the writer wishes to correct any possible misconceptions the reader may have developed upon reading the passage. Sentence 2 further elaborates on Sentence 1. Sentences 4 and 5 are sound concluding remarks and should come at the end of the paragraph.

30. The best answer is F. Although the passage touches on answer choices G and J, they are not among the writer's main points. In addition, while the passage does demonstrate the good that can come from a family spending time together, the passage's main point is that the writer loves her family and interacts well with them, even though what the family does for fun may appear bizarre to some people.

31. The best answer is C. This underlined verb is part of a past-tense passive construction with the preceding auxiliary verb "was." Therefore, the past participle "chosen" is the correct form.

32. The best answer is H. As written, "its" is the possessive determiner. The correct form is "it's," which is the contraction of "it is," a subject pronoun and verb.

33. The best answer is D. As always, take the "DELETE" answer choice seriously. It is a clue to look for wordiness or redundancy created by the underlined portion. In this case, there is redundancy between "representing" and "symbolically." If the bald eagle represents the spirit of freedom and excellence, then it can be called a symbol of those ideas.

34. The best answer is G. "Instead of" is not appropriate here; it creates an awkward start to the sentence.

35. The best answer is C. The underlined portion should mean "with the exception of," so "except" is correct. "Accept" is a verb, one meaning of which is "take willingly."

36. The best answer is J. This prepositional phrase acts as a modifier, so it is best placed immediately after what it modifies. As written, the sentence is grammatically correct, but its meaning is not clear. "The bird" is not "in a boat or along a lakeshore." It's the "people" who are "in a boat or along a lakeshore" looking for bald eagles.

37. The best answer is C. The underlined portion should be the third-person plural possessive determiner "their" to mark the noun "population." The form "their" agrees with the third-person plural subject of the main clause: "bald eagles."

38. The best answer is G. The sentence should indicate that "human activity" caused the decline in the bald eagle population. Only answer choice G marks "human activity" as a cause.

39. The best answer is B. Notice first that the adverb "then" cannot be used in comparative constructions. Therefore, eliminate answer choices C and D. The difference between "less" and "fewer" has to do with the difference between non-count and count nouns. If a noun cannot be counted (such as hope, love, sand, air), use "less." If a noun can be counted (such as "1,000 [bald eagles]" in this case), use "fewer."

40. The best answer is F. The singular subject of this sentence "Increased public awareness" requires the singular verb form "has."

41. The best answer is C. The major clue in the sentence to be added is the adverb "also." This indicates that a related sentence should precede it. Sentence 3 of the paragraph is about government responses to the bald eagle's decline. The sentence to be added is about private parties' conservation efforts. Therefore, this sentence should follow Sentence 3.

42. The best answer is J. The form of "harass" should parallel the form of "threaten" after the conjunction "and." Only answer choices H and J have the bare form of "harass." Between these two answer choices, only answer choice J is idiomatic, using a form of "continue" with a verb in the infinitive form ("to" + "harass").

43. The best answer is C. The sentence up to the word "population" is a well-formed clause that can end in a period. Answer choice B, while grammatically correct, does not make sense in the sentence. Answer choices A and D are awkward and not grammatically correct.

44. The best answer is J. While answer choices G and J have the same meaning (the other two answer choices are grammatically incorrect), answer choice J benefits from being more concise and is in the active voice.

45. The best answer is C. The passage addresses the bald eagle from a population health perspective. Few details are given about habitat and diet, and none are given about how (or whether) habitat and diet vary geographically.

46. The best answer is G. The phrase beginning with "making" should modify the entire clause that precedes it. It is the fact that Robinson played football, basketball, track, and baseball that made him the first student to letter in four sports. Answer choice F leaves sentence fragments, while answer choice H would create a run-on. Answer choice J is not grammatically correct because "making" is a gerund that lacks tense, and there is no subject to complete a clause after the comma and conjunction "and."

47. The best answer is A. The writer includes this sentence because without it, some readers may not understand why so talented an athlete as Robinson would not have played in the majors. Answer choice C includes the word "obstacles," one of which was certainly the racial barrier in baseball, but because the passage is written in an even, unbiased style, it is not clear that the author feels any "regret" about Robinson's struggle for justice in sports.

48. The best answer is F. The phrase beginning with "at least" modifies the entire clause, "Segregation couldn't last forever." Therefore, it is correctly joined to it with a comma. In the immediate context, answer choice G seems acceptable, but by reading further you can see that "because" introduces a dependent clause, and the sentence ends without the independent clause it requires.

49. The best answer is B. The simple past tense verb "chose" is correct here. As it is written, the sentence is incomplete.

50. The best answer is H. This introductory phrase modifies the clause beginning with the subject "Rickey." Answer choice H uses a form (the gerund) that can behave as a modifier of a clause.

51. **The best answer is A.** The phrase "Starting with" creates an awkward sentence not appropriate in standard written English.

52. **The best answer is G.** "Threats to both Robinson and his family" were included in the "heckling," so only answer choice G is appropriate.

53. **The best answer is D.** "Help" and "assist" have nearly the same meaning; therefore, one must be eliminated to avoid redundancy.

54. **The best answer is H.** This sentence begins, "in 1949," so the main verb should be in the past tense.

55. **The best answer is C.** The nouns "awards," "accolades," "honors," and "distinctions" are synonyms that could be used in this sentence. Only "gifts" does not fit the context.

56. **The best answer is H.** The phrase "ten-year-long" behaves as one modifier, so it cannot be divided by commas. Therefore, answer choices F and G can be eliminated. Answer choice J is incorrect because the single hyphen links "year" and "long," when "ten" and "year" should be linked as well.

57. **The best answer is B.** The sentence lists only one of Robinson's accomplishments: the founding of the bank in Harlem. Therefore, the singular verb "was" is appropriate.

58. **The best answer is J.** This portion should be omitted because Robinson's death is mentioned at the beginning of the sentence. Remember, the ACT rewards eliminating redundancy.

59. **The best answer is A.** First, a comma or a colon is required before quotations of complete sentences. Second, the usage of the preposition "with" in answer choice A is not standard and may be awkward to some readers.

60. **The best answer is H.** This passage is about the success of Jackie Robinson. Although he did endure segregation for a time, the passage does not comment on Major League Baseball's segregation in general. This passage has a narrower scope than what the question stem describes.

61. **The best answer is D.** The adjectives "prosperous" and "successful" have nearly the same meaning, so one should be eliminated to avoid redundancy.

62. **The best answer is G.** The phrase "as a poor use of labor and resources" is the complement of the adjective "criticized," so it must not be set apart with a comma or any other punctuation. Verify this by reading the sentence to yourself without the phrase "by the government."

63. **The best answer is A.** The underlined portion should be an adverb to modify the adjective "popular" that follows. Most adverbs end in "-ly," as is the case here.

64. **The best answer is H.** The question stem asks you to choose the sentence that leads into the next paragraph. To do this, read the first portion of the next paragraph and choose the sentence that best matches what you read. Only answer choice H specifically describes the rationing of food, which is mentioned in the first phrase of the second paragraph.

65. **The best answer is A.** When sentence order is inverted, as it is here, a comma normally comes before the sentence's subject. Rephrase the sentence in standard word order to see this change: "Millions of Americans joined the effort with the help of government and business programs and resources."

66. **The best answer is H.** The gerund phrase beginning with "leaving" does not require any adverb, preposition, conjunction, or other word before it. The entire gerund phrase modifies the second clause of the sentence ("Americans would be able to provide many of their own fruits and vegetables"), so the gerund phrase should be set apart from the second clause with a comma.

67. **The best answer is A.** According to the passage, the Victory Gardens were established and maintained during the war, so only answer choice A makes sense in this context.

68. **The best answer is J.** The past perfect form of the verb "transform" is appropriate to describe a duration of time (the years people were maintaining the Victory Gardens) that was completed in the past. (Maintenance of Victory Gardens ended when the war ended.)

69. **The best answer is C.** The only punctuation appropriate before a relative clause headed by "which" is the comma. Answer choice B has a comma, but also the conjunction "and," which does not make sense in this context.

70. **The best answer is J.** The pronoun "them" is ambiguous, and should be replaced by a noun to more clearly indicate who is making the statement.

71. **The best answer is A.** The last part of the sentence, "taking the fight to the enemy," gives the impression of actual combat, like that which the predominantly young, male military was engaged in. The first part of the sentence, then, offers a contrast to this youthful image of war by showing people of all ages working toward the same goal of defeating the enemy: with gardening rather than weapons.

72. **The best answer is F.** This third-person possessive determiner correctly refers to the third-person plural noun phrase "Americans young and old."

73. **The best answer is B.** Sentence 1 describes the extent of Victory Gardens in the United States and ends with a figure of how much food was produced by them. It is a good first sentence for the paragraph. Sentence 3 should follow Sentence 1 because Sentence 3 further elaborates on how the great amount of produce grown in the Victory Gardens was put to use. Sentence 4 successfully concludes the paragraph.

74. **The best answer is H.** Relative clauses with a human logical subject require the relative subject pronoun "who," and not "that." Remember that "whom" is an object pronoun, which is not indicated here. The pronoun "who" acts as the subject of the verb "answered."

75. **The best answer is A.** The question stem specifically indicates "one way civilians actively supported the American cause during World War II." Because the passage is about the Victory Gardens program and no other programs, this essays fulfills the writer's goal.

▰▰▰   SCORING WORKSHEET

On each ACT multiple-choice test (English, Mathematics, Reading, and Science) you will receive a SCALED SCORE on a scale of 1 to 36. Use the following guidelines to determine your approximate SCALED SCORE on the ACT English Practice Test that you just completed.

Step 1 Determine your RAW SCORE.

Your RAW SCORE is the number of questions that you answered correctly. Because there are 75 questions on the ACT English Test, the highest possible RAW SCORE is 75.

Step 2 Determine your SCALED SCORE using the following Scoring Worksheet

English	—————————— × 36 = —————————— + 75 = ——————————	
	RAW SCORE	
		− 2 (*correction factor)
		——————————
		SCALED SCORE

   *The correction factor is an approximation based on the average from several recent ACT tests. It is most valid for scores in the middle 50 percent (approximately 16–24 scaled composite score) of the scoring range. The scores are all approximate. Actual ACT scoring scales vary from one administration to the next based upon several factors.

CHAPTER 7

ACT ENGLISH PRACTICE TEST 2

This chapter should help you evaluate your progress in preparing for the ACT English Test. Make an honest effort to answer each question, and then review the explanations that follow. Review Chapter 3, "Grammar Review," Chapter 4, "Strategies and Techniques," and Chapter 5, "Applying Strategies, Building Skills," if you continue to struggle with the questions on this simulated practice test.

ACT ENGLISH PRACTICE TEST 2
Answer Sheet

ENGLISH

1 Ⓐ Ⓑ Ⓒ Ⓓ	21 Ⓐ Ⓑ Ⓒ Ⓓ	41 Ⓐ Ⓑ Ⓒ Ⓓ	61 Ⓐ Ⓑ Ⓒ Ⓓ
2 Ⓕ Ⓖ Ⓗ Ⓙ	22 Ⓕ Ⓖ Ⓗ Ⓙ	42 Ⓕ Ⓖ Ⓗ Ⓙ	62 Ⓕ Ⓖ Ⓗ Ⓙ
3 Ⓐ Ⓑ Ⓒ Ⓓ	23 Ⓐ Ⓑ Ⓒ Ⓓ	43 Ⓐ Ⓑ Ⓒ Ⓓ	63 Ⓐ Ⓑ Ⓒ Ⓓ
4 Ⓕ Ⓖ Ⓗ Ⓙ	24 Ⓕ Ⓖ Ⓗ Ⓙ	44 Ⓕ Ⓖ Ⓗ Ⓙ	64 Ⓕ Ⓖ Ⓗ Ⓙ
5 Ⓐ Ⓑ Ⓒ Ⓓ	25 Ⓐ Ⓑ Ⓒ Ⓓ	45 Ⓐ Ⓑ Ⓒ Ⓓ	65 Ⓐ Ⓑ Ⓒ Ⓓ
6 Ⓕ Ⓖ Ⓗ Ⓙ	26 Ⓕ Ⓖ Ⓗ Ⓙ	46 Ⓕ Ⓖ Ⓗ Ⓙ	66 Ⓕ Ⓖ Ⓗ Ⓙ
7 Ⓐ Ⓑ Ⓒ Ⓓ	27 Ⓐ Ⓑ Ⓒ Ⓓ	47 Ⓐ Ⓑ Ⓒ Ⓓ	67 Ⓐ Ⓑ Ⓒ Ⓓ
8 Ⓕ Ⓖ Ⓗ Ⓙ	28 Ⓕ Ⓖ Ⓗ Ⓙ	48 Ⓕ Ⓖ Ⓗ Ⓙ	68 Ⓕ Ⓖ Ⓗ Ⓙ
9 Ⓐ Ⓑ Ⓒ Ⓓ	29 Ⓐ Ⓑ Ⓒ Ⓓ	49 Ⓐ Ⓑ Ⓒ Ⓓ	69 Ⓐ Ⓑ Ⓒ Ⓓ
10 Ⓕ Ⓖ Ⓗ Ⓙ	30 Ⓕ Ⓖ Ⓗ Ⓙ	50 Ⓕ Ⓖ Ⓗ Ⓙ	70 Ⓕ Ⓖ Ⓗ Ⓙ
11 Ⓐ Ⓑ Ⓒ Ⓓ	31 Ⓐ Ⓑ Ⓒ Ⓓ	51 Ⓐ Ⓑ Ⓒ Ⓓ	71 Ⓐ Ⓑ Ⓒ Ⓓ
12 Ⓕ Ⓖ Ⓗ Ⓙ	32 Ⓕ Ⓖ Ⓗ Ⓙ	52 Ⓕ Ⓖ Ⓗ Ⓙ	72 Ⓕ Ⓖ Ⓗ Ⓙ
13 Ⓐ Ⓑ Ⓒ Ⓓ	33 Ⓐ Ⓑ Ⓒ Ⓓ	53 Ⓐ Ⓑ Ⓒ Ⓓ	73 Ⓐ Ⓑ Ⓒ Ⓓ
14 Ⓕ Ⓖ Ⓗ Ⓙ	34 Ⓕ Ⓖ Ⓗ Ⓙ	54 Ⓕ Ⓖ Ⓗ Ⓙ	74 Ⓕ Ⓖ Ⓗ Ⓙ
15 Ⓐ Ⓑ Ⓒ Ⓓ	35 Ⓐ Ⓑ Ⓒ Ⓓ	55 Ⓐ Ⓑ Ⓒ Ⓓ	75 Ⓐ Ⓑ Ⓒ Ⓓ
16 Ⓕ Ⓖ Ⓗ Ⓙ	36 Ⓕ Ⓖ Ⓗ Ⓙ	56 Ⓕ Ⓖ Ⓗ Ⓙ	
17 Ⓐ Ⓑ Ⓒ Ⓓ	37 Ⓐ Ⓑ Ⓒ Ⓓ	57 Ⓐ Ⓑ Ⓒ Ⓓ	
18 Ⓕ Ⓖ Ⓗ Ⓙ	38 Ⓕ Ⓖ Ⓗ Ⓙ	58 Ⓕ Ⓖ Ⓗ Ⓙ	
19 Ⓐ Ⓑ Ⓒ Ⓓ	39 Ⓐ Ⓑ Ⓒ Ⓓ	59 Ⓐ Ⓑ Ⓒ Ⓓ	
20 Ⓕ Ⓖ Ⓗ Ⓙ	40 Ⓕ Ⓖ Ⓗ Ⓙ	60 Ⓕ Ⓖ Ⓗ Ⓙ	

ENGLISH TEST
45 Minutes—75 Questions

DIRECTIONS: In the passages that follow, some words and phrases are underlined and numbered. In the answer column, you will find alternatives for the words and phrases that are underlined. Choose the alternative that you think is best, and fill in the corresponding bubble on your answer sheet. If you think that the original version is best, choose "NO CHANGE," which will always be either answer choice A or F. You will also find questions about a particular section of the passage or the entire passage. These questions will be identified by either an underlined and numbered portion or a number in a box. Look for the answer that clearly expresses the idea, is consistent with the style and tone of the passage, and makes the correct use of standard written English. Read the passage through once before answering the questions. For some questions, you should read before and beyond the indicated portion before you answer.

PASSAGE I

> The following paragraphs may or may not be in the most logical order. You may be asked questions about the logical order of the paragraphs, as well as where to place sentences logically within any given paragraph.

Juan Rodríguez Cabrillo: Portuguese Explorer

[1]

Just off the tip of Point Loma, San Diego, California,
    1
the Cabrillo National Monument sits. The monument,
    1

with its fourteen-foot-high statue, of Portuguese explorer
                    2
Juan Rodríguez Cabrillo is a striking commemoration of
    2
an important event in American history. But few today know

much about the man, which is honored there.
                    3

[2]

His was the first European expedition to what later

became the U.S. west coast. Cabrillo was Portuguese, while
                                        4
as a young man, he joined the Spanish forces of the
conquistador Hernán Cortés in the conquest of Mexico.

1. A. NO CHANGE
    B. The Cabrillo National Monument sits in San Diego, California, just off the tip of Point Loma.
    C. Just off the tip of Point Loma, sits the Cabrillo National Monument in San Diego, California.
    D. In San Diego, just off the tip of Point Loma, California, sits the Cabrillo National Monument.

2. F. NO CHANGE
    G. fourteen-foot-high statue of Portuguese explorer Juan Cabrillo,
    H. fourteen-foot-high statue of Portuguese, explorer Juan Cabrillo,
    J. fourteen-foot-high statue of Portuguese explorer, Juan Cabrillo,

3. A. NO CHANGE
    B. man who
    C. man that
    D. man, who

4. F. NO CHANGE
    G. Cabrillo was Portuguese, therefore
    H. Cabrillo was Portuguese, but
    J. Cabrillo was Portuguese, moreover

GO ON TO THE NEXT PAGE.

<u>Soon becoming a conquistador himself</u> and ultimately
5

<u>set sail on an exploration up the Pacific Coast</u> in search of
6
trade opportunities.

[3]

⑦ Every October, a festival commemorates Cabrillo with a reenactment of his landing at San Diego Bay. Local San Diegans and tourists enjoy Portuguese, Mexican, and indigenous food, music, and dancing in celebration of Cabrillo's historic discovery.

[4]

Today, Cabrillo's statue overlooks a scenic public park. The view encompasses San Diego's harbor and skyline; on clear days, a glance to the south reveals the Tijuana coastline. Starting in December and continuing through March, visitors can <u>watch grey, whales,</u> migrate south to
8
their breeding grounds off the coast of Baja, Mexico, and back up again to their summer feeding area in the Arctic Ocean.

[5]

Cabrillo's journey <u>begins</u> in what is now Acapulco,
9
Mexico, and ended far to the north at the Russian River in northern California. Despite its historical importance, Cabrillo's expedition was not <u>a universal success.</u>
10
For example, none of his place names have survived. Cabrillo initially named the San Diego area after <u>San Miguel (St. Michael)—the area</u> received its current
11
name when it was surveyed in 1602. He also missed the

discovery of San Francisco Bay. <u>It is famous for the</u>
12

<u>Golden Gate Bridge</u> Juan Rodríguez Cabrillo never profited
12,

5. **A.** NO CHANGE
   B. He soon became one
   C. Cabrillo soon became a conquistador himself
   D. Cabrillo soon became one himself

6. **F.** NO CHANGE
   G. set sail to explore the Pacific Coast
   H. set sail on exploring up the Pacific Coast
   J. set sail on Pacific Coast exploration

7. Which of the following sentences would be the most effective introductory sentence for Paragraph 3?
   A. Juan Rodríguez Cabrillo landed at San Diego Bay on September 28, 1542.
   B. Honor is very important to the Portuguese.
   C. San Diego sits at the southwestern tip of the continental United States.
   D. Most exploration of the Pacific Coast was done by Spaniards.

8. **F.** NO CHANGE
   G. watch grey, whales
   H. watch grey whales,
   J. watch grey whales

9. **A.** NO CHANGE
   B. began
   C. is beginning
   D. has begun

10. **F.** NO CHANGE
    G. a total and universal success
    H. an entirely complete success
    J. absolutely a universal success

11. Which of the following alternatives to the underlined portion would be LEAST acceptable?
    A. San Miguel (St. Michael); however, the area
    B. San Miguel (St. Michael), the area
    C. San Miguel (St. Michael). The area
    D. San Miguel (St. Michael); the area

12. **F.** NO CHANGE
    G. Famous for the Golden Gate Bridge.
    H. The Golden Gate Bridge was built there.
    J. DELETE the underlined portion.

GO ON TO THE NEXT PAGE.

from his exploration of California. During the expedition, on November 23, 1542, Cabrillo slipped on a rock, fracturing his shin. The injury worsened, and Cabrillo died of gangrene the <u>following</u> January.
₁₃

13. The best placement for the underlined portion would be:
   A. where it is now.
   B. before the word *injury*.
   C. after the word *died*.
   D. before the word *Cabrillo*

Questions 14 and 15 ask about the preceding passage as a whole.

---

14. Which of the following concluding statements would most effectively restate the main focus of the essay?
   F. A true adventurer, Juan Rodríguez Cabrillo epitomized the sixteenth-century spirit of discovery.
   G. A true visionary, Juan Rodríguez Cabrillo exemplified the sixteenth-century artist.
   H. A true gentleman, Juan Rodríguez Cabrillo typified the spirit of scholarship of his age.
   J. A true Spaniard, Juan Rodríguez Cabrillo embodied the European exploitation of indigenous people.

15. Which of the following sequences of paragraphs makes the essay most logical?
   A. NO CHANGE
   B. 1, 3, 2, 4, 5
   C. 4, 1, 2, 3, 5
   D. 1, 2, 5, 4, 3

PASSAGE II

The Chinese New Year

Every winter, the Chinese New Year—a major holiday for ethnic Chinese—is celebrated internationally. Many Westerners <u>were</u> familiar with the Chinese New Year
₁₆
because of the 12-year cycle of animals in the Chinese zodiac. Each year has a representative animal: rat, ox, tiger, rabbit, dragon, snake, horse, sheep, monkey, rooster, dog, or pig. The animal is honored at New Year celebrations and is thought to give its characteristics <u>by</u> the coming year.
₁₇

16. F. NO CHANGE
   G. are
   H. have been
   J. becoming

17. A. NO CHANGE
   B. to
   C. into
   D. DELETE the underlined portion.

GO ON TO THE NEXT PAGE.

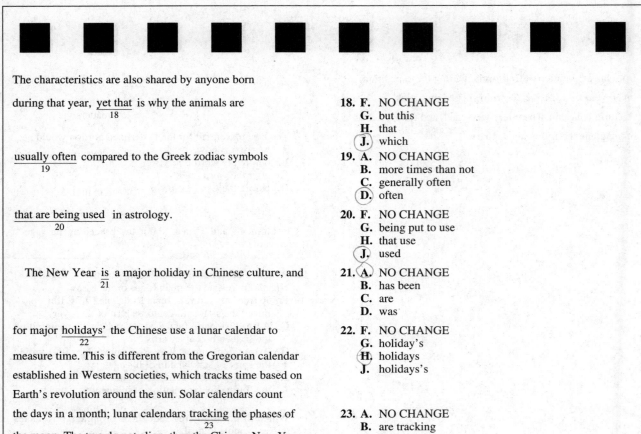

The characteristics are also shared by anyone born
during that year, yet that is why the animals are
                     18

usually often compared to the Greek zodiac symbols
   19

that are being used in astrology.
   20

  The New Year is a major holiday in Chinese culture, and
               21

for major holidays' the Chinese use a lunar calendar to
              22
measure time. This is different from the Gregorian calendar
established in Western societies, which tracks time based on
Earth's revolution around the sun. Solar calendars count
the days in a month; lunar calendars tracking the phases of
                                      23
the moon. The two do not align, thus the Chinese New Year

does not correspond to a specific date on the Western
                     24

calendar. The holiday is usually calculated to fall on the
second new moon after the winter solstice. In practical
terms, the New Year can begin any time between January 22
and February 20.

  The New Year festival usually lasts two weeks, beginning
on the first day of the first lunar month of the Chinese
calendar and ending on the fifteenth day. Traditionally,
different activities are practiced each day. Most of the
traditions honor family and ensure good fortune for the
                                25

18. F. NO CHANGE
    G. but this
    H. that
    J. which

19. A. NO CHANGE
    B. more times than not
    C. generally often
    D. often

20. F. NO CHANGE
    G. being put to use
    H. that use
    J. used

21. A. NO CHANGE
    B. has been
    C. are
    D. was

22. F. NO CHANGE
    G. holiday's
    H. holidays
    J. holidays's

23. A. NO CHANGE
    B. are tracking
    C. tracked
    D. track

24. F. NO CHANGE
    G. by
    H. for
    J. within

25. Which of the following alternatives to the underlined por-
    tion would be LEAST acceptable?
    A. guarantee
    B. secure
    C. perform
    D. promise

coming year. Families visit with their elders, and everyone enjoys special meals consisting of tasty, traditional fare.
20

According to the Chinese mythology, the coming of the New Year coincides with the arrival of a monster that appears each year to eat whatever humans it can find. The monster is frightened away by loud noises and the color red. Therefore, fireworks, and red decorations became popular at New
27
Year's celebrations. Today, these same traditions are thought to ward off evil spirits and encourage good luck. Chinese people also spread good luck in giving red envelopes
28
containing money to children and young, unmarried adults. The envelopes often have gold lettering representing wealth. By comparison, all people, Chinese or not, can relate to this
29

aspiration. 30

26. Given that all the choices are true, which one would best conclude the sentence while helping readers visualize the holiday meal?
   F. NO CHANGE
   G. that can take many hours or even days to prepare.
   H. because family members may live great distances apart.
   J. because Chinese people hold food in high esteem.

27. A. NO CHANGE
   B. fireworks and red decorations,
   C. fireworks, and red decorations,
   D. fireworks and red decorations

28. F. NO CHANGE
   G. on
   H. for
   J. by

29. A. NO CHANGE
   B. Certainly,
   C. Nevertheless,
   D. Therefore,

30. Given the writer's discussion of the Chinese New Year rituals in this paragraph, would the following sentence appropriately conclude the paragraph?

   When was the last time you had everything you wanted?

   F. Yes, because the paragraph starts by discussing the origin of Chinese New Year well-wishing and narrows its focus to just one, the wish for abundance.
   G. Yes, because the paragraph starts by discussing one myth and broadens its topic to mention others.
   H. No, because the sentence unexpectedly shifts the subject of the paragraph from a discussion of a Chinese New Year tradition to a direct question about the condition of the reader.
   J. No, because it is a rhetorical question that the reader does not have sufficient information to answer.

PASSAGE III

Ireland: Worth the Trip

[1]

If you ever have the chance, plan a visit to Ireland. This lovely island nation is small—with just over
31
four million inhabitants, but warmly inviting to locals
31
and strangers alike.

31. A. NO CHANGE
   B. small, with just over four million inhabitants,
   C. small. With just over four million inhabitants,
   D. small with just over four million inhabitants

GO ON TO THE NEXT PAGE.

[2]

[1] Despite being much farther north than the contiguous United States, the Irish countryside is lush and green (thus the name, "The Emerald Isle"), and the temperature rarely dips below freezing, even in the middle of winter. [2] The island even has small palm trees growing along its coast! [3] Ireland is located in the northern reaches of the Atlantic Ocean. [4] However, thousands of years of cultivation have left few large trees in Ireland. Instead, rolling fields of grass dotted with sheep cover the sparsely populated hillsides. 32

[3]

Away from the cities, small villages with few inhabitants
_____
                              33
are connected by one- and two-lane roads called *boreens* (from the Gaelic for "little road"). Vehicles and pedestrians are protected from Atlantic winds by six-foot stone walls that line both sides of the boreens. Despite what the
                                               ‾‾‾‾‾‾‾
                                                 34
greenery may suggest, Ireland has very rocky soil, and the stones are collected from the local farmlands. Specially
                                                          ‾‾‾‾‾‾‾‾
                                                            35
trained masons fit the rocks together without using cutting tools to shape them or mortar to hold them together, constructing completely solid walls, strong enough to withstand gale-force winter storms. 36

[4]

Although effective against the wind, stone walls are not enough for protection inhabitants from the frequent, chilly
         ‾‾‾‾‾‾‾‾‾‾‾‾‾
              37
rain. To warm up and dry off, Irish people can stop by their

32. For the sake of the logic and coherence of this paragraph, Sentence 3 should be placed:
   F. where it is now.
   G. before Sentence 1.
   H. after Sentence 1.
   J. after Sentence 4.

33. A. NO CHANGE
   B. Small villages away from the cities with few inhabitants
   C. Small villages, with few inhabitants away from the cities
   D. Small villages with few inhabitants

34. F. NO CHANGE
   G. Because of
   H. According to
   J. Never mind

35. A. NO CHANGE
   B. special
   C. specialized
   D. especially

36. Which of the following sentences, if added here, would most logically conclude this paragraph?
   F. Masons are an important part of Irish society.
   G. Transportation is very important for local trade.
   H. Irish rocks are sometimes exported to other countries.
   J. In this way, far-flung communities are safely connected to one another.

37. A. NO CHANGE
   B. to protect
   C. to protecting
   D. by protecting

GO ON TO THE NEXT PAGE.

local pub. Pubs in Ireland <u>are</u> different from bars in the
₃₈
United States in that they serve a purpose beyond drinking.
Often a whole community, including children, will gather in
a pub for meals and conversation about the day's events.
<u>Whether</u> closely associated with alcohol, pubs can become
₃₉
famous for the quality of their "pub grub," the quick and

satisfying food that often <u>include</u> regional specialties such
₄₀
as fresh local fish.

[5]

In the evening, pubs are also good places to hear local
musicians in full session. <u>These open parties, called céilís,</u>
₄₁
<u>often involving energetic Irish dancing.</u> Don't be surprised
₄₁
if you see signs advertising "good music and good *craic*."
(That's Irish slang for "fun!")

[6]

<u>But anyway, I recommend.</u> a trip to Ireland. With
₄₂

it's beautiful countryside and open hospitality, Ireland is
₄₃
truly a treasure to discover.

38. **F.** NO CHANGE
   G. is
   H. were
   J. they're

39. **A.** NO CHANGE
   B. Because
   C. Still
   D. Although

40. **F.** NO CHANGE
   G. including
   H. includes
   J. included

41. **A.** NO CHANGE
   B. These are open parties—called *céilís*—which often have involved energetic Irish dancing.
   C. These open parties, called *céilís*, often involve energetic Irish dancing.
   D. Called *céilís*, these open parties are involving energetic Irish dancing.

42. **F.** NO CHANGE
   G. Ultimately, I would have to recommend
   H. Despite all this, I would strongly suggest
   J. I definitely recommend

43. **A.** NO CHANGE
   B. one's
   C. its
   D. their

Questions 44 and 45 ask about the preceding passage as a whole.

---

44. The writer wishes to add the following sentence in order to give the reader advice about visiting Ireland:

   Residents know that the most satisfying fare is often served in unassuming surroundings.

The new sentence would best support and be placed at the end of Paragraph:
   F. 2.
   G. 3.
   H. 4.
   J. 5.

GO ON TO THE NEXT PAGE.

45. Suppose the editor of a newspaper had told the writer of this essay to examine objectively the positive and negative aspects of visiting Ireland. Does the essay successfully fulfill the assignment?
  A. Yes, because the writer focuses on Ireland's tightly united communities.
  B. Yes, because the author mentions Ireland's frequent inclement weather and the problems it causes.
  C. No, because the author gives a description of Irish topography without cultural bias.
  D. No, because the writer emphasizes the advantages of visiting Ireland and recommends doing so.

PASSAGE IV

French Learning

Every country has its own system for educating its children; it's interesting to look _at_ how another country
46

chose to do something as important as training the
47
next generation of young adults. Unlike the United States, where individual states have control over their schools, France _represents an example_ of a
48

centralized system. The French Ministry of _National_
49
Education, Advanced Instruction and Research controls
49
course content and employs all teachers and staff. There

are other important _difference_ as well.
50

   Primary education in France is _much as is education_
51
primarily in the United States, although all children in
51
France _begin the first year with preschool_. French public
52
preschools are free, and the teachers have the same educational degrees and training as elementary-school teachers. Elementary school proper begins with what Americans would call kindergarten and continues through

46. F. NO CHANGE
  G. to
  H. for
  J. with

47. A. NO CHANGE
  B. is choosing to doing
  C. choose to do
  D. chooses to do

48. F. NO CHANGE
  G. is an example
  H. examples
  J. makes an example

49. A. NO CHANGE
  B. National Education, Advanced, Instruction, and Research
  C. National Education, Advanced Instruction, and Research
  D. National Education Advanced Instruction and Research

50. F. NO CHANGE
  G. differences
  H. different
  J. differs

51. A. NO CHANGE
  B. like the primary education is
  C. similar to primary education
  D. much like primary education is, essentially,

52. F. NO CHANGE
  G. during the first year begin with preschool
  H. preschool begin their first year
  J. begin with preschool

GO ON TO THE NEXT PAGE.

the fifth grade. These years are split into three learning

sequences Cycle I (age two to four), Cycle II (elementary
___
53

years one through three), and Cycle III (elementary years

four through six). Children can pass within cycles based on

their age, but they have to master specific skills (for

example, reading and math) in order to advance.

    Secondary schools called *collèges* cover the next four

years, from ages twelve to fifteen. By successfully

completing the *collèges* curriculum, a student earns a *brevet*

des collèges, a sort of intermediate diploma that allows a

student to quit school legally. The system is designed so that

a student who quits traditional academic study can transfer

to another program, such as like a technical or vocational
                     _____
                      54

school. Students in academics who are not interested
            _____
               55

are strongly encouraged to transfer at this time.

Though the purpose of transferring is to reduce the
_____
         56

frustration of nonacademic students while freeing up

resources for the ones who remain. It's the student who

ultimately decides, however—any student with sufficient

grades are moving up to the next level or select an
       _____
         57

alternate path.

↓ *two sentence policy*

    Lycée, or high school, lasts for only three years. After
       _____
        57

the first year, students are given the opportunity to choose an

area of concentration, which can be purely academic, such

as science or literature, or more applied, such as accounting

or marketing. Students do not have to pass any particular

exams to enter a specialization. They do, however, need the

approval of their teachers. If a teachers' committee does not

53. Which of the following alternatives to the underlined portion would be LEAST acceptable?
   A. series
   B. classifications
   C. events
   D. developments

54. **F.** NO CHANGE
   G. likely
   H. such as
   J. such as one offered by

55. The best placement for the underlined portion would be:
   A. where it is now.
   B. after the word *interested*.
   C. after the word *who*.
   D. after the word *transfer*.

56. **F.** NO CHANGE
   G. The purpose
   H. While, the purpose
   J. The purpose, on the other hand,

57. **A.** NO CHANGE
   B. has moved up
   C. will have moved up
   D. can move up

58. **F.** NO CHANGE
   G. or high school
   H. or, high school
   J. or high, school

GO ON TO THE NEXT PAGE.

feel a student has the knowledge, skills, and abilities to succeed in a particular area, <u>they</u> will be redirected to
₅₉
another concentration.

59. **A.** NO CHANGE
    B. it
    C. you
    D. the student

At the end of *lycée*, students sit for an exam called the *baccalauréat*, or simply the *bac*, which is a combination of an intensive critical-thinking skills assessments and examinations covering the *lycée* curriculum. Once students pass this final testing hurdle, they <u>can be applied</u> for college
₆₀
admission.

60. **F.** NO CHANGE
    G. will have applied
    H. are applying
    J. can apply

PASSAGE V

The Legend of Robin Hood: Fact or Fiction?

People who <u>knew</u> Robin Hood only through Hollywood
₆₁
movies might be a little surprised to discover that the original stories are markedly more complicated. Robin Hood may have robbed from the rich <u>(as they were the ones</u>
₆₂
<u>with the money, after all)</u> —but did he give to the poor?
₆₂
Not necessarily. There are other differences to reconcile, as well.

61. **A.** NO CHANGE
    B. knows
    C. know
    D. are knowing

62. The writer wants to classify Robin Hood's robbery victims accurately. Given this purpose, which choice would work best?
    F. NO CHANGE
    G. (while they were in their fancy houses)
    H. (who made up the upper class in medieval England)
    J. DELETE the underlined portion.

The first records of Robin Hood are from the early thirteenth century, a few years after the reign of King John (called "Prince John" in the legends). While it is possible that there was a real historical figure at the heart of the Robin Hood stories, many historians believe his existence was unlikely. By 1261, "Robin Hood" <u>becoming</u> just a
₆₃
generic term used to describe thieves and other common criminals. By the fourteenth century, more detailed legends were being written down. Since then, Robin has been portrayed in various lights: as a relentless do-gooder, a pious gentleman, and even a treasonous murderer. Some of these later <u>legends, borrowed</u> events from the lives of
₆₄

63. **A.** NO CHANGE
    B. becomes
    C. had become
    D. had became

64. **F.** NO CHANGE
    G. legends borrowed
    H. legends, borrowing
    J. legends having borrowed

documented historical figures, but only beginning in the nineteenth century does Robin Hood <u>takes</u> the role
65
of savior of the poor and defender of righteousness.

[1] Robin Hood's companions were not always who we would expect, either. [2] <u>As such characters as</u> Will Scarlet
66
and Little John historically appear early, a female companion would not have been socially acceptable considering Robin Hood's outlaw lifestyle. [3] Consequently, Robin Hood had no romantic interest in the original tales. [4] Maid Marian did not appear with him until the sixteenth century. [5] Marian, <u>was derived</u> from a
67
very old legend in which she is a shepherdess character, was a late borrowing from the May Day festivals. [6] May Day, a popular holiday in England, celebrates the beginning of spring. [7] Eventually, though, the two were <u>tied together</u>
68
<u>and united.</u> [8] Robin Hood and his men celebrated the day,
68
and Maid Marian did too, but in disparate works of literature. [69] [9] This notion of Robin Hood sustaining an inclusive, nearly democratic society friendly to the poor and women is an adaptation to modern times.

<u>Since</u> Marian entered the legend, the character of Robin
70
Hood had already changed dramatically. He gained an aristocratic title, Earl of Huntingdon, and began to represent a legitimate kingship battling <u>tyranny despotism</u> with a good
71
measure of violence. Over generations, however, the

savagery was shed, and what resulted was the <u>charmingly</u>
72
<u>charismatic</u> outlaw so popular today. Robin Hood is,
72

65. A. NO CHANGE
    B. take from
    C. take by
    D. take on

66. F. NO CHANGE
    G. Moreover, such characters as
    H. However, such characters as
    J. Even though such characters as

67. A. NO CHANGE
    B. had been derived
    C. derives
    D. derived

68. F. NO CHANGE
    G. united by being tied together.
    H. united.
    J. united as if tied together.

69. For the sake of logic and coherence of this paragraph, Sentence 8 should be placed:
    A. where it is now.
    B. before Sentence 2.
    C. before Sentence 5.
    D. before Sentence 7.

70. F. NO CHANGE
    G. So
    H. By the time
    J. Although

71. A. NO CHANGE
    B. tyrannically despotic
    C. tyrannical despotism
    D. tyrants with despots

72. F. NO CHANGE
    G. charm
    H. charming charisma
    J. charming

GO ON TO THE NEXT PAGE.

after all, a literary creation, so the reader must accept him and his exploits as fiction. Considering the real history of the <u>Middle Ages resisting</u> the ruling class would have been
₇₃
forbiddingly difficult and bloody, certainly not fodder for

children's stories. 74

73. **A.** NO CHANGE
   B. Middle Ages resist
   C. Middle Ages, resisting
   D. Middle Ages. Resisting

74. Given that all are true, which of the following sentences, if inserted here, would best conclude this paragraph?
   F. Robin Hood has always been a popular character.
   G. Robin Hood's stories have had a lasting impact on English literature.
   H. While critics have not always valued Robin Hood's legends, the character remains a staple of English culture.
   J. In reality, Robin Hood's best modern incarnations retain many of his fearsome qualities found in early legends.

Question 75 asks about the preceding passage as a whole.

75. Suppose the writer's goal had been to write a brief descriptive essay about the evolution of the Robin Hood tales. Would this essay fulfill that goal?
   A. Yes, because the essay focuses on how Robin Hood may never have existed.
   B. Yes, because the essay focuses on how the Robin Hood tales have been adapted over many centuries.
   C. No, because the essay objectively describes how changing times affect the plot and characterization of the Robin Hood tales.
   D. No, because the essay fails to show whether Robin Hood actually stole from the rich to give to the poor.

END OF THE ENGLISH TEST
STOP! IF YOU HAVE TIME LEFT OVER, CHECK YOUR WORK ON THIS SECTION ONLY.

ANSWERS AND EXPLANATIONS

1. **The best answer is B.** The ACT rewards clarity. This sentence has standard structure: subject ("The Cabrillo National Monument"), verb ("sits"), complement ("in San Diego, California, just off the tip of Point Loma").

2. **The best answer is G.** No comma should be used between a noun ("statue") and its complement ("of Portuguese explorer Juan Rodríguez Cabrillo"). Therefore, eliminate answer choice F. No comma should be used between an adjective and the noun it modifies: "Portuguese [adj.] explorer [n.]." Therefore, answer choice H can be eliminated. Finally, when a noun is preceded by a noun phrase that acts as a job title, rank, or essential feature, no comma can intervene: "Portuguese explorer Juan Rodríguez Cabrillo."

3. **The best answer is B.** The proper relative subject pronoun to use with humans is "who." Although answer choice D includes "who," it should be eliminated because a comma is not required after "man."

4. **The best answer is H.** The conjunction "but" correctly marks seemingly contradictory information. Here, the fact that Cabrillo was Portuguese but sailed on behalf of Spain seems contradictory.

5. **The best answer is C.** The underlined portion should have a clear subject and a verb. While answer choices C and D seem equally correct, answer choice D is awkward because the pronoun "one" does not have a clear antecedent. Moreover, to be "one" of a group, the group must be plural. The only preceding mention of "conquistador" is singular. Answer choice B is too vague.

6. **The best answer is G.** Among the answer choices, answer choice G is simple and clear, making use of the infinitive verb form "to explore." Answer choices F, H, and J are awkward.

7. **The best answer is A.** Paragraph 3 is about a festival commemorating Cabrillo's discovery of San Diego Bay. The other answer choices do not mention this event.

8. **The best answer is J.** No comma should be used between the adjective "grey" and the noun it modifies, "whales." Therefore, answer choices F and G can be eliminated. In addition, no comma can be used between subject and verb, so answer choice H can be eliminated: "whales" (subject), "migrate" (verb).

9. **The best answer is B.** Cabrillo's journey started in the past and is completed; therefore, the simple past form "began" is best.

10. **The best answer is F.** The sentence as it is written simply and clearly expresses the intended idea. The remaining answer choices include redundancy.

11. **The best answer is B.** Independent clauses cannot be linked with only a comma. This specific error is called comma splicing, and is frequently included in ACT English tests. If a comma is used to join independent clauses, a conjunction (such as "and" or "but") or some longer phrase must also be used.

12. **The best answer is J.** The Golden Gate Bridge is irrelevant to a discussion of an exploratory voyage that took place centuries ago. Although true, the location of the bridge in San Francisco Bay distracts from the main idea of the paragraph and the essay.

13. **The best answer is A.** The adjective "following" modifies "January."

14. **The best answer is F.** The passage is about the legacy of Cabrillo as an explorer and discoverer of places along the Pacific Coast. This idea is best expressed in the statement in answer choice F.

15. **The best answer is D.** Paragraph 1 is a brief introduction to what information the essay will include. Paragraph 2 defines who Cabrillo is, and how he came to be on the Pacific Coast of North America. Paragraph 5 should come next because it details Cabrillo's voyage of discovery and ends with his accidental death. Paragraph 4 follows logically from Paragraph 5 by describing how Cabrillo is memorialized. Paragraph 3 gives further detail on the memorial traditions.

16. **The best answer is G.** The simple present tense is appropriate to match the simple present tense throughout the passage. Note that although many of the sentences are in passive voice, the auxiliary verbs in these constructions are in simple present tense (is/are + past participle).

17. **The best answer is B.** The indirect object of the verb "give" is generally headed with the preposition "to." In this case, "its characteristics" is the direct object, and "the coming year" should be the indirect object.

18. **The best answer is J.** The two clauses are not at all contradictory, so using "yet" or "but" (as in answer choices F and G) would be inappropriate.

Answer choice H may not be used because "that" cannot introduce subordinate clauses when preceded by a comma. In contrast with "that," "which" may introduce subordinate clauses when preceded by a comma; therefore, answer choice J is a simple and clear revision.

19. **The best answer is D.** This test item requires you to eliminate wordiness and redundancy. Because "usually," "generally," and "often" have nearly the same meaning, it is redundant to use two of them together. Eliminate answer choices A and C. Answer choice B, although grammatically correct, expresses in four words what answer choice D expresses in one word.

20. **The best answer is J.** This test item requires you to eliminate wordiness. Because "used" (answer choice J) is grammatically correct and the shortest answer choice, it is the best of the answer choices.

21. **The best answer is A.** The sentence is best as written, using the third-person, singular, simple present tense "is" to agree with the third-person, singular subject "The New Year" and parallel the simple present tense found throughout the break passage.

22. **The best answer is H.** The noun phrase "major holidays" is the object of the preposition "for." Therefore, it must be a noun without any possessive markings.

23. **The best answer is D.** Semicolons divide two well-formed clauses. This means that each clause joined by a semicolon must have a subject, verb, and any necessary verb complements. Eliminate answer choice A because the gerund "tracking" does not have tense, and thus cannot be the main verb of a clause. Answer choice D is the best of those that remain because it is in simple present-tense form, which parallels the form of the verb "count" in the clause preceding the semicolon.

24. **The best answer is F.** In this idiomatic phrase, the correct preposition to use is "to."

25. **The best answer is C.** While all of the answer choices are closely related, "perform" does not fit the context, and is not the best choice.

26. **The best answer is F.** The crucial phrase in the question stem is "helping readers visualize the holiday meal." Answer choices G, H, and J do not include any images of the meal. Alternatively, answer choice F includes language that describes the meal and helps the reader envision what the meal might consist of.

27. **The best answer is D.** The subject of this sentence is "fireworks and red decorations." With two elements joined with "and," commas cannot intervene, nor can commas separate subject from verb ("became").

28. **The best answer is J.** The phrase beginning with "giving" describes how "Chinese people also spread good luck." Therefore, the best preposition to head the phrase beginning with "giving" is "by."

29. **The best answer is B.** Beginning this sentence with "certainly" marks the statement as a truism. It is obvious to the reader that all people want abundant wealth, love, success, health, and so on. No comparison is being made between this sentence and the previous one, as answer choice A would indicate. In addition, this statement is not a contradiction, as answer choice C would indicate, nor is it the effect brought about by some cause, as answer choice D would indicate.

30. **The best answer is H.** The writer's goal in this passage is to explain the Chinese New Year. The question of whether the reader has ever had everything he or she wanted is distracting and irrelevant.

31. **The best answer is B.** The phrase "with just over four million inhabitants" is a prepositional phrase acting as a nonrestrictive modifier of the adjective "small." It is nonrestrictive because it can be removed from the sentence without altering the greater meaning or rendering the sentence grammatically incorrect. Nonrestrictive phrases and clauses must be set apart from what they modify using commas. The ACT will not ask you to mix a dash with a comma, as in answer choice A.

32. **The best answer is G.** Sentence 3 clearly introduces the topic of Irish geography. It would be appropriate as the first sentence of the paragraph. The next sentence would be Sentence 1, which expands on the statement that Ireland is located in the far-northern Atlantic Ocean.

33. **The best answer is D.** The word "village," especially when modified by the prepositional phrase "with few inhabitants," implies being outside major cities. Therefore, the sentence is more concise when the adverbial phrase "away from the cities" is eliminated.

34. **The best answer is F.** The preposition "despite" correctly introduces a seemingly contradictory notion. In this case, it would seem contradictory that the land would have lots of green plants if the soil were very rocky.

35. **The best answer is A.** The adverb "specially" correctly modifies the verb "trained."

36. **The best answer is J.** This sentence successfully concludes the discussion of the walled roads connecting distant villages.

37. **The best answer is B.** The ACT generally rewards active voice. Therefore, it is best to use the verb phrase "to protect." The sentence as written lacks a complete verb.

38. **The best answer is F.** Verbs used to describe the present state of nouns (in this case, "pubs in Ireland") should be in simple present tense.

39. **The best answer is D.** The conjunction "although" correctly marks a seemingly contradictory notion: pubs are best known for drinking, but they may have quality food, too.

40. **The best answer is H.** The singular noun "food" requires the singular verb "includes."

41. **The best answer is C.** This answer choice has standard word order (subject, verb, object) and the main verb "involve" is correctly in the simple present tense. It is also in the active voice.

42. **The best answer is J.** This answer choice is clearest, and the simple present tense "recommend" is concise. Although answer choice F uses this same verb form, the interjection "but anyway" is informal and less desirable in writing than in oral communication.

43. **The best answer is C.** The correct form is the possessive determiner "its," which marks the conjoined noun phrase "beautiful countryside and open hospitality" and whose antecedent is "Ireland," which comes later in the sentence.

44. **The best answer is H.** The noun "fare" refers to food, and "unassuming surroundings" most likely refers to pubs, which are best known for drinking, not eating. Therefore, this sentence should be added to the end of Paragraph 4.

45. **The best answer is D.** The passage is a lengthy description of the favorable aspects of visiting Ireland. The writer uses words such as "lovely" and "beautiful" and punctuation like dashes and exclamation points to give a sense of excitement to the piece. The passage fails the newspaper editor's assignment because it does not objectively consider the negative aspects of Ireland.

46. **The best answer is F.** The correct preposition to use in this idiomatic phrase is "at."

47. **The best answer is D.** This verb should parallel the simple present tense used throughout the passage. Additionally, "country" is a singular noun that requires a singular verb.

48. **The best answer is G.** Idiomatically, something "is an example of" something else. As it is written, the sentence contains redundancy—an example is a representation, so it's not necessary to use both words.

49. **The best answer is C.** It is necessary to separate the three items in this list with commas. Answer choice B contains an extraneous comma after "Advanced."

50. **The best answer is G.** The preceding adjective "important" indicates that the underlined portion should be a noun. To choose between answer choices F and G, notice that the sentence begins, "There are," which calls for a plural noun.

51. **The best answer is C.** The phrase "similar to primary education" is the clearest, most concise, and grammatical of the answer choices.

52. **The best answer is J.** This is the clearest and most concise answer choice. It is free of the redundancy present in the other answer choices. It is obvious that when students begin going to school, they are in their first year of school.

53. **The best answer is D.** The words "sequences," "series," "classifications," and "events" are mostly synonymous and match the context. While "developments" could be sequential, this choice does not fit the context.

54. **The best answer is J.** Although this answer choice is not the shortest, it is much better suited to the sentence and more precise than the others. It is more logical to say that a "technical or vocational school" *offers programs* than to say that "a technical or vocational school" is an example of "another program." Schools normally have multiple programs of study.

55. **The best answer is B.** This question requires you to place the prepositional phrase directly after the word that it modifies. In this case, "in academics" makes most sense as the complement to the adjective "interested." Answer choice A creates redundancy; it is obvious that students are involved in academics. Placement of the prepositional phrase as called for by answer choices C and D would be awkward.

56. **The best answer is G.** It is clearest and most concise. Answer choices F and H can be eliminated because they create incomplete sentences. Answer choice J is not the best because it contains the idiom "on the other hand," which is a cliché and does not make sense in context.

57. The best answer is D. The entire passage is a description of the educational path in France. It is written in the simple present tense, which is commonly used to describe action without reference to the past, present, or future.

58. The best answer is F. The phrase "or high school" is an appositive and must be set off with commas.

59. The best answer is D. This subject refers to "a student," the subject from the preceding clause. Because it is third-person and singular, neither answer choice A, which is plural, nor answer choice C, which is second-person, can be used. Answer choice B, "it," never refers to people. Therefore, the only possible answer choice is D, which repeats the antecedent.

60. The best answer is J. This sentence should mean that passing the *bac* is a requirement for applying to college. Only answer choice J conveys this meaning, and does so concisely.

61. The best answer is C. This sentence requires the simple present-tense verb "know." Answer choice B includes the singular form "knows," which does not match the plural subject "people."

62. The best answer is J. The sentence already identifies the robbery victims as "the rich." Adding a long parenthetical clause is somewhat distracting, but moreover, the answer choices do not add any ideas that would not already be clear to the reader.

63. The best answer is C. The past perfect tense is appropriate here because it references a period of time in the past without a clear beginning or end. In this case, the end of the usage of "Robin Hood" as a generic term for a thief is unspecified.

64. The best answer is G. The subject "some of these legends" must not be separated from the main verb "borrowed" by a comma.

65. The best answer is D. When speaking or writing about characters in books, it is conventional to use the simple present tense. In addition, the phrase "take on" is idiomatic in this context.

66. The best answer is J. This first clause should be a dependent clause marked as an apparent contradiction to the main clause. The writer intends to convey that although Robin Hood started having companions in the tales, these companions included no women for a long time.

67. The best answer is D. The comma after the subject "Marian" indicates that the underlined portion begins nonrestrictive information. In this case,

a long adverbial phrase is required. Answer choices A and B incorrectly use a verb form of the root "derive." Only answer choice D is an adjective that can head the long modifier set apart from the sentence with commas. Notice that the entire adverbial phrase can be omitted without making the sentence grammatically incorrect. "Marian" is the subject of the main verb "was."

68. The best answer is H. "Tied together" and "united" have nearly the same meaning. Avoid redundancy by eliminating one of them.

69. The best answer is D. Sentence 8 indicates that Robin Hood and Maid Marion celebrated May Day, but apparently not together (*disparate works of literature*). The sentence is best placed between Sentence 7 and Sentence 9.

70. The best answer is H. The second, main clause of the sentence references a period of time in the past (when Robin Hood changed dramatically) prior to another time in the past (when Marian entered the legend). Therefore, the main clause is in past-perfect form. The best way to introduce the first clause is with the phrase "by the time," which parallels the notion of an extended period of time in the past leading up to another time in the past.

71. The best answer is C. The object of the gerund "battling" should be a noun or well-formed noun phrase. Only answer choice C is a well-formed noun phrase, comprising the adjective "tyrannical" and the noun "despotism."

72. The best answer is J. The underlined portion modifies the noun "outlaw," so it must be an adjective or adjective phrase. Only answer choices F and J satisfy this requirement. Between the two, answer choice J is best because it eliminates the redundancy between the roots "charm" and "charisma," which have nearly the same meaning.

73. The best answer is C. The subject of the main clause of this sentence is "resisting the ruling class." The phrase "considering the real history of the Middle Ages" is introductory material that modifies the entire clause; therefore, it should be set apart from the main clause with a comma.

74. The best answer is J. The passage emphasizes how the conception of Robin Hood has varied over time. In this paragraph, the writer asserts that Robin Hood should be considered fiction because much of the true nature of his alleged exploits is lost. In the last sentence, Robin Hood's actions are inferred to have been "bloody" and "not fodder for children's stories," meaning only appropriate for adults. Answer choice J gives the writer's opinion about what makes for a historically accurate representation of Robin Hood.

75. The best answer is B. The passage is a brief account of the origins and history of the Robin Hood tales. The word "adapted" in answer choice B appropriately responds to the question stem's term "evolution."

■ SCORING WORKSHEET

On each ACT multiple-choice test (English, Mathematics, Reading, and Science) you will receive a SCALED SCORE on a scale of 1 to 36. Use the following guidelines to determine your approximate SCALED SCORE on the ACT English Practice Test that you just completed.

Step 1 Determine your RAW SCORE.

Your RAW SCORE is the number of questions that you answered correctly. Because there are 75 questions on the ACT English Test, the highest possible RAW SCORE is 75.

Step 2 Determine your SCALED SCORE using the following Scoring Worksheet

English —————————————— × 36 = —————————— + 75 = ——————————————
                    RAW SCORE   **− 2** (*correction factor)

                                                                                        ——————————————
                                                                                        SCALED SCORE

*The correction factor is an approximation based on the average from several recent ACT tests. It is most valid for scores in the middle 50 percent (approximately 16–24 scaled composite score) of the scoring range. The scores are all approximate. Actual ACT scoring scales vary from one administration to the next based upon several factors.

PART II

THE ACT READING TEST

CHAPTER 8

FORMAT AND SCORING

As explained in the Introduction, the ACT includes four multiple-choice tests (English, Mathematics, Reading, and Science) and an optional essay. This chapter will provide more information on the format of the ACT Reading Test and briefly discuss how this test is scored.

The ACT Reading Test has four passages of about 600–800 words each, followed by ten questions, for a total of forty questions. You will have 35 minutes to complete the Reading Test. The Reading Test is not meant to test your knowledge about a particular subject. Instead, it is designed to measure your reading comprehension—that is, how well you understand, evaluate, and assimilate written material across a variety of subjects. You should answer the questions based only on the information presented in the passage or passages, not on any prior knowledge that you might have of the subject. You might be asked to draw a conclusion (inference), but you should only do so based on what the writer's words actually say or imply.

The test authors choose subject matter that they think will be representative of the type of material that you will have to read in college. All of the passages on the actual ACT come from material that has been previously published. Therefore, you can rely on the fact that the passages are well edited and will be correct in terms of their grammar, punctuation, and overall structure.

The four passages will be of four different types, as follows:

- **Prose fiction** (excerpts from novels and short stories)
- **Humanities** (passages with topics from arts and literature, often biographies of famous authors, artists, musicians, etc.)
- **Social sciences** (History, Sociology, Psychology, and other areas of Social Studies)
- **Natural sciences** (Biology, Chemistry, Physics, etc.)

ANATOMY OF AN ACT READING QUESTION

As explained in the Introduction, each multiple-choice Reading Test question includes four answer choices (A, B, C, and D for odd-numbered questions or F, G, H, and J for even-numbered questions). The answer choices correspond to the circles (bubbles) on your answer sheet.

Here is the basic structure of an ACT Reading Test passage and question.

> Scientists know very little about the eating habits of our ancestors who lived over two and a half million years ago. To solve this problem, scientists have started examining chimpanzees' hunting behavior and diet to find clues about our own prehistoric past.
>
> It is not difficult to determine why studying chimpanzees might be beneficial. Modern humans and chimpanzees are actually very closely related. Experts believe that chimpanzees share about 98.5% of our DNA sequence. If this is true, humans are more closely related to chimpanzees than to any other animal species.

Passage

1. The main purpose of the passage is to: **Question Stem**

A. explore biological and physiological similarities between humans and chimpanzees.
B. examine the hunting behavior and diet of chimpanzees and compare it to human activity.
C. discuss the health benefits of eating and hunting meat while simultaneously predicting the effect of this behavior on chimpanzee offspring.
D. bring attention to the pioneering research of Dr. Jane Goodall in Tanzania.

Answer Choices

A heading that includes information about the passage type, title, and author precedes each Reading Test passage. This information might prove useful in understanding the passage, so don't forget to read it. The different question types found on the ACT Reading Test and strategies for each of the types will be discussed in Chapter 11, "Strategies and Techniques."

THE ACT READING TEST SCORE

Each of the ACT multiple-choice tests is given a score on a scale of 1–36. In 2014, the average ACT Reading Test score in the United States was 21.4. Your score will be rounded to the nearest whole number before it is reported. The schools that you select to receive score reports will get three ACT Reading Test scores: your total score based on all forty questions, a subscore based on the Social Studies and Natural Science passages, and a subscore based on the Prose Fiction and Humanities passages. Because most colleges and universities focus only on the total score, we have not included specific information on calculating subscores. Check with the admissions departments at your schools of choice to find out how (or if) they use Reading Test subscores.

Your ACT Reading Test score will be used along with the scores from the other multiple-choice tests to calculate your composite score. Refer to the Scoring Worksheets provided with the explanations for the Reading Practice Tests in this book to calculate your approximate scaled score (1–36) on each test.

WHAT'S NEXT?

Chapter 9 includes an ACT Reading Diagnostic Test, which you should use to determine your current readiness for the real ACT Reading Test. Then, read Chapters 10–12 to learn the best approach to answering the questions on the simulated tests included in this book (Chapters 13 and 14), and on your actual ACT.

CHAPTER 9

ACT READING DIAGNOSTIC TEST

The following Diagnostic Test will help you to evaluate your current readiness for the ACT Reading Test. Make an honest effort to answer each question, then review the explanations that follow. Don't worry if you are unable to answer many or most of the questions at this point. Chapter 10, "Speed Reading," Chapter 11, "Strategies and Techniques," and Chapter 12, "Applying Strategies, Building Skills," contain information and resources to help you to maximize your ACT Reading scores. Once you have identified your areas of strength and weakness, you should review those particular chapters in the book.

ACT READING DIAGNOSTIC TEST
Answer Sheet

READING

1 (A) (B) (C) (D)	11 (A) (B) (C) (D)	21 (A) (B) (C) (D)	31 (A) (B) (C) (D)
2 (F) (G) (H) (J)	12 (F) (G) (H) (J)	22 (F) (G) (H) (J)	32 (F) (G) (H) (J)
3 (A) (B) (C) (D)	13 (A) (B) (C) (D)	23 (A) (B) (C) (D)	33 (A) (B) (C) (D)
4 (F) (G) (H) (J)	14 (F) (G) (H) (J)	24 (F) (G) (H) (J)	34 (F) (G) (H) (J)
5 (A) (B) (C) (D)	15 (A) (B) (C) (D)	25 (A) (B) (C) (D)	35 (A) (B) (C) (D)
6 (F) (G) (H) (J)	16 (F) (G) (H) (J)	26 (F) (G) (H) (J)	36 (F) (G) (H) (J)
7 (A) (B) (C) (D)	17 (A) (B) (C) (D)	27 (A) (B) (C) (D)	37 (A) (B) (C) (D)
8 (F) (G) (H) (J)	18 (F) (G) (H) (J)	28 (F) (G) (H) (J)	38 (F) (G) (H) (J)
9 (A) (B) (C) (D)	19 (A) (B) (C) (D)	29 (A) (B) (C) (D)	39 (A) (B) (C) (D)
10 (F) (G) (H) (J)	20 (F) (G) (H) (J)	30 (F) (G) (H) (J)	40 (F) (G) (H) (J)

READING TEST

35 Minutes—40 Questions

DIRECTIONS: This test includes four passages, each followed by ten questions. Read each passage and choose the best answer to each question. After you have selected your answer, fill in the corresponding bubble on your answer sheet. You should refer to the passages as often as necessary when answering the questions.

Passage I

PROSE FICTION: This passage is adapted from Louisa May Alcott's "An Ivy Spray and Ladies' Slippers" from *A Garland for Girls* © 1887.

"It can't be done! So I may as well give it up and get a new pair. I long for them, but I'm afraid my nice little plan for Laura will be spoiled," said Jessie Delano to herself, as she shook her head over a pair of small,
5 dilapidated slippers almost past mending. While she vainly pricked her fingers over them for the last time, her mind was full of girlish hopes and fears, as well as anxieties too serious for a light-hearted creature of sixteen.

A year ago the sisters had been the petted
10 daughters of a rich man; but death and misfortune came suddenly, and now they were left to face poverty alone. They had few relations, and had offended the rich uncle who offered Jessie a home, because she refused to be separated from her sister. Poor Laura
15 was an invalid, and no one wanted her; but Jessie would not leave her, so they clung together and lived on in the humble rooms where their father died, trying to earn their bread by the only accomplishments they possessed. Laura painted well, and after many
20 disappointments was beginning to find a sale for her dainty designs and delicate flowers. Jessie had a natural gift for dancing; her former teacher, a kind-hearted Frenchwoman, offered her favorite pupil the post of assistant teacher in her classes for children.

25 It cost the girl a struggle to accept a place of this sort and be a humble teacher, patiently twirling stupid little boys and girls round and round over the smooth floor where she used to dance so happily when she was the pride of the class and the queen of
30 the closing balls. But for Laura's sake she gratefully accepted the offer, glad to add her mite to their small store, and to feel that she could help keep the wolf from the door. They had seemed to hear the howl of this dreaded phantom more than once during that
35 year, and looked forward to the long hard winter with an anxiety which neither would confess to the other. Laura feared to fall ill if she worked too hard, and then what would become of this pretty young sister who loved her so tenderly and would not be tempted
40 to leave her? And Jessie could do very little except

rebel against their hard fate and make impracticable plans. But each worked bravely, talked cheerfully, and waited hopefully for some good fortune to befall them, while doubt and pain and poverty and care
45 made the young hearts so heavy that the poor girls often fell asleep on pillows wet with secret tears.

The smaller trials of life beset Jessie at this particular moment, and her bright wits were trying to solve the problem how to spend her treasured five dollars on slippers for
50 herself and paints for Laura. Both were much needed, and she had gone in shabby shoes to save up money for the little surprise on which she had set her heart; but now dismay fell upon her when the holes refused to be cobbled, and the largest of bows would not hide the worn-out toes
55 in spite of ink and blacking lavishly applied.

"These are the last of my dear French slippers, and I can't afford any more. I hate cheap things! But I shall have to get them; for my boots are shabby, and everyone has to look at my feet when I lead. Oh
60 dear, what a horrid thing it is to be poor!" and Jessie surveyed the shabby little shoes affectionately, as her eyes filled with tears; for the road looked very rough and steep now when she remembered how she used to dance through life as happy as a butter-
65 fly in a garden full of sunshine and flowers.

"Now, Jess, no nonsense, no red eyes to tell tales! Go and do your errands, and come in as gay as a lark, or Laura will be worried." And springing up, the girl began to sing instead of sob, as she stirred
70 about her dismal little room, cleaning her old gloves, mending her one white dress, and wishing with a sigh of intense longing that she could afford some flowers to wear, every ornament having been sold long ago. Then, with a kiss and a smile to her patient
75 sister, she hurried away to get the necessary slippers and the much-desired paints, which Laura would not ask for, though her work waited for want of them.

1. According to the narrator, Jessie refused to live with her uncle because:
   A. her uncle had a cold and drafty house.
   B. her uncle was unpleasant and ugly.
   C. Jessie refused to live away from her sister Laura.
   D. Jessie's sister Laura refused to go with her.

GO ON TO THE NEXT PAGE.

██

2. Considering the events of the entire passage, it is most
    reasonable to infer that Jessie says "a horrid thing it is to
    be poor" (line 60) because she:
    F. dislikes her poor neighbors.
    G. was impoverished by her father's death.
    H. despises people who beg for money.
    J. works in a charity soup kitchen.

3. As it is used in line 5, the word *dilapidated* most nearly
    means:
    A. neglected.
    B. forgotten.
    C. wasted away.
    D. worn-out.

4. Which of the following statements best describes the inter-
    actions between Jessie and Laura?
    F. Laura thinks that Jessie is foolish for staying with
        her, and often gets angry with her sister for minor
        problems.
    G. Jessie resents Laura's disability and wishes she had
        decided to go live with her uncle.
    H. Jessie and Laura spend most of their time complaining
        about their bad fortune and trying to make each other
        more miserable.
    J. Jessie and Laura each pretend to be happy for the
        other's sake but are privately both very worried about
        their future.

5. Which of the following does the passage suggest is the
    reason Jessie wants expensive new shoes?
    A. Jessie is selfish and does not think about what her sis-
        ter may need.
    B. Jessie likes pretty things.
    C. Many people look at Jessie's shoes.
    D. Jessie insists no other shoes fit her well.

6. The phrase "no red eyes to tell tales" (lines 66–67) most
    strongly suggests that Jessie:
    F. is trying to stop crying in front of her sister.
    G. does not want her tears to ruin her good looks.
    H. is sickly from excessive work and poor eating.
    J. always cries about her problems.

7. It is reasonable to infer from the passage that Laura would
    not ask Jessie to buy her paints (lines 76–77) because:
    A. Laura is lazy and doesn't want to help support their
        little family.
    B. Laura will buy the paints herself after she sells her
        latest work.
    C. Laura believes she can finish the work with the paints
        she has.
    D. Laura doesn't want to impose on Jessie with her own
        needs.

8. The relationship between Jessie and Laura would most
    accurately be described as:
    F. indifferent yet polite.
    G. loving and considerate.
    H. a matter of convenience only.
    J. based upon common interests and activities.

9. As it is used in line 31, the word *mite* most nearly means:
    A. small amount of time.
    B. tiny parasite.
    C. small contribution.
    D. insignificant object.

10. Jessie's former dance teacher offers her a job as an assis-
    tant teacher after:
    F. Jessie's father first falls ill.
    G. Laura does not ask Jessie for new paints.
    H. Jessie's uncle is offended and the girls are left on their
        own.
    J. Laura's paintings begin to sell for a lot of money.

Passage II

SOCIAL SCIENCE: *Rosa Parks: Mother of American Civil Rights*

Spanning 1955–1968, the civil rights movement is frequently defined by scholars as the movement aimed at abolishing segregation, social inequality, and the overall unfair treatment of African Americans in the
5 United States. It is difficult to understand fully the birth of the civil rights movement without mentioning Rosa Parks. Often referred to as the "mother" of the movement, Parks was arrested on December 1, 1955, after refusing to surrender her seat to a white man on a seg-
10 regated Montgomery, Alabama, city bus. When asked why she made such a decision, Parks replied, "I knew someone had to take the first step, and I made up my mind not to move."

Strangely, the prevailing notion in America is
15 that Parks' rebellion was an isolated act of personal defiance, perhaps brought about by exhaustion at the end of a long shift. Nothing could be further from the truth. Rosa Parks was actually a long-time active member of the civil rights movement in Alabama. Prior to her
20 demonstration on the Montgomery bus, she served as both the secretary and youth leader of the Montgomery affiliate of the National Association for the Advancement of Colored People. Parks and her husband were also members of the Voters' League. Regarding that
25 fateful day, Parks later wrote, "I was not tired physically, or no more tired than I usually was at the end of a working day. I was not old, although some people have an image of me as being old then. I was forty-two. No, the only tired I was, was tired of giving in."

30 Rosa Parks was not the only African American to test the segregation laws on public transportation. However, her education, personal history, and dignified carriage made her an ideal representative of the movement. It was her stand against inequality that set into motion
35 the Montgomery Bus Boycott organized by Martin Luther King, Jr. After 381 days of boycotting, the local law was lifted. Parks' arrest also inspired a renewed legal challenge to segregation laws and, in 1956, the Supreme Court ruled that the Montgomery ordinance under which
40 Parks had been arrested and fined was unconstitutional. While Parks' case was not the one chosen for the Supreme Court challenge, Parks' action remained the impetus for outlawing racial segregation on public transportation and the beginning of a new chapter in American history.

45 Parks suffered financially and personally as a result of her activism, but continued to speak out about the cause she so strongly believed in. Loss of employment and disagreements with local civil rights leaders forced her to move away from Montgomery, and in 1957, she
50 and her husband Raymond moved to Detroit, Michigan. During her first years in Detroit, Rosa Parks worked as a seamstress; beginning in 1965, she worked as a secretary and receptionist in the office of U.S. Representative John Conyers. She continued as a member of his staff for
55 twenty-three years.

Following the death of her husband in 1977, Rosa Parks proved once again her dedication to the rights and freedoms of all American citizens. To celebrate her husband's life, Parks established the Rosa and Raymond
60 Parks Institute for Self-Development, an organization dedicated to motivating the youth of America to achieve their highest potential. Rosa Parks saw the momentum for change in the energy of America's youth. Using programs like Pathways for Freedom, an annual summer
65 program for teens focused on the civil rights movement and its place in American history, she kept the dream of equality alive.

In 1996, Parks was publicly recognized for her contributions to the quest for equality and the betterment of
70 society as a whole. President Clinton awarded her with the Presidential Medal of Freedom, the nation's highest civilian honor. She also received the Congressional Gold Medal in 1999 and was awarded over forty-three honorary doctorates from universities around the world.
75 This public recognition is just the beginning of a long list of honors Parks received over the course of her life.

On October 24, 2005, Rosa Parks died peacefully in her Detroit home. She left behind a legacy that will inspire generations to come. The United States
80 would most certainly not be the same country if not for Parks' bravery on that December day in 1955. Rosa Parks once said, "I would like to be known as a person who is concerned about freedom and equality and justice and prosperity for all people." Just as she
85 hoped, her legacy of tolerance and fair play lives on.

11. The passage suggests that most Americans assume that Rosa Parks kept her bus seat because:
A. she founded the civil right movement.
B. she did not understand the segregation laws.
C. there were no other seats on the bus.
D. she did not want to move after a hard workday.

12. The passage implies that Rosa Parks stated how old she was on the day of her arrest for which of the following reasons?
F. She was giving a timeline of events in her life.
G. She wanted to emphasize her maturity and wisdom at the time of her arrest.
H. She was trying to counter the belief that she was weak at the time.
J. She was explaining why she was so tired on that particular day.

13. According to the passage, what was the purpose of Pathways for Freedom?
A. It was a summer program for teens that taught civil rights history.
B. It taught elementary school children about the Underground Railroad.
C. It provided year-round education about American history.
D. It emphasized the role of Montgomery, Alabama, in the civil rights movement.

GO ON TO THE NEXT PAGE.

14. According to the passage, what is Rosa Parks' legacy?
    F. A message of respect and equality for all people
    G. The importance of civil disobedience in enacting change
    H. The importance of ordinary people in matters of public policy
    J. The significance of public transportation in 1950s America

15. According to the passage, why was Rosa Parks chosen as a symbol of the civil rights movement?
    I. She was the only African American to refuse to give up her bus seat to a white person.
    II. She was calm and dignified.
    III. She had a history of support for the civil rights movement.
    A. I only
    B. I and II only
    C. II and III only
    D. I, II, and III

16. According to the passage, what were Rosa Parks' duties as an employee of Representative Conyers?
    F. Youth leader
    G. Secretary and receptionist
    H. Political activist
    J. Bus driver

17. All of the following were results of Rosa Parks' protestation EXCEPT:
    A. local transportation laws were changed to outlaw segregation on Montgomery buses.
    B. the Supreme Court ruled that segregation of public transportation was unconstitutional.
    C. Parks was forced to leave her home in Montgomery, Alabama.
    D. Parks spent an extended period of time in jail.

18. According to the passage, the Rosa and Raymond Parks Institute for Self-Development was established to:
    F. teach techniques for improving self-esteem.
    G. motivate young people to maximize their potential.
    H. improve women's rights.
    J. retrain retirees who need work.

19. All of the following were clearly identified in the passage as awards Rosa Parks was conferred EXCEPT:
    A. the presidential Medal of Freedom.
    B. the Congressional Gold Medal.
    C. the Medal of Honor.
    D. honorary doctorates.

20. As it is used in lines 32–33, the word *carriage* most nearly means:
    F. demeanor.
    G. management.
    H. transportation.
    J. posture.

GO ON TO THE NEXT PAGE.

Passage III

HUMANITIES: *The following passages discuss two well-known authors and some of their literary achievements.*

Passage A

Shakespeare was raised in a fairly prosperous household. His father was a glove maker and town official. Very few detailed records exist regarding Shakespeare's life. However, court records indicate that Shakespeare's father
5 was prosecuted for participating in illegal wool trade.

At the age of 18, Shakespeare married Anne Hathaway, a lady eight years his senior. During the early years of their marriage, Hathaway gave birth to two daughters and a son. Unfortunately, Shakespeare's only
10 son died at the tender age of 12. Shakespeare continued working, and by his mid-thirties, was a top actor. During this time, he also gained recognition as a playwright. Shakespeare even formed his own acting company called "The Lord Chamberlain's Men." Later, this renowned
15 group became known as "The King's Men."

Some controversy exists regarding the true authorship of Shakespeare's works. It is believed by some that Shakespeare, as owner of the acting company, signed his own name to all works done by those under his employ.
20 Despite this controversy, Shakespeare is best known for his ability to understand and portray the vast array of human emotions. He was a master of both tragedy and comedy and perfected these two important dramatic genres. Shakespeare's talent was as unique as it was
25 highly regarded.

Shakespeare's works continue to entertain and inspire audiences. Troupes all over the world, both amateur and professional, regularly perform classic tragedies such as "Romeo and Juliet" and "Macbeth," as well as comedies
30 such as "Much Ado About Nothing."

Passage B

American literature encompasses many different and unique styles and genres. One of the most interesting of these is the Southern Gothic subgenre. As its name implies, Southern Gothic literature is reflective of life in
35 the American South. Southern Gothic maintains some of the characteristics of Gothic writing, such as plot development of the supernatural or the ironic. However, Southern Gothic does not focus on creating tension and suspense like other Gothic genres. Instead, Southern Gothic
40 storylines examine Southern society and its underlying and often implicit social structure.

Southern Gothic writers generally spurn the stereotype of the gentleman on the plantation and the glamorous Southern belle. Instead, the authors develop characters
45 who are sinister or reclusive and not particularly pleasant on the surface. However, these characters usually have redeeming qualities that allow and encourage the reader to empathize with their situations or dilemmas.

Many American authors are known for their Southern
50 Gothic style. Playwright Tennessee Williams (1911–1983)

is among the most celebrated of these writers. Williams' long list of plays and novels include Pulitzer Prize–winning dramas "A Streetcar Named Desire" (1948) and
55 "Cat on a Hot Tin Roof" (1955). It is said that many of Williams' characters were based on his own family. For instance, it is speculated that the pitiable character Laura in "The Glass Menagerie" is modeled after Williams' mentally incapacitated sister, Rose. Williams' experi-
60 ences living in New Orleans and his family connections to the South gave him plenty of inspiration. Williams used this influence to create masterpieces that continue to leave lasting impressions on his audiences.

Questions 21–23 ask about Passage A.

---

21. In Passage A, the word *master* (line 22) refers to Shakespeare's:
   A. attitude.
   B. experiences.
   C. professionalism.
   D. accomplishments.

22. The tone of the author of Passage A in lines 24–25 ("Shakespeare's talent . . . regarded.") is best described as:
   F. satirical.
   G. impudent.
   H. deferential.
   J. disrespectful.

23. The last paragraph of Passage A (lines 26–30) indicates that Shakespeare:
   A. wrote more tragedies than comedies.
   B. was considered a better actor than a writer.
   C. is still a source of inspiration for actors around the globe.
   D. often performed as a professional actor in many of his own plays.

Questions 24–26 ask about Passage B.

---

24. Passage B is developed primarily through:
   F. quotations from specific biographies.
   G. dialogue between two main characters.
   H. narration of an explicit literary occurrence.
   J. presentation of an idea with a supporting example.

25. Based on the passage, the information about Southern society in line 41 is most likely meant to suggest that:
   A. its examination is unnecessary.
   B. its structure is not openly discussed.
   C. its story is neither fully nor accurately told.
   D. its entertainment value is spurned by modern society.

GO ON TO THE NEXT PAGE.

██

26. The phrase ". . . Pulitzer Prize–winning . . ." in line 53 emphasizes the:
    F. politics involved in writing plays.
    G. popularity of the Gothic style of writing.
    H. acceptance of the Southern Gothic sub genre.
    J. recognition Williams earned with his writing.

Questions 27–30 ask about both passages.

---

27. Compared to Passage A, Passage B provides more information about:
    A. a specific style of writing.
    B. the wife of a famous playwright.
    C. how to become a successful author.
    D. overcoming poverty and family tragedy

28. According to both passages, plays written by Tennessee Williams were probably most like:
    F. Shakespeare's tragedies.
    G. Shakespearean comedies.
    H. modern-day situation comedies.
    J. sonnets written by Shakespeare.

29. Both passages are primarily concerned with the theme of:
    A. comparing writing poetry with writing plays.
    B. contrasting the works of popular playwrights.
    C. a brief introduction to an important playwright and dicussion of his work.
    D. American writing styles and specific American genres during the fifteenth century.

30. It can be reasonably inferred that both Shakespeare and Tennessee Williams developed their characters through:
    F. studying dramatic genres.
    G. a deep understanding of human emotion.
    H. a clear disdain for all other writing styles.
    J. emphasizing tragic situations over comedic ones.

GO ON TO THE NEXT PAGE.

Passage IV

NATURAL SCIENCE: This passage is adapted from *The Working of Steel: Annealing, Heat Treating and Hardening of Carbon and Alloy Steel,* by Fred H. Colvin and K. A. Juthe © 1922.

In spite of all that has been written about steel, there are many hazy notions in the minds of many engineers regarding its manufacture. There are four processes now used for the manufacture of steel. These are: The Bessemer,
5 open hearth, crucible, and electric furnace methods.

The Bessemer process consists of charging molten pig iron into a huge, brick-lined pot called the Bessemer converter, and then blowing a current of air through holes in the bottom of the vessel into the liquid metal. The
10 air blast burns the white-hot metal, and the temperature increases. The action is exactly similar to what happens in a firebox under a forced draft. And in both cases, some parts of the material burn easier and more quickly than others. Thus it is that some of the impurities in the pig
15 iron—including the carbon—burn first, and if the blast is shut off when they are gone, little of the iron is destroyed. Unfortunately sulfur, one of the most dangerous impurities, is not expelled in the process. Where the steel is finished, the converter is tilted, or swung on its trunnions,
20 the blast turned off, and the steel poured out of the top.

The open-hearth furnace consists of a big brick room with a low arched roof. It is charged with pig iron and scrap through doors in the sidewalls. Through openings at one end of the furnace come hot air and gas, which
25 burn in the furnace, producing sufficient heat to melt the charge and refine it of its impurities. Lime and other nonmetallic substances are put in the furnace. These melt, forming a "slag" which floats on the metal and aids materially in the refining operations.

30 In the Bessemer process, air is forced *through* the metal. In the open-hearth furnace, the metal is protected from the flaming gases by a slag covering. Therefore, it is reasonable to suppose that the open-hearth final product will not contain as much gas as the Bessemer product.

35 Crucible steel is made by melting material in a clay or graphite crucible. Each crucible contains about forty pounds of iron, forty pounds of clean "mill scrap," and sufficient rich alloys and charcoal to make the mixture conform to the desired chemical analysis. The crucible
40 is covered, lowered into a melting hole, and entirely surrounded by burning coke. After about four hours, the metal is converted into a white-hot liquid. Several crucibles are then pulled out of the hole and their contents carefully poured into a metal mold, forming an ingot.

45 The fourth method of manufacturing steel is by the electric furnace. These furnaces are of various sizes and designs, according to the electrical principles used. One design is the squat kettle, made of heavy sheet steel with a dished bottom, and mounted so it can be tilted forward

50 slightly and completely drained. This kettle is lined with special firebrick, which will withstand the most intense heat and resist the cutting action of hot metal and slag. For a roof, a low dome of firebrick is provided. The shell and lining is pierced in front for a pouring spout, and on
55 either side by doors, through which the raw material is charged.

Two or three carbon "electrodes"—eighteen-inch cylinders of specially prepared coke or graphite—extend through holes in the roof. Electrical connections are made
60 to the upper ends, and a very high current sent through them. This causes tremendous arcs to form between the lower ends of the electrodes and the metal below, which are the only source of heat in this style of furnace.

Electric furnaces can be used to do the same work
65 as is done in crucible furnaces—melting a charge of carefully selected pure raw materials. On the other hand, they can be used to produce very-high-grade steel from cheap and impure metal, similar to open-hearth furnaces. They can push the refining even further than the open-
70 hearth furnace does, for two reasons: first, the bath is not swept continuously by a flaming mass of gases; second, the temperature can be run up higher, enabling the operator to make up slags, which are difficult to melt but very useful to remove small traces of impurities from
75 the metal.

31. The passage states that the Bessemer method produces a product with more gas than the open-hearth method because:
A. the Bessemer method forces air through the metal.
B. the Bessemer method is less effective than the open-hearth method.
C. the open-hearth method does not use gas to purify the iron.
D. the Bessemer method is older than the open-hearth method.

32. The passage asserts that less gas remains in molten steel produced by the open-hearth method because:
F. no gas is used in the open-hearth method.
G. molten lime and other materials create a surface covering that protects the metal from gasses.
H. the ingredient materials are purer than those used in other methods.
J. the brick furnace allows the gas to burn off before it can contaminate the metal.

33. The main point of the last paragraph is that:
A. slags are very important in the purification of metal.
B. some furnaces produce high-grade steel when starting with purer metals, while other furnaces are effective with cheaper metals.
C. electric furnaces can achieve an extremely high temperature.
D. because of its versatility, the electrical furnace is the most effective of the four steel-producing methods.

GO ON TO THE NEXT PAGE.

34. As it is defined in the passage, crucible steel is made:
    I.   by converting metal into a white-hot liquid.
    II.   by mixing iron, clean "mill scrap," and other alloys.
    III. by heating metal to melting temperature by burning coke.
    F. I only
    G. II only
    H. II and III only
    J. I, II, and III

35. According to the passage, heat for steel refining can be provided by all of the following EXCEPT:
    A. burning coke.
    B. electric current.
    C. burning gas.
    D. wind power.

36. The passage asserts that the Bessemer furnace is like a firebox in that:
    F. forced air increases the temperature and results in uneven burning.
    G. forced air adds dangerous sulfur to the combustible material.
    H. both are used to create high-grade steel.
    J. "firebox" is a casual term for "Bessemer furnace."

37. It can reasonably be inferred that the amounts of "rich alloys and charcoal" (line 41) used in the crucible method:
    A. do not change from batch to batch.
    B. are greater than the amounts of "mill scrap" used.
    C. are greater than the amounts of iron used.
    D. vary depending on the type of steel being made.

38. The passage states that electric furnaces for steel production have which of the following equipment?
    F. Forced-air systems
    G. Clay or graphite crucibles
    H. Firebrick roofs
    J. Combustible gas inlets

39. The passage states that all steel-producing furnaces use:
    A. coke as a fuel source.
    B. forced air to eliminate impurities.
    C. iron as a base metal for steel.
    D. brick ovens to contain the raw materials.

40. The author suggests that an overview of steel-production techniques is important because:
    F. little has been written about the properties of steel.
    G. general knowledge is important for its own sake.
    H. too few engineers understand how steel is made.
    J. the general public is interested in steel production.

END OF THE READING TEST
STOP! IF YOU HAVE TIME LEFT OVER, CHECK YOUR WORK ON THIS SECTION ONLY.

ANSWERS AND EXPLANATIONS

Passage I

1. **The best answer is C.** According to the passage, Jessie "had offended the rich uncle who offered Jessie a home, because she refused to be separated from her sister." The other answer choices are not supported by the passage.

2. **The best answer is G.** The passage states that Jessie and Laura "lived on in the humble rooms where their father died, trying to earn their bread. …" This means that they were left poor by their father's death. This change in Jessie's life is also reflected at the end of the fifth paragraph: "for the road looked very rough and steep now when she remembered how she used to dance through life as happy as a butterfly. …"

3. **The best answer is D.** The passage says of Jessie's shoes, "a pair of small, dilapidated slippers almost past mending …." These are the shoes Jessie wore to her dance class, so it is most logical that they are *worn-out* from use. In fact, the passage goes on to say that in a later discussion of the shoes.

4. **The best answer is J.** The last sentence of the passage gives insight into the girls' relationship with each other: Jessie kisses and smiles at her sister and then leaves to get the paints Laura needs but "would not ask for." By saying that Laura would not ask for her paints, the author wants to convey that she doesn't want to impose on her sister. Earlier in the narrative, Jessie was upset and crying over her broken shoes, but for her sister, she maintains a good attitude. This best supports answer choice J.

5. **The best answer is C.** According to the passage, Jessie says, "everyone has to look at my feet when I lead." This best explains why Jessie would want nice shoes.

6. **The best answer is F.** This phrase is spoken by Jessie to herself. It means that Jessie does not want to show Laura that she was crying about some problem, as evidenced by the redness of Jessie's eyes. The other answer choices are not supported by the passage.

7. **The best answer is D.** The passage makes clear that the girls are very considerate toward and avoid imposing on each other. This best supports answer choice D. Nothing in the passage supports the other answer choices.

8. **The best answer is G.** The passage makes clear that Jessie loves her sister and is willing to make sacrifices for her. Nothing in the passage indicates that their relationship is at all casual, so answer choices F, H, and J can be eliminated.

9. **The best answer is C.** Based on context, you can determine that the phrase "add her mite to" most likely means "do her part for" or "make a contribution to." The word *mite* is particularly apt here because it emphasizes the smallness of what Jessie was able to do. Throughout the passage, the meagerness of all Jessie owns, earns, and can do for herself and her sister is emphasized.

10. **The best answer is H.** The passage describes the death of the girls' father and the consequences it had for the girls. These events are given chronologically. After refusing to live with her uncle, Jessie takes a job dancing to support herself and Laura.

Passage II

11. **The best answer is D.** The first sentence of the second paragraph indicates that the "prevailing notion" about Rosa Parks' refusal to move from her seat for a white man is that she did so because of "exhaustion at the end of a long shift."

12. **The best answer is H.** The quotation near the end of the second paragraph is Parks' response to the misconception many Americans have of how old she was on the day she refused to give up her seat on the bus. That misconception holds that Parks was weak or helpless at the time, and many people take that to mean that she was old. Parks' statement of her age at the time contradicts this.

13. **The best answer is A.** Pathways for Freedom is defined in an appositive immediately following its mention in the passage: "an annual summer program for teens focused on the civil rights movement and its place in American history …."

14. **The best answer is F.** The last sentence of the passage states, "the legacy of tolerance and fair play lives on." The other answer choices are not supported by the passage.

15. **The best answer is C.** All three options seem plausible, but you must recall that the passage says that Parks was only one among many who refused to give up her bus seat to a white person. The first sentence of the third paragraph states: "Rosa Parks was not the only African American to test the segregation laws on public transportation." Therefore, Roman numeral I must be excluded. The passage supports Roman numerals II and III, so answer choice C is correct.

16. **The best answer is G.** The passage specifically states that Parks "worked as a secretary and receptionist in the office of U.S. Representative John Conyers."

17. **The best answer is D.** There is nothing in the passage about an *extended* period of time Parks spent in jail. The first paragraph does mention her arrest for violating segregation law on the bus, but there is no indication of a stay in jail.

18. **The best answer is G.** The "Rosa and Raymond Parks Institute for Self-Development" is defined in the appositive that follows it: "an organization dedicated to motivating the youth of America to achieve their highest potential."

19. **The best answer is C.** The sixth paragraph says that Parks received the Presidential Medal of Freedom, the Congressional Gold Medal, and forty-three honorary doctorates. The Medal of Honor is not mentioned in the passage.

20. **The best answer is F.** The second sentence of the third paragraph describes attributes of Rosa Parks: "her education, personal history, and dignified carriage." The adjective *dignified* means showing dignity of manner. So Parks' *carriage* means how she carried, or presented, herself in public. This describes *demeanor*, answer choice F. Answer choices G, H, and J do not relate to the passage and can be eliminated.

Passage III

21. **The best answer is D.** The context surrounding word *master* indicates that Shakespeare was a very accomplished and successful writer. Therefore, it is likely the word was used to refer to Shakespeare's many accomplishments.

22. **The best answer is H.** The word *deferential* means "respectful." The author indicates that

Shakespeare's talent was "highly regarded," which would make *deferential* the best option.

23. **The best answer is C.** The last paragraph is primarily about Shakespeare's continuing influence on audiences and performers, making answer choice C the best option.

24. **The best answer is J.** The introductory sentence of Passage B presents the idea that American literature covers many different writing styles. The passage then goes on to discuss one of those styles and a notable author.

25. **The best answer is B.** The phrase "Southern society and its underlying and often implicit social structure" indicates that its underlying structure is not something that is openly discussed. Rather, it is evidenced through the behavior and lifestyle of its members.

26. **The best answer is J.** The Pulitzer Prize is a much-coveted award given to writers. The fact that Tennessee Williams won such an award reflects the recognition he garnered as a writer.

27. **The best answer is A.** While Passage A provides a brief overview of Shakespeare's life and some of his works, Passage B delves more deeply into a description of the Southern Gothic style of writing.

28. **The best answer is F.** According to the passage, Southern Gothic writers "develop characters who are sinister or reclusive and not particularly pleasant on the surface. However, these characters usually have redeeming qualities that allow and encourage the reader to empathize with their situations or dilemmas." This best matches the plots of Shakespeare's tragedies.

29. **The best answer is C.** Each passage introduces a writer and briefly discusses his life, influences, and works. The other answer choices are not supported by details in the passages.

30. **The best answer is G.** According to Passage A, "Shakespeare is best known for his ability to understand and portray the vast array of human emotions." Passage B echoes this sentiment in the sentences "Williams' experiences living in

New Orleans and his family connections to the South gave him plenty of inspiration. Williams used this influence to create masterpieces that continue to leave lasting impressions on his audiences."

Passage IV

31. **The best answer is A.** This question is answered in the fourth paragraph: "In the Bessemer process, air is forced *through* the metal. ... Therefore, it is reasonable to suppose that the open-hearth final product will not contain as much gas as the Bessemer product."

32. **The best answer is G.** The passage states that, "In the open-hearth furnace, the metal is protected from the flaming gases by a slag covering." *Slag* is defined in the last two sentences of the third paragraph: "Lime and other nonmetallic substances are put in the furnace. These melt, forming a 'slag' which floats on the metal. ..." This directly supports answer choice G.

33. **The best answer is D.** The last paragraph of the passage states that electric furnaces can do what the other production options do, making them the most versatile choice. The first sentence states: "Electric furnaces can be used to do the same work as is done in crucible furnaces. ..." The second sentence says that electric furnaces "can be used to produce very-high-grade steel from cheap and impure metal," which is an obvious advantage to using electric furnaces. Finally, the paragraph states that electric furnace temperatures can be raised high enough to create slags useful for further purifying the metal. It is clear that the author finds the electric furnace to be the superior choice of those he describes in the passage. This supports answer choice D.

34. **The best answer is J.** The fifth paragraph includes all three options: "a white-hot liquid" (I), "forty pounds of iron, forty pounds of clean 'mill scrap,' and ... alloys" (II), and "surrounded by burning coke" (III). Therefore, answer choice J is correct.

35. **The best answer is D.** The passage states that the open-hearth process uses "hot air and gas" and that the crucible process uses "burning coke." Obviously, the electric furnace uses electric current. Therefore, answer choice D is the exception. The passage makes no mention of wind power.

36. **The best answer is F.** The passage states that, "The air blast burns the white-hot metal, and the temperature increases. The action is exactly similar to what happens in a firebox under a forced draft. And in both cases, some parts of the material burn easier and more quickly than others." This directly supports answer choice F. The other answer choices are not supported by the passage.

37. **The best answer is D.** The conjoined noun phrase "rich alloys and charcoal" is modified by the adjective *sufficient*, which means *enough*. In addition, the ingredients "forty pounds of iron" and "forty pounds of clean 'mill scrap'" are modified by *about*, which suggests that the amounts are subject to variation. It is logical that the "rich alloys and charcoal" would likewise vary. Eliminate answer choice A. Answer choices B and C are not logical because the quantities of iron and mill scrap are given to show that they are the main ingredients. Answer choice D is the most logical inference.

38. **The best answer is H.** The sixth paragraph describes the electric furnace: "For a roof, a low dome of firebrick is provided." The other answer choices are characteristic of other refining equipment described in the passage.

39. **The best answer is C.** All steel is made from iron. The iron raw material is mentioned with respect to the Bessemer process, the open-hearth process and the crucible process. Although the word *iron* does not appear in the description of the electric furnace, the last paragraph does state that electric furnaces can do the same work as crucible furnaces. Therefore, it is reasonable to assume that electric furnaces melt iron to make steel, making answer choice C best. The other answer choices may be characteristic of some refining processes described in the passage, but not all of them.

40. **The best answer is H.** The first sentence of the passage indirectly states the author's purpose: "In spite of all that has been written about steel, there are many hazy notions in the minds of many engineers regarding its manufacture." (The passage then goes on to illuminate the steel-manufacturing processes.) Answer choice H is directly supported by information in the passage.

▬▬ SCORING WORKSHEET

On each ACT multiple-choice test (English, Mathematics, Reading, and Science) you will receive a SCALED SCORE on a scale of 1 to 36. Use the following guidelines to determine your approximate SCALED SCORE on the ACT Reading Diagnostic Test that you just completed.

Step 1 Determine your RAW SCORE.

Your RAW SCORE is the number of questions that you answered correctly. Because there are 40 questions on the ACT English Test, the highest possible RAW SCORE is 40.

Step 2 Determine your SCALED SCORE using the following Scoring Worksheet

Reading —————— × 36 = —————— ÷ 40 = ——————
          RAW SCORE   + 2 (*correction factor)

——————
                          SCALED SCORE

   *The correction factor is an approximation based on the average from several recent ACT tests. It is most valid for scores in the middle 50 percent (approximately 16–24 scaled composite score) of the scoring range. The scores are all approximate. Actual ACT scoring scales vary from one administration to the next based upon several factors.

Your SCALED SCORE should be rounded to the nearest number according to normal rules. For example, 31.2 ≈ 31 and 31.5 ≈ 32. If you answered 28 quetions correctly on the Reading Test, for example, your SCALED SCORE would be 25.

CHAPTER 10

SPEED READING

The ACT Reading Test requires you to read and comprehend sometimes difficult material. While you will learn in Chapter 12 that it is not necessary to read every word of a reading passage on the ACT, increasing the rate at which you read will certainly come in handy.

The term *speed reading*, much like it sounds, refers to training yourself to read at a faster rate (and with better comprehension) than you do currently. This, of course, is easier said than done. The primary goal of speed reading is to take in as much information as possible in the shortest time possible, while maintaining a high level of understanding. Repeatedly working with the strategies and techniques presented in this chapter should result in a measurable increase in both your reading speed and comprehension.

SOME BENEFITS OF SPEED READING

There are countless benefits to acquiring speed-reading skills, both in the short term and throughout life. Even beyond the classroom, the ability to quickly process large volumes of information is invaluable. Perhaps the greatest benefit of speed reading is an increased rate of information absorption.

When you are able to read faster and absorb more information into your short-term memory, you can often more easily see a document's structure and meaning. This skill is incredibly helpful on the ACT Reading Test. In addition to achieving better comprehension, you will find that your eyes are not working nearly as hard as they normally would, so reading becomes less tiring.

EXPECTATIONS OF SPEED READING

While there are several applications for speed reading on the ACT, it is important to note that for the purposes of the ACT exam, speed reading should be one of the last skills on which you focus. Once you have mastered the other skills presented throughout this book, consider practicing the strategies presented in this chapter to give yourself an extra edge.

In addition, although speed reading is a valuable skill worth pursuing, this chapter is meant merely as an introduction to the technique. Like with all skills, repeated practice is necessary to fully master speed reading.

DETERMINING YOUR BASELINE READING SPEED

The first step in becoming a "speed reader" is to determine your baseline reading speed—that is, the speed at which you read comfortably with comprehension. For the sake of comparison, research shows that the average person reads at a pace of about 250 words per minute. The following exercise will help

> **Study Tip**
> The strategies included in this chapter are specifically geared toward reaching your maximum potential on the ACT Reading Test.

you to determine your baseline reading speed, which might be slower or faster than average:

First, find a stopwatch or a watch with a second hand. You will need to time yourself for one minute while reading the following passage at your typical reading pace—the speed at which you are the most comfortable reading. At the end of the one-minute period, be sure to note the line number where you stopped.

This excerpt is adapted from Remember the Alamo *by Amelia E. Barr* © 1888.

1   In A.D. sixteen hundred and ninety-two, a few Franciscan monks began
2 to build a city. The site chosen was a lovely wilderness hundreds of miles
3 away from civilization on every side, but the spot was as beautiful as the
4 garden of God. It was shielded by majestic mountains, watered by two
5 rivers, carpeted with numerous flowers, and shaded by noble trees joyful
6 with the notes of a multitude of singing birds. To breathe the balmy
7 atmosphere was to be conscious of some rarer and finer life, and the
8 beauty of the sunny skies—marvelous at dawn and evening with tints of
9 gold and purple—was like a dream of heaven.

10   One of the rivers was fed by a hundred springs situated in the midst
11 of charming bowers. The monks called it the San Antonio, and on its
12 banks they built three noble Missions. The shining white stone of the
13 neighborhood rose in graceful domes and spires above the green trees.
14 Sculptures, basso-relievos, and lines of gorgeous coloring adorned the
15 exteriors. Within, were splendid altars and the appealing charms of
16 incense, fine vestures, and fine music; while from the belfries, bells sweet
17 and resonant called to those who paused spell-bound and half-afraid to
18 listen.

19   Certainly these priests had to fight as well as to pray. The Indians did
20 not suffer them to take possession of their paradise without passionate
21 and practical protest. But what the monks had taken, they kept, and
22 the fort and the soldier followed the priest and the Cross. Before long,
23 the beautiful Mission became a beautiful city, about which a sort of
24 fame full of romance and mystery gathered. Throughout the south and
25 west, up the great highway of the Mississippi, on the busy streets of
26 New York, and among the silent hills of New England, men spoke of
27 San Antonio.

28   Sanguine French traders carried to the city rich ventures in fancy
29 wares from New Orleans; and Spanish dons from the wealthy cities of
30 Central Mexico, and from the splendid homes of Chihuahua, came there
31 to buy. And from the villages of Connecticut, and the woods of Tennessee,
32 and the lagoons of Mississippi, adventurous Americans entered the Texan
33 territory. They went through the land, buying horses and lending their
34 ready rifles and stout hearts to every effort of that constantly increasing
35 body of Texans, who, even in their swaddling bands, had begun to cry
36 Freedom!

The following chart will allow you to determine your initial, or baseline, reading speed in words per minute (wpm). Find the number in the left column that is closest to the line number at which you stopped reading after one minute, then move to the right in the table to determine your approximate baseline reading speed.

Line number	Approximate words per minute (wpm)
7	100
10	150
15	200
18	250
21	300
25	350
28	400
30	425

INCREASING YOUR BASELINE READING SPEED

If your baseline reading speed is slower than you would like, it is possible to increase that speed by changing the way you read.

The way that most people read is something like the following:

The..boy..runs..fast..when..he..is..racing..with..his..friends.

Each word is read separately, one at a time, and the eye stops at individual words. Not only is this inefficient, it is unnecessary. The human brain can comprehend words at almost twice the rate that the human eye can read them in this jerky, stop-and-go process. This type of reading contributes to the tendency of many people to find reading boring; their minds often wander because too much time is spent between words. Increasing the number of words that your eye is able to see when you look at a page is one of the easiest ways to increase your reading speed.

Following are some more specific techniques for improving your overall reading speed.

TECHNIQUES FOR IMPROVING YOUR READING SPEED

There are several methods to increase the number of words your eyes see at any given time, and to increase your overall reading speed. This section provides an overview of the steps you can take to read faster with better comprehension.

Eliminate the "Stops" in Your Reading

> **Study Tip**
> Use your finger as a pointer, and follow it with your eyes as it moves along the text.

As we mentioned earlier, most people pause at each word in a sentence. Because the brain is capable of processing information considerably faster than the unaided eye sees words, the goal is to help your eyes more quickly send the information—the words—to your brain for processing.

One way to achieve this is to use a pointer, such as your finger or a pencil, to give your eyes something on which they can focus. Place the pointer just below each line of text as you read, and move it along the line, following the tip of it with your eyes. You should practice moving the object faster and faster while still maintaining comprehension.

The overall purpose of this exercise is to smooth out your reading pace, allowing your eyes to skip over the spaces between words. Not only will this increase your reading speed, but it will also improve comprehension. Consider the following examples: if you read a comic strip panel by panel, taking a minute-long break between each panel, it would be much harder to follow the story. The same applies when watching a half-hour television program in ten, three-minute chunks, taking a break between each one. Although reading happens at a much faster pace, the concept is the same: keeping the intake of information as fluid as possible increases your ability to piece together the developing ideas.

Despite how smoothly you may be able to read, your eyes will still stop moving at times. These pauses, known as *fixations*, are the moments when your eyes are physically looking at the words on the page. This is unavoidable, but decreasing the number of times your eyes stop, or at least the length of time that they stop between words should significantly increase your reading speed. Making better use of these fixations by "seeing" as many words as possible when your eyes do stop is one of the fundamental aspects of speed reading.

Turn Off Your Internal Narrator

When we first learn to read, it is often aloud in a classroom setting. This initial experience of reading out loud then translates into a life-long habit of *sub-vocalization*, or reading out loud in your head. This helps people to understand what they are reading, but it is usually unnecessary and dramatically limits the maximum number of words that an individual can read in a given period of time.

For the purpose of the ACT Reading Test, and other similar activities where getting a sense of the main idea is the primary purpose, you should attempt to silence that voice in your head. The process of speaking the words out loud cripples your reading speed; some people will even move their lips as though they were actually saying the words they are reading.

One way to overcome this bad habit is to quietly hum to yourself while you practice reading. If the part of your brain that would typically vocalize what you read is occupied with humming, with practice you should be able to take in more words with the same level of comprehension as if you had spoken each word aloud. Over time, the humming will become less necessary, and you will be able to process words without subvocalizing.

Reduce Regressions

A *regression*, or *skip-back*, is simply reading what you've already read. This is often a subconscious tendency and contributes to a cycle of continuous regressions in some readers. It begins when we are very young and are attempting to remember what we have just read. If we doubt our ability to recall the details, we automatically re-read them and thus reinforce the doubts about our memory. Over time, these repeated regressions actually reduce our ability to focus on what is being read, as our brains have come to expect that most things will be re-read.

These regressions disrupt the forward flow of reading and have a negative impact on not only speed but also the ability to initially comprehend what is read. It is incredibly challenging to read at increasingly faster speeds if you are continuously doubting your ability to comprehend what you just read.

Perhaps the best way to reduce the tendency toward regression, besides being exceptionally focused on your reading, is to use an index card or a piece of paper. Start at the top of the page, and use the index card to cover each line of text as you finish reading it. This way, even though you may subconsciously want to go back and read a previous line, the text will be blocked. At first, you may notice a decrease in comprehension, but eventually you will regain confidence in your ability to remember what you have just read and your comprehension will increase. Eventually, the urge to go back and re-read portions

---

Study Tip

Accidental subvocalization will still happen; be sure to correct the behavior as soon as you catch yourself doing it. As with all of the speed-reading techniques presented, practice is absolutely necessary to achieve the greatest benefits.

of the text will subside, and you will notice yourself reading entire pages faster while remembering more of what you read.

STRATEGIES TO INCREASE SPEED-READING COMPREHENSION

This section includes strategies that will improve your overall reading ability when used in conjunction with speed reading, especially if your ultimate goal is to improve your understanding of ACT Reading Test passages.

Read Introductory Material

The first thing to be aware of is the text before the text. If there is any introductory material, headings, or subheadings, make sure to read and take advantage of them. This supplemental information will serve as signposts on the road to improved understanding of the text. Often, it will provide you with a slight preview of what you are about to read, so that you will approach the passage with some idea of what you can expect to get from it.

Focus on Main Concepts

Spend as little time as possible comprehending individual words, unless they are key concepts. Focus instead on an overall understanding of the author's aims and how the structure of a given piece of writing contributes to those goals. Spending the majority of your time on supporting details is not nearly as efficient as determining the concepts that the author is trying to stress, and then relating the central ideas back to those main points.

Don't Push It!

Once you have achieved some mastery of speed reading, be sure not to overestimate your own rate of comprehension. Try to avoid pushing yourself to the upper limit of your reading speed, as comprehension tends to decrease slightly at that point. You should try to hover slightly below your maximum speed as much as possible, as this gives your brain the greatest opportunity to process the text and make sense of what you are reading.

SOME POTENTIAL PROBLEMS WITH SPEED READING

Although speed reading is a valuable skill, it does have its disadvantages. Perhaps the greatest of these is that some people are inclined to make speed reading their default reading strategy. It should be seen as one of many reading strategies at your disposal, but not the only one.

Some of the techniques previously discussed for improving reading speed can actually pose problems for certain types of reading. For example, on the ACT English Test, subvocalization is almost a necessity. Reading sentences "aloud in your head" allows you to catch errors in grammar and sentence construction that you would likely pass over while speed reading. The goal when reading ACT English Test passages is not merely to get an overall idea of the passage, but to focus on spotting errors and improving the writing.

Additionally, although regressions reduce the forward momentum of your reading, for certain material such as philosophy or complex science, it is very difficult to comprehend all of the information on the first pass through a document, even at a normal reading speed. If you find yourself comprehending very

> **Study Tip**
> Remember to practice these strategies to maximize your comprehension.

little from more difficult reading material, you should not attempt to speed read through it. Further, it is okay to regress at times when concepts and ideas are not making sense; often, if one major concept does not connect, the ideas that follow will be even more difficult to understand.

Finally, there are times when you should read slowly, enjoying the text. Often times, especially with some prose or poetry, the beauty of the language and the specific word choices made by the author will be lost by reading too quickly. You should still be able to comprehend the ideas presented, but the author's voice will be considerably more difficult to discern. At the fastest speeds, almost all writing will begin to seem somewhat stiff and mechanical. Be aware of situations where the meaning behind the words is especially important, and times when you may simply want to slow down and appreciate the art of writing.

▬▬ SPEED READING DRILLS

Throughout this chapter, we have stressed the importance of practicing the various speed reading techniques presented. This section includes two exercises designed to push you to read at an increasingly faster pace while utilizing the skills and techniques discussed earlier.

Before turning to either of these drills, however, you should recalculate your baseline reading speed. You will produce the most accurate measure of your new reading speed by using new material, such as a novel that you may currently be reading. Your practice material should contain few, if any, pictures, and should be in a reasonable font size. In addition, because the ACT Reading Test is a paper-and-pencil test, you should use actual books or magazines when you practice. Studies show that humans read differently when reading text on a computer screen than they do when reading words printed on paper.

Recalculating Your Reading Speed

Using your trusty stopwatch (or watch with a second-hand), time yourself reading new material for one minute. When the time is up, count the number of lines that you were able to read, and write down that number. Next, determine the average words per line by counting the total number of words in five lines and dividing that number by five. Multiply the total number of lines you were able to read by the average words per line to get your new baseline words per minute speed.

> **Study Tip**
> Number of lines × Average words per line = Baseline Reading Speed

The Double (2×) Drill

Now that you have a new baseline speed (which should already show some improvement), you need to stretch your speed reading muscles! The first exercise is called the *double drill*.

The purpose of a double drill is to get through twice the number of lines that you can currently read in one minute. Find some fresh reading material, and count off twice the number of lines that you were previously able to read in one minute. Now, give yourself another one-minute period to read that entire section. For example, if you read ten lines of text in one minute, you should mark off twenty lines of new material. The goal is to force yourself to read these twenty lines in the time it took you to read ten lines.

At first, this will seem incredibly difficult. Do not worry about comprehension, as the aim is just to physically get through the material. With time, your eyes will acclimate themselves to moving at ever-increasing rates, and speed reading will start to feel more natural. At this later point comprehension will become the primary focus, but for now concentrate on speed.

Spend the next ten minutes repeating the double drill on the SAME material—if you were reading twenty lines, then use those same twenty lines for each drill. You should be picking up a bit more information on each pass through the material so that after ten minutes worth of double drills, you will be able to comprehend a good deal of what you've been reading. It may be helpful afterward to ask yourself questions such as "What was the main idea of each paragraph I read?" to test your understanding following the drills.

The Triple (3×) Drill

Your goal for the *triple drill* is to read three times the number of lines that you can currently read in one minute (based on the initial number of lines when calculating your baseline).

You may wonder what the point of these triple drills is. According to experts, in order to achieve your normal level of comprehension while speed reading, you must practice actually reading material at three times that speed. Continuously increasing your base speed and practicing triple drills will produce greater levels of understanding at faster reading speeds.

Starting with new material (it can be from the same book, but make sure you have not looked at the section you are going to use for these drills), count off three times the number of lines you were able to read when calculating your new baseline speed. Force yourself, again in only one minute, to read all of this material.

It is normal and expected that your comprehension will decrease dramatically during the triple drill. You will probably retain little, if any, of the information after you first read it at three-times your normal speed. Do ten of these triple drills—like you did with the double drills—trying to get a slightly better grasp of the passage each time. When you have completed this task, ask yourself questions again, trying to measure your comprehension.

▬▬ PRACTICE, PRACTICE, PRACTICE!

You will likely find speed reading quite challenging because you have probably been reading fairly slowly for years. This habit will be hard to break. In fact, without realizing it, you may slow down and speed up multiple times while you read, failing to notice any real improvement in your reading speed or comprehension. It is even possible to see a decrease in both speed and comprehension depending on your level of distraction at the time.

Now that you have the tools to increase your reading speed and comprehension, you must continue to practice the drills on a regular basis. At least twice a week, ideally every other day, you should set aside a half-hour block of time for drills. In this half hour you should do one set of ten double drills as a speed reading warm-up, followed by two sets of ten triple drills. Test yourself on new reading material, and at the end of each set of drills reflect on how much of the material you were able to comprehend.

Recalculate your reading speed at the end of each week, and use this new baseline for your double and triple drills in the following weeks. Over time, the techniques discussed in this chapter will become second nature and you will be reading faster with greater comprehension.

> **Study Tip**
> Repeated practice is necessary to become a confident speed reader!

■■■　WHAT'S NEXT?

Chapter 11 covers additional strategies and techniques that will help you improve the skills necessary for success on the ACT Reading Test. Apply your new skills to the simulated practice ACT Reading Tests included in Chapters 12 and 13. Additional practice material is available in *McGraw-Hill's 10 ACT Practice Tests*.

CHAPTER 11

STRATEGIES AND TECHNIQUES

Study Tip

Remember to fill in every answer "bubble" on your answer sheet since there is no extra penalty for guessing incorrectly as there is on some other tests, like the SAT.

If you choose to answer all of the questions on the ACT Reading Test, you will have about 8 minutes to work on each of the four passages and still have enough time to mark the answers on your answer sheet. For many students, it makes sense to slow down a bit, focus on two or three of the passages, and simply guess on the remaining questions. Whether you choose to work on all four of the passages or not will depend on where you are on the scoring scale. The truth of the scoring patterns on the ACT exam is that if you get 30 out of the 40 questions correct, you end up with a scaled Reading Score of about 28. (There is minor variation in scaled scores from one exam to the next.) A 28 on the Reading Test means that your reading score would be well within the top 10 percent of reading scores nationwide.

The current national average ACT Reading Test score is around a 21 on the scale. This means that the average ACT-taker correctly answers about one half of the questions on the Reading Test. Of course, we recommend that you strive to do your best and we hope that all readers of this book will be well into the above-average range on the ACT.

If you are closer to the average ACT Reading test taker, and find that you are only able to really understand two passages and their accompanying questions in the time allowed, you are still likely to get credit for a few more correct responses by guessing on the remaining 20 questions. In fact, since there are four answer choices for each question, you should predict that you would get about 25 percent correct when guessing at random. This means that guessing on 20 questions should yield about five correct answers. If you manage to get only 15 correct of the 20 questions that go with the two passages that you work on carefully, you would still have a scaled score of approximately 20 or 21.

◼◼◼ "SACRIFICING" A READING PASSAGE

As we just discussed, many students will not have time to attempt all four of the passages on the Reading Test. In this case, you should choose a passage or two that will be "sacrificed" in the interest of time management. There are a few factors to consider when deciding which passage(s) you will sacrifice. For example, you should certainly look at the subject matter. Most students have distinct preferences for one or two of the passage types mentioned previously. Conversely, there is probably at least one type of passage that always gives you trouble and accounts for the bulk of the questions that you regularly miss on practice Reading Tests. Let your practice testing help you to decide whether to attack all four passages. If you decide to focus on two or three passages on test day, let your practice guide you when deciding which passages to sacrifice.

ACT READING TEST GENERAL STRATEGIES

Don't read these passages as though you were studying for a high school exam. The open-book aspect of the ACT Reading Test means that you should read in a way that helps your brain to work through the information efficiently. You will not have to remember the information for a long period of time, so don't spend time studying or memorizing. You should read loosely and only dwell on information that you are sure is important because you need it to answer a question. This type of reading should be very goal oriented. If the information you are looking at does not help to answer a question, you should not linger over it.

Following are some strategies to apply to the ACT Reading Test.

Read the Question Stems First

The single most powerful strategy for reading is to read the question stems first. The question stems are the prompts, or *stimuli*, that appear before the four answer choices. The questions might contain useful information. They might refer to specific names or terms repeatedly or contain references to the line numbers that are printed down the left side of the passage. This can be very useful in focusing your attention and energy on the parts of the passage that are likely to lead to correct answers to questions.

While reading the question stems can be helpful, reading the answers choices usually is not. Don't read them before you read the passage. Most of the answer choices are wrong and, in fact, are referred to by testing professionals as "distractors." If you read them before you read the passage, you will be much more likely to get confused.

Each of the passages has numbered lines. Some of the questions will refer to a particular line or lines. When you read a question that contains a line reference, locate those lines in the passage and make a note in the margin so that you know where to begin to find the answer to the question. For example, put parentheses around the line referenced text, and write the question number next to the parentheses.

As you read the questions, attempt to put them into your own words to increase your understanding of what's being asked. Then, once you've read the question stems, move to the passage itself.

Determine the Main Idea of the Passage

As you begin to read the passage, your first step should be to determine the main idea. This technique can help you to answer the "big-picture" questions and assist you in locating information necessary to answer the other question types (discussed later in this chapter). The main idea has the following three components:

Topic (what is the passage about?)
Scope (what aspect of the topic does the passage focus on?)
Purpose (why did the author write the passage?)

If you can answer these three questions, you understand the main idea. Consider the following scenarios:

1. The world's tropical rain forests are being decimated at an alarming rate. Each day, thousands of acres of trees are destroyed in both developing and industrial countries. Nearly half of the world's species of plants and animals will be eliminated or severely threatened over the next 25 years due to this rapid deforestation. Clearly, it is imperative that something be done to curtail this rampant destruction of the rainforests.

2. Tropical rain forests are crucial to the health and welfare of the planet. Experts indicate that over 20 percent of the world's oxygen is produced by the Amazon rain forest alone. In addition, more than half of the world's estimated 10 million species of plants, animals, and insects live in the tropical rain forests. These plants and animals of the rain forest provide us with food, fuel wood, shelter, jobs, and medicines. Indigenous humans also inhabit the tropical rain forests.

The **topic** of both passages is tropical rain forests. However, the **scope** of each passage is very different. The first passage discusses destruction of the tropical rain forests, whereas the second passage introduces the diversity of the rain forests and indicates why the rain forests are important. The **purpose** of the first passage is a call to action, while the second passage is primarily informative.

The introductory paragraph of the reading passage often indicates the topic or topics being discussed, the author's point of view, and exactly what the author is trying to prove (if anything). Read a little more slowly at the beginning of the passage until you get a grip on the three components of the main idea, then shift into higher gear and skim the rest of the passage.

Skim the Passage

Don't use context clues the first time that you skim through a passage. When you come to a word or phrase that is unfamiliar, just read past it. You will most likely have time to come back if you need to. But there is a strong chance that you won't need to bother figuring out exactly what that one word or phrase means in order to answer the bulk of the questions that follow the passage. If you waste some of your precious time, you'll never get it back. With perseverance and practice, you will start to get comfortable with a less-than-perfect understanding of the passage.

You should also pay close attention to paragraph breaks. While reading through paragraphs, follow these tips to help you gather information more effectively:

• Try to determine the subtopic for each paragraph quickly.
• Focus on the general content of each paragraph.
• Determine the purpose of each paragraph.

Note that the first sentence is not always the topic sentence. Don't believe those people who say that you can read the first and last sentence of each paragraph and skip the rest of the sentences completely. You are better off skimming over all of the words even if you end up forgetting most of what you read almost immediately. Remember that the idea at this stage is not to waste time. Keep moving through the material.

In addition, you should read actively throughout the passage-based Reading-sections. That is, think about things such as the tone and the purpose of the passage. This technique will help you to stay focused on the material, and, ultimately, will allow you to select the best answer to the questions.

Study Tip
The goal with skimming is to get a general understanding of the structure of the passage. This is key so that you can find pertinent facts when you refer to the passage as you answer questions.

Study Tip
You can write in your test booklet. So, when you see a topic word, circle it. If you can sum up a paragraph in a word or two, jot it down in the margin.

Likewise, while vocabulary is not tested directly on the ACT, there is certainly an advantage to knowing what the words mean as you try to decipher a passage. We have included a vocabulary list (Appendix A), which includes words that have appeared on past ACT tests and may appear again. Even if none of the words on the list shows up on your exam, you should at least get an idea of the type of word that is likely to be seen and the level of difficulty that you can expect to find on your test.

Paraphrase the Question Stems

Once you have found the information in the passage that will provide the answer you are looking for, try to answer the question in your mind. Put the question in your own words so that it makes more sense to you. Do this before you look at the answer choices. Remember that three out of every four answer choices are incorrect. Not only are they incorrect, but also they were written by experts to confuse you. They are less likely to confuse you if you have a clear idea of an answer before you read the answer choices. It often helps to consciously simplify as you read. Try using the phrase, "So what they are really saying is …." This technique works for question stems and answer choices, as well as for the passages.

> **Study Tip**
> You can paraphrase on your first pass through the question stems. You can also sometimes predict an answer before you read the passage. Be sure to check the context before you mark your final answer.

Predict Answers to the Questions

Try to predict an answer for the question, and then skim the choices presented and look for your answer. You might have to be a little flexible to recognize it. Your answer might be there dressed up in different words. If you can recognize a paraphrase of your predicted answer, choose it. Mark the question in your test booklet if you are unsure.

Note that it is possible for an answer choice to be both true *and* wrong. The answer that you choose must respond correctly to the question being asked. Simply being true is not enough to make an answer correct. The best answer will always be supported by details, inference, or tone.

Read and Answer the Questions

Start at the beginning of each group of questions. Read the first question and make sure that you understand it. Go back to the part of the passage that will probably contain the answer to your question. Some of the questions on the ACT ask you to draw conclusions based on the information that you read. However, even these questions should be answered based on the information in the passage. There will always be some strong hints, or evidence, that will lead you to an answer.

Some of the questions contain references to specific lines of the passage. The trick in those cases is to read a little before and a little after the specific line that is mentioned. At least read the entire sentence that contains the line that is referenced.

On the other hand, some of the questions don't really tell you where to look for the answer, or, they are about the passage as a whole. In those cases, think about what you learned about the passage while you were skimming it. Note the subtopics for the paragraphs, and let them guide you to the part of the passage that contains the information you are looking for.

One of the important skills rewarded by the ACT is the ability to sift through text and find the word or concept for which you are looking. This skill improves with practice.

Remember that the most complicated-sounding answer choice is not always correct. Too many ACT-takers have cost themselves points over the years by applying the following flawed logic: "If I can't understand it, it must be correct because this is a hard test!"

Finally, be careful always to consider all of the choices before you select your answer, even if your predicted answer is among the choices. The difference between the best answer and the second best answer is sometimes very subtle.

Don't be afraid to refer back to the passage repeatedly, and don't be reluctant to skip around within the question group that accompanies each of the passages. In fact, many students report success with a strategy of actually skipping back and forth *between* passages. This plan won't work for everyone. It probably would just create confusion for most test takers. But, if you feel comfortable with it after trying it on practice tests, we can't think of any reason not to do it on test day.

Use the Process of Elimination

Elimination is the process that most test takers use for all the questions that they answer. It is reliable, but slow. It is useful to you as a backup strategy for the questions for which either you cannot predict an answer, or your prediction is not listed as a choice. Once you have eliminated an answer choice that is not supported by the passage, cross it off in your test booklet.

It can be hard to break the habit of always applying the process of elimination. You have developed this habit because you have been given too much time on most exams that you have taken. There are a couple of different reasons that teachers tend to allow long periods of time for exams. The first is that teachers must allow enough time for even the slower students to have a fair chance to answer questions. The second is that testing time for students is often break time for the instructor. He or she might be able to catch up on paper work or read a newspaper during the time that students are testing. These factors tend to lead to students who get used to a leisurely pace on exams.

Apply Logic

It is important to know the difference between information that is stated directly in the passage, and inferences and assumptions. You might be asked questions based on factual information found in the reading passages. Or, you might be asked to make an inference based on information provided in the reading passage.

An *inference* is a conclusion based on what is stated in the passage. You can infer something about a person, place, or thing by reasoning through the descriptive language contained in the reading passage. In other words, the author's language *implies* that something is probably true.

An *assumption*, on the other hand, is unstated evidence. It is the missing link in an author's argument. Following is a classic example of a conclusion based on stated evidence and unstated evidence (assumption):

> *Socrates is a man.*
> *Therefore, Socrates is mortal.*

Because you are given that Socrates is a man, the conclusion that Socrates is mortal *must* be based on the assumption that men are mortal.

> *Socrates is a man. (Stated evidence)*
> *Men are mortal. (Unstated evidence)*
> *Therefore, Socrates is mortal. (Conclusion)*

Some of the evidence is not stated, but the final conclusion leads you to the existence of that missing evidence, or assumption.

■■■ ACT READING TEST QUESTION TYPES

Following is a list of the types of questions you are likely to encounter on the ACT Reading Test.

- Main Idea/Point of View
- Specific Detail
- Conclusion/Inference
- Extrapolation
- Vocabulary in Context

We have included a description of each question type, along with specific approaches to tackling the questions. You will begin to recognize the different question types as you work through the sample questions and practice exams.

Main Idea/Point of View

These questions might ask about the main idea of the passage as a whole, or about a specific paragraph. They also ask about the author's point of view or perspective and the intended audience.

> **Strategy:** Answer these questions according to your understanding of the three components of the main idea mentioned previously (**topic**, **scope**, and **purpose**). It is also worth noting that the incorrect choices are usually either too broad or too narrow. You should eliminate the answer choices that focus on a specific part of the passage and also eliminate the answer choices that are too general and could describe other passages besides the one on which you are working.

Specific Detail

These questions can be as basic as asking you about some fact that is easily found by referring to a part of the passage. Often, they are a bit more difficult because they ask you to interpret the information that is referred to.

> **Strategy:** Refer to the passage to find the answer to these questions. Use line or paragraph references in the questions if they are given. Sometimes the answer choices are paraphrased, so don't just choose the answers that contain words that appeared in the passage. Make sure that the choice you select is responsive to the question being asked.

Conclusion/Inference

These questions require the test taker to put together information in the passage and use it as evidence for a conclusion. You will have to find language in the passage that will cause you to arrive at the inference that the question demands. (To "*infer*" is to draw a conclusion based on information in the passage.)

> **Strategy:** Although you have to do a bit of thinking for these questions, you should be able to find very strong evidence for your answers. If you find yourself creating a long chain of reasoning and including information from outside the passage when "selling" the answer to yourself, stop and reconsider. The ACT rewards short, strong connections between the evidence in the passage and the answer that is credited.

Extrapolation

These questions ask you to go beyond the passage itself and find answers that are probably true based on what you know from the passage. They can be based on the author's tone or on detailed information in the passage.

Strategy: You need to be sensitive to any clues about the author's tone or attitude and any clues about how the characters in the passage feel. Eliminate any choices that are outside the scope of the passage. As with inference questions, the ACT rewards short, strong connections between the passage and the correct answers.

Vocabulary in Context

These questions will ask what a specific word or phrase from the passage means. The context of the passage should lead you to an educated guess even if you don't know the specific word or phrase being asked about.

Strategy: The best way to answer these questions is the simplest way; just read the answer choices back into the sentence mentioned in the question stem and choose the one that changes the meaning of the sentence the least. These questions are almost always accompanied by a line reference. Often, the answer to the question is found in the line before or the line after the referenced line or lines.

WHAT'S NEXT?

Chapter 12 includes exercises designed to help you master the ACT Reading Test questions. Focus on those areas that give you the most trouble, and be sure to review the explanations. Chapters 13 and 14 contain simulated ACT Reading Tests in format, as well as explanations for each question.

CHAPTER 12

APPLYING STRATEGIES, BUILDING SKILLS

The exercises in this chapter are designed to help you practice the skills that are generally tested on the ACT Reading Test—namely, critical thinking skills. The ACT Reading Test rewards quick, active reading, which requires more mental energy than the reading most students are used to. As we mentioned in Chapter 11, you should not read the passages on the ACT Reading Test slowly and deliberately. Instead, you should read for the main idea, then skim for details, and refer back to the passage as needed to answer the questions.

The following exercises, while not always in ACT format, will help you to become an active reader who can skillfully apply the critical thinking necessary for success on the ACT Reading Test.

IDENTIFY TOPIC, SCOPE, AND PURPOSE—MAIN IDEA

Remember that **topic**, **scope**, and **purpose** are the three components of the main idea of ACT reading passages. Read the following excerpts, and identify the **topic**, **scope**, and **purpose** of each.

1. The theory that global warming is the result of human activity is not proven. Furthermore, there is insufficient evidence to support the idea that slightly increased temperatures on Earth would result in the kind of harm that some fear. There is simply not enough evidence about global warming to support making dramatic changes in human activity that would certainly cause significant economic and social problems around the world.

   Measuring Earth's temperature is an inexact science at best. Scientists do not agree on what the current average surface temperature is, much less on what the temperature was more than 100 years ago, before modern instruments were available to measure surface temperature. There is actually satellite data showing that there has been a slight cooling during the last twenty years or so. Even those scientists who report that there has been a temperature increase are only claiming about one-half of one degree Celsius, an amount that is easily attributed to natural variations that have no connection to human activity.

TOPIC_____

SCOPE _____

PURPOSE_____

_____

2. Louis XIV's reign can be characterized by the remark often attributed to him, "I am the state." Although there is some disagreement regarding the attribution, historians agree that the statement neatly sums up the attitude of "The Sun King." Also known as "The Grand Monarch" due to his expansion of French territory and his focus on improving and exporting French culture, Louis sat on the throne of France for over fifty years and built his country into a dominant force in Europe, and, arguably, the world. Among his many accomplishments, he increased France's territory in Europe and her empire abroad. He built several masterpieces of architecture, including Versailles, and improved and expanded several others, such as the Louvre. Louis was also successful in adding Spain to his dynasty. In fact, the current King of Spain, Juan Carlos, is his direct descendant. Even within the United States, Louis XIV's influence is still felt; the state of Louisiana was named for him.

Although he was successful in military and cultural pursuits, his reign was hard on the populace of France as he continually raised taxes to finance his wars and lavish palaces.

Ruling as an absolute monarch with no checks on his power, Louis XIV answered to no one. His ruthless expansionism and excessive taxation led not only to bitter feelings among the lower classes but, some argue, to the French Revolution over fifty years after his death.

TOPIC_____

SCOPE _____

PURPOSE_____

_____

3. Frank Frazetta undoubtedly ranks among the greatest painters of all time, and his work will be studied by future generations in the same way that today's students study the works of Michelangelo and DaVinci. While his paintings were primarily done for paperback book covers and movie posters, his work transcends its commercial roots and has influenced an entire generation of illustrators and painters. His themes of barbaric violence and artistic nudity overwhelm some more faint-hearted viewers. However, even the squeamish must admit the talent and skill that Frazetta brings to bear on his work. His idealized human forms are famous for being lifelike and, at the same time, appearing stronger and more attractive than any actual humans that we have ever met in our own lives. Although he has many imitators, none have been able to capture the power and dynamism of a Frazetta character.

TOPIC_____

SCOPE _____

PURPOSE_____

_____

4. Aviator Charles A. Lindbergh was undeniably a man of genius. In 1927, he was the first to fly from New York to Paris. Such success is not the result of academic excellence, but the result of ingenuity and determination.

Throughout his childhood and early adulthood, Charles Lindbergh was not interested in erudition. In 1918, with the United States in the throes of World War I, Lindbergh eagerly agreed to return to the farm to grow food for the war effort in exchange for his high school diploma. Though the small Minnesota farm thrived under his care, his passion was not for agriculture, but for things mechanical. When he expressed these interests to his parents (a congressman and a teacher), they encouraged him to obtain a more formal education.

Lindbergh attended the University of Wisconsin to study engineering. However, Lindbergh's penchant for "hands-on" learning, combined with a lack of scholarly discipline and study skills, resulted in academic probation after barely two years. Realizing that the only practical knowledge he had gained in college was through his participation in the Reserve Officers' Training Corps (R.O.T.C.), Lindbergh dropped out of college, never to return.

TOPIC_____

SCOPE _____

PURPOSE_____

_____

5. The origin of the first Americans has been, and continues to be, a subject of debate. Some people argue that Christopher Columbus, the explorer widely credited with discovering America, was the first American. However, about 500 years before Columbus was born, a Norse (Viking) captain named Leif Eriksson set up a colony in present-day Newfoundland, Canada. In addition, an ancient Oriental ship bell found off the coast of California led some to speculate that perhaps early Japanese or Chinese fishermen reached the Pacific Coast of North America.

Despite the fact that these various people visited or settled in America long ago, the first Americans were the Native Americans who lived on American soil for thousands of years before the arrival of Christopher Columbus, Leif Eriksson, or Asian fishermen. How many thousands of years? Again, this depends on your point of view. Until the early twentieth century, it was generally accepted that humans had inhabited the North American continent for approximately 3,000 years.

This view was reevaluated after the discovery of bison bones bearing the marks of ancient stone knives in 1908. The bones were not carefully examined until 1922, when archaeologists began to accept that humans had probably inhabited America for about 10,000 years. This estimate was revised relatively quickly, as stone spears found in the 1930s suggested that the first Americans were here at least 11,000 years ago.

TOPIC_____

SCOPE _____

PURPOSE_____

■■■ LOCATE AND INTERPRET SIGNIFICANT DETAILS

The passage below is followed by questions about specific details contained within the passage. Practice looking for key words and phrases in both the question stem and answer choices to help you locate the correct information in the passage. Then, select the best answer from among the choices listed.

Sir Isaac Newton has generally been regarded as the founder of modern physical science. He was the first to promulgate a set of natural laws governing both terrestrial and celestial motion, and he laid the groundwork for subsequent innovations in mathematics, astronomy, chemistry,
5   and physics.
Noted for his achievements in exploring and defining gravitational forces, Newton's first major scientific accomplishment was the invention, design, and construction of a reflecting telescope. His ingenuity led to an advance in telescope technology; versions of the mirror that
10 he created are still used in some modern telescopes. Later, while still a student at Cambridge, he read works on optics and light by the English physicists Robert Boyle and Robert Hooke, and discovered measurable patterns in the light refracted by a glass prism. Based on the results of his experiments, he postulated that light consisted of streams of minute
15 particles. His attempts to publish this unconventional idea were thwarted by critics.
Despite experiencing numerous setbacks, Sir Isaac Newton is known today as a brilliant scientist, who helped to advance the fields of mathematics, astronomy, chemistry, and physics.

1. The passage states that Newton was the first person to:
   A. develop a refracting telescope.
   B. publicize laws of motion.
   C. measure gravitational forces.
   D. study under Robert Boyle.

2. Which of the following questions is NOT answered by information in the passage?
   F. What type of telescope mirror did Newton create that is still in use?
   G. What physicists' works did Newton read while at Cambridge?
   H. What achievements is Newton most noted for?
   J. What object prompted Newton's discovery of measurable patterns of light?

3. According to the passage, Newton postulated which of the following theories about light?
   A. It consisted of seven distinct colors across a varied spectrum.
   B. Waves of light traveled faster than waves of sound.
   C. It was made up of streams of tiny particles.
   D. Light waves consisted of large fragments seen collectively.

4. All of the following are mentioned in the passage as fields furthered by Newton EXCEPT:
   F. physics.
   G. mathematics.
   H. astrology.
   J. chemistry.

5. The author indicates that one reason Newton's publishing attempts were thwarted was:
   A. his economic status.
   B. his lack of experience.
   C. his young age.
   D. his unconventional ideas.

◼ UNDERSTAND SEQUENCES OF EVENTS AND COMPREHEND CAUSE-EFFECT RELATIONSHIPS

The passage below is followed by questions that ask you to evaluate sequences of events and cause-and-effect relationships. Read the questions, then select the best answer from among the choices listed.

Is the human being primarily driven by instinct or by learned behavior? The "Nature vs. Nurture" argument is an almost constant topic of discussion for some scientists and others. Regardless of whether our thoughts and actions are determined by our biological makeup, it is
5 evident to most observers that certain biological factors do play a role in our development and behavior. Even those on the "nurture" side of the debate acknowledge that genetics can create tendencies toward certain types of behavior in some individuals. There is very little agreement as to how much of a role nature plays in controlling human behavior. To a
10 certain degree, the various physiological processes that are occurring in our bodies each and every day determine many facets of our lives. The scientists who support the "nature" argument wonder how, exactly, the mechanisms work. This thinking has fueled research to determine which of these biological processes cause or contribute to certain emotions.
15 For example, some scientists now believe that the feeling of "love" can be traced to a specific hormone in our bodies. The "chemistry of love" has become an important sociological topic as men and women discuss the roots of certain behaviors in mating rituals and relationships. Infatuation has been linked to the production of a neurochemical called
20 *phenyl ethylamine* or, PEA. PEA is one of the substances in the brain that causes feelings of elation, exhilaration, and euphoria. By allowing electrical impulses in the brain to bridge the gaps, called *synapses*, between neurons, PEA stimulates and increases brain activity in general and seems to work on some specific areas of the brain that are associated
25 with feelings of love in its early stages. This biological process may

help to explain the emotional highs that human beings feel when they experience infatuation—the intense feelings that some individuals have during the beginning of a romantic relationship.

30 One drawback, however, is that the body can sometimes become addicted to these neurological chemicals, and feel depressed and "down" without near constant re-release of the chemicals. Some psychiatrists now identify "lovesick" individuals as having a specific craving for PEA. In a revolutionary study, a group of "lovesick" men and women were given a variety of antidepressant drugs, called MAO (monoamine oxi-

35 dase) inhibitors. These drugs helped to boost the levels of PEA in the brains of these patients by slowing the natural processes that deplete the brain's supply of neurotransmitters over time. As a result, these subjects soon reported a less-perceived need for affection from others.

1. According to the passage, research into the effects of biological processes on human emotion was initiated by:
   A. observation of genetic tendencies, or predispositions, toward certain activities.
   B. attempts to disprove the "nature" side of the Nature vs. Nurture argument.
   C. curiosity about the degree to which biological processes determine human behavior.
   D. isolation of specific strings of genes that are thought to directly impact various emotion centers within the brain.

2. The second paragraph (lines 15–28) suggests that if PEA did not stimulate certain areas of the brain, then:
   F. humans would not experience the intense feelings associated with infatuation.
   G. the desire for human affection would increase in most people.
   H. feeling strong emotions at the onset of a relationship would be common.
   J. men and women would cease to be attracted to one another.

3. According to the passage, a lovesick person who is feeling depressed is experiencing that emotional state most probably because the:
   A. individual is experiencing a sudden disappointment.
   B. amount of PEA in the brain has been depleted.
   C. person toward whom the infatuation is directed is not interested.
   D. level of PEA in the brain has increased.

4. The author implies that treatment with MAO inhibitors is likely to cause:
   F. no change in an individual's mental state.
   G. an increase in the desire for affection.
   H. boosted feelings of longing.
   J. a reduction in perceived emotional need.

5. Based on information in the passage, you can infer that psychiatrists believe "lovesickness" is the result of:
   A. a biological fluctuation in brain synapse activity.
   B. a combination of various environmental factors.
   C. an addiction to specific neurological chemicals.
   D. an abundance of certain chemical inhibitors.

■ DETERMINE THE MEANING OF WORDS, PHRASES, AND STATEMENTS IN CONTEXT

The passage below is followed by questions that ask you to determine the meaning of words, phrases, and statements within the context of the passage. Read the questions, then select the best answer from among the choices listed.

> While some claim that modern society infringes on the environment, there are others who believe that good stewardship of the earth and environmentalism can go hand in hand. According to the latter, a hands-off approach isn't always the best one. For example, nature uses fire
> 5 to assist in maintaining the proper balance of underbrush, new-growth trees, and other vegetation. But allowing a naturally occurring fire to burn out of control could be devastating to both wildlife and humans in nearby communities. In addition to the immediate damage to property and loss of life, the loss of trees and vegetation can contribute to further
> 10 devastation. Landslides can accompany heavy rains when hillsides have been stripped of trees by fire, resulting in the loss of topsoil necessary to support immediate renewed growth and interfering with local water sources.
>   Controlled burning, a human intervention, can be used to contain
> 15 such fires. However, it cannot be done on land with dense underbrush and an overabundance of small, new-growth trees. In order to successfully manage a controlled burn, this vegetation must be thinned out. Workers must "knock down" the fuel load before the fire is introduced; otherwise, the fire will burn uncontrollably.
> 20 One California landowner said, "Sometimes current environmental laws don't make sense to me. If I failed to get rid of the trash on my property, I'd be in violation of zoning regulations. To my way of thinking, underbrush and excess new-growth trees are nature's garbage, yet many want us to let it just pile up."

1. The *hands-off approach* mentioned in lines 3–4 most nearly refers to:
   A. letting your neighbors solve their own problems.
   B. allowing nature to manage itself.
   C. not clearing the underbrush before a controlled burn.
   D. expecting problems to suddenly get better.

2. As it is used in line 2, the word *stewardship* most nearly means:
   F. management of a household.
   G. conservation of animals.
   H. responsible care-taking of resources.
   J. manipulating the environment for profit.

3. When the author says, "Workers must 'knock down' the fuel load" (line 18), he most likely means that:
   A. the underbrush and new growth must be removed.
   B. large dead trees must be chopped down.
   C. stockpiles of fuel must be spread throughout the forest.
   D. fuel must be compressed before the fire will ignite.

4. As it is used in line 1, the word *infringes* means:
   F. breaks down.
   G. interferes with.
   H. prevents.
   J. corrects.

5. In the context of the passage, what does the California landowner mean when he states "To my way of thinking?"
A. You should agree with me.
B. It makes no sense to me.
C. It is my belief that.
D. I disagree with this.

■ DRAW GENERALIZATIONS

The passage below is followed by questions that ask you to draw generalizations based on information in the passage. Read the questions, then select the best answer from among the choices listed.

This passage is adapted from Jane Eyre *by Charlotte Bronte © 1897.*

Seeing me, she roused herself: she made a sort of effort to smile, and framed a few words of congratulations; but the smile expired, and the sentence was abandoned unfinished. She put up her spectacles and pushed her chair back from the table.

5 "I feel so astonished," she began, "I hardly know what to say to you, Miss Eyre. I have surely not been dreaming, have I? Sometimes I half fall asleep when I am sitting alone and fancy things that have never happened. It has seemed to me more than once when I have been in a doze, that my dear husband, who died fifteen years since, has come in

10 and sat down beside me; and that I have even heard him call me by my name, Alice, as he used to do. Now, can you tell me whether it is actually true that Mr. Rochester has asked you to marry him? Don't laugh at me. But I really thought he came in here five minutes ago, and said that in a month you would be his wife."

15 "He has said the same thing to me," I replied.
"He has! Do you believe him? Have you accepted him?"
"Yes."
She looked at me bewildered.
"I could never have thought it. He is a proud man; all the Rochesters

20 were proud: and his father at least, liked money. He, too, has always been called careful. He means to marry you?"
"He tells me so."
She surveyed my whole person: in her eyes I read that they had there found no charm powerful enough to solve the enigma.

25 "It passes me!" she continued; "but no doubt it is true since you say so. How it will answer I cannot tell: I really don't know. Equality of position and fortune is often advisable in such cases; and there are twenty years of difference in your ages. He might almost be your father."
"No, indeed, Mrs. Fairfax!" I exclaimed, nettled; "he is nothing like

30 my father! No one, who saw us together, would suppose it for an instant. Mr. Rochester looks as young, and is as young, as some men at five and twenty."
"Is it really for love he is going to marry you?" she asked.
I was so hurt by her coldness and skepticism, that the tears rose to

35 my eyes.

1. As she is revealed in the passage, Mrs. Fairfax is best described as:
   A. understanding and genuine.
   B. warm yet hostile.
   C. surprised and disapproving.
   D. frigid yet supportive.

2. Based on the passage, Miss Eyre's feelings about her relationship with Mr. Rochester can best be described as:
   F. unbelievable.
   G. erratic.
   H. diplomatic.
   J. self-assured.

3. Which of the following statements best paraphrases lines 25–28?
   A. Mrs. Fairfax feels as though Mr. Rochester is not good enough for Miss Eyre, and that they should not marry.
   B. Mrs. Fairfax is unsure if Mr. Rochester knew what he was asking when he proposed.
   C. Miss Eyre and Mr. Rochester are going to have a difficult time making ends meet.
   D. Miss Eyre and Mr. Rochester are mismatched, which might lead to an unhappy marriage.

4. As he is depicted in the passage, Mr. Rochester is best described as a man who is usually:
   F. arrogant and methodical.
   G. cautious and self-respecting.
   H. wary and frugal.
   J. prideful and brash.

5. Based on lines 34 and 35, which of the following best characterizes Miss Eyre's feeling toward Mrs. Fairfax?
   A. Miserable and vexed
   B. Offended and upset
   C. Emboldened and animate
   D. Buoyant and dejected

■ ANALYZE THE AUTHOR'S OR NARRATOR'S VOICE AND METHOD

The passage below is followed by questions that ask you to identify and analyze the author's or narrator's voice and method of writing. Read the questions, then select the best answer from among the choices listed.

For some, backpacking is the ultimate vacation. The wilderness has a way of cleansing the spirit. What was once for me a tedious, tiring activity is now an essential part of my summer recreation. My passion for backpacking took hold many years ago when I crossed paths with a
5   hiker in the backcountry of Isle Royale National Park. The excitement in his eyes was infectious as he gazed out on Lake Superior. "By the shores of Gitche Gumee,/By the shining Big-Sea-Water,/Stood the wigwam of Nokomis,/Daughter of the Moon, Nokomis." He continued with more verses. "Have you read Longfellow's Song of Hiawatha?" he asked.

10 I had not. "Read it," he replied, "and you'll feel the passion the native people had for this lake, this land. It was their lifeblood." I understood what he meant. In the wilderness is found physical and spiritual sustenance, so every step along the trail brings you closer to peace. My goal in back packing was no longer the destination. Like the people in Longfellow's epic, I
15 now seek harmony with the Earth through immersion in its scenic riches.

After many summers on the trail, I've established my preferred routine. I rise and retire with the sun. Sunrises and sunsets are times for calm reflection. After breakfast and before dinner, I slowly walk around the area near my tent, taking note of the plants, animals, and minerals
20 that surround me. If I'm lucky, there is a creek or a pond to discover. Sometimes I find a fallen log or a huge boulder perfect for sitting. In these times I surrender myself to the wilderness, allowing the sights, sounds, and smells to pass through me. In silence, I ponder the natural system at play, and in occasional moments of lucidity, words pour from
25 my brain to my hand to my notepad.

Sometimes what I write in the wilderness is poetry, other times it's prose. Years later I look at my notepads to stir up vivid memories of my travels. This creative process has made backpacking immeasurably more rewarding. The backcountry stimulates both primal instincts and 30 high
30 forms of creativity. Nowhere else do I feel as rawly human. I write when others snap photographs. For me, a picture isn't worth a thousand words. A journal of reflections imbued with nature's spectacle is far more valuable.

1. Which of the following statements most accurately expresses the author's feelings when sitting atop a large boulder?
   A. Nostalgic and energized by the absolute serenity
   B. Seamlessly connected to the movement of nature
   C. Overwhelmed by the beauty of the environment
   D. Possessed by a clarity of thinking and creative thought

2. Which of the following is NOT an accurate description of the passage?
   F. A story about an individual's love of hiking and backpacking
   G. A glimpse into the creative inspiration and processes of an author
   H. A portrait of a writer connecting a love of backpacking to his work
   J. A look at the influence of nature on various styles of poetry and prose

3. Which of the following best describes the way the first paragraph (lines 1–15) functions in the passage?
   A. It reveals the reasons for the author's love of backpacking.
   B. It reinforces the author's position on the notion of nature inspiring art.
   C. It challenges many conceptions of America's backcountry.
   D. It disproves the hikers' wisdom that the journey is not about the destination.

4. According to the last paragraph, which of the following statements would the author most likely make with regard to nature photography?
   F. It lacks a descriptive quality that is only present in writing.
   G. It is a remarkable form of art that should receive the same praise as writing.
   H. It is the perfect companion to a journal of written reflections.
   J. It is proof that good photographers cannot be good writers.

5. The author develops the first paragraph (lines 1–15) mainly through:

    A. reliving a series of conversations to find a deeper sense of meaning.

    B. elaborating upon a verse of poetry so as to create a worldview.

    C. relating a chance conversation and the way in which it reshaped his opinion.

    D. describing a series of life experiences and the differences between them.

■■■ MAKE COMPARISONS AND CONTRASTS

The passage below is followed by questions that ask you to process the information in the passage and make comparisons and contrasts. Read the questions, then select the best answer from among the choices listed.

The reign of Justinian (A.D. 527–565) marked the final end of the Roman Empire. During Justinian's reign, his military recovered former Roman territories in Africa, Italy, and Spain. However, throughout Justinian's wars, Roman citizens faced many hardships: the Aqueducts

5 around Rome suffered damage, returning parts of the countryside to marshes; marauding enemies devastated the surrounding countryside; and, probably of most significance, the Italian economy suffered greatly. The prolonged wars' impact on the treasury of the empire was a result of several factors. For one, Justinian appeared to have difficulty establishing

10 priorities. He put military plans into action before he had the means to provide his commander with enough troops to do the job effectively. The financial problems also resulted in inadequate supplies and compensation for those troops. In order to feed and pay the troops, money traditionally was raised by collecting property taxes from the citizens of

15 Constantinople, in the eastern part of the empire. Reportedly, only about a third of those taxes were actually collected, which added to the funding problems.

The Bubonic Plague was also a factor at this time. It began in Constantinople in A.D. 542 and affected the entire Roman Empire until

20 A.D. 558. The plague ended the period of economic growth during which locating funds hadn't been a problem, even when all of the property taxes were not collected. The onset of the plague worsened the problems caused by financial resources that were already stretched too thin. Although John the Economist devised ways for Justinian to collect

25 money, there simply wasn't enough money to collect. To make matters worse, in the economic climate that resulted from the dual devastation of war raids and the plague, and during a time when his army depended on him for supplies and support, Justinian cut an already inadequate military budget so that he could have more funds available for the

30 reconstruction of Constantinople.

Some historians also report that Justinian never appeared to have a clear battle plan. He made many of his decisions without considering the consequences. For example, the commander Belisarius was seemingly randomly assigned to different areas of the country. Justinian first

35 gave him the job of winning the west, only to recall him to defend the east against the Persians. Then, Belisarius was recalled to Italy in A.D. 544, only later to be ordered to fight the Vandals in North Africa. This erratic use of resources is more likely a result of Justinian's inability to set priorities than his lack of planning.

1. According to the author, a significant difference between Justinian and previous Roman emperors was:
   A. the other emperors' unsuccessful efforts to collect taxes.
   B. Justinian's inability to rank the importance of goals.
   C. the other emperors' mismanagement of the Roman army.
   D. Justinian's failed attempts to conquer areas of Africa.

2. According to the author, a significant difference between the economic impacts of the Bubonic Plague and the failings of the military was that:
   F. Justinian's mismanagement of military spending led to a period of growth following the onset of the plague.
   G. Justinian's costly response to the plague did not hamper his spending plan to improve the status of the military.
   H. the impact of the plague was worsened by an economic downturn that was initially the result of military failures.
   J. the impact of the failing military was worsened as a result of the economic downturn caused by the plague.

3. According to the author, the significant difference between the plague and the damaged aqueducts is that only one:
   A. had a direct impact on the economy of the Roman Empire.
   B. was a hardship suffered by Roman citizens under Justinian's rule.
   C. contributed to the end of the Roman Empire.
   D. could be cited as a major failure of Justinian himself.

4. The author compares the collection of property taxes during a growing economy and during an economic downturn, and states that one way in which property tax collection differed during the growing economy was that:
   F. property tax collection rates increased significantly.
   G. it was not worth the Empire's time to collect property taxes in Constantinople.
   H. John the Economist was doubtful that property tax collection would balance the Roman budget.
   J. complete property tax collection was not necessary to find enough money to run the Empire.

5. In the last paragraph the author alludes to but apparently does NOT share which of the following points of view?
   A. The plague put further pressure on Justinian to reduce military expenditures and thus forced him to relocate several of his generals.
   B. Belisarius was frequently reassigned because of Justinian's poor planning.
   C. It was a tactical mistake to recall Belisarius from his position in the west, because the implications of such a move were not fully considered.
   D. Justinian lacked the ability to formulate and execute objectives for the Empire.

ANSWERS AND EXPLANATIONS

IDENTIFY TOPIC, SCOPE, AND PURPOSE—MAIN IDEA

You might have arrived at slightly different answers. The idea with these exercises is to learn to quickly identify the main idea of a reading passage.

1. **TOPIC:** Global Warming

    SCOPE: It is nearly impossible to measure slight variations in global temperatures therefore global warming is not a serious issue.

    PURPOSE: To show that there is no way to prove that humans are responsible for the increase in temperatures, nor should we expect catastrophic consequences from minor temperature increases.

2. **TOPIC:** King Louis XIV

    SCOPE: His accomplishments and expansion of power.

    PURPOSE: To identify the lasting effects of his reign both at home and abroad, potentially including the French Revolution.

3. **TOPIC:** Frank Franzetta's art

    SCOPE: The unique style of his lifelike, yet extreme characters that transcends his art's commercial roots.

    PURPOSE: To express the opinion that Franzetta has influenced a generation of artists, and one day his work will be studied like that of the great masters is today.

4. **TOPIC:** Charles A. Lindbergh

    SCOPE: His less than impressive formal education.

    PURPOSE: To show that his New York-to-Paris flight was a mark of his personal determination and ingenuity, despite his lack of education.

5. **TOPIC:** The first Americans

    SCOPE: There is considerable disagreement over who was here first.

    PURPOSE: To point out that science has proven that people were here for thousands of years prior to the discovery of North America by formal expeditions.

LOCATE AND INTERPRET SIGNIFICANT DETAILS

1. **The best answer is B.** As stated in the passage, Sir Isaac Newton "… was the first to promulgate a set of natural laws governing both terrestrial and celestial motion …." This best supports answer choice B.

2. **The best answer is F.** Of the four questions asked in the answer choices, only answer choice F is not addressed by the passage. Answer choice G is addressed in lines 10–12: "… while still a student at Cambridge, he read works on optics and light by the English physicists Robert Boyle and Robert Hooke …." Answer choice H is addressed in lines 6–7: "… Noted for his achievements in exploring and defining gravitational forces…." Answer choice J is answered in lines 11–13: "he … discovered measurable patterns in the light refracted by a glass prism." While the passage discusses Newton's ingenuity in designing a telescope mirror, it does not identify the type of telescope mirror, so answer choice F is the best answer.

3. **The best answer is C.** According to the passage, Newton "… postulated that light consisted of streams of minute particles." The adjective "minute" means "very small." The other answer choices are not supported by details in the passage.

4. **The best answer is H.** As stated in the passage, "… Sir Isaac Newton is known today as a brilliant scientist, who helped to advance the fields of mathematics, astronomy, chemistry, and physics." Of the four answer choices, astrology is the only field not listed.

5. **The best answer is D.** According to the passage, as it relates to Newton's particle theory, "attempts to publish this unconventional idea were thwarted by critics." The other answer choices are not supported by details in the passage.

UNDERSTAND SEQUENCES OF EVENTS AND COMPREHEND CAUSE–EFFECT RELATIONSHIPS

1. **The best answer is C.** According to the passage, research into the effects of biological processes on human emotion was fueled by the question of "… how much of a role nature plays in controlling human behavior." This best supports answer choice C.

2. **The best answer is F.** According to the second paragraph of the passage, "… PEA stimulates and increases brain activity in general and seems to work on some specific areas of the brain that are associated with feelings of love in its early stages. This biological process may help to explain the emotional highs that human beings feel when they experience infatuation …." Based on this information, PEA is responsible for the human emotion of infatuation. Without PEA and its stimulation of various parts

of the brain, one can assume that humans wouldn't experience infatuation.

3. **The best answer is B.** As indicated by the passage, in regard to PEA, "… the body can sometimes become addicted to these neurological chemicals, and feel depressed and 'down' without near constant re-release of the chemicals." Based on this information, you can infer that this depression is caused by a lack of PEA.

4. **The best answer is J.** According to the passage, "lovesick" men and women were treated with MAO inhibitors. "These drugs helped to boost the levels of PEA in the brains of these patients …. As a result, these subjects soon reported a less-perceived need for affection from others." This information demonstrates a cause-effect relationship. If lovesick people take MAO inhibitors, they will experience a reduction in perceived emotional need.

5. **The best answer is C.** According to the passage, "… the body can sometimes become addicted to these neurological chemicals, and feel depressed and 'down'…." The passage then goes on to say that "lovesick" individuals have a "specific craving for PEA." Based on this information, you can infer that psychiatrists think "lovesick" individuals are addicted to neurological chemicals, specifically PEA.

DETERMINE THE MEANING OF WORDS, PHRASES, AND STATEMENTS IN CONTEXT

1. **The best answer is B.** As it is used in the passage, the *hands-off approach* most nearly means allowing nature to manage itself. This can be determined from the following: "… a hands-off approach isn't always the best one. For example, nature uses fire to assist in maintaining the proper balance of underbrush, new-growth trees, and other vegetation, but allowing a naturally occurring fire to burn out of control could be devastating to both wildlife and humans in nearby communities."

2. **The best answer is H.** Based on the information in the passage, *stewardship* is used in regard to how humans interact with and care for the earth. Answer choice F can be eliminated because the passage is about humans' interaction with the environment, rather than a household. Because the word *good* is used with *stewardship*, you can infer that stewardship is a positive way to care for the earth. Answer choice J is negative, so it can be eliminated. The passage speaks more generally to the environment as a whole than to animals, so answer choice G can be eliminated. The remaining result, choice H, *responsible care-taking of resources*, is the best answer.

3. **The best answer is A.** According to the second paragraph, "Controlled burning, a human intervention, can be used to contain such fires. However, it cannot be done on land with dense underbrush and an overabundance of small, new-growth trees … *Workers must 'knock down' the fuel load* before the fire is introduced; otherwise, the fire will burn uncontrollably." Based on this information, in order for a controlled burning to take place, *workers must knock down the fuel load* by removing dense underbrush and new-growth trees.

4. **The best answer is G.** According to information in the first paragraph, "While some claim that modern society *infringes* on the environment, there are others who believe that good stewardship of the earth and environmentalism can go hand in hand." The context of the passage suggests a comparison because of the introductory word "while": "*infringes*" versus "good stewardship of the earth and environmentalism." Because "good" is attached to "stewardship of the earth and environmentalism," you can infer that "*infringes*" will have a negative connotation. The definition of *infringe* is to "violate or engage in trespassing," which best fits the context of the passage.

5. **The best answer is C.** According to the passage, the California landowner doesn't agree with the environmental laws. "Sometimes current environmental laws don't make sense to me. If I failed to get rid of the trash on my property, I'd be in violation of zoning regulations. *To my way of thinking*, underbrush and excess new-growth trees are nature's garbage, yet many want us to let it just pile up." The context indicates that the landowner is expressing an opinion or belief, which best supports answer choice C.

DRAW GENERALIZATIONS

1. **The best answer is C.** Throughout the passage, Mrs. Fairfax expresses surprise over the news of Miss Eyre's and Mr. Rochester's engagement. Statements made by Mrs. Fairfax such as, "I feel so astonished," and, "It passes me!" as well as details like, "She looked at me bewildered," demonstrate Mrs. Fairfax's surprise. Furthermore, the passage states that, regarding Jane, Mrs. Fairfax "surveyed my whole person: in her eyes I read that they had there found no charm powerful enough to solve the enigma." Throughout the passage Mrs. Fairfax's skepticism is noted.

2. **The best answer is J.** Miss Eyre responds to Mrs. Fairfax's questions with a sense of decisiveness. When asked if she accepted Rochester's request for marriage, Miss Eyre replied with a simple, "Yes." In regard to Mrs. Fairfax's comparison of

Mr. Rochester to Miss Eyre's father, Miss Eyre replied, "No, indeed, Mrs. Fairfax!... he is nothing like my father! No one, who saw us together, would suppose it for an instant. Mr. Rochester looks as young, and is as young, as some men at five and twenty." These statements reflect Miss Eyre's sense of *self-assuredness* in regard to her relationship with Mr. Rochester.

3. **The best answer is D.** The statement made by Mrs. Fairfax indicates that she is unsure of the outcome of a marriage between Miss Eyre and Mr. Rochester because there seems to be no "equality of position and fortune." Answer choice D best paraphrases this sentiment. Although the passage indicates that Mrs. Fairfax believed Miss Eyre and Mr. Rochester should not marry, it is not because she thinks Mr. Rochester is not good enough for Miss Eyre, making answer choice A incorrect.

4. **The best answer is H.** As stated in the passage, "He is a proud man; all the Rochesters were proud: and his father at least, liked money. He, too, has always been called careful." *Wary* means *watchful* or *cautious*, which is similar to *careful*. In addition, Mr. Rochester is referred to as one who is *careful* with money, which means that he is aware of and sparing with his finances. The word *frugal* means *economical in expenditure*, so answer choice H makes the most sense.

5. **The best answer is B.** In regard to Mrs. Fairfax, Miss Eyre says, "I was so hurt by her coldness and skepticism, that the tears rose to my eyes." This statement marks the pain that Miss Eyre felt as a result of Mrs. Fairfax's doubt and best supports answer choice B.

ANALYZE THE AUTHOR'S OR NARRATOR'S VOICE AND METHOD

1. **The best answer is D.** The passage states, "Sometimes I find a fallen log or a huge boulder perfect for sitting. … In silence, I ponder the natural system at play, and in occasional moments of lucidity, words pour from my brain to my hand to my notepad." Based on this information, you can infer that sitting on a boulder provides the author with great *lucidity*, or *clearness of mind*. It is during this time that the author is able to write freely.

2. **The best answer is F.** While the passage is about backpacking, the focus of the narrative is not the physical activity of backpacking itself, but rather the effect this physical activity has on the author's state of mind and creativity. Answer choices G, H, and J all address this idea.

3. **The best answer is A.** The first paragraph provides a background into the author's love of backpacking. The author begins with a detail about how backpacking used to be "a tedious, tiring activity," but then moves on to explain why it's become a favorite part of summer. The author closes the paragraph by detailing a personal goal: "I now seek harmony with the Earth through immersion in its scenic riches." As a whole, this paragraph gives insight into why the author loves backpacking, and helps to set up the rest of the passage.

4. **The best answer is F.** In regard to nature photography the author states, "For me, a picture isn't worth a thousand words. A journal of reflections imbued with nature's spectacle is far more valuable." Based on this information, you can infer that the author feels pictures lack the ability to detail nature in the same meaningful way that writing can.

5. **The best answer is C.** The first paragraph details a conversation held between the author and a fellow hiker the author happened to encounter ("crossed paths"). This conversation helped the author reach a conclusion about nature: "I understood what he meant. In the wilderness is found physical and spiritual sustenance, so every step along the trail brings you closer to peace." The other answer choices are not supported by information in the passage.

MAKE COMPARISONS AND CONTRASTS

1. **The best answer is B.** As stated in the passage, "The prolonged wars' impact on the treasury of the empire was a result of several factors. For one, Justinian appeared to have difficulty establishing priorities." Based on this information, you can conclude that Justinian displayed an inability to rank the importance of his goals.

2. **The best answer is H.** The passage states that, "The plague ended the period of economic growth and worsened the problems caused by resources that were already stretched too thin." According to the passage, resources were stretched thin because of Justinian's prolonged wars. This information best supports answer choice H.

3. **The best answer is D.** Based on information in the passage, both the Aqueduct damage and the Bubonic Plague had a significant impact on the Roman Empire's economy during Justinian's reign. The Aqueducts' damage returned many parts of the countryside to marshes, and the Bubonic Plague ended economic growth and worsened the problems caused by resources already stretched to the breaking point. While both of these factors played a significant

role in the destruction of the Roman Empire, only the damages to the Aqueducts were faulted directly to Justinian himself. Justinian didn't handle the aftermath of the plague well, but he had no control over its onset.

4. **The best answer is J.** In regard to property tax collection in a growing economy the passage states, "The plague ended the period of economic growth during which locating funds hadn't been a problem, even when all of the property taxes were not collected." This suggests that complete property tax collection was not necessary during times of economic growth; there was money to be found elsewhere.

5. **The best answer is B.** The passage states, "Some historians also report that Justinian never appeared to have a clear battle plan of action for his conquests." As a result, it is implied, Belisarius was frequently reassigned to different areas of the country. However, the author seems not to agree with other historians when he states, "This erratic use of resources is more likely a result of Justinian's inability to set priorities than of his lack of planning." The author alludes to the possibility that Justinian's lack of planning resulted in Belisarius' frequent reassignments, but then rejects that option in favor of Justinian's inability to set priorities.

WHAT'S NEXT?

Chapters 13 and 14 present simulated ACT Reading Tests. Apply the strategies and techniques you learned in the previous chapters to correctly answer as many of these questions as possible in the time allowed.

CHAPTER 13

ACT READING PRACTICE TEST 1

This chapter will allow you to practice the ACT Reading Test strategies that were introduced in the earlier chapters of this book. Make an honest effort to answer each question and review the explanations that follow. Review Chapter 10, "Speed Reading," Chapter 11, "Strategies and Techniques," and Chapter 12, "Applying Strategies, Building Skills," as necessary.

ACT READING PRACTICE TEST 1
Answer Sheet

READING

1 (A) (B) (C) (D)	11 (A) (B) (C) (D)	21 (A) (B) (C) (D)	31 (A) (B) (C) (D)
2 (F) (G) (H) (J)	12 (F) (G) (H) (J)	22 (F) (G) (H) (J)	32 (F) (G) (H) (J)
3 (A) (B) (C) (D)	13 (A) (B) (C) (D)	23 (A) (B) (C) (D)	33 (A) (B) (C) (D)
4 (F) (G) (H) (J)	14 (F) (G) (H) (J)	24 (F) (G) (H) (J)	34 (F) (G) (H) (J)
5 (A) (B) (C) (D)	15 (A) (B) (C) (D)	25 (A) (B) (C) (D)	35 (A) (B) (C) (D)
6 (F) (G) (H) (J)	16 (F) (G) (H) (J)	26 (F) (G) (H) (J)	36 (F) (G) (H) (J)
7 (A) (B) (C) (D)	17 (A) (B) (C) (D)	27 (A) (B) (C) (D)	37 (A) (B) (C) (D)
8 (F) (G) (H) (J)	18 (F) (G) (H) (J)	28 (F) (G) (H) (J)	38 (F) (G) (H) (J)
9 (A) (B) (C) (D)	19 (A) (B) (C) (D)	29 (A) (B) (C) (D)	39 (A) (B) (C) (D)
10 (F) (G) (H) (J)	20 (F) (G) (H) (J)	30 (F) (G) (H) (J)	40 (F) (G) (H) (J)

READING TEST

35 Minutes—40 Questions

DIRECTIONS: This test includes four passages, each followed by ten questions. Read each passage and choose the best answer to each question. After you have selected your answer, fill in the corresponding bubble on your answer sheet. You should refer to the passages as often as necessary when answering the questions.

Passage I
PROSE FICTION: Painful Memories

Fifteen years had passed since she'd seen her father and five since she'd even heard from him. After what he'd done to her mother, that suited Nina fine. Embarrassed to call him her father, she simply referred to him
5 as "Rick." It helped her to ignore the biological ties she hated so much. After the death of her mother two years ago, Nina thought she had abandoned her father's memory altogether. That is, until the phone call came.

"I'm sorry to bother you, ma'am, but are you Nina
10 Sanders?" a barely audible voice whispered over the phone.

"What?" Nina asked. "I can't hear you."

"I'm sorry." He sounded contrite. "Are you Nina Sanders?"

15 "Yes, I am. What can I do for you?" Nina turned to lean against the kitchen table. Noticing a scuffmark on the floor, she began rubbing at it with her shoe.

The voice grew louder. "I'm sorry to have to bother you like this, Nina. My name is Jack VanSetten. I was a
20 friend of your father's, Rick Sanders."

Nina looked up from the floor. "What does he want?" she asked, her voice becoming hard.

"Well, it's just … I know you two weren't exactly close or.…"

25 "That's the understatement of the year," Nina muttered. She looked back down. The scuffmark had refused to budge.

"What?" Jack asked.

"Nothing." Nina forced her voice back to neutral.
30 "So why are you calling me? I haven't talked to the guy in five years, and frankly, I like it that way."

"I understand, it's just … Nina, he died yesterday."

There was silence on the line. Nina's stomach began to turn. She felt the grilled cheese sandwich she'd had
35 for lunch begin to work its way up the back of her throat.

Jack coughed and continued, "He asked that you make the memorial arrangements."

Nina felt all of the blood rush from her head. Gripping the kitchen table to steady herself, she asked,
40 "Why?"

"I don't know, Nina. He just—the cancer made him think a lot. He just said he wanted you to do the memorial arrangements, and I promised him that I'd take care of it," Jack's voice had steadied itself again.

45 "Well, Jack, that's your problem, not mine. I'm not doing anything for him."

"Please, at least consider it. He was your father."

"No, he wasn't. At least, not for a long time."

"Nina, please. You were all he had. I mean, after
50 you and your mother left …."

"Don't you dare put blame on my mom and me! You don't even know us!" Nina could hear her voice rising in anger.

"I'm sorry. I wasn't trying to. I just …." Jack paused
55 a moment. "Nina, his life fell apart. You know that. But the man's dead now. Can't you give him a break? Please, Nina, do this one thing." She could hear the pleading in his quiet voice.

"Why should I?" she asked.

60 "There is no good reason, Nina, except that you have a chance to be the bigger person. Stop punishing him. I can help a little, but he asked for you."

It was Jack's turn to wait. Nina began chewing on her thumbnail, a nervous habit she'd had for as long as
65 she could remember. She didn't want to do anything for her father, even if he was dead, but for some reason she knew she had to. Maybe it was the grilled cheese, or maybe it was the knotting in her stomach, but something made her feel like she had no choice. She let the silence
70 fill the line between them, then, finally, answered.

"Fine."

"Fine?"

GO ON TO THE NEXT PAGE.

███████████████████████████████████████

"Yeah, fine."

"Thanks, Nina." His relief was palpable. Nina hated
75 him for it.

"Whatever," she said, and then hung up the phone.

Now, a week later, all Nina wanted to do was crawl
into bed, pull the sheets over her head, and not come
out for days. Instead, she grabbed a spoon out of the
80 dishwasher and, plunging it into a carton of ice cream,
let herself collapse on the living room couch. After fum-
bling around for the remote control, Nina flipped on
the TV, not really watching it. Cradling the ice cream
carton, she leaned her head against the couch and sighed
85 heavily. The funeral had been awful, but at least now
it was over. Nina's body became still as she sadly
muttered three short words, "My father's dead."

1. Which of the following best describes the structure of
the passage?
   A. A dialogue between two people attempting to deal
   with an unsettling situation.
   B. An account of the narrator's relationship with her
   father, revealed through their conversations.
   C. A character sketch of two people as related by a
   narrator who knows them both well.
   D. A detailed narration of the dynamics that exist
   between the narrator and certain members of her
   family.

2. It can be reasonably inferred from the beginning of the
passage that Nina views Rick as:
   F. her loving father.
   G. a close family friend.
   H. just another individual.
   J. an acquaintance of her father.

3. The passage states that, prior to the phone call, Nina had
done which of the following with the memory of her
father?
   A. Abandoned it altogether
   B. Recalled it fondly
   C. Escaped it completely
   D. Cherished it dearly

4. In line 13, the passage states that the man on the phone
sounded "contrite," which most nearly means that the
man was:
   F. patiently tolerant.
   G. quietly difficult.
   H. sincerely apologetic.
   J. especially pensive.

5. As depicted in the fifth paragraph, Nina's fixation on the
scuffmark most strongly suggests that:
   A. she was nervous about talking to Jack.
   B. she was not focused on the phone call.
   C. she maintained a remarkably clean home.
   D. she had been expecting this call for days.

6. Which of the following statements about why Rick
Sanders wanted Jack to call Nina is supported by the
passage?
   F. Rick's illness led to a change of heart.
   G. Jack convinced Rick to reconcile with his daughter.
   H. Jack and Nina had lost touch over the past ten years.
   J. Nina recently had been trying to contact Rick.

7. According to the passage, Nina responded to the news of
her father's death with:
   A. profound grief.
   B. heartless indifference.
   C. shock and apprehension.
   D. joy and relief.

8. Details in lines 41–44 most strongly suggest that Jack:
   F. does not care what Nina decides.
   G. thinks that Nina is being selfish.
   H. believes that Rick and Nina were close.
   J. wants to honor his promise to Rick.

9. Which of the following statements most nearly captures
the sentiment behind the comment "Nina hated him for it"
(lines 74–75)?
   A. Nina was offended by what Jack had said about her
   father.
   B. Nina was relieved by Jack's answer.
   C. Nina did not want the responsibility thrust upon her
   by Jack.
   D. Nina felt as though she had been exploited by Jack.

10. It can be reasonably inferred from the last paragraph
(lines 77–87) that Nina:
   F. ultimately wished that she had refused to make the
   memorial arrangements.
   G. ultimately felt grief in response to the death of her
   father.
   H. does not deal well with death in general.
   J. had spent weeks pretending that her father was still
   alive.

GO ON TO THE NEXT PAGE.

Passage II
SOCIAL SCIENCE: Federalism: Protector of Freedom

Federalism has evolved dramatically since its roots in the writings of Calvinist philosopher Johannes Althusius (1557–1630). Nevertheless, proponents of federalism continue to believe that governing authority is
5 best when it is divided between a central governing body and semi-autonomous subunits. In modern federal societies, the powers and authority granted to the subunits and central body vary greatly. In general, however, the center is responsible for defending its subunits and
10 creating a national foreign policy. It also serves to create a cohesive, though not restrictive, domestic policy.

In practice, federal power is constitutionally divided between two or more territorial levels of government, such as state and county. The different levels
15 of government have some absolute authority and can act independently in certain areas of governing, though they must cede power in other areas. A useful example is the United States of America, which comprises fifty states and assorted territories, each with their own set of
20 legal codes, united under one central government with an overarching set of laws. Americans must follow the laws of both their state and federal governments, while the governments themselves have the responsibility to avoid overt conflict within those laws. Sometimes, as
25 is the case with euthanasia or medical marijuana, conflicts still occur. Resolution is left to the courts of law. Federalism differs fundamentally from other types of government, such as France's essentially single level of authority. While France has regional departments, the
30 country is heavily centralized in its daily governance and the departments cannot set their own regional laws. Federalism is not, therefore, a prerequisite for successful government; nevertheless, properly executed federalism can result in an improved quality of life for all citizens.

35 Proponents of federalism have promoted the idea that federalism protects liberty and freedom. It is certainly true that states can avert foreign threats and prevent war by joining together and becoming powerful enough to discourage enemies from attacking them. This
40 was a strong incentive for the original thirteen American colonies. In addition, federalism can prevent conflict and aggression among the states themselves. A good example of this occurred in the early nineteenth century border dispute between the state of Ohio and the then-territory
45 of Michigan. The dispute, known as the Toledo War (or Ohio-Michigan War), arose when the governments of Ohio and Michigan both claimed sovereignty over a thin strip of land along their mutual border. When Michigan included the strip in its application for statehood, Ohio's
50 Congressional delegation was able to halt Michigan's admission to the Union. Both sides then raised militia and placed troops along the disputed border. The federal government was able to broker a successful compromise that avoided armed conflict and allowed Michigan to
55 join the United States peaceably. As Ohio was able to effectively influence federal policy to protect its own interests, this example further shows how federalism allows formerly sovereign governments of small states to have influence as a subunit. In other words, as a
60 subunit, even a small state can gain limited autonomy by having a voice in the central government.

Federalism can also protect minorities and individuals against injustice from their local governing bodies or from the central government itself. The center has
65 the authority to check the power of its subunits and intervene when necessary. In theory, the center will protect all of its citizens from any subunit injustice, as was the case with the American civil rights movement. In turn, the subunits can band together to protest any
70 injustice done by the central governing body. In the case that minorities are not powerful enough to influence central government directly, they are likely to have influence through their subunit governments. Ideally, broad political participation keeps the system fair for
75 all citizens.

Federalism does more than protect freedoms and democracy. It can also promote economic prosperity. Normally, federal states have freer trade among themselves than they would have as completely independent
80 states. Small states can band together and create larger and more prosperous economies by sharing and trading natural resources. Finally, federalist states can also use their unity to bargain with otherwise larger and more powerful nations. In theory, all of this promotes
85 economic competitiveness in an increasingly global economy. In practice, one can see the need to be economically competitive as the underlying impetus for the creation of the European Union.

11. According to the passage, the conclusion made about the limited autonomy gained by a small state was based on:
   A. Michigan's desire to gain control over Ohio during the Ohio-Michigan War.
   B. Ohio's ability to influence federal policy to protect its own interests.
   C. Michigan's admission to the Union.
   D. Ohio's economic competitiveness in an increasingly global economy.

12. The main idea of the first paragraph is that the success of federalism stems from:
   F. the ability of the federal government to create a restrictive domestic policy.
   G. the absolute freedom of state governments on issues within their borders.
   H. the division of power between a central authority and several smaller groups.
   J. the concentration, at the state level, of foreign policy decisions.

13. The author cites all of the following as positive aspects of federalism EXCEPT:
   A. duplication of various legal codes.
   B. reduction of conflict between the states.
   C. promotion of economic prosperity.
   D. defense of minority rights and freedoms.

GO ON TO THE NEXT PAGE.

14. The author calls the interactions between a central governing body and semi-autonomous subunits:
 F. economically unsound.
 G. supportive of cohesive domestic policy.
 H. disruptive of national foreign policy.
 J. politically unjust.

15. Which of the following is NOT listed in the passage as a development in the Toledo War?
 A. Michigan and Ohio placed militia along the disputed border.
 B. Michigan claimed the land in its application for statehood.
 C. Ohio ceded the entire strip of land to Michigan.
 D. Ohio's congressional delegation halted Michigan's statehood.

16. As it is used in line 26, the word *resolution* most nearly means:
 F. clarity.
 G. opinion.
 H. reduction.
 J. decision.

17. By the statement in line 32, the author most nearly means that France:
 A. is an example of quality government without the separation of powers.
 B. should be emulated despite the lack of regional autonomy.
 C. will eventually adopt federalism as its primary form of government.
 D. would gain greater international respect by switching to federalism.

18. The author calls the American civil rights movement an example of:
 F. the subunits protecting the citizens.
 G. the subunits protecting each other.
 H. the center protecting the citizens.
 J. the center protecting the subunits.

19. The author claims that which of the following will keep the system fair for all parties?
 A. Economic isolation
 B. Completely independent states
 C. Retention of natural resources
 D. Broad political participation

20. The author uses the remark "one can see the need to be economically competitive as the underlying impetus for the creation of the European Union" (lines 86–88) primarily as an example of:
 F. the failure of other schools of thought to address the problems presented by international trade.
 G. the ability of federalism to respond to a changing global economy.
 H. the potential weakness of federalism when faced with a unification of national subunits.
 J. the application of various principles of federalism so as to ensure mutual defense.

GO ON TO THE NEXT PAGE.

Passage III
HUMANITIES: *The Canterbury Tales:* Opinions on gender and marriage

Geoffrey Chaucer was one of the most successful poets of the fourteenth century and one of the few medieval authors whose influence extends to the popular culture of today. Chaucer's most renowned work
5 is unquestionably *The Canterbury Tales*, a collection of short stories linked together by a pilgrimage from London to the holy site at Canterbury, England. The pilgrimage was very popular in Chaucer's day and allowed the author to bring together a few dozen characters from
10 various social classes and walks of life. Some of the characters, like the Host, Harry Bailly, are based on real people. Others, like the Parson, are little more than archetypes. The poem itself is unfinished and contains several inconsistencies that reflect the need for further
15 revision. Still, *The Canterbury Tales* remains popular because of its vivid characters and fascinating vignettes. Among these stories, *The Wife of Bath* has stood out as the most controversial and interesting of them all. Medieval scholars have tirelessly studied *The Wife of
20 Bath* in order to capture the main character's meaning.

Upon first reading, the main character—Alyson, the Wife—appears to embody the very fears of medieval clerical misogyny, or, by the same acts, to be a true representation of a stereotypic feminist. Alyson insists
25 on speaking her mind (loudly), rejecting the negative opinions and sexual constraints traditionally placed upon women. She is lewd, and has the audacity to use *The Bible* to attack clerical arguments from *The Bible* dealing with chastity and virginity. In the Middle Ages, a preaching
30 woman could be considered heretical and burned at the stake. With this in mind, the Wife may have a good reason for keeping her sense of humor.

And she does have a sense of humor. Alyson is well aware of her own failings, even as she defends those
35 faults to the company. As for her verbosity, the Wife says she can't help it: all women talk too much. For proof, she later cites the famous story of King Midas, who was given ass's ears as punishment by the god, Apollo. Midas, she says, told his misfortune to his wife, who,
40 afraid she would burst from keeping the secret, whispered it to the banks of a river where it spread over the country. The Wife tells her listeners they can read the rest in *Ovid*. But here is where the Wife's account diverges. In *Ovid*, Midas trusts his secret to his barber,
45 a man. It is a man who cannot keep the secret safe, who talks too much. Moreover, Midas has received the ass's ears because he was unable to listen wisely. Chaucer doesn't tell us if we should believe that Alyson is an ignorant illiterate who doesn't know her *Ovid*, or if she is subtly
50 tweaking the critics who think men are inherently superior to women.

Dovetailing neatly with the themes of her prologue is the story Alyson tells her fellow pilgrims. In many ways, it is a traditional Arthurian romance. The
55 protagonist of the story, a young knight, commits an assault. In order to save himself from capital punishment, he is allowed to go on a one-year quest to discover what women most desire. The simple answer, he learns, is *maistrie*, or authority, over their husbands.
60 But in Chaucer nothing is simple. When the knight is at last convinced to give *maistrie* to his own wife, she surprises him by promising to be obedient, faithful, and loving. The dichotomy of power, of male versus female, is destroyed in the act of surrender.

65 Is this Chaucer's recipe for social harmony, or is it merely wish fulfillment on the part of the Wife herself? Literary scholars have desperately tried to discover Chaucer's own views of marriage and society through his characters. Their pursuit, often as tangled as Chaucer's own narrative, allows us to consider yet again the questions Chaucer asks of us.

21. Which of the following statements best expresses the main idea of the passage?
   A. The mix of interesting characters and events in the Canterbury Tales serves as a lasting legacy for English poet Geoffrey Chaucer.
   B. Analyzing the Wife of Bath's prologue and tale has allowed scholars to definitively understand Chaucer's opinions on marriage.
   C. The Wife of Bath is an incredibly interesting character who continues to be a topic of scholarly discussion.
   D. The prologue of the Wife of Bath's tale was a shocking feminist critique of society, written centuries ahead of its time.

22. The passage suggests that Chaucer's most important contributions to literature were his:
   F. simple narratives revealing the inconsistencies of human nature.
   G. innovative writing techniques, used to relate historical fiction.
   H. easily reproduced theatrical manuscripts and creative subject matter.
   J. dynamic characters and memorable vignettes, used to present social commentary.

23. One of the main points of the last paragraph is that through his writing, Chaucer attempted to promote in his readers a sense of:
   A. mystery.
   B. nostalgia.
   C. respect.
   D. trust.

24. The author states that the pilgrimage allowed Chaucer to bring together all of the following EXCEPT:
   F. caricatures of real people.
   G. successful poets of the fourteenth century.
   H. archetypal characterizations.
   J. characters of differing social classes.

25. The author most likely includes the information in lines 47–51 to suggest:
   A. the Wife's ignorance and lack of proper education.
   B. the many interpretations of certain aspects of *The Canterbury Tales*.
   C. Chaucer's inability to retell mythological history.
   D. Chaucer's exceptional skill in misdirection.

GO ON TO THE NEXT PAGE.

26. According to the passage, the fact that *The Canterbury Tales* had several inconsistencies reflected:
    F. Chaucer's inexperience at writing a collection of stories.
    G. an intentional attempt by the author to be vague and mysterious.
    H. the unfinished state of the piece and a need for revision.
    J. a lack of depth, and characters who changed their stories frequently.

27. The second paragraph (lines 21–32) establishes all of the following about the Wife EXCEPT:
    A. she is in favor of accepted clerical viewpoints.
    B. she is in favor of women's sexual freedom.
    C. she is considerably vulgar.
    D. she is incredibly opinionated.

28. As it is used in line 35, the word *verbosity* most nearly means:
    F. excessive speech.
    G. unnecessary volume.
    H. polite brevity.
    J. refined voice.

29. According to the passage, which of the following was the wife of Midas afraid of?
    A. Failing to spread the secret
    B. Listening to the god Apollo
    C. Lying to her husband
    D. Telling the secret

30. Which of the following words best describes how the knight referred to in the fourth paragraph (lines 52–64) most likely feels when his wife surrenders to him?
    F. Optimistic
    G. Frustrated
    H. Virtuous
    J. Complete

GO ON TO THE NEXT PAGE.

Passage IV
NATURAL SCIENCE: *The following passages discuss different points of view regarding Pluto's status as a planet.*

Passage A

Until recently, Pluto has been considered a planet. Most astronomers now argue that it is more accurately categorized as an asteroid or comet. However, some evidence remains to suggest that Pluto was prematurely stripped
5 of its planetary status.

The solar system's asteroid belt is a remnant of the proplyd, or protoplanetary disk, that preceded the planets. Gravitational interference by Jupiter prevented some material from consolidating in the process that created the
10 planets. Included in the leftover material are asteroids—solid objects much smaller than any planet—with masses that vary considerably. The largest of the known asteroids are found in the main asteroid belt between the orbits of Mars and Jupiter, and not at the fringe of the inner
15 solar system where Pluto resides.

Another example of non-planetary objects, comets, are thought to originate in the Oort cloud, a massive area of comet nuclei occupying the outer reaches of the solar system. It is theorized to have formed following the col-
20 lapse of the original nebula that formed the sun five billion years ago. According to the hypothesis, comet nuclei are stable at the outer reaches of the solar system until interaction with planetary gravitation—usually Pluto's—causes a comet to enter a highly elliptical orbit around
25 the sun. As a comet nears the sun, a tail becomes visible as light reflects off the trail of ice particles and dust it leaves behind. Several passes through the solar system destroy the comet, which is replaced by another of the billions of comets orbiting in the Oort cloud. Pluto shows
30 no tail at any point in its circuit.

Additionally, with a diameter of more than 1,400 miles, Pluto is almost 1,000 times larger than an average comet and more than twice the size of 1 Ceres, the largest of the asteroids, which comprises nearly a third of the
35 total mass of the asteroid belt.

A planet can be described as a non-moon, sun-orbiting object that does not generate energy through nuclear fusion and is large enough to be pulled into a spherical shape by its own gravity. Pluto is not a moon,
40 as it does not orbit another planet. Although Pluto's orbital path is irregular compared to the other planets of the solar system, it undisputedly orbits the sun. Even by strict definition alone, Pluto is a planet, and assuredly not an asteroid or a comet.

Passage B

45 In 2006, Pluto was demoted from a planet to a "dwarf planet." It is now considered a member of the Kuiper

Belt, which is a group of substantial comets at the edge of the solar system. Kuiper belt, scattered disk, and Oort cloud objects together comprise the large trans-Neptunian
50 objects, which are the least understood celestial bodies in the solar system. As such, much care must be taken in the classification of phenomena in distant orbits of the sun. Calling Pluto a planet—on par with the other eight planets in our solar system—is an ideal example of jumping to
55 unfounded conclusions because of erroneous or incomplete science.

First, Pluto is composed of icy material, as are the comets in the Kuiper Belt, while the other planets of the solar system are either rocky or gaseous. Mercury, Venus,
60 Earth, and Mars are small, rocky, and near the sun. Jupiter, Saturn, Uranus, and Neptune are larger, gaseous, and more distant from the sun. As a small, solid body farthest from the sun, Pluto seems to violate the natural order obeyed by the eight true planets.

65 Likewise, the discovery of trans-Neptunian object (TNO) 2003 UB_{313} which is similar in composition and orbit to Pluto, shows Pluto is unlike the other planets. This celestial body, which orbits the sun beyond Neptune, is even more massive than Pluto. Contemporary observa-
70 tions show that Pluto is much too small to be a planet. It is less than half the diameter of the next smallest planet, Mercury. Seven moons, including Earth's, are larger than Pluto. The body is so small, in fact, that all of its own moons have likely yet to be discovered. The latest two
75 were found in 2005, and only after reexamining Hubble Space Telescope imagery from 2002 and 2003 in which the moons were overlooked.

Finally, the eccentricity of Pluto's orbit indicates that it is not a planet. While commonly considered the ninth
80 planet, for 20 years of its 249-year orbit, Pluto is actually closer to the sun than is Neptune, placing it in eighth position. More than 70 Kuiper Belt comets share this irregular orbit, proving Pluto is more similar to them than to proper planets.

Questions 31–34 ask about Passage A.

31. Lines 21–30 suggest that, for defenders of Pluto's planetary status, "a highly elliptical orbit" and "a tail" are held to be:
A. mutually exclusive.
B. crucial comet features.
C. unpredictably variable.
D. essential planet attributes.

32. In line 30, "circuit" most nearly means:
F. mass.
G. current.
H. ice particle.
J. cyclic motion.

GO ON TO THE NEXT PAGE.

33. In Passage A, all of the following are referred to as evidence of Pluto's planetary status EXCEPT the:
   A. existence of moons orbiting Pluto.
   B. orbit of Pluto exclusively around the sun.
   C. visible tail of dust and ice, which Pluto does not have.
   D. size of Pluto compared with that of comets and asteroids.

34. The author of Passage A considers Pluto's size (lines 32–35) as evidence for it being a planet because:
   F. planets vary greatly by mass.
   G. it is significantly larger than any known asteroid.
   H. its gravitation destroys the orbit of Oort cloud comets.
   J. very few large comets and asteroids have been discovered.

Questions 35–37 ask about Passage B.

35. In context, "substantial" (line 47) most nearly means:
   A. large.
   B. valid.
   C. durable.
   D. corporeal.

36. Which statement about Pluto, if true, would most directly support the view described in lines 69–74?
   F. Pluto shares many characteristics of the inner, rocky planets of the solar system.
   G. Pluto's size is much closer to that of the celestial bodies found in the Kuiper Belt.
   H. A planet discovered between Pluto and Neptune would be similar to Pluto but have a stable, circular orbit.
   J. An analysis of Pluto's composition is unlikely to make a distinction between ice and certain types of rock.

37. Which research outcome would best illustrate the argument made in Passage B?
   A. Detailed analysis of Pluto's orbit reveals that it is gradually becoming round.
   B. A moon that is much larger than Pluto is found orbiting one of the eight proper planets.
   C. Pluto's gravitation perturbs the orbit of comets more significantly than previously believed.
   D. Telescope surveys of the Oort cloud reveal that trans-Neptunian objects do not reach the size of Pluto.

Questions 38–40 ask about both passages.

38. Both authors agree that Pluto:
   F. is not composed of icy material.
   G. has an irregular orbit around the sun.
   H. is too massive to be considered a comet.
   J. fails to meet the criteria required to be considered a planet.

39. Passage A and Passage B share a general tone of:
   A. open hostility.
   B. analytical neutrality.
   C. unflinching certitude.
   D. affectionate nostalgia.

40. The information in Passage B contradicts which assumption about Pluto as described in Passage A?
   F. Its small size does not preclude it from being a planet.
   G. Its icy composition reveals it is more like a comet than a planet.
   H. The discovery of additional moons would support Pluto's planetary status.
   J. It has a highly elliptical orbit like that of comets passing through the inner solar system.

END OF THE READING TEST
STOP! IF YOU HAVE TIME LEFT OVER, CHECK YOUR WORK ON THIS SECTION ONLY.

ANSWERS AND EXPLANATIONS

Passage I

1. **The best answer is A.** The bulk of this passage is occupied by the conversation held between two people, Nina and Jack VanSetten. This conversation has undertones of tension and awkwardness, as signaled by various statements such as, "'What does he want?' she asked, her voice becoming hard"; "'Don't you dare put blame on my mom and me! You don't even know us!' Nina could hear her voice rising in anger"; and "'Thanks, Nina.' His relief was palpable. Nina hated him for it." Statements like these clearly indicate an unsettling situation, making answer choice A best.

2. **The best answer is H.** According to the passage, "Embarrassed to call him her father, she simply referred to him as 'Rick.' It helped her to ignore the biological ties she hated so much." This statement serves as evidence that Nina had a distant and negative relationship with her father. Therefore, answer choices F and G can be eliminated. Likewise, Rick is her father, so he can't be an acquaintance to himself. Eliminate answer choice J.

3. **The best answer is A.** The passage states, "After the death of her mother two years ago, Nina thought she had abandoned her father's memory altogether." This is seen in answer choice A.

4. **The best answer is H.** According to the passage, Jack VanSetten began the conversation in "a barely audible voice." When Nina couldn't hear him, he replied with, "I'm sorry." Because Jack VanSetten started the conversation in a reserved manner, and then apologized to Nina, it is likely that he was expressing genuine remorse and was sincere in his apology.

5. **The best answer is B.** It is evident in the beginning of the passage that Nina doesn't know who is calling her, and doesn't expect the call to be of much importance. Instead of focusing on the call, she occupies herself with the scuffmark. This best supports answer choice B.

6. **The best answer is F.** In the passage Jack states, "I don't know, Nina. He just–the cancer made him think a lot. He just said he wanted you to do the memorial arrangements, and I promised him that I'd take care of it." This statement suggests that after having much time to think about things, Rick had a change of mind and heart.

7. **The best answer is C.** According to the passage, after hearing the news of her father's death, Nina felt sick. "There was silence on the line. Nina's stomach began to turn. She felt the grilled cheese sandwich she'd had for lunch begin to work its way up

the back of her throat." This reaction indicates that Nina felt both surprised and anxious about the news, which best supports answer choice C.

8. **The best answer is J.** According to the passage, when Nina asked why her father wanted her to make the memorial arrangements, Jack responded with, "I don't know, Nina. He just—the cancer made him think a lot. He just said he wanted you to do the memorial arrangements, and I promised him that I'd take care of it." Instead of being preoccupied with why Rick Sanders asked that his daughter make the memorial arrangements, Jack seems to be concerned with the promise he'd made to his friend, which best supports answer choice J.

9. **The best answer is C.** Prior to the statement, "Nina hated him for it," Nina agreed to making her father's memorial arrangements, despite her desire to decline the request. Jack VanSetten was relieved at her acceptance. You can infer that Jack's relief would irritate Nina because she wasn't looking forward to the task he put before her.

10. **The best answer is G.** As depicted in the last paragraph of the passage, Nina seems to be exhausted by the process of making her father's memorial arrangements. Just going through the movements of preparing a snack and watching TV, Nina's mind is somewhere else. Eventually, she lets her thoughts take control: "Cradling the ice cream carton, she leaned her head against the couch and sighed heavily … Nina's body became still as she sadly muttered three short words, 'My father's dead.' " Nina finally acknowledges her grief, which best supports answer choice G.

Passage II

11. **The best answer is B.** The passage states, "As Ohio was able to effectively influence federal policy to protect its own interests, this example further shows how federalism allows formerly sovereign governments of small states to have influence as a subunit. In other words, as a subunit, even a small state can gain limited autonomy by having a voice in the central government." This best supports answer choice B.

12. **The best answer is H.** The first paragraph of the passage states, "… governing authority is best when it is divided between a central governing body and semi-autonomous subunits." This best supports answer choice H.

13. **The best answer is A.** As stated in the passage, federalism "… can prevent conflict and aggression among the states themselves," "… protect minorities and individuals against injustice from

their local governing bodies or from the central government itself," and "… can also promote economic prosperity." Therefore, answer choices B, C, and D can be eliminated. This leaves answer choice A, the duplication of various legal codes, excluded from the positive aspects of federalism listed in the passage.

14. The best answer is G. In regard to the interactions between a central governing body and semi-autonomous subunits, the passage says they serve to create a "… cohesive, though not restrictive, domestic policy." This best supports answer choice G.

15. The best answer is C. As stated in the passage, "When Michigan included the strip in its application for statehood, Ohio's Congressional delegation was able to halt Michigan's admission to the Union. Both sides then raised militia and placed troops along the disputed border." This information allows for the elimination of answer choices A, B, and D. Information in the passage does not support the claim that Ohio ceded the entire strip of land to Michigan.

16. The best answer is J. As indicated by paragraph two of the passage, when governments can't come to a conclusion regarding a specific issue, "Resolution is left to the courts of law." In other words, it is up to the courts to come to a decision regarding the issue at hand. Of the four answer choices, answer choice J, *decision*, is most synonymous with *resolution*.

17. The best answer is A. According to the passage, France's government involves a single level of authority, with many regional departments. Although France doesn't employ federalism, the country still has a successful government. In this way, the author is demonstrating how a government doesn't have to employ federalism in order to be a good government. The other answer choices are not supported by the passage.

18. The best answer is H. The passage states, "In theory, the center will protect all of its citizens from any subunit injustice, as was the case with the American civil rights movement." This best supports answer choice H.

19. The best answer is D. According to the passage, "Ideally, broad political participation keeps the system fair for all citizens." The other answer choices are not supported by the passage.

20. The best answer is G. The author states that federalism "… promotes economic competitiveness in an increasingly global economy." In an answer to the need to be globally competitive in the world, the European Union was established. This serves as an

example that federalism both promotes and responds to a changing global economy, answer choice G.

Passage III

21. The best answer is C. As stated in the passage, "… *The Wife of Bath* has stood out as the most controversial and interesting of them all … Medieval scholars have tirelessly studied *The Wife of Bath* in order to capture the main character's meaning." This best supports answer choice C. The other answer choices are either too broad or not supported.

22. The best answer is J. According to the passage, "*The Canterbury Tales* remains popular because of its vivid characters and fascinating vignettes," which are drawn from "various social classes and walks of life." This best supports answer choice J.

23. The best answer is A. The last paragraph of the passage indicates that many questions surround both Chaucer and his writing. In regard to *The Wife of Bath*, "Is this Chaucer's recipe for social harmony, or is it merely wish fulfillment on the part of the Wife herself? Literary scholars have desperately tried to discover Chaucer's own views of marriage and society through his characters." As demonstrated in the passage, Chaucer and his writings exhibit mysterious undertones, making answer choice A best.

24. The best answer is G. As stated in the passage, Chaucer's use of the pilgrimage allowed him "to bring together a few dozen characters from various social classes and walks of life. Some … are based on real people. Others … are little more than archetypes." Based on this information, answer choices F, H, and J can be eliminated. While answer choice G, *successful poets of the fourteenth century*, is included in the passage, it is unrelated to Chaucer's use of the pilgrimage.

25. The best answer is B. The information in the lines referenced in the question stem offers two different ways in which the Wife's incorrect account of *Ovid* can be interpreted. The author likely includes this information as an example of the many ways that Chaucer's work can be interpreted. Therefore, answer choice B is best.

26. The best answer is H. As stated in the passage, "The poem itself is unfinished and contains several inconsistencies that reflect the need for further revision." This best supports answer choice H.

27. The best answer is A. As stated in the second paragraph of the passage, the Wife "… insists on speaking her mind (loudly), rejecting the negative opinions and sexual constraints traditionally placed upon women. She is lewd ...." Based on this information, you can eliminate answer choices B, C, and D. According to the passage, the Wife actually believes the opposite of the sentiment expressed in answer choice A.: "She ... has the audacity to use *The Bible* to attack clerical arguments from *The Bible* dealing with chastity and virginity." Therefore, answer choice A is best.

28. **The best answer is F.** The passage states, "As for her verbosity, the Wife says she can't help it: all women talk too much." The information following the colon can be used to help determine the meaning of *verbosity*. The Wife explains her own *verbosity* by highlighting the common opinion that all women talk too much. Therefore, you can infer from the context that *verbosity* is synonymous with *excessive talking*, answer choice F. The other answer choices are not supported by the context of the passage.

29. **The best answer is D.** As stated in the passage, "Midas, she says, told his misfortune to his wife, who, afraid she would burst from keeping the secret, whispered it to the banks of a river where it spread over the country." Midas' wife feared "bursting" forth with the secret, which best supports answer choice D.

30. **The best answer is G.** The passage indicates that the knight didn't want to give his wife authority. In fact, he had to be convinced to do so. After finally granting his wife authority, her subsequent surrender must instill in him a sense of frustration for having worked so hard to gain her submission, only to have her so easily give it.

Passage IV

31. **The best answer is B.** According to the passage, "As a comet nears the sun, a tail becomes visible," and "Pluto shows no tail at any point in its circuit." Because the author of Passage A believes that Pluto is a planet, the fact that it does not share this feature of a comet supports the author's position.

32. **The best answer is J.** In the context of the passage, the word "circuit" is used to reference Pluto's orbit. Therefore, "circuit" most nearly means "cyclic motion."

33. **The best answer is A.** Passage A does not mention the existence of Pluto's moons. Only Passage B does so.

34. **The best answer is G.** According to the author, "Pluto is almost 1,000 times larger than an average

comet and more than twice the size of 1 Ceres, the largest of the asteroids, which comprises nearly a third of the total mass of the asteroid belt." This information best supports Answer Choice G.

35. **The best answer is A.** In Passage B, the author mentions "a group of substantial comets" and then goes on to further explain that "Kuiper belt, scattered disk, and Oort cloud objects together comprise the large trans-Neptunian objects." This information best supports Answer Choice A.

36. **The best answer is G.** According to the passage, "Contemporary observations show that Pluto is much too small to be a planet. It is less than half the diameter of the next smallest planet, Mercury. Seven moons, including Earth's, are larger than Pluto. The body is so small, in fact, that all of its own moons have likely yet to be discovered." This would suggest that the author believes Pluto is too small to be a planet.

37. **The best answer is B.** The argument against Pluto being a planet relies, in part, on Pluto's size: "Contemporary observations show that Pluto is much too small to be a planet. It is less than half the diameter of the next smallest planet, Mercury. Seven moons, including Earth's, are larger than Pluto." Therefore, if another moon larger than Pluto were discovered, this argument would be supported.

38. **The best answer is G.** According to Passage A, "Although Pluto's orbital path is irregular compared to the other planets of the solar system, it undisputedly orbits the sun." Likewise, Passage B states "Pluto is actually closer to the sun than is Neptune, placing it in eighth position. More than 70 Kuiper Belt comets share this irregular orbit, proving Pluto is more similar to them than to proper planets."

39. **The best answer is C.** Although the authors disagree on Pluto's status as a planet, they each provide convincing evidence in support of their positions. The information in the passages best supports Answer Choice C.

40. **The best answer is F.** According to Passage A, even though Pluto is small, it shares many attributes of the other planets and should, therefore, be considered a planet. Passage B also indicates that Pluto is much smaller than the other planets, which, according to Passage A, should not preclude its planetary status.

▆▆▆ SCORING WORKSHEET

On each ACT multiple-choice test (English, Mathematics, Reading, and Science) you will receive a SCALED SCORE on a scale of 1 to 36. Use the following guidelines to determine your approximate SCALED SCORE on the ACT Reading Practice Test that you just completed.

Step 1 Determine your RAW SCORE.

Your RAW SCORE is the number of questions that you answered correctly. Because there are 40 questions on the ACT English Test, the highest possible RAW SCORE is 40.

Step 2 Determine your SCALED SCORE using the following Scoring Worksheet

---

Reading ——————— × 36 = ——————— ÷ 40 = ———————
            RAW SCORE   **+ 2**   (*correction factor)

                                                    ———————
                                                    SCALED SCORE

---

   *The correction factor is an approximation based on the average from several recent ACT tests. It is most valid for scores in the middle 50 percent (approximately 16–24 scaled composite score) of the scoring range. The scores are all approximate. Actual ACT scoring scales vary from one administration to the next based upon several factors.

Your SCALED SCORE should be rounded to the nearest number according to normal rules. For example, $31.2 \approx 31$ and $31.5 \approx 32$. If you answered 28 quetions correctly on the Reading Test, for example, your SCALED SCORE would be 27.

CHAPTER 14

ACT READING PRACTICE TEST 2

This chapter will allow you to practice the ACT Reading Test strategies that were introduced in the earlier chapters of this book. Make an honest effort to answer each question and review the explanations that follow. Review Chapter 10, "Speed Reading," Chapter 11, "Strategies and Techniques," and Chapter 12, "Applying Strategies, Building Skills," as necessary.

ACT READING PRACTICE TEST 2
Answer Sheet

READING

1 Ⓐ Ⓑ Ⓒ Ⓓ	11 Ⓐ Ⓑ Ⓒ Ⓓ	21 Ⓐ Ⓑ Ⓒ Ⓓ	31 Ⓐ Ⓑ Ⓒ Ⓓ
2 Ⓕ Ⓖ Ⓗ Ⓙ	12 Ⓕ Ⓖ Ⓗ Ⓙ	22 Ⓕ Ⓖ Ⓗ Ⓙ	32 Ⓕ Ⓖ Ⓗ Ⓙ
3 Ⓐ Ⓑ Ⓒ Ⓓ	13 Ⓐ Ⓑ Ⓒ Ⓓ	23 Ⓐ Ⓑ Ⓒ Ⓓ	33 Ⓐ Ⓑ Ⓒ Ⓓ
4 Ⓕ Ⓖ Ⓗ Ⓙ	14 Ⓕ Ⓖ Ⓗ Ⓙ	24 Ⓕ Ⓖ Ⓗ Ⓙ	34 Ⓕ Ⓖ Ⓗ Ⓙ
5 Ⓐ Ⓑ Ⓒ Ⓓ	15 Ⓐ Ⓑ Ⓒ Ⓓ	25 Ⓐ Ⓑ Ⓒ Ⓓ	35 Ⓐ Ⓑ Ⓒ Ⓓ
6 Ⓕ Ⓖ Ⓗ Ⓙ	16 Ⓕ Ⓖ Ⓗ Ⓙ	26 Ⓕ Ⓖ Ⓗ Ⓙ	36 Ⓕ Ⓖ Ⓗ Ⓙ
7 Ⓐ Ⓑ Ⓒ Ⓓ	17 Ⓐ Ⓑ Ⓒ Ⓓ	27 Ⓐ Ⓑ Ⓒ Ⓓ	37 Ⓐ Ⓑ Ⓒ Ⓓ
8 Ⓕ Ⓖ Ⓗ Ⓙ	18 Ⓕ Ⓖ Ⓗ Ⓙ	28 Ⓕ Ⓖ Ⓗ Ⓙ	38 Ⓕ Ⓖ Ⓗ Ⓙ
9 Ⓐ Ⓑ Ⓒ Ⓓ	19 Ⓐ Ⓑ Ⓒ Ⓓ	29 Ⓐ Ⓑ Ⓒ Ⓓ	39 Ⓐ Ⓑ Ⓒ Ⓓ
10 Ⓕ Ⓖ Ⓗ Ⓙ	20 Ⓕ Ⓖ Ⓗ Ⓙ	30 Ⓕ Ⓖ Ⓗ Ⓙ	40 Ⓕ Ⓖ Ⓗ Ⓙ

READING TEST

35 Minutes—40 Questions

DIRECTIONS: This test includes four passages, each followed by ten questions. Read each passage and choose the best answer to each question. After you have selected your answer, fill in the corresponding bubble on your answer sheet. You should refer to the passages as often as necessary when answering the questions.

Passage I
PROSE FICTION: Family History Discovered

As a boy, I was fortunate to have a close family; all of us lived in the same town. I saw my grandparents often, and they'd tell me story after story of a past world and of the people who dwelled in it.
5 I remember one summer night I strolled through a thicket with my grandfather, picking up leaves and sticks along the way. Sometimes I knew from which tree they had fallen, but my grandfather had to give me hints for most of them.

10 "You had better bring your bathing suit, because that one is a …" he prompted me, showing his sense of humor.

"A beech?" I replied, not feeling entirely sure of myself. My grandfather nodded and smiled.

15 We continued to wander through the copse and, bit-by-bit, he told me a story about where he and his family had come from and the acres of woods he had explored as a boy.

"The woods in French Canada are hearty and old,"
20 he told me. "All of those trees are regrowth after the widespread logging from over a century ago. There were so many different kinds of trees when I was your age, and I tried to learn as much as I could about them all. We had plenty of maples, and your great-grandmother knew just
25 how to boil the sap to make syrup. It had to be done very slowly for it to turn out right."

My grandfather's immediate family came from Quebec; his distant relatives hailed from France. He always wanted to take me to his hometown near Mon-
30 treal, but we hadn't yet had the opportunity.

When we came in from our walk that night, my grandfather brought one of his dusty shoeboxes down from the attic and sat down next to me. It amazes me now, how I've never seen the same shoebox emerge twice
35 from the attic; his family records are astounding. In all of these dusty boxes are old sepia photographs of family members; some portray relatives going about their daily business, others were taken at special occasions, and some are merely candid shots that illustrate treasured moments
40 from the past.

"Here is your great-grandmother kneading dough in the kitchen," my grandfather told me as he held up a fading photograph of a woman surrounded by pies.

The edges were splitting on a different photograph,
45 of boys skating on a pond, hockey sticks raised in celebration of a goal. Upon seeing this one, my grandfather remarked, "That was your great-uncle and I the winter after he got his first pair of ice skates."

One by one, I felt the emotion captured by these
50 images, and I got the nagging feeling that I might never otherwise know about these people from my family's past.

"I am so glad that you kept all of these photos and are here to share their stories with me," I said to my grandfather, wanting him to know just how much it meant to me.

55 "Well, if you really want to know the stories, we had better get started," he commented while grinning. "There are at least another hundred boxes upstairs waiting for us."

After that day, I often joined my grandfather to
60 learn about my French-Canadian ancestry, so that, when he was gone, I could be the custodian of those stories.

The culmination of our time together was a detailed family tree, with its base formed by our French ancestors
65 who first arrived on this continent. Our search for information uncovered amazing historical documents such as ships' manifests and handwritten marriage certificates. If we were lucky, we'd find more than just a name. Dates recognizing births and deaths were fairly easy to
70 find; occupations and other bits of our ancestors' life stories became increasingly difficult to uncover as we dug deeper into the past. Now, years later, I am continuing to preserve this history so that some day my progeny may learn from these stories and take comfort in know-
75 ing that, though life may end, family goes on forever.

GO ON TO THE NEXT PAGE.

1. Which of the following statements best characterizes the narrator of this passage?
   A. A teenager looking toward the future and commenting on the traditions he hopes to continue
   B. An adult reflecting on the time spent with his grandson and the value of those experiences for both of them
   C. An adult who regrets not knowing more about his family, but who enjoys spending time outdoors with his current relatives
   D. An adult reflecting on cherished moments from his youth and how they continue to influence him even now

2. As it is used in line 15, the word *copse* most likely means:
   F. an expansive and rolling field of crops.
   G. a small forest or thicket of trees.
   H. a clearing found within a dense forest.
   J. a neglected or overgrown piece of land.

3. It can be reasonably inferred from the passage that the narrator provided the information in the first paragraph about having a close family in order to:
   A. suggest that the events to follow would not have been likely to occur otherwise.
   B. highlight his family experience as an ideal type upon which to model.
   C. prepare the reader for a disappointing series of events.
   D. begin a discussion of why family ties are important in French-Canadian culture.

4. When the narrator mentions that his grandfather's "family records are astounding" (line 35), he most nearly means that:
   F. the photograph collection was incredibly expansive and wide-ranging.
   G. his grandfather kept many useless, elaborate records.
   H. the narrator was overwhelmed by the details of the information about his family.
   J. the documents collected by his grandfather were partial and incomplete.

5. In the passage, what is the narrator's response to being shown a variety of photos about his ancestors (lines 49–51)?
   A. An understanding of his ancestors as a result of a shared past and common experiences
   B. Frustration from having not learned about these family members sooner

C. Relief that he was able to learn about these relatives before it was too late
   D. Despair at never having met the people in the photographs

6. According to the passage, which of the following events happened last in the narrator's life?
   F. Sorting through handwritten marriage certificates
   G. Preserving a nearly complete family history
   H. Identifying twigs and leaves in the forest
   J. Seeing a photograph of his grandmother baking

7. Which of the following words best describes the narrator's feelings about the time spent with his grandfather looking at pictures?
   A. Empathy
   B. Suspense
   C. Elation
   D. Appreciation

8. As presented in the passage, what is the narrator's attitude toward the final product of his time spent with his grandfather?
   F. Sorrow over not starting the process sooner
   G. Distress as a result of being the new caretaker of the pictures
   H. Melancholy from a lack of new projects to focus on
   J. Pride at having detailed a lasting family history

9. It can be reasonably inferred from the passage that the narrator's grandfather is:
   A. listless and nostalgic.
   B. jovial yet sincere.
   C. patient and wistful.
   D. demanding but compassionate.

10. The last paragraph (lines 63–75) primarily reinforces the author's:
    F. desire to have children so that he may pass on the family history.
    G. genuine admiration of the time spent with his grandfather.
    H. commitment to continuing the work he started with his grandfather.
    J. record of overcoming difficult circumstances to fulfill personal goals.

Passage II

SOCIAL SCIENCE: The Hart–Cellar Act: Changing the nature of immigration

Modern immigration, also known as post-1965 immigration, has forever changed American society. In 1965, amendments to the Immigration and Nationality Act, more commonly known as the Hart–Cellar Act, greatly
5   increased non-European immigration. In the decades since the Hart–Cellar Act became law, immigration has continued to increase steadily in the United States.

Some experts disagree on whether the Hart–Cellar Act was the primary reason for the shift in modern
10 immigration. In 1968, the Hart–Cellar Act's goals were to unite fragmented families and to bring in foreign labor. The Hart–Cellar Act eliminated national quotas that were biased against immigrants from Southern and Eastern Europe. In addition, the Hart–Cellar Act
15 removed the long-standing ban on Asian immigrants. The abolition of the national quotas encouraged immigrants from Eastern Europe, Southern Europe, and Asia to come to America. Unfortunately, the original Hart–Cellar Act and its later amendments also established
20 the first cap on immigrants from the Western Hemisphere. This greatly affected immigration from Central America, South America, and Mexico.

Compared with the immigrants of the nineteenth and early twentieth centuries, post-1965 immigrants
25 are distinctly diverse. These new immigrants settle in different areas, come from a wide variety of countries, and have different socioeconomic backgrounds. In fact, unlike the Ellis Island immigrants, modern immigrants hail principally from non-European nations.
30 Modern immigration has had a significant impact on the size and design of America's population. Since the 1960s, new immigrants have represented over one-third of America's total growth. Although all ethnic groups contribute to America's growth, Asian
35 and Hispanic immigrant populations continue to grow larger and faster than all of the others. Only thirty years ago, Asians and Hispanics made up an infinitesimal percentage of the American population. Since then, the size of these groups has almost quadrupled.

40 In the 1800s, immigrants from Europe tended to settle on the East Coast or in the Midwest. States like Michigan, Virginia, New York, Pennsylvania, Illinois, Massachusetts, and New Jersey became havens for new Americans. If these immigrants preferred
45 the cosmopolitan life, they usually headed for booming cities like New York, Detroit, Chicago, Philadelphia, St. Louis, and Boston. In the twenty-first century, immigrants continue to flock to these areas. However, today's immigrants also settle on the West Coast, in
50 the Southwest, and in the Southeast. Texas, Arizona, Florida, California, Washington, and Oregon are among the states with the largest immigrant populations.

Many of the modern immigrants arrive in America with jobs, college degrees, or technical training, in stark
55 contrast to the immigrants of the nineteenth century. Networks produced by family ties, friendships, and business contacts enable immigrants to prosper in America far more quickly than they were able to in the past.

Since the 1970s, family or friends already in the United
60 States sponsored more than two-thirds of the new immigrants. Other humanitarian institutions, both public and private, also help new immigrants become established in America. In addition to helping immigrants find jobs and homes, these organizations assist in eliminating the
65 abuse and discrimination that many immigrants face.

It is no wonder that family ties play such a major role in modern immigration. The Hart–Cellar Act of 1965 and its ensuing amendments made family reunification a priority. This important measure provided immediate
70 family members of American citizens with unlimited visas. Extended relatives were also granted visas based on availability.

Thanks to the Hart–Cellar Act and other legislation, America has become more than a melting pot.
75 With its modern immigration policies, America has become a land filled with united and prosperous families. The Hart–Cellar Act, along with other immigration legislation, has brought increased diversity and new challenges. Like the immigrants before them, modern
80 immigrants require assistance and compassion. However, the strengths and benefits that many of the new immigrants bring far outweigh a temporary cost to society.

11. The discussion of immigrants as a portion of total population growth in the third paragraph serves which of the following purposes?
   A. It weakens the assertion that all immigrants contribute to the population growth of the United States.
   B. It establishes the need for making family unification a priority of all immigration legislation.
   C. It provides statistical evidence in favor of immigration quotas for the prevention of overpopulation.
   D. It supports the claim that immigration will have a significant impact on the size of America's population.

12. The examples in the sixth paragraph (lines 66–72) are offered as support for which of the following goals of the Hart–Cellar Act?
   F. Eliminating regional immigration quotas
   G. Reversing historical discrimination against immigrants
   H. Uniting fragmented immigrant families
   J. Increasing foreign trade in the United States

13. The author of the passage would be most likely to agree with which of the following statements about the immigration reforms of the late 1950s?
   A. The expense of encouraging Eastern Hemisphere immigration was placing restrictions on Western Hemisphere immigration.
   B. The quota systems that were implemented following the passage of the Hart–Cellar Act were almost as fundamentally flawed as those that existed under previous immigration legislation.
   C. The greatest unintended consequence of the legislation was that knowledge of skilled trades came to be valued higher than familial relationships.
   D. The costs incurred by society as a result of the increased immigrant population outweighed the benefits for many years following the reforms.

GO ON TO THE NEXT PAGE.

14. According to the passage, which one of the following states is NOT among those with the largest new immigrant populations?
   F. Florida
   G. Oregon
   H. California
   J. New York

15. According to the passage, which of the following groups of immigrants tended to settle on the East Coast or in the Midwest?
   A. Hispanic immigrants in the 1800s
   B. European immigrants in the 1800s
   C. Hispanic immigrants in the 1900s
   D. Asian immigrants in the 1900s

16. The passage most strongly suggests that the status of immigration in the United States today is a result of which of the following?
   F. Post-twentieth century immigration legislation
   G. Pre-1965 immigration legislation
   H. Post-1965 immigration legislation
   J. Pre-nineteenth century immigration legislation

17. According to the passage, the two fastest-growing immigrant populations are:
   A. Asian and Hispanic.
   B. Hispanic and African.
   C. African and Asian.
   D. Hispanic and European.

18. The primary function of the fifth paragraph (lines 53–65) is to:
   F. praise the work of humanitarian institutions in helping immigrants to relocate to the United States.
   G. refocus the discussion on the deplorable working and housing conditions faced by many new immigrants.
   H. challenge the supposition that the Hart–Cellar Act was a successful piece of immigration legislation.
   J. articulate the reasons why immigrants today are increasingly likely to thrive compared to those of the nineteenth century.

19. According to the passage, the Hart–Cellar Act lifted the immigration ban against individuals of what ethnicity?
   A. Hispanic
   B. Asian
   C. American
   D. European

20. The main idea of the seventh paragraph (lines 73–82) is that:
   F. the size of the American melting pot expanded to include a variety of new cultures and peoples.
   G. modern immigration legislation would have failed had it not been for the strength of family relationships and support structures.
   H. the Hart–Cellar Act was remarkably successful and, as a result, America is the prosperous, multicultural nation that it is today.
   J. on balance, the costs and benefits of increased immigration even out and America will continue to encourage family reunification.

GO ON TO THE NEXT PAGE.

Passage III

HUMANITIES: This passage is adapted from *Artist and Public* by Kenyon Cox © 1914.

In the history of art, as in the history of politics and in the history of economics, our modern epoch is marked off from all preceding epochs by one great event: the French Revolution. The artist Fragonard, who survived that Revo-
5 lution to lose himself in a new and strange world, is the last of the old masters; David, some sixteen years his junior, is the first of the moderns. Now if we look for the most fundamental distinction between our modern art and the art of past times, I believe we shall find it to be this:
10 the art of the past was produced for a public that wanted it and understood it, by artists who understood and sympa-
thized with their public; the art of our time has been, for the most part, produced for a public that did not want it and misunderstood it, by artists who disliked and despised
15 the public for which they worked. When artist and public were united, art was homogeneous and continuous. Since the divorce of artist and public, art has been chaotic and convulsive.

That this divorce between the artist and his
20 public—this dislocation of the right and natural relations between them—has taken place is certain. The causes of it are many and deep-seated in our modern civilization, and I can point out only a few of the more obvious ones.

The first of these is the emergence of a new public.
25 The art of past ages had been distinctively an aristocratic art, created for kings and princes, for the free citizens of slave-holding republics, for the spiritual and intellectual aristocracy of the church, or for a luxurious and frivolous nobility. As the aim of the Revolution was the
30 destruction of aristocratic privilege, it is not surpris-
ing that a revolutionary like David should have felt it necessary to destroy the traditions of an art created for the aristocracy. In his own art of painting he succeeded so thoroughly that the painters of the next generation
35 found themselves with no traditions at all. They had not only to work for a public of enriched bourgeois or pro-
letarians who had never cared for art, but they had to create over again the art with which they endeavored to interest this public. How could they succeed? The rift
40 between artist and public had begun, and it has been wid-
ening ever since.

If the people had had little to do with the major arts of painting and sculpture, there had been, however, all through the Middle Ages and the Renaissance, a truly
45 popular art—an art of furniture making, of wood-carv-
ing, of forging, of pottery. Every craftsman was an artist in his degree, and every artist was but a craftsman of a superior sort. Our machine-making, industrial civilization, intent upon material progress and the satisfaction of
50 material wants, has destroyed this popular art; and at the same time that the artist lost his patronage from above, he lost his support from below. He has become a superior person, but he has no longer a splendid nobility to employ him or a world of artisans to surround him and
55 understand him.

And to the modern artist, so isolated, with no tradition behind him, no direction from above and no support

from below, the art of all times and all countries has become familiar through modern means of communication
60 and modern processes of reproduction. Having no com-
pelling reason for doing one thing rather than another, or for choosing one or another way of doing things, he is shown a thousand things that he may do and a thousand ways of doing them. Not clearly knowing his own mind
65 he hears the clash and reverberation of a thousand other minds, and having no certainties he must listen to count-
less theories.

21. It can be reasonably inferred that the primary purpose of this passage is to:
   A. attempt to rekindle an appreciation of art within the new public.
   B. establish a standard of evaluating modern art in light of its divergence from previous artistic movements.
   C. articulate one author's view as to why modern art and modern artists exist in their current forms.
   D. present evidence as to why technology has ruined artists and the pursuit of artistic excellence.

22. Fragonard is presented by the author as being:
   F. an artist who thrived following the French Revolution.
   G. an artist who had little impact on the history of art.
   H. a great, early French artist.
   J. the first of the modern painters.

23. Which of the following best describes the way the second paragraph functions in relation to the passage as a whole?
   A. It outlines an idea that will be expanded on throughout the rest of the passage.
   B. It offers an opinion that is later proven to be false by the introduction of new evidence.
   C. It contradicts the essay's assertion that modern art is delineated from classic art.
   D. It suggests an alternate lens for interpreting newly developing trends in the world of art.

24. It can be reasonably inferred from the third paragraph (lines 24–41) that one of the biggest potential problems of David's success was:
   F. the dissolution of common knowledge existing among free citizens at the time.
   G. the resulting lack of any traditions for modern artists to build upon.
   H. the accidental creation of a spiritual and intellectual nobility.
   J. the destruction of artistic traditions created for an aris-
tocracy.

25. Based on the author's discussion of the demands new art-
ists faced, it can be reasonably inferred that the author's attitude toward modern artists is one of:
   A. disdain.
   B. petulance.
   C. contention.
   D. sympathy.

GO ON TO THE NEXT PAGE.

26. As it is used in lines 46–47, the phrase "an artist in his degree" most nearly means that:
   F. craftsmen were trained in classical artistic techniques.
   G. the work of craftsmen was perfected to the greatest extent of their abilities.
   H. craftsmen paid very close attention to accepted standards of detail and style.
   J. craftsmen were more focused on the look of a piece than its function.

27. According to the passage, the industrialization of society is significant because it:
   A. destroyed the popular arts of painting and sculpture.
   B. produced mechanical and technological art that did not conform to the standards of society.
   C. removed the support of the public from various artistic endeavors.
   D. erased the historical traditions of the major arts and forced artists to re-create the past.

28. The author uses all of the following statements to describe the modern artist EXCEPT that he:
   F. has no compelling reason to do one thing or another.
   G. must listen to countless theories.
   H. is shown a thousand things that he may do.
   J. must isolate himself from other artists.

29. As it is used in line 51, the word *patronage* most nearly means:
   A. esteem.
   B. abhorrence.
   C. encouragement.
   D. separation.

30. It can be reasonably inferred from the passage that the biggest difference between the artists of the past and the artists of the present is that:
   F. artists of the past were outcasts, while artists of the present are celebrities.
   G. artists of the past were owned by their public, while artists of the present are unconditionally supported by their public.
   H. artists of the past sympathized with their public, while artists of the present influence their public.
   J. artists of the past understood their public, while artists of the present renounce their public.

GO ON TO THE NEXT PAGE.

Passage IV

Natural Science: The following passages discuss two different perspectives regarding human dependence on computer technology.

Passage A

Human reliance on information technology today is quickly progressing all over the world. The technological developments in the areas of computing, networking, and software engineering have aided the transitions from
5 paper to paperless transactions, and text and data media to multimedia. Today, speed, efficiency, and accuracy in the exchange of information have become primary tools for increasing productivity and innovation. Activities as diverse as health care, education, and manufac-
10 turing have come to depend on the generation, storage, and transmission of electronic information. Computers are not only used extensively to perform the industrial and economic functions of society but are also used to provide many services upon which human life depends.
15 Medical treatment, air traffic control, and national security are a few examples. Even a small glitch in the operation of these systems can put human lives in danger. Computers are also used to store confidential data of a political, social, economic, or personal nature. This
20 fairly recent and progressive dependence on computer technology signals a real danger for the human race.

Current computer systems offer new opportunities for law breaking and the potential to commit traditional types of crimes in nontraditional ways. For example,
25 the threat of identity theft is magnified by our reliance on computers to assist us in everyday activities such as shopping and paying bills. Identity theft refers to all types of crime in which someone wrongfully obtains and uses another person's personal data by way of fraud or decep-
30 tion, typically for economic gain. By making personal and credit information available on the Internet, people open themselves up to the possibility of a criminal obtaining this information and using it for nefarious purposes. This is but one instance of the negative impact that over-
35 reliance on computer technology can have on society.

As humans continue to make technological advances, so too do they rely more heavily upon those innovations. This is a dangerous progression that must be tempered with common sense and self-restraint. We cannot allow
40 computer technology to control so many aspects of our lives, lest we become victims of our own ingenuity.

Passage B

On the eve of December 31, 1999, millions of people around the world prepared for the worst—major power outages, the loss of communication networks, airplanes
45 falling from the sky, the end of life as we knew it—all because of the uncertainty surrounding computer systems switching from the year 1999 to the year 2000. However, the end did not come, and today it seems that humans are more dependent upon computer technology

50 than ever before. The so-called "Y2K" phenomenon came and went without so much as a lightbulb flicker. This means, of course, that any threat of future disasters resulting from human dependence on technology is unfounded, and we, as a global society, should continue
55 to rely upon computers to enhance our everyday lives.

It is difficult for most of us to imagine a life without computers. Innovations we might never have imagined are now commonplace. The speed with which we can communicate and the ease with which we can accomplish
60 complicated tasks are but two of the many advantages computer technology offers us. For example, the Federal Drug Administration recently approved a surgical robot for use in certain surgeries. The robot has three arms that can be moved with pinpoint accuracy. This tech
65 nology magnifies the skills of an experienced surgeon, who can manipulate the robot's arms while sitting in a chair across the room. In addition, the use of computers in the classroom is now being hailed as an educational revolution. Computer technology is currently integrated
70 into the curriculum of thousands of classrooms, transforming the learning environment of students worldwide.

Human dependence on technology is a natural progression in the advancement of our species. Computer technology, specifically, will continue to allow people in
75 all nations on Earth to learn, grow, heal, and move forward in their efforts to maximize the human potential. It is imperative that we not only maintain our current relationship with computer technology, but that we also develop and nurture this relationship to the fullest extent possible.

Questions 31–33 ask about Passage A.

---

31. In line 33, *nefarious* most nearly means:
A. wicked.
B. sensible.
C. economic.
D. prosperous.

32. The author most likely uses the phrase "a small glitch" (line 16) in order to:
F. acknowledge the fact that human reliance on computer technology is completely safe.
G. cast doubt on the accuracy of any personal data collected on the Internet by criminals.
H. criticize human technological advances in the areas of education, medicine, and national security.
J. emphasize the idea that it is dangerous for humans to rely so heavily on computer technology.

33. The author in Passage A argues that:
A. human dependence on computer technology can sometimes have a negative impact on society.
B. human dependence on computer technology is a key component to the advancement of the species.
C. human dependence on computer technology is a positive indicator of the advancement of the species.
D. human dependence on computer technology should never be allowed under any circumstances.

GO ON TO THE NEXT PAGE.

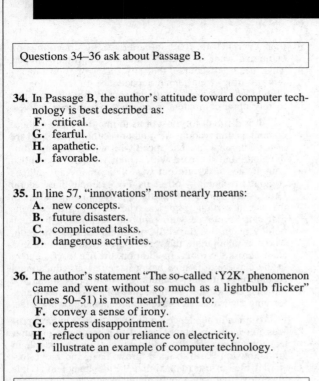

34. In Passage B, the author's attitude toward computer technology is best described as:
  F. critical.
  G. fearful.
  H. apathetic.
  J. favorable.

35. In line 57, "innovations" most nearly means:
  A. new concepts.
  B. future disasters.
  C. complicated tasks.
  D. dangerous activities.

36. The author's statement "The so-called 'Y2K' phenomenon came and went without so much as a lightbulb flicker" (lines 50–51) is most nearly meant to:
  F. convey a sense of irony.
  G. express disappointment.
  H. reflect upon our reliance on electricity.
  J. illustrate an example of computer technology.

Questions 37–40 ask about both passage.

37. What would be the likely response of the author of Passage B to the discussion of identity theft in lines 27–35 of Passage A?
  A. Identity theft provides evidence of the "Y2K" phenomenon.
  B. Identity theft presents a technological challenge that can be solved.
  C. Identity theft emphasizes the more positive advances of technology.
  D. Identity theft is an indication that computer technology has progressed too far.

38. The author of Passage A and the author of Passage B disagree most strongly about:
  F. the role of robotics in advancing medical treatment.
  G. the dangers of increasing technological dependence.
  H. the national security applications of computer technology.
  J. the implications of including personal information on the Internet.

39. Which of the following statements provides the most accurate comparison of the tone of each passage?
  A. Passage A presents a less hopeful outcome than does Passage B.
  B. Passage A presents a more hopeful outcome than does Passage B.
  C. Both passages begin by expressing concern over technological advancement but conclude with an analysis of the benefits of such advancement.
  D. Both passages begin by examining the pitfalls of human dependence on computer technology but conclude by presenting the advantages of our relationship with computers.

40. Both Passage A and Passage B highlight:
  F. the dangers inherent in information technology.
  G. the reaction of humans to advancements in information technology.
  H. the certainty of the dangers posed by our reliance on computer technology.
  J. the ways in which people have come to depend upon computer technology.

END OF THE READING TEST
STOP! IF YOU HAVE TIME LEFT OVER, CHECK YOUR WORK ON THIS SECTION ONLY.

ANSWERS AND EXPLANATIONS

Passage I

1. **The best answer is D.** In the passage, the narrator states, "Now years later, I am continuing to preserve this history so that some day, my progeny may learn from these stories and take comfort in knowing that, though life may end, family goes on forever." The narrator's desire to continue preserving history marks the fond memories associated with the practice.

2. **The best answer is G.** As indicated by the passage, the narrator and his grandfather "strolled through a thicket" as they discussed their family history. The passage then continues, "We continued to wander through the *copse*." Because *copse* is used to describe the setting, its definition can best be determined by referring back to the narrator's original description of the setting, which was a thicket. Therefore, the best answer is the one that is most similar to a thicket.

3. **The best answer is A.** As described in the first paragraph of the passage, the narrator found his close family to be advantageous. For example, the narrator states, "I saw my grandparents often, and they'd tell me story after story of a past world and of the people who dwelled in it." This statement implies that without his grandparents close by to share their stories, it would have been difficult for him to learn of his family's past. This idea is demonstrated by answer choice A.

4. **The best answer is F.** In the passage, the narrator says of his grandfather, "It amazes me now, how I've never seen the same shoebox emerge twice from the attic; his family records are astounding." This statement demonstrates the narrator's awe over his grandfather's all-encompassing family records.

5. **The best answer is C.** The passage indicates that the narrator is thankful for the time spent viewing the photographs. "One by one, I felt the emotion captured by these images, and I got the nagging feeling that I might never otherwise know about these people from my family's past. 'I am so glad that you kept all of these photos and are here to share their stories with me,' I said to my grandfather, wanting him to know just how much it meant to me." This statement demonstrates the narrator's

feelings that without his encounter with his grandfather's records, he may never have known the many stories of his past.

6. **The best answer is G.** As indicated by the narrator in the last paragraph of the passage, "Now years later, I am continuing to preserve this history so that some day, my progeny may learn from these stories and take comfort in knowing that, though life may end, family goes on forever." The narrator's reference to the present and future mark the last event of the passage.

7. **The best answer is D.** In regard to the time spent looking over the photographs, the narrator says to his grandfather, "I am so glad that you kept all of these photos and are here to share their stories with me." This demonstrates the narrator's appreciation for the time spent with his grandfather.

8. **The best answer is J.** Throughout the last paragraph of the passage, the narrator makes statements such as, "Our search for information uncovered amazing historical documents such as ships' manifests and handwritten marriage certificates," and, "Now years later, I am continuing to preserve this history so that some day, my progeny may learn from these stories and take comfort in knowing that, though life may end, family goes on forever." These statements reveal the pride the narrator feels at discovering and detailing his past.

9. **The best answer is B.** Throughout the passage the narrator highlights his grandfather's earnestness when sharing the family history. The narrator also demonstrates his grandfather's humorous personality. For example, the narrator relays the following when describing his walks through the thicket with his grandfather: "Sometimes I knew from which tree they had fallen, but my grandfather had to give me hints for most of them. 'You had better bring your bathing suit, because that one is a...' he prompted me, showing his sense of humor." This scene, as well as the grandfather's dedication to the family history, is best characterized through answer choice B.

10. **The best answer is H.** The narrator plans on "continuing to preserve this history so that some day, my progeny may learn from these stories and take comfort in knowing that, though life may end, family goes on forever." In this way, the narrator will continue the work that his grandfather began.

Passage II

11. **The best answer is D.** In the second paragraph, the passage states that, "Modern immigration has had a significant impact on the size and design of America's population." Near the end of that paragraph, the author discusses the fact that immigrants since the 1960s represent one-third of the total population growth. The information about percentage of total population growth supports the claim regarding the significance of immigration, making answer choice D the best answer. The other answer choices are not supported by the passage.

12. **The best answer is H.** According to the paragraph, "The Hart–Cellar Act of 1965 and its ensuing amendments made family reunification a priority." The examples that follow serve as support for this statement.

13. **The best answer is A.** The passage states, "The abolition of the national quotas encouraged immigrants from Eastern Europe, Southern Europe, and Asia to come to America. Unfortunately, the original Hart–Cellar Act and its later amendments also established the first cap on immigrants from the Western Hemisphere. This greatly affected immigration from Central America, South America, and Mexico." This statement demonstrates the idea that while Eastern Hemisphere immigration increased, it was at the expense of Western Hemisphere immigration.

14. **The best answer is J.** The passage states that, "Texas, Arizona, Florida, California, Washington, and Oregon are among the states with the largest immigrant populations." Because New York is the only answer choice not included in the above statement, answer choice J is the best answer.

15. **The best answer is B.** According to the passage, "In the 1800s, immigrants from Europe tended to settle on the East Coast or in the Midwest."

16. **The best answer is H.** The passage states, "Modern immigration, also known as post-1965 immigration, has forever changed American society." This statement suggests that post-1965 immigration legislation is largely responsible for today's immigration status.

17. **The best answer is A.** As stated in the third paragraph of the passage, "Although all ethnic groups contribute to America's growth, Asian and His- panic immigrant populations continue to grow larger and faster than all of the others." These two ethnic groups are found in answer choice A.

18. **The best answer is J.** The fifth paragraph of the passage states, "Many of the modern immigrants arrive in America with jobs, college degrees, or technical training, in stark contrast to the immigrants of the nineteenth century. Networks produced by family ties, friendships, and business contacts enable immigrants to prosper in America far more quickly than they were able to in the past." This demonstrates the higher chances of success experienced by modern immigrants in comparison to nineteenth-century immigrants.

19. **The best answer is B.** According to the second paragraph of the passage, "In addition, the Hart–Cellar Act removed the long-standing ban on Asian immigrants."

20. **The best answer is H.** According to the seventh paragraph, "Thanks to the Hart–Cellar Act and other legislation, America has become more than a melting pot. With its modern immigration policies, America has become a land filled with united and prosperous families." Answer choice H best demonstrates the ideas of this statement.

Passage III

21. **The best answer is C.** As stated by the author, "That this divorce between the artist and his public—this dislocation of the right and natural relations between them—has taken place is certain. The causes of it are many and deep-seated in our modern civilization, and I can point out only a few of the more obvious ones." It is clear through this statement that the author's intent is to discuss that which brought modern art and its artists to their current form. This intent is best captured in answer choice C.

22. **The best answer is H.** As seen in the first paragraph of the passage, the author describes Fragonard as "the last of the old masters." Because the "old" in this statement refers to the earlier artists, and because the master artist in this statement can also be defined as the great artist, answer choice H most closely echoes the author's intent when describing Fragonard.

23. **The best answer is A.** The author uses the second paragraph to set up an idea upon which to expand over the course of the passage: "The causes of it are many and deep-seated in our modern civilization, and I can point out only a few of the more obvious ones."

24. **The best answer is G.** According to the passage, David's success was problematic. "As the aim of the Revolution was the destruction of aristocratic privilege, it is not surprising that a revolutionary like David should have felt it necessary to destroy the traditions of an art created for aristocracy. In his own art of painting he succeeded so thoroughly that the painters of the next generation found themselves with no traditions at all." This idea is found in answer choice G.

25. **The best answer is D.** Throughout the passage, the author implies that the current state of art is not the fault of modern artists, but rather the result of choices made by earlier artists. This attitude seems to be one of sympathy.

26. **The best answer is G.** The phrase "an artist in his degree" refers to the efforts put forth by the craftsman of the Middle Ages and Renaissance. Because craftsmen work toward perfecting their individual skills, they were considered to be artists in their own right. This idea is best demonstrated by answer choice G.

27. **The best answer is C.** According to the passage, "Our machine-making, industrial civilization, intent upon material progress and the satisfaction of material wants, has destroyed this popular art; and at the same time that the artist lost his patronage from above, he lost his support from below. He has become a superior person, but he has no longer a splendid nobility to employ him or a world of artisans to surround him and understand him." This best supports answer choice C.

28. **The best answer is J.** The author lists various attributes in the fifth paragraph of the passage to describe modern artists. "Having no compelling reason for doing one thing rather than another, or for choosing one or another way of doing things, he is shown a thousand things that he may do and a thousand ways of doing them. Not clearly knowing his own mind he hears the clash and reverberation of a thousand other minds, and having no certainties he must listen to countless theories." Because the only answer not found in this list of attributes is that the modern artist must isolate himself from other artists, answer choice J is best.

29. **The best answer is C.** According to the passage, "at the same time that the artist lost his patronage from above, he lost his support from below"; *patronage* seems to reflect the encouragement and financial support that artists received from the nobility who employed them. A patron is a person who supports with money or efforts, making answer choice C best. The other answer choices are not supported by the context of the passage.

30. **The best answer is J.** According to the first paragraph of the passage, "Now if we look for the most fundamental distinction between our modern art and the art of past times, I believe we shall find it to be this: the art of the past was produced for a public that wanted it and understood it, by artists who understood and sympathized with their public; the art of our time has been, for the most part, produced for a public that did not want it and misunderstood it, by artists who disliked and despised the public for which they worked." This statement illustrates the split between modern artists and the modern public. It is best summarized by the idea that artists of the past understood their public, while artists of the present renounce their public.

Passage IV

31. **The best answer is A.** The word *nefarious* means "wicked." According to the passage, "people open themselves up to the possibility of a criminal obtaining this information and using it for nefarious purposes. This is but one instance of the negative impact that overreliance on computer technology can have on society." This best supports answer choice A.

32. **The best answer is J.** The context of the passage indicates that "Computers are not only used extensively to perform the industrial and economic functions of society but are also used to provide many services upon which human life depends. Medical treatment, air traffic control, and national security are a few examples. Even a small glitch in the operation of these systems can put human lives in danger." A "glitch" is a "defect." These details best support Answer Choice J.

33. **The best answer is A.** Throughout Passage A, the author indicates that humans rely heavily on technology. The author also mentions several dangers associated with such reliance.

34. The best answer is J. Passage B sheds a more positive light on our dependence on computer technology. Throughout the passage, the author mentions several ways in which computers have helped to advance technology and enhance our lives.

35. The best answer is A. The word "innovation" means "something new." The author uses this word to show that new concepts involving technology are enhancing our lives in many different ways.

36. The best answer is F. "Irony" refers to "an outcome of events contrary to what was, or might have been, expected." Because millions of people expected the world to end on December 31, 1999, and it, in fact, did not, the author's comment displays a sense of irony.

37. The best answer is B. The author of Passage B takes a much more positive tone regarding our reliance on computer technology, mentioning several ways in which it has enhanced our lives. Therefore, it is most likely that he would attempt to suggest a solution to the problem of identity theft and not consider it the danger that the author of Passage A does.

38. The best answer is G. Overall, the author of Passage A takes a more negative approach to human reliance on computer technology, citing several instances in which it can be dangerous. Conversely, the author of Passage B discusses advancements in science and education that have come about as a result of human dependence on computer technology.

39. The best answer is A. Throughout Passage A, the author takes a more negative approach to human reliance on computer technology, citing several instances in which it can be dangerous. On the other hand, the author of Passage B discusses advancements in science and education that have come about as a result of human dependence on computer technology.

40. The best answer is J. While the tone of each passage is different, both passages focus on different ways in which people have come to depend on computer technology.

▬▬▬   SCORING WORKSHEET

On each ACT multiple-choice test (English, Mathematics, Reading, and Science) you will receive a SCALED SCORE on a scale of 1 to 36. Use the following guidelines to determine your approximate SCALED SCORE on the ACT Reading Practice Test that you just completed.

Step 1 Determine your RAW SCORE.

Your RAW SCORE is the number of questions that you answered correctly. Because there are 40 questions on the ACT Reading Test, the highest possible RAW SCORE is 40.

Step 2 Determine your SCALED SCORE using the following Scoring Worksheet.

Reading   ——————— × **36** = ——————— ÷ **40** = ———————

                 RAW SCORE   **+ 2** (*correction factor)

                                                                    ———————

                                                                    SCALED SCORE

   *The correction factor is an approximation based on the average from several recent ACT tests. It is most valid for scores in the middle 50 percent (approximately 16–24 scaled composite score) of the scoring range. The scores are all approximate. Actual ACT scoring scales vary from one administration to the next based upon several factors.

Your SCALED SCORE should be rounded to the nearest number according to normal rules. For example, $31.2 \approx 31$ and $31.5 \approx 32$. If you answered 28 questions correctly on the Reading Test, for example, your SCALED SCORE would be 25.

PART III

THE ACT WRITING TEST

CHAPTER 15

FORMAT AND SCORING

The ACT Writing Test is optional. Your decision to take it or not should be based on the requirements of the colleges and universities to which you are applying. As of the writing of this book, a large number of schools around the country require the ACT Writing Test, so it is in your best interest to check with your schools of choice before you register for the ACT. If you take the Writing Test, it will come after the other ACT sections. You will have a short break after the ACT Science Test before beginning the Writing Test, which you will have 40 minutes to complete.

THE ACT WRITING TEST FORMAT

The Writing Test consists of a "prompt" or "stimulus," which is a brief discussion of a topic that you must respond to, and some blank, lined space in which to write your answer. If you run out of space on this test, you are simply writing too much! There is a more detailed discussion of controlling the length of your response in Chapter 17, "Writing Strategies and Techniques." The essay readers are not looking for long answers; they are looking for quality answers. We discuss exactly what the essay readers are looking for a bit later in this chapter.

The ACT Writing Test is designed to measure your writing skills. The test writers choose topics that reflect change in the modern world. You are given three perspectives to consider. Your goal is to pick a position and support it throughout your essay. The readers will reward you with more points if you stay on your main idea throughout your essay and back up your position by giving specific examples and information. You will certainly do well if you have a clear, logical structure and if your language is correct and free of errors in grammar or vocabulary. Don't take any vocabulary risks when writing this essay. If you are not sure what a word means, don't use it. Do not fill your essay with vernacular, slang, jargon, or profanity.

You will be given some "scratch paper" on this part of the ACT. In Chapter 17, "Writing Strategies and Techniques," we'll tell you how to use the scratch paper. Be certain that you *do* use it! This is not the time to just jump in and start writing a stream-of-consciousness, shoot-from-the-hip answer off the top of your head. You might not have time to do a full first and second draft of this essay but you should make use of the time you are given to be sure that you plan out what you are going to say before you actually start writing your essay.

At this point in your ACT testing day, you are likely to be at least a bit tired. Try to focus on the fact that you are almost finished and do what you can to keep your focus for the last forty minutes.

Study Tip

There is a big overlap between the English section of the ACT and the Writing Test. If you can recognize proper English and recognize common errors in the multiple-choice questions on the ACT English Test, you should be able to avoid making those same errors on the Writing Test.

▬▬ THE ACT WRITING TEST ESSAY PROMPT

The essay prompt will be a few sentences long and will mention an issue that can cause some disagreement. It will include three different perspectives on the issue and instructions to construct an essay in which you take a position and support it.

The page following the prompt will be blank on both sides, except for a note that says that anything that you put on those two pages will not be scored. This is the scratch paper.

Four lined answer pages follow the blank pages. You are to confine your response to those four pages. It may not sound like a lot of space, but we have found that the students who write the most and complain about not having enough room to finish are usually spending too much time on irrelevant discussion or include needless repetition in their essays. You may use a pencil only. No ink is allowed. You should probably write with a medium pressure since, if you don't press hard enough, your words might not scan. If you press too hard, you will have a hard time keeping your essay neat if you need to erase.

The essay prompt essentially describes a debate on an issue that you are likely to have some strong feelings about. If you do have strong feelings, you should just stick with your first response to the issue and work from there. If you don't, the fact that ACT will give you three different responses to the issue means that you can just choose one of them as your starting point. If you have a different response from the ones that are mentioned in the stimulus, then you may write about it. However, this choice is significantly more difficult for most students and should be considered a very advanced technique.

> **Study Tip**
>
> It is always a good idea to get a fresh pair of eyes to review your work. It does not take long for an experienced reader to give feedback that can be immensely valuable to a student.

We have included several essay prompts in later chapters upon which you should base your practice essays. As was noted earlier in this book, humans acquire skills through practice. Since the Writing Test is a test of your writing skills, you should practice writing in order to score better. Specifically, you should practice the type of writing that is rewarded by the scoring rubric (discussed in the next section). The best way to make sure that you are on track is to have someone with experience in this area (your tutor or a teacher, for example) give you specific feedback on the good and not-so-good parts of your practice essays. You can gain something by reading your own essays and comparing them to a rubric. Additionally, you may use our Guided Self-Critique found at the end of this chapter to help you do some analysis on your own. However, remember that writers tend to develop blind spots when it comes to areas that need improvement in their own essays.

▬▬ THE ACT WRITING TEST SCORE

The Writing Test scoring system has undergone some change recently, but the overall goal is still the same: Write a well-structured, convincing essay that conforms to the conventions of Standard Written English. Two graders will each score your essay on a scale of 1-6 (6 is best) across four "domains." Your score will be reported on a 2-12 range, combining the scores of each grader. A thorough review of the information available from ACT reveals that the type of writing that will be rewarded with a top score has not changed. ACT is merely attempting to provide more detailed information to educators and admissions offices. The "new" rubric rewards clarity and logic in exactly the same way as the "old" rubric did.

The most important thing to know about this essay is that there is no correct answer! The readers are looking at the essay as an example of your ability to write a clear, concise, persuasive piece within the time allowed. Do not waste time by trying to figure out which position the test writers want you to choose.

To ensure fairness and accuracy, the two readers independently evaluate each essay. The readers do not know who you are, or how you scored on other sections of the ACT. To keep things simple, we are disregarding the "domains" in the list below of the things to keep in mind when you are practicing to write an essay that will get you a higher score on the ACT.

Score of 6

The essay takes a clear position and discusses other perspectives, including perspectives that may differ from the author's. The essay is logical and complete. There are good transitions and very little or no irrelevant information. There is a solid introduction and conclusion that are consistent with each other and with the argument presented. The essay predicts and deals with counterarguments. While there may be a few errors, they are minor and infrequent. Grammar, spelling, and punctuation are nearly perfect. Vocabulary is effective and appropriate.

Score of 5

The essay takes a clear position on the topic and might give an overall context. The essay deals with some of the complex issues surrounding the topic and at least raises some counterarguments. There are specific examples given. Organization is clear and concise even if it is not creative. Transition signals are used. The author uses language competently and there is some variation in word choice. Any errors present are relatively minor and not distracting.

Score of 4

The essay demonstrates an understanding of the issue and the purpose of the essay is clear. The author states a position on the main issue and at least raises some potential counterarguments. There is adequate development of ideas and some specific reasons and/or examples are given. There is some logical sequence. Most transitions are simple. There is some variety in sentence length and word choice. There are some distracting errors but the essay is still understandable.

Score of 3

The essay reveals that the author has some understanding of the task. There is a clear position but no real overall context is provided. There may be some mention of counterarguments but they are cursory or not clearly stated. The essay may be repetitious or redundant. The essay stays within the general subject but may stray from the specific issue. The organization is simple and predictable. Transitions, if any, are simple and predictable. Introduction and conclusion are present but not well developed. Word choice is generally appropriate and sentences lack variety in length or structure. There are distracting errors that impact understandability.

Score of 2

The essay shows that the author misunderstood the assignment. There is no position taken on the main issue or there are no reasons given. There may be a general example or two but no specific examples offered. There are problems with the relevance of some of the statements made. Transition words may be incorrect or misleading. There are several distracting errors that affect the understandability of the essay.

Score of 1

The author demonstrates almost no grasp of the assignment. The essay fails to take a position or fails to support a position taken. The essay may be excessively redundant. There is little or no structure or coherence. There are several errors that nearly prevent understanding the author's point, if any.

Score of 0

The answer document is blank, the essay is on a topic of the author's own choosing, or the essay is either completely or nearly illegible.

Note that the readers are allowed to assign a score of 6 to an essay that is just a little bit less than perfect. The readers know that you have limited time to write, that you are writing the essay after you have just taken what may be the toughest exam of your life up to now, and that your fatigue and stress levels are likely to be elevated as a result.

Although neatness is not specifically mentioned, the colleges that you are applying to will have access to your essay. This means that the people who are deciding on your applications may take your neatness into account. It may also have an impact on the readers as they assign a score to your essay.

So, make it easy on your reader to interpret those differences in your favor. Keep your essay neat and your handwriting legible. There is nothing in the rules that prevents you from printing rather than writing in cursive. If your printing will be easier for readers and admissions officials to read, then, by all means, print.

Colleges are likely to make use of the scoring information in different ways. You should do some thorough research of the colleges that you are applying to and find out how they interpret ACT results in general, and Writing scores specifically.

Guided Self-Critique

There is no substitute for a review by an experienced grader. However, you can do some self-analysis of your essay by asking yourself the following questions:

1. Have I chosen a position and clearly stated it?
2. Have I organized my thoughts so that the reader can follow easily?
3. Have I used my best college-level vocabulary correctly?
4. Have I acknowledged and dealt with counter arguments effectively?
5. Have I used transition words to help my reader follow my argument?
6. Have I discussed all of the presented perspectives?
7. Is my tone appropriate to the task (not too conversational or excessively self-referential)?

Study Tip

Visit www.act.org for more information on the Writing score.

8. Have I explained any underlying assumptions that my reader may not share?
9. Are all of my paragraphs and sentences contributing support to my position?
10. Have I avoided discussing irrelevant examples/topics?
11. If I were reading this essay for the first time, would I be convinced? Would I be impressed with the quality of the writing?

Use these questions along with the scoring guidelines to come up with a fair and realistic evaluation of your essay.

■■■ WHAT'S NEXT?

Chapter 16 includes an ACT Writing Diagnostic Test, which you should use to determine your current readiness for the real ACT Writing Test. Then read Chapters 17 and 18 to learn the best approach to writing a good essay based on the simulated prompts included in this book (Chapters 19 and 20), and on your actual ACT. Be sure to review Chapter 3, "Grammar Review," to ensure that you are using language correctly in your writing.

CHAPTER 16

ACT WRITING DIAGNOSTIC TEST

This section will assist you in evaluating your current readiness for the ACT Writing Test. Make an honest effort to write the best essay you can within the forty-minute time limit. Chapter 3, "Grammar Review," Chapter 17, "Strategies and Techniques," and Chapter 18, "Applying Strategies, Building Skills," contain information and resources to help you to write a successful ACT essay. Once you have identified your areas of strength and weakness, you should review those particular chapters in the book.

WRITING TEST

DIRECTIONS: This test is designed to assess your writing skills. You have forty minutes to plan and write an essay based on the given perspectives. Read and carefully consider these perspectives. Each suggests a particular way of thinking about the issue. Organize your ideas in a focused and logical way, and use the English language to clearly and effectively express your position.

Write your essay on separate sheets of paper. On the actual ACT you will receive approximately two and a half pages of scratch paper on which to develop your essay, and approximately four pages of notebook paper on which to write your essay. We recommend that you limit yourself to this number of pages when you write your practice essays.

When you have finished writing, refer to the Scoring Rubrics discussed in Chapter 15 to estimate your score. We have also included sample essays at the end of this chapter to which you can compare your essay. Read the scoring explanation for each sample essay to see why a particular score was awarded—this will help you to improve your writing.

Minimum Grade Point Average Requirement

In some states, high school students are required to maintain an adequate grade point average (GPA) in order to be allowed to legally work. Many educators see a link between good grades and responsibility in the work place. Is such a rule beneficial to students and society at large? In light of the changing nature of work and education, is such a rule realistic? Is it enforceable? It is worth considering the impact such rules can have.

Perspective One	Perspective Two	Perspective Three
Academic success and achievement are more important to a young person's future than earning a few extra dollars that will probably be spent on frivolous, temporary pleasures. Working in an entry-level job should be considered only after establishing basic academic skills.	Work experience can be extremely valuable. Preventing students with low academic achievement from gaining it is punishing them twice. Some people are not cut out for higher education, and they should not be prevented from getting an early start on their careers.	A rule requiring a minimum GPA before allowing part-time employment is an unconscionable restriction on students' basic liberty. The government should stay out of decisions that are more properly left to students and their families.

Essay Task

Write a unified, coherent essay in which you evaluate multiple perspectives on the implications of maintaining a certain GPA in order to work. In your essay, be sure to:

- analyze and evaluate the perspectives given
- state and develop your own perspective on the issue
- explain the relationship between your perspective and those given

Your perspective may be in full agreement with any of the others, in partial agreement, or wholly different. Whatever the case, support your ideas with logical reasoning and detailed, persuasive examples.

▰▰ SAMPLE ESSAYS WITH SCORING EXPLANTATIONS

Essay: Score of 6

Today's society is more competitive than ever. The United States has evolved away from an agricultural and industrial economy toward one dominated by business, technological, and commercial services. Never has it been so important to distinguish oneself from the hordes of other young people trying to join the highly skilled workforce. For this reason, no amount of achievement in high school should be sacrificed to earn a few bucks at an hourly job. Having a minimum grade point average for work permits is a responsible measure to ensure high school students have their priorities in order.

Four focused years of high school can mean the difference between advancing into a college or other training program of one's choosing and being limited to a life of unskilled labor. In the American college system, high school grades are crucial, and minimum admissions standards for higher education seem only to be increasing. Freshmen applications outpace the growth of classroom and housing space. Students who work during high school but don't earn good grades may have plenty of spending money, but they are neglecting their investment in their future. Proof abounds that degree-holders make dramatically greater money than their counterparts who don't have college under their belts.

On a philosophical level, requiring a minimum grade point average for work permits reinforces the ethic in our democratic society that personal intellectual growth should supersede the pursuit of wealth. If we let a student enter the workplace while doing poorly in school, we are tacitly indicating that it is acceptable for the student to be uneducated if he or she can bring home a paycheck. Thomas Jefferson identified the risk of not taking education seriously: "Whenever the people are well informed, they can be trusted with their own government." Education is the key to freedom, and high school students who pay little heed to the former risk giving up the latter.

Some may argue that certain students simply do not have the natural abilities to achieve the minimum grade point average, and mandating one infringes on these students' right to keep a job. This argument fails because most jobs (certainly the desirable ones) minimally require a high school diploma. Bad grades can keep students from reaching that milestone, and they may decide to drop out, unaware of the monumental challenges they will face entering the working world with a nearly empty résumé.

In short, four years of high school flashes by, but students' performance there has profound consequences for the rest of their lives. Working is a great use of time when school affairs are already in check. However, students must remember, "first things first." Take care of school; you have a whole life of work ahead of you.

Scoring Explanation

This essay demonstrates effective skill in responding to the writing task.

The essay takes a position on the issue (*Having a minimum grade point average for work permits is a responsible measure to ensure high school students have their priorities in order*) and offers a critical context for discussion (*Never has it been so important to distinguish oneself from the hordes of other young people trying to join the highly skilled workforce*). Complexity is addressed as the writer anticipates and responds to a counterargument (*This argument fails because most jobs [certainly the desirable ones] minimally require a high school diploma*). The writer also shows sophistication by considering both the practical aspects of the issue (*Four focused years of high school can mean the difference between advancing into a college or other training program of one's choosing and being limited to a life of unskilled labor*) and the abstract (*On a philosophical level, requiring a minimum grade point average for work permits reinforces the ethic in our democratic society that personal intellectual growth should supersede the pursuit of wealth*). Development of ideas is ample, specific, and logical. The writer expands on each aspect and develops ideas in a way that clarifies their implications (*Students who work during high school but don't earn good grades may have plenty of spending money, but they are neglecting their investment in their future.... Education is the key to freedom, and high school students who pay little heed to the former risk giving up the latter*). Clear focus on the specific issue in the prompt is maintained.

Organization of the essay is clear if predictable. Most of the ideas are logically sequenced (*On a philosophical level, requiring a minimum grade point average for work permits reinforces the ethic in our democratic society that personal intellectual growth should supersede the pursuit of wealth. If we let a student enter the workplace while doing poorly in school, we are tacitly indicating that it is acceptable for the student to be uneducated if he or she can bring home a paycheck*). Transitions are not often used in this essay (*For this reason, In short, However*), but the ones there are are well-integrated into the essay (*Never has it been so important to distinguish oneself from the hordes of other young people trying to join the highly skilled workforce. For this reason, no amount of achievement in high school should be sacrificed to earn a few bucks at an hourly job*). The lack of transitions is compensated for by the strong logical flow of ideas. The introduction and conclusion are clear, effective, and do not repeat each other. The introduction in particular is well developed.

The essay shows a good command of language, with precise and varied sentences and word choice (*Never has it been so important to distinguish oneself from the hordes of other young people trying to join the highly skilled workforce ... requiring a minimum grade average for work permits reinforces the ethic in our democratic society that personal intellectual growth should supersede the pursuit of wealth*).

There are few, if any, errors to distract the reader.

Essay: Score of 5

In high school, grades are most important. Many people believe that any and all steps should be taken to maximize the achievement of students in high school. After all, unlike elementary and middle school, high school grades have consequences. These days, it's becoming harder and harder to find a job out of high school. Therefore, it is important to go to college or become trained in a job skill. Most higher education won't consider you without at least a high school diploma and sometimes a minimum grade point average. One way to ensure that high school students are devoting enough time to school is by restricting work permits to those students who are making the grade. High school students should put off working if they need the time to improve their grades. After all, there's a whole lifetime of working ahead of us.

The reason for high school is to develop critical thinking skills and important knowledge and skills for the workplace, college, and life in our American democracy. There is nothing more important for a teenager to do than attend school and complete the work. Without education, we are destined to an ignorant life and reduced opportunities. If you blow off class to make a buck, you are potentially wasting a future of higher wages in favor of a quick dollar today. If you flunk out your junior year, how many more years will it take you to get your GED? At the clothing store where I work, you can't become a shift leader without a high school diploma. That's a difference of over $4 an hour. Not taking high school seriously could mean you sit at a lower wage for months or years. Clearly, the value of working a nearly minimum wage job during high school pales in comparison to the value of getting your grades right before working, even if that means waiting until you graduate to find a job.

If you don't make decent grades in high school, you can't go to college, and people with degrees make much more money than young people on the minimum-wage path. Most of the colleges I'm applying to have freshman classes with very good test scores and average GPAs around 3.3. These applicants are the best students from many great schools. If you hope to compete with so many new high school graduates, you need to set everything aside that you must to get good grades. Even if you buy into the argument that grades aren't everything, you need to see that they're a vital part of the system as it exists today. A history of bad grades simply can't be explained away.

In our American democratic society, developing reason is of paramont importance. Devoting yourself to academic excellence is seen as admirable and honorable. It gives you confidence to make the most of yourself. When your young, curious, and full of energy, you should do whatever it takes to get good grades. The state can help by requiring good grades before issuing a work permit. Teens have years and years of work ahead of them, so they should sieze on the educational opportunities they have now before it's too late.

Scoring Explanation

This essay demonstrates competent skill in responding to the task.

The essay shows a clear understanding of the task. The essay takes the position in favor of students maintaining a certain grade point average in order to obtain a work permit (*High school students should put off working if they need the time to improve their grades*). The issue is placed in the broader context of increasing future earning potential by maximizing the high school learning experience (*it's becoming harder and harder to find a job out of high school. Therefore, it is important to go to college or become trained in a job skill.*

Most higher education won't consider you without at least a high school diploma and sometimes a minimum grade point average).

The essay shows recognition of complexity by partially evaluating the implications of attempting to earn good wages without a high school diploma (*If you blow off class to make a buck, you are potentially wasting a future of higher wages in favor of a quick dollar today*) or trying to attend a good university without strong grades (*If you hope to compete with so many new high school graduates, you need to set everything aside that you must to get good grades*). The writer does not completely explore a counterargument, but hints at one in the third paragraph (*Even if you buy into the argument that grades aren't everything, you need to see that they're a vital part of the system as it exists today*).

Development of ideas is specific and logical. Most ideas are elaborated, with clear movement between general statements (*Without education, we are destined to an ignorant life and reduced opportunities*) and specific reasons, examples and details (*At the clothing store where I work, you can't become a shift leader without a high school diploma. That's a difference of over $4 an hour*). Focus on the specific issue in the prompt is maintained.

The organization of the essay is clear, although transitions could be better used to guide the reader through the writer's argument. Ideas are logically sequenced within paragraphs, especially the second paragraph which moves smoothly from general ideas to specific points and then on to a conclusion. The essay's introduction and conclusion are clear and generally well developed, though the relevance of civic responsibility *American democracy*) is never explained.

Language is competent and clear. Sentences are varied and somewhat sophisticated in structure (*In our American democratic society, developing reason is of paramount importance*) and word choice is sometimes varied and precise (*reduced opportunities, pales in comparison*). The essay contains a few spelling errors (*paramont, sieze*) and some syntactical errors, but they are rarely distracting.

Essay: Score of 4

Work permits are a way for the government to make sure that students aren't working too much. Even though there is a limit to how many hours a student can work once they get the permit, even a legal number of hours per week can be too much for some students. To decide who should be able to work and who shouldn't, students should have to make a minimum grade point average before earning a work permit.

First, high school is the most important part of teenagers lives. Without school, students would be ignorant, and employers don't want ignorant people to work for them. It is important to get good grades through hard work in order to be prepared for a career. Many students don't realize this though, and they don't believe adults who tell them, so having the law require good grades in order to work is a good idea. My friend Ray works about twenty-five hours per week at a fast food place and earns around a B–average at school. I know he could do better if he spent less time working and more time studying. Because my state doesn't require good grades to work, Ray can keep spending all the money he gets from work on his fancy stereo and chrome accessories for his truck. It would be helpful for him if the law made him get good grades to continue earning money.

Second, the state is better off if their students get good grades. Anything that would help should be made law. Kids who get good grades are happier, better behaved, and more productive members of society. Kids who get bad grades might end up dropping out or having low self-esteem, which can lead to crimes, gang behavior, and drug use. The state wouldn't need to spend so much money on keeping all the teenage hoodlums in check. Plus good grades can get you into college, which means more skilled workers for the state. They earn more money for their families in the long run, so working in high school is no big deal. Wasting high school just to make around minmum wage is a bad decision.

In conclusion, for the sake of students and the state, work permits should be issued only when students make a minimum grade point average. Some people might say that work and school are unrelated, but this is untrue. High school should be the most important parts of students lives.

Scoring Explanation

The essay demonstrates adequate skill in responding to the task.

The writer takes a position (*To decide who should be able to work and who shouldn't, students should have to make a minimum grade point average before earning a work permit*) and offers some context for discussion (*Work permits are a way for the government to make sure that students aren't working too much*). The essay also shows some recognition of complexity by acknowledging multiple perspectives and providing some response to a counterargument to the writer's position (*Even though there is a limit to how many hours a student can work once they get the permit, even a legal number of hours per week can be too much for some students*).

Development of ideas is adequate, with two ideas discussed and with some movement between general statements (*the state is better off if their students get good grades*) and specific reasons, examples, and details (*Kids who get bad grades might end up dropping out or having low self-esteem, which can lead to crimes, gang behavior, and drug use*). Focus on the specific issue in the prompt is maintained throughout the essay.

The organization of the essay is apparent but predictable, with obvious transitions (*First, Second, In conclusion*). There is some evidence of logical sequencing in the body of the essay (*It is important to get good grades through hard work in order to be prepared for a career. Many students don't realize this though, and they don't believe adults who tell them, so having the law require good grades in order to work is a good idea. … I know he could do better if he spent less time working and more time studying*). The introduction and conclusion are both clear, though the introduction is better developed.

The writer demonstrated adequate ability with language, using a variety of sentence types (*Kids who get good grades are happier, better behaved, and more productive members of society … They earn more money for their families in the long run, so working in high school is no big deal.*). Word choice is simple, but clear and appropriate. There are few distracting errors (*their* instead of *its* in the third paragraph) to impede understanding.

Essay: Score of 3

I feel that students should not be required to maintain a minimum grade point average in order to work outside of school. It's not a fair policy. Just because a student doesn't have the best grade point average doesn't mean that they can't do a good job at work. Especially since not all students are meant to take an academic route. I mean, yeah, school is good for all students, but I think to require students to meet grade point average requirements discriminates against the kids that see themselves as more skilled in the workforce than in school.

Also, some students have to work because of their economic situation I know I have friends that work so they can pay for clothes and have money to do stuff like go to the movies and go out to dinner. If our school had a grade point requirement, some of my friends wouldn't be able to work and then they would never have money to buy anything. That's another reason why a grade point average requirement is a bad idea.

Schools shouldn't be able to interfere with a student's right to work. It's one thing to have a grade point requirement for school sports and activities but when a school has a grade point requirement in order to give a student a work permit, they are taking it too far. Schools should leave some areas alone. Student employment thats one of them.

Scoring Explanation

This essay shows a developing skill in responding to the task.

The essay takes a clear position (*I feel that students should not be required to maintain a minimum grade point average in order to work outside of school*), but does not provide the necessary context for discussion. Instead, it veers from the task at hand (*Just because a student doesn't have the best grade point average doesn't mean that they can't do a good job at work*).

It mentions a counterargument (*not all students are meant to take an academic route*), but fails to properly develop it. There is only a single appropriate use of a transition (*Also*). The opening and closing sentences signal an introduction and a conclusion, but the essay as a whole lacks development. Sentences are somewhat varied in length, but there are numerous grammatical and structural errors (*Also, some students have to work because of their economic situation I know I have friends that work so they can pay for clothes and have money to do stuff like go to the movies and go out to dinner*) and (*Student employment thats one of them*). Errors are at all times distracting.

ACT WRITING DIAGNOSTIC TEST 237

Essay: Score of 2

If you ask high school students if they want to have to go to a job after school and still have to do homework and other stuff most of them would say no. To be able too have a job kids should have to get good grades before. Having to worry about a job and also school is having lots of students be stresed to much. I would like to have a job insted of just school so that I would make some extra money but I would be nervus about school and grades.

In school there are already enough things that students have to do and have to worry about and its lots of work that would be lots harder if they had to work after school. Students do not have any time to hang out with there friends or do other things if they have to go to a job to. If they has to work after school than they won't do the homework that is do the next day.

Because kids already have lots of stuff to deal with at school. They shouldn't have to go work at a job also. If they do want to go to work because they are needing to make money real bad then they should have to have got real good grades first so that they still learn school and also learn working at a job.

Scoring Explanation

This essay demonstrates weak skill in responding to the task.

Although the essay takes a position on the issue (*To be able to have a job kids should have to get good grades before*), there is a lack of focus on the thesis throughout the rest of the essay. For example, the essay discusses the difficulties of holding a job while going to school full-time (*Having to worry about a job and also school is having lots of students be stressed to much … In school there are already enough things that students have to do … Students don't have any time to hang out with there friends*), but does not explain why a minimum grade point average should be required before students can begin working. While there is some organizational structure evident in this essay through the division of the essay into paragraphs, the absence of transitions still leaves the essay lacking in fluidity. Word choice and sentence structure are simple, and frequent punctuation and grammar errors (*If they has to work after school than they won't do the homework that is do the next day*) are distracting.

Essay: Score of 1

I am deciding to write that students should not have to have a certain good grades to get a work permit to work after school at there job. So what if there grades aren't as good if you can make some money. I know that I like my job that I had from last year when we were at school. I think that every students should go to a job and also should play sports. I played football during school and I made lots of new freinds and our team has a awesome season and we beet our rival team. I like football practice and work at my job more then I like school and boring homework. Lots of students thinks the same things as me.

Scoring Explanation

This essay fails to achieve the task.

While the essay does assume a position (*students should not have to get a work permit to work after school at there job*), the essay offers no support for the thesis. Instead, it moves off topic by discussing the importance of both working and playing a sport (*I think that every students should go to a job and also should play sports*). The essay is poorly organized, exhibiting no evidence of an introduction or a conclusion. Frequent use of grammar, spelling, and punctuation errors (*I played football during school and I made lots of new freinds and our team has a awesome season and we beet our rival team*) are distracting and weaken the argument.

CHAPTER 17

STRATEGIES AND TECHNIQUES

This chapter includes the necessary steps for writing the best ACT Writing Test essay that you can within the forty-minute time period. Perform each step in order, and do one thing at a time—this is not the time for improvisation or multitasking! If you were to simply read the stimulus and then write your essay from the beginning to the end, you would certainly be doing several tasks at once. You would be creating the logical structure of your essay; searching your memory for vocabulary words; anticipating counterarguments; trying to correctly apply the rules of grammar, punctuation, and spelling; and remembering some good, relevant examples to plug into your essay structure. In short, students who write without planning are setting themselves up for a disappointing score. This chapter begins with a discussion of the ACT Writing Test essay prompt, and continues with an introduction to the structure of a well-written essay and some specific strategies to help you to write your best under test conditions.

THE ACT ESSAY PROMPT

Study Tip

Be sure to explain the connection between the examples that you are using and your conclusion. Don't assume that the reader will agree with your viewpoint regarding the significance of a given fact.

The ACT Writing Test does not require any specialized knowledge on your part. You are not tested on what you might know about a particular subject. Instead, you are given an opportunity to demonstrate your ability to reason clearly and write coherently and concisely. College admissions people are looking for logical reasoning, clarity, organization, writing mechanics, and proper language usage. You are expected to think clearly and critically about the issue and create a thoughtful, well-reasoned essay supporting your position.

Remember, there is never a "correct" answer on the ACT Writing Test. Your task is simply to write a good essay from whatever perspective you choose. In addition, how *well* you write is much more important than how *much* you write. You should write enough to clearly support your position within the allotted time.

There are many possible responses to any issue prompt. You might agree or disagree in part or in whole. You might attack the underlying assumptions in the statement that is given. You might indicate that the statement you are writing about has only limited applicability in certain situations. You should use at least one example to support your position. You can use more than one example as long as the examples you select are relevant and you stay focused on your main idea.

The issues in the prompts are carefully chosen so that they aren't biased toward any college major or profession. However, luck is a bit of a factor on the ACT Writing Test. If you are presented with an issue that you know something about, you will probably feel more comfortable writing about it. But be careful to respond to the issue presented and the assignment given. Don't answer a question that wasn't asked just because you happen to know something about the subject matter.

WHAT MAKES A GOOD ESSAY

Effective writing is well organized and focused. A good writer displays skill in structuring sentences and uses precise and relevant vocabulary. Following is an introduction to the elements of a good essay.

The Paragraph

Sentences are grouped into paragraphs, each of which represents a unique thought or line of reasoning. Each paragraph should have a topic sentence that clearly defines the purpose of the paragraph. Consider the following paragraph:

> *Blue is certainly my favorite color.* All day, I find myself staring at the sky or the lake. The color seems to match anything—just consider denim jeans, the most popular pants in the world! Blue is the color of true indigo, a rare and alluring natural pigment. The blue backdrop in the American flag represents vigilance, perseverance, and justice.

The first sentence is the topic sentence, a notion that all the other sentences in the paragraph work together to support. Your topic sentence should clearly state the objective of the paragraph.

There is no absolute rule about how many sentences should make up a paragraph. The best test is to consider whether a topic is introduced and fully supported, and whether the paragraph keeps from straying to secondary or minor points. Paragraph length is also an important consideration. Readers struggle with a lot of little paragraphs or just a few very large ones, so be sure to vary the lengths of your paragraphs as you write. The next sections outline the components of a well-constructed paragraph.

Logical Order

Sentences within a paragraph should be arranged in an order that corresponds to time or mental reasoning. Consider this example of poor logical order:

> During the mating season, male robins are characterized by brilliant black feathers on their heads. Robins can lay two sets of eggs in a season. The bird is commonly seen snatching worms from the earth to feed hatchlings. Soon, the females arrive to choose their mates and breed. They return to northern breeding grounds earlier than the females in order to compete with each other for the best nesting sites.

Following is the same series of sentences placed in a more logical order:

> During the mating season, male robins are characterized by brilliant black feathers on their heads. They return to northern breeding grounds earlier than the females in order to compete with each other for the best nesting sites. Soon, the females arrive to choose their mates and breed. Robins can lay two sets of eggs in a season. The bird is commonly seen snatching worms from the earth to feed hatchlings.

This paragraph could benefit from a topic sentence that unifies it, as shown below:

> *Early spring is a wonderful time to watch amazing bird activity.* During the mating season, male robins are characterized by brilliant black feathers on their heads. They return to northern breeding grounds earlier than the females in order to compete with each other for the best nesting sites. Soon, the females arrive to choose their mates and breed. Robins can lay two sets of eggs in a season. The bird is commonly seen snatching worms from the earth to feed hatchlings.

Correct Pronoun Use

When composing paragraphs, pay close attention to pronouns. Use your best judgment to determine if the reader may forget an antecedent. Consider the following example:

> Larry is my brother. As kids, he and I would terrorize the neighborhood. During the summer, we would keep street hockey games going long into the evening. On the empty lot, he liked to build dirt ramps.

By the time the reader comes to the last sentence, the antecedent of *he* is too distant a memory. *Larry* should be substituted.

Similarly, repetition of words can make writing dull, as shown next:

> The *tree* in my backyard was tall and gnarled. I marveled at that centuries-old *tree* every day as a kid. I wished the *tree* could tell stories about this land.

Other words could be substituted for *tree* to increase variety in the sentences, as follows:

> The *oak* in my backyard was tall and gnarled. I marveled at that centuries-old tree every day as a kid. I wished *that wise man* could tell stories about this land.

Figurative language, such as the personification of the tree in the last sentence of the previous example, makes reading more interesting. Avoid clichés, however, which are figures of speech that have lost their novelty due to overuse.

Effective Word Choice

Be sure to explain the connection between the facts you are using and your conclusion. Don't assume that the reader will agree with your viewpoint regarding the significance of a given fact. For instance, imagine an essay about schools. A prejudicial statement in the essay, such as "… *which is merely a public school*," reveals the writer's bias, and may not actually contribute to a convincing essay.

Consider "100 percent" words carefully. Words such as *every, everyone, all, entire, whole, none, no one, zero, always,* and *never* are absolute terms, which should generally be avoided. If you think critically about a topic, you usually find that there are likely exceptions, as shown next:

> **(1)** *It is always hot in Arizona.*

This cannot be true if Arizona has ever had cool weather.

> **Rephrase:** *It is usually hot in Arizona.*

> **(2)** *No doctor likes to reveal bad news.*

This cannot be true if there ever was a doctor who liked revealing bad news.

> **Rephrase:** *Compassionate doctors do not like to reveal bad news.*

Use *most* and *majority* carefully. These words mean "more than 50 percent" specifically, so be sure not to make overly broad statements. Consider the following examples:

> **(3)** *Most Americans like football.*

Certainly many Americans like football, but without specific data, it is impossible to know if football fans exceed half of the total population.

> **Rephrase:** *Many Americans like football.*

> *(4) A majority of the guests enjoyed the meal.*

Unless you know the total number of guests and the specific number of guests who enjoyed the meal, you cannot assume they number over half, regardless of general impression.

> **Rephrase:** *I believe a majority of the guests enjoyed the meal.*

No Redundant or Irrelevant Language

Good writing does not include information irrelevant to the topic of a sentence or paragraph. An effective paragraph conveys its information precisely and concisely. Many writers who strive to lengthen their work make the mistake of including redundant information. Consider the following paragraph:

> My first baseball game was *awesome* and *amazing*. My father bought us *third-row seats, not right in front*, along the first-base line right by the wall. I enjoyed all the action as I munched on nachos and a hotdog. *I like a lot of relish on my hotdogs.* Our team won the game, and I got to spend quality time with my dad. I would love to do it again.

Awesome and *amazing* are synonyms; they have nearly the same meaning. One should be eliminated. *Third-row* implies that the *seats* are *not right in front*, making the latter phrase unnecessary. The sentence "*I like a lot of relish on my hot dogs.*" is irrelevant because the paragraph is about the writer's enjoyment of watching a baseball game, not the writer's choice of condiments.

The Relationship Between Paragraphs

Paragraphs must have a certain amount of independence from each other, yet they should have similar tone and style, and provide the reader with a meaningful transition from one topic to the next.

For example, do not use a pronoun in one paragraph whose antecedent is in a previous paragraph, as shown next:

> … John was an interesting fellow. I only knew him from one class in high school, but he instantly made an impression on me.

> The first time I met *him* was on the steps outside the building.

Replace *him* in the new paragraph with its antecedent, *John*.

Use "transition" words and phrases within and between paragraphs to introduce new topics or evidence. There are four basic categories of transition words. Following is a list of those categories along with some sample transition words:

- **Contrast:** *but, however, on the other hand, conversely, alternatively, although, even though*
- **Similarity:** *likewise, similarly*
- **Evidence:** *since, because, in light of, first, second, third*
- **Conclusion:** *therefore, thus, as a result, so, it follows that, in conclusion*

Study Tip

Transition words help to lead the reader through your essay, and can improve the overall flow of your essay.

Observe how transition words are used to tie the following sentences and paragraphs together:

> Youth baseball pitchers are discouraged from practicing complicated pitches, *since* developing shoulders and elbows may not tolerate the powerful twisting and snapping action required to produce effective curveballs, screwballs, and the like. Little League Baseball, *however*, does not officially recognize any evidence that particular pitches lead to increased instances of injury, *since* the only studies on the subject have been conducted with college-age or older pitchers.
>
> *On the other hand*, evidence does exist that injury is minimized when the total number of pitches thrown by a young player is minimized. *As a result*, USA Baseball has issued recommendations for safe total pitch counts according to player age.

▬▬ COMMON MISTAKES TO AVOID

Review these common errors that test takers make in their essays. If you know what to avoid, you'll not only be a better writer, but you'll have a much easier time on the ACT English multiple-choice test.

Too General

Effective writing uses specific examples. Think of the best teachers you have had. They tend to tell you the general concept that they are teaching and then give one or more specific, memorable examples. This strategy works because of the memorable examples.

For example, if you are told that there is no progress without determination and hard work, you might accept the statement as true and you may even remember it. However, you will have a much better chance of fully grasping the idea and remembering it later if you are given a specific example such as Thomas Edison, who tried thousands and thousands of different filament materials in his light bulbs before finally settling on one that gave acceptable light and lasted a reasonable period of time.

Too often, students make broad, general statements in their essays without giving any specific support. Make sure that you provide clear, simple examples of the general statements that you make.

Too Emotional and Opinionated

While it is true that the stimulus will ask you for an opinion, you should not make the entire essay about your feelings. You should state what your opinion is and then back up your opinion with well-reasoned logical support. Tell the reader *why* you feel the way you do rather than just saying *how* you feel.

Overly Complicated

Many coaches and teachers have suggested that students apply the K.I.S.S. principle. While there is a slightly less polite formulation, we'll explain the K.I.S.S. Principle as an acronym for "Keep It Short and Sweet." Do not use three words when one will do.

For example, write, "*There are better proposals.*" Do not write, "*I believe that I am correct when I state that the previously proposed solution to this complicated problem will be less than completely effective as compared to other potential solutions that have been brought forth recently.*"

The essay readers are not going to be blown away by your ability to use a dozen words to state a simple idea. They are going to be blown away if you are able to make your point cleanly and clearly.

Risky Vocabulary

As we mentioned previously, if you are not sure what a word means, or whether it would be appropriate to your essay, don't use it. Many an otherwise good essay has been sunk by a word or two used incorrectly, which made the essay grader question the author's writing abilities.

Poor Penmanship

As discussed in Chapter 15, "Format and Scoring," the reader has to assign a score to your essay that depends on his or her interpretation of the terms in the rubric (scoring guide). In order to help the reader interpret those terms in your favor, you should write, or print, as neatly as you can. Make it easy for the readers to find the good things about your essay that will allow them to give you all of the points that your hard work deserves.

Shaky Logic

Your ACT Writing Test essay should describe your position on a given topic. The essay should have a conclusion about the topic and support for that conclusion.

Choose relevant examples that are connected to your topic in a direct way. One way to do this is to use examples that show a cause-effect relationship. For example, *"I really think I would enjoy teaching high school Spanish. Students are generally in a brighter mood in language classes. Happy students learn more, and through classroom learning they come to respect the teacher."*

While you may disagree with the conclusion of the above argument, you have to admit that there is a cause-effect connection between the evidence presented and the position that the author takes.

Unsafe Assumptions

There are two components to an assertion: evidence and conclusion. Evidence leads to conclusion. You need at least two pieces of evidence to support one conclusion. If you only give one piece of evidence, you are making an assumption. Logic professors refer to assumptions as "suppressed premises," which is just a fancy way to say "unstated evidence." If you leave too much of your evidence unstated, your argument starts to get weak.

For example, if an essay says, *"Curfews are dangerous because what if I have to be somewhere after midnight?"* The reader immediately starts to wonder, "Where could you have to be so late? What would you be doing?" There are simply too many unanswered questions. If the reader agrees with the position that the writer is taking, he or she might "help" with the assumptions and provide examples and answers to the unanswered questions. The reader might read the statement above and fill in an example from his or her own life or one that he or she would consider plausible. Minimize the number of unanswered questions by providing evidence to support your conclusion.

Too Conversational

The ACT Writing Test essay is supposed to be an example of your command of standard written English. Read Chapter 3, "Grammar Review," if you are still uncertain about how to effectively apply the rules of grammar.

Avoid the generic *you*: "*You could feel the tension in the room when Jeff had a pizza delivered to American History class.*" The pronoun does not actually mean "you, the reader." The person making that statement should have said, "*I could feel the tension …*" or "*We could all feel the tension ….*"

In conversation we often try to be inclusive and gender-neutral, although English has no third-person singular gender-neutral pronouns. *They, their, them,* and *theirs* must only be used as plurals in writing. Be careful not to use them when you're referring to singular subjects (a student, the teacher, and so on).

Always remember that your essay needs to be a formal document. It is not appropriate to write in the same idiom that you use with friends in informal conversation.

■■■ STEPS TO WRITING WELL

Now that you have a grasp of what a good essay contains, you should follow these steps in the order they are presented to maximize your ACT Writing Test score.

Carefully Read the Prompt

Know what the task is before you begin. Read the essay prompt a couple of times to be certain that you understand what you are reading. The stimulus is short, so reading carefully will not take up much of your time. One or two minutes will probably be sufficient.

Do not rush through this step, however, as rushing can cost valuable points and make some of your hard work worthless.

For instance, many students write essays that argue vehemently against school *uniforms* when responding to a prompt that mentions school *dress codes*, but never actually mentions uniforms. While it is possible to write an essay that takes the idea of dress codes one step further and actually advocate for school uniforms, an essay that argues against something that is never even mentioned reveals a clear misunderstanding of the stimulus. An essay that does not directly and accurately address the stimulus will probably only be assigned a score of 3, which is particularly tragic when it is otherwise extremely well written.

Think About the Prompt

If the topic is something that you have thought about, or discussed in the past, then you may already have an opinion. If not, then take a short time to formulate one. The test writers are careful to choose topics that have at least two sides that can be successfully argued.

Remember that one of the criteria in the rubric is taking a position on the issue. This is not the time to be overly diplomatic. Take a side and defend your choice. This decision process should not take very long, a few minutes at most.

Study Tip

Don't be afraid to use your test booklet to underline, circle, or make other notations to help you understand the prompt. It may prevent you from making a mistake in responding to the prompt.

Study Tip

There is no correct or incorrect position. Either side can be supported, so choose the side for which you have more relevant examples.

Plan Your Essay

Start your essay with a clear statement of your position on the issue. The reader should have no doubt about which side you are on.

Use the scratch paper that is provided to outline the structure of your essay. Your outline does not have to include complete sentences. It does have to include the ideas that you will put into your final draft. You need to be sure that you have a clear picture of where you are going and how you will get there before you start to write on the answer pages.

Many test takers use a cluster diagram, which is a visual representation of how details are used to support a main idea. In a cluster diagram, supporting details are linked to the central idea. If you plan your specific evidence, each evidence item should appear as a bubble attached to the statements that surround the main idea. This task is sometimes called *webbing* because the result is something that resembles a web with lines radiating from the center. (Figure 17.1 shows an example of a cluster diagram used to plan an essay about technology.)

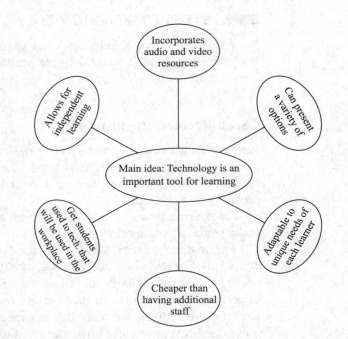

Figure 17.1

Be sure that you have a clear introduction, a body, and a conclusion that echoes the introduction. You may choose to write a traditional five-paragraph essay, but it is possible to write a very effective essay with more or fewer paragraphs. Organization and flow is more important than length.

You will hear some of the other test takers around you scratching furiously with their pencils from the beginning of the forty-minute period. Sometimes that sound can make you feel like you are getting behind. You are not. Remember that the planning stage is the most important stage. If you do solid planning and outlining, it will be as though you are turning in a second draft of your essay, rather than a rushed first draft.

Write Your Essay on the Lined Pages

The final step in the essay writing process is to, well, write your essay! You've read and understood the prompt, have decided upon your position, and have outlined your response. Now it's time to tackle the essay. Discuss each of the three presented perspectives at least briefly. Of course, you should advocate for your position. But, you must deal with counterarguments effectively and explain why you disagree. Your essay is meant to make an argument, and arguments are much more effective when they do not ignore potential problems and weaknesses with their main points. Do not fall into the trap of simply pointing out positive aspects of your position and negative aspects of other, competing positions. Striking a blow against the opposition is not precisely the same as supporting your position. Most perspectives have both positive and negative implications; discuss both, and present a balanced picture that leads the reader to supporting your conclusions. Be sure to include the following four categories of information in your essay:

- **Positive for your position**—*I believe that dress codes in school should be supported because such codes would allow students to focus on school work, rather than on the latest fashions.*
- **Negative for your position**—*However, because some students express themselves through their choice of clothing, dress codes might reduce a student's freedom of expression.*
- **Positive for the other side**—*There are those who believe that dress codes are an example of just one more restriction placed on young people today.*
- **Negative for the other side**—*Nevertheless, dress codes can be an important means of imposing necessary order on a teenager's sometimes chaotic life.*

An effective essay uses facts from all four categories. You can think of your side as "correct" and the other side as "incorrect." When you write a paragraph that is focused on the "correct" side of the issue, you should mention at least one aspect of your choice that might be seen as a negative by some people. Of course, you should be sure to mention plenty of positive information to overcome the potential downside that you are admitting to.

Apply the same technique when you discuss the opposition's position. You should admit that the other side of the debate has at least one strong point. Then, refute the other side of the argument with ample evidence so that your side ends up looking like the clear winner. This is known as *dealing with potential counterarguments*, and it is the most effective way of presenting a persuasive written argument.

Refer back to Chapter 16, "ACT Writing Diagnostic Test," for examples of both good and bad essays. Take another look at the essay evaluations to see how the strategies and techniques in this chapter were applied to the essays that received the highest scores.

◼◼ REVISING AND EDITING

You will probably have little time to read over your essay, so do not expect to be able to catch all of your mistakes. Errors in mechanics should be fixed, but not at the expense of correcting faulty reasoning or gaps in support of your opinions. If your essay fails on a conceptual level, your score will suffer. Take care of your logic and evidence errors first, and then correct spelling, punctuation, and grammar. Do this neatly, with a minimum of scratch-outs. To eliminate something that you have written, draw a single line through it. Do not make a big patch over each word.

▰▰▰   WHAT'S NEXT?

Chapter 18 includes exercises designed to help you master the ACT Writing Test. Focus on those areas that give you the most trouble, and be sure to review the exercise explanations and sample essay evaluations.

CHAPTER 18

APPLYING STRATEGIES, BUILDING SKILLS

This chapter contains exercises designed to help you write more effectively and in accordance with the ACT Writing Test scoring rubrics outlined in Chapter 15. The ACT English exercises in Chapter 5 will also help you to improve your writing. Remember to practice your writing skills sufficiently before test day.

WRITING A GOOD ESSAY

Effective writing is well organized and focused. A good writer displays skill in structuring sentences and uses precise and relevant vocabulary. The exercises on the following pages will help you to hone your writing skills.

Correcting Sentences

Efficient development of sentences is rewarded on the ACT Writing Test. A good sentence has all of the elements in the right place and is clear and concise. Read the following sentences and select the best choice for the underlined portion from among those listed.

Pronoun Use

1. When a city faces high rates of unemployment, people often blame government officials for <u>its</u> lack of leadership.
   A. CORRECT AS IS
   B. their
   C. one's
   D. your

2. Learning to identify the constellations can be a satisfying hobby, particularly if <u>they live</u> in an area of mostly clear skies.
   A. CORRECT AS IS
   B. some live
   C. it lives
   D. one lives

3. Today, canoeing is mostly a form of entertainment and exercise, but <u>they</u> began as a mode of transportation.
   A. CORRECT AS IS
   B. it
   C. some
   D. one

4. Because the production company failed to properly advertise its upcoming play, <u>their attendance</u> on opening night was, not surprisingly, very low.
   A. CORRECT AS IS
   B. its attendance
   C. our attendance
   D. the attendance

5. Dogs may love to chew on bones, but pet owners need to be mindful of <u>his or her chewing habits</u> to avoid digestive obstructions.
   A. CORRECT AS IS
   B. its chewing habits
   C. their dogs' chewing habits
   D. some chewing habits

6. Two years ago, one of our international students was Pietro Martinico, <u>who</u> came from Sicily.
   A. CORRECT AS IS
   B. that
   C. which
   D. he who

7. Teachers provide in-depth language understanding, and children are rewarded for improving <u>his or her</u> communication skills.
   A. CORRECT AS IS
   B. ones'
   C. there
   D. their

8. During the Great Depression, at least 13 million people <u>lost them jobs</u>.
   A. CORRECT AS IS
   B. lost his or her jobs
   C. lost they're job
   D. lost their jobs

9. Until they were widely harvested for <u>any</u> ivory tusks in the twentieth century, African elephants were plentiful throughout the savannahs of Africa.
   A. CORRECT AS IS
   B. its
   C. they're
   D. their

10. As a rule of thumb, I avoided any classes requiring psychology research, because <u>they</u> generally involved some form of pain or deprivation for little credit.
    A. CORRECT AS IS
    B. some
    C. one
    D. any

Word Choice

1. The first step in the Scientific Method is to define the problem, which can sometimes be the <u>more</u> difficult step of all.
   A. CORRECT AS IS
   B. less
   C. most
   D. many

2. The company did not pay annual bonuses to some managers because it believed that doing so <u>rewards</u> them for cutting essential staff.
   A. CORRECT AS IS
   B. has rewarded
   C. will reward
   D. rewarded

3. Attempting to remove two feet of snow from your driveway, even if you use a <u>high-powered snow blower</u>, can be a daunting task.
   A. CORRECT AS IS
   B. snow blower of high power
   C. snow blower with high power
   D. snow blower having high power

4. In 2004, Pablo Picasso's painting *Boy with a Pipe* sold for over $100 million, <u>and it was</u> the highest price ever paid for one of his paintings.
   A. CORRECT AS IS
   B. being
   C. becoming
   D. which was

5. Although Caleb performs well in all of his classes, he finds classes with a <u>smaller amount</u> of students to be the most beneficial.
   A. CORRECT AS IS
   B. less amount
   C. less number
   D. smaller number

6. Aware of the flu epidemic spreading around school, Jacob didn't need to see a doctor to find out why he wasn't feeling <u>good</u>.
   A. CORRECT AS IS
   B. as healthy as he could be feeling
   C. well
   D. good enough

7. One of Melanie's favorite things to do after a long day at work is change into pajamas and <u>lie</u> down for a nap.
   A. CORRECT AS IS
   B. lies
   C. lays
   D. laying

8. Before taking off for a week-long vacation at the family cottage, Emma wanted to <u>insure</u> that all of her apartment's doors and windows were locked.
   A. CORRECT AS IS
   B. assure
   C. ensure
   D. go over

9. It took fifteen minutes of my mother poking and prodding my little brother before he was <u>already</u> to go.
   A. CORRECT AS IS
   B. completely already
   C. completely all ready
   D. all ready

10. It's unfortunate that ten years have passed and still there has been no communication <u>between</u> Jonathan and his father.
    A. CORRECT AS IS
    B. among
    C. within
    D. amongst

Redundant Language

1. The escalating rate of tuition <u>is rising and many students are kept from attending college</u>; some blame the school administrators for poor allocation of funds, but the administrators themselves blame the lack of state and private funding.
   A. CORRECT AS IS
   B. is rising and keeps many students from attending college
   C. has risen to keep many students from attending college
   D. is keeping many students from attending college

2. <u>The marathon's finish line having been reached at the end of the race,</u> many of the exhausted runners collapsed into chairs and began guzzling water.
   A. CORRECT AS IS
   B. When having reached that marathon's finish line at the end
   C. When they reached the marathon's finish line
   D. At the marathon's finish line, when they reached the end

3. June 24th is still considered Midsummer Day, marking the <u>halfway point, the point that is</u> between planting and harvesting summer crops.
   A. CORRECT AS IS
   B. point of time between the times of
   C. halfway point that is the one between
   D. halfway point

4. Willa Cather wrote her first novel in 1911 <u>at the age of thirty-eight years old</u>.
   A. CORRECT AS IS
   B. and she was thirty-eight years old that year
   C. when she was thirty-eight
   D. at the time when she was thirty-eight years of age

5. Indeed the variations <u>could be endless for an eternity</u>, with the addition of each new color creating slightly different versions.
   A. CORRECT AS IS
   B. could go on endlessly for an eternity
   C. could be an endless eternity
   D. could be endless

6. Perhaps the greatest of all my holiday memories is the <u>first time I initially saw</u> the Rockefeller Center's tree illuminated.
   A. CORRECT AS IS
   B. the first time I saw
   C. the primary time of all times I first saw
   D. the time at which I initially saw

7. There is considerable debate over how much <u>individual political power</u> is held by each member of the Supreme Court.
   A. CORRECT AS IS
   B. individualized political related power
   C. individualized political power
   D. political power

8. Before the thief had time to devise an escape plan, he found himself <u>surrounded on all sides</u> by police.
   A. CORRECT AS IS
   B. completely surrounded
   C. enclosed in totality
   D. surrounded

9. The purpose of the assignment was to <u>summarize</u> the book's plot and themes.
   A. CORRECT AS IS
   B. briefly recap
   C. summarize briefly
   D. summarize and recap

10. Over four <u>decades and more than forty years</u> of planning and building had come to a halt and the structure was complete.
    A. CORRECT AS IS
    B. decades amounting to more than forty years
    C. decades—over forty years—
    D. decades

Parallelism

1. The first motor convoy to travel across the country did so in 1919 and <u>consisting</u> of 81 United States Army vehicles.
   A. CORRECT AS IS
   B. consisted
   C. was consisting
   D. did consist

2. Activities as diverse as healthcare, education, and manufacturing have come to depend on the <u>generation, storage, and transmitting</u> of electronic information.
   A. CORRECT AS IS
   B. generating, storage, and transmitting
   C. generation, storage, and transmission
   D. generating, storing, and transmission

3. Most news stories, whether in print, broadcast on television, or posted on the web, are created by individuals responsible for a series of different tasks such as <u>sorting through press releases to determine which are newsworthy</u>, deciding which facts to use, preparing the actual story, and creating an appropriate headline.
   A. CORRECT AS IS
   B. to sort through press releases and determining which are newsworthy
   C. to sort through and determine which press releases are newsworthy
   D. sorting through press releases and so determining which are newsworthy

4. Concern for the well-being of young children has <u>led many states to enacting laws</u> requiring the use of child safety seats.
   A. CORRECT AS IS
   B. led many states enacting laws to
   C. led many states to enact laws
   D. many states leading to enact laws

5. Scientists believe that, unlike most of the 2,500 mosquito species, one particular species in the Florida Keys is restricted to a nectar diet <u>but not a blood meal, and it lays</u> eggs in the soil, rather than in standing water.
   A. CORRECT AS IS
   B. instead of a blood meal, and laying
   C. not a blood meal, and is laying
   D. rather than a blood meal, and lays

6. The speed at which the Earth, and other planets such as Mars, Saturn, and Pluto, <u>revolves are</u> determined by eccentricity and distance.
   A. CORRECT AS IS
   B. revolve are
   C. revolve was
   D. revolves is

7. The Sears Tower is lauded not only as being among the tallest buildings in North America, but also <u>as having the most breathtaking views</u> of the city of Chicago.
   A. CORRECT AS IS
   B. having had the most breathtaking views
   C. being the building with the most breathtaking views
   D. it has the most breathtaking views

8. The new <u>museum, consisting of hundreds of exhibits from the medieval time period, and is subsidized by the state's board of tourism</u>.
   A. CORRECT AS IS
   B. museum is subsidized by the state's board of tourism, it consists of hundreds of exhibits from the medieval time period
   C. museum to consist of hundreds of exhibits from the medieval time period, and to be subsidized by the state's board of tourism
   D. museum, consisting of hundreds of exhibits from the medieval time period, is subsidized by the state's board of tourism

9. They have flown to elk and deer wintering areas, ridden horses and snowmobiles through the mountains, and <u>throwing</u> back their heads and attempted to communicate with the wolves.
   A. CORRECT AS IS
   B. throw
   C. threw
   D. thrown

10. It was clear that I was going to need something—<u>a hug, a smile, a friendly handshake</u>—to get me through the day.
    A. CORRECT AS IS
    B. a hug, smile, a friendly handshake
    C. hug, a smile, a friendly handshake
    D. a hug, some smiling, a friendly handshake

Misplaced Modifiers

Read the following sentences and select the best choice for the placement of the underlined portion of the sentence from among those listed.

1. The debate fell apart when the student who was speaking lost <u>quickly</u> her place in her notes.
   A. Where it is now.
   B. After the word *place*.
   C. After the word *debate*.
   D. After the word *notes*.

2. There was much tension in the air as the restaurant owner served the food critic <u>on a designer plate</u> his award-winning cedar plank salmon.
   A. Where it is now.
   B. After the word *salmon*.
   C. After the word *owner*.
   D. After the word *as*.

3. It was a beautiful summer night, and <u>stretching across the horizon,</u> I could see a mass of fuchsia, orange, and yellow clouds as the sun began to set.
   A. Where it is now.
   B. After the word *mass*.
   C. After the word *clouds*.
   D. Before the word *began*.

4. Because of its upbeat music and flashy steps, <u>swing dancing is making a comeback</u> on college campuses around the country.
   A. Where it is now.
   B. Before the word *because*.
   C. After the word *campuses*.
   D. After the word *country*.

5. *Glory* is meant to evoke the movie <u>during the Civil War</u> of the same name, which tells the story of a black regiment.
   A. Where it is now.
   B. After the word *name* (but before the comma).
   C. After the word *story*.
   D. After the word regiment (ending the sentence with a period).

Dangling Modifiers

In the sentences below, modifiers may or may not be positioned correctly in the sentence. If the sentence is CORRECT AS IS, place a "C" in the space provided. If the sentence has a modifier out of place, rewrite the sentence to correct the error.

1._____ After keeping an oath of secrecy for twenty years, the mystery was revealed.

_____

_____

2._____ As I entered the building, a strange feeling came upon me.

_____

_____

3._____ Windsurfing on Lake Michigan, a sandbar was spotted.

_____

_____

4._____ After cleaning the bathroom, the toilet overflowed.

_____

_____

5._____ While barking, Elizabeth could tell how strong the dog's impulses were.

_____

_____

Active/Passive Voice

The sentences below are constructed in either the passive or the active voice. If the sentence is written correctly in the active voice, place a "C" in the adjacent blank. If the sentence is written in passive voice, rewrite it in the active voice in the space provided.

1._____ While some imprudent actions were performed by Garvey during his career, it must be remembered that his life was devoted to a cause in which he believed.

_____

_____

2. _____ A lack of artistic talents was shown by Fairfield Porter compared to his siblings.

_____

_____

3. _____ The queen not only enjoyed immense political power, but also maintained the loyalty of her subjects.

_____

_____

4. _____ After a final count, it was determined that the contest was won by Dennis.

_____

_____

5. _____ Differing from many of his fellow painters, Rembrandt painted people in a realistic and humble manner.

_____

_____

6. _____ After five consecutive years of applicants failing the entrance exam, school officials think it's time to make a change.

_____

_____

7. _____ It was found by a recent study that senior surgeons use intuition significantly more often than do most residents or mid-level doctors.

_____

_____

8. _____ A bit of wind created ripples on the water, but we could only remark that this same breeze would aid us on our way back to shore.

_____

_____

9._____ The face of the agricultural industry was changed by Eli Whitney's cotton gin.

_____

_____

10._____ It was believed by many students that Mrs. Mauro was the best teacher of reading.

_____

_____

Improving Paragraphs

Sentences within a paragraph should be arranged in an order that corresponds to time or mental reasoning. Likewise, paragraphs must have a certain amount of independence from each other, yet they should have similar tone and style, and provide the reader with a meaningful transition from one topic to the next.

Read the following sets of paragraphs and questions, then select the best answer from among those listed. Be sure to pay specific attention to the logical order of sentences within the paragraphs. There should also be an overall sense of cohesion between the ideas within a paragraph and within each group of paragraphs.

---

(1) Ocean currents from south of the equator. (2) Ultimately, they can have a huge impact on weather patterns all the way to the North Pole. (3) Probably the best-known ocean currents are the El Niño and La Niña. (4) Both of these tropical Pacific Ocean currents are influencing of producing global heat waves, flooding, and droughts. (5) Changes in ocean currents, including temperature and flow, tend to occur in twenty- to thirty-year cycles.

(6) Beginning in the late 1990s, two other ocean current patterns, known as the PDO and the AMO, became more active. (7) Their flows have gone up in speed, and the water temperatures have also risen. (8) Again, these changes have brought unusual levels of precipitation to land, primarily to the North American continent. (9) The greenhouse effect relates to the impact that man has on the environment. (10) Ocean currents also have an effect on the frequency and strength of tropical storms and hurricanes.

(11) Much controversy has developed in determining its degrees of impact on the weather. (12) The ultimate hope is that man and nature begin to develop a more symbiotic relationship. (13) Studies show that the heat that radiates from a major city changes the air around it. (14) These urban heat islands emit warm air during the day, which reduces the rainfall in those areas. (15) Weather patterns may also be influenced by manmade objects such as vehicles and buildings.

1. Of the following, which is the best way to revise and combine Sentences 1 and 2 (reproduced below)?

Ocean currents from south of the equator. Ultimately, they can have a huge impact on weather patterns all the way to the North Pole.

A. Ultimately, ocean currents from south of the equator can have a huge impact all the way to the North Pole on their weather patterns.

B. Ocean currents, ultimately, can have a huge impact up to the North Pole's weather patterns.

C. Ocean currents from south of the equator can have a huge impact on weather patterns extending to the North Pole.

D. From south of the equator to the North Pole, ocean currents can have a huge impact on weather patterns.

2. Of the following, which is the best way to phrase Sentence 4 (reproduced below)?

Both of these tropical Pacific Ocean currents are influencing of producing global heat waves, flooding, and droughts.

A. CORRECT AS IS

B. These tropical Pacific Ocean currents influence the production of global heat waves, flooding, and droughts.

C. Global heat waves, flooding, and droughts are all being produced from both of these tropical currents coming from the Pacific Ocean.

D. Both of these tropical currents from the Pacific Ocean are influential in producing global heat waves, flooding, and droughts.

3. In Sentence 7, the phrase "*gone up*" is best replaced by:

A. arisen.

B. increased.

C. speeded up.

D. jumped up.

4. Which of the following sentences should be omitted to improve the unity of the second paragraph?

A. Sentence 6

B. Sentence 7

C. Sentence 8

D. Sentence 9

5. In context, which of the following is the best way to phrase the underlined portion of Sentence 11 (reproduced below)?

Much controversy has developed in determining <u>its degrees of impact</u> *on the weather.*

A. CORRECT AS IS

B. the degree of man's impact

C. to what degree it impacts

D. to how much of a degree man impacts

6. Which of the following is the most logical order for the sentences in the third paragraph?

A. CORRECT AS IS

B. 11, 15, 14, 12, 13

C. 15, 11, 13, 14, 12

D. 12, 15, 13, 11, 14

---

(1) Robert Frost is perhaps one of America's best poets. (2) Maybe the most beloved poet of all time. (3) While Frost is known as a New Englander, he actually lived his first 11 years in California. (4) Born in 1874, Frost moved east after the death of his father. (5) He attended high school in Massachusetts where he became an avid writer. (6) Though he continued to write during his college years, he never earned a college degree nor did he find much success with publishing his poetry.

(7) At the age of 38, Frost moved to England where he quickly joined the literary circles of English writers. (8) A year later, Frost's first book of poetry, *A Boy's Will*, was successfully published and sold. (9) This started the beginning

of Frost's acceptance as a literary giant. (10) Prior to this, Frost had been working at mills and grammar schools; he also ran a farm. (11) Shortly after the publication of Frost's second anthology, *North of Boston*, he and his family reestablished their home in the States.

(12) Frost's literary talent met with great success back in the United States. (13) While Frost maintained the family's New Hampshire farm, he also wrote and published prolifically. (14) In 1923, Frost earned the first of his four Pulitzer Prizes for his work and was the first poet to read at a presidential inauguration in 1961. (15) Probably one of Robert Frost's best known and most often quoted poems is "The Road Not Taken," particularly the last lines: "Two roads diverged in a wood, and I / I took the one less traveled by, and that has made all the difference."

7. Of the following, which is the best way to revise and combine Sentences 1 and 2 (reproduced below)?

   Robert Frost is perhaps one of America's best poets. Maybe the most beloved poet of all time.
   A. Perhaps Robert Frost is one of America's most beloved poets for all time.
   B. Robert Frost is perhaps one of America's best and most beloved poets.
   C. One of America's best and most beloved poets is perhaps Robert Frost.
   D. Robert Frost, one of America's best poets, is perhaps the most beloved.

8. Of the following, which is the best way to phrase Sentence 6 (reproduced below)?

   Though he continued to write during his college years, he never earned a college degree nor did he find much success in publishing his poetry.
   A. CORRECT AS IS
   B. He continued to write during college while he never earned a degree and didn't publish his poetry.
   C. While he wrote during his college years, he wasn't published and received no degree.
   D. Going to college did not earn him a degree nor did he get his writings published.

9. In Sentence 9, the phrase *started the beginning* is best replaced by:
   A. started the beginnings.
   B. marked the beginning.
   C. marks the start.
   D. starts the marking.

10. Which of the following sentences should be omitted to improve the unity of the second paragraph?
    A. Sentence 7
    B. Sentence 8
    C. Sentence 9
    D. Sentence 10

11. In context, which of the following is the best way to phrase the underlined portion of Sentence 12 (reproduced below)?

Frost's literary talent met with great success back in the United States.
A. CORRECT AS IS
B. talent literally met with great success
C. literary talent meeting with great success
D. great success with literary talents

12. Which of the following is the most logical order for the sentences in the third paragraph?
A. CORRECT AS IS
B. 14, 12, 15, 13
C. 15, 13, 14, 12
D. 13, 15, 12, 14

(1) We had assembled all our gear, making sure to remember the camera, and were ready to head out. (2) We were finally going to take that ghost town tour. (3) To Rhyolite, Nevada, we were going. (4) Rhyolite, once a thriving gold-mining center, was now a small set of abandoned buildings and ruins. (5) We loaded the dog and backpack into the car and set off happily.

(6) Driving up into the foothills where Rhyolite is situated, a visitor can immediately spot one of the few intact structures. (7) This is the Tom Kelly house, built of nearly 50,000 beer and medicine bottles mashed into the clay. (8) It is clear that this home was once considered to be a rather magnificent edifice with its glass windows and wide-sweeping front porch. (9) Out in the expansive yard are fine displays of rusted farm tools. (10) Crude glass mosaic art forms are scattered about. (11) A curator of sorts sits on a chair just outside the bottle house, with a cat in her lap, just waiting to enlighten the next visitor about Rhyolite's many charms. (12) The scruffy cat does not like lying on the lady's lap. (13) The house itself is locked tight, due to what the cat lady describes as "pilferers."

(14) Unfortunately, driving the two miles into Beatty to purchase new batteries is not a solution; this camera is outfitted with a battery *pack* that requires recharging with its special charger. (15) I take my tiny new digital camera out of the backpack, longing to capture Rhyolite's quaintness forever, only to discover the camera's battery pack is dead. (16) We spend only a few more minutes exploring the other Rhyolite foundations and then silently get back into the car. (17) This angers my father, who is looking forward to a bit of Rhyolite on his computer desktop. (18) We will return to this ghost town another time, and you can be sure we will be carrying two cameras, both freshly charged! (19) My father is further incensed.

13. Of the following, which is the best way to revise and combine Sentences 2 and 3 (reproduced below)?

We were finally going to take that ghost town tour. To Rhyolite, Nevada, we were going.

A. We were going to Rhyolite, Nevada finally, to take that tour of a ghost town.
B. We were finally going to take that tour of the ghost town, Rhyolite, Nevada.

    C. Finally we were going to Rhyolite, Nevada, and take that ghost town tour.

    D. We were finally going to go to Rhyolite, Nevada, to take that tour of the ghost town there.

14. Of the following, which is the best way to phrase Sentence 5 (reproduced below)?

We loaded the dog and backpack into the car and set off happily.

    A. CORRECT AS IS

    B. We loaded the dog in the car and the backpack and happily set off in the car.

    C. We happily into the car loaded the dog and the backpack and set off.

    D. We loaded, happily, the dog and backpack into the car and set off.

15. In Sentence 7, the phrase *mashed into the clay* is best replaced by:

    A. that were stuck into clay.

    B. clay imbedded.

    C. that had been put into clay.

    D. imbedded in clay.

16. Which of the following sentences should be omitted to improve the unity of the second paragraph?

    A. Sentence 9

    B. Sentence 10

    C. Sentence 11

    D. Sentence 12

17. In context, which of the following is the best way to phrase the underlined portion of Sentence 17 (reproduced below)?

This angers my father, <u>who is looking forward to</u> *a bit of Rhyolite on his computer desktop.*

    A. CORRECT AS IS

    B. who will really be looking forward to

    C. as he had been looking forward to

    D. who has for a long time been looking forward to

18. Which of the following is the most logical order for the sentences in the third paragraph?

    A. CORRECT AS IS

    B. 15, 17, 14, 19, 16, 18

    C. 17, 14, 19, 18, 16, 15

    D. 16, 19, 15, 18, 14, 17

■■■ ANSWERS AND EXPLANATIONS

Pronoun Use

1. **The best answer is B.** Because "government officials" is plural, it is necessary to use the plural possessive pronoun "their."
2. **The best answer is D.** Although there is no antecedent in this sentence, the pronoun should refer to the person learning to identify the constellations. Therefore, it is best to use the general reference personal pronoun "one."
3. **The best answer is B.** The antecedent in this sentence is the gerund "canoeing," which is singular. Therefore, the singular pronoun "it" is correct.
4. **The best answer is D.** The sentence as it is written incorrectly replaces the singular noun "production company" with the plural possessive pronoun "their," and also suggests that the production company itself attended the play. While answer choice B correctly uses the singular possessive pronoun "its," this choice also indicates that the production company was in attendance, which is not likely the intended meaning of the sentence. The relative pronoun "the" clearly and effectively conveys the intended meaning.
5. **The best answer is C.** The context of the sentence indicates that owners should monitor the habits of their dogs. The pronouns "his or her" indicate the chewing habits of the owners and not of the dogs. Answer choice C best expresses that multiple dog owners need to be mindful of the chewing habits of their multiple dogs.
6. **The best answer is A.** The sentence is correct as it is written because it uses the personal pronoun "who" to introduce the clause describing Pietro Martinico. This sentence requires "who" because the clause refers to a person.
7. **The best answer is D.** This sentence requires the use of a possessive pronoun. The antecedent (children) is plural, so the plural possessive pronoun "their" is correct. The other pronouns are singular and "there" is an adverb, not a pronoun.
8. **The best answer is D.** The subject of the sentence is "13 million people" so you must use the plural possessive pronoun "their." Also, when talking about employment, 13 million people cannot share one job, so you must use the plural noun "jobs."
9. **The best answer is D.** The plural antecedent "African elephants" requires the plural pronoun "their." "They're" is the contraction of "they are."
10. **The best answer is A.** The plural antecedent "classes" requires the plural pronoun "they." Therefore, the sentence is correct as written. The author of the sentence specifically avoids certain classes because of the psychology research; the author does not avoid the research in general.

Word Choice

1. **The best answer is C.** The superlative "most" should be used to indicate the greatest in degree; according to the sentence, the first step often has the greatest degree of difficulty, therefore, "most" should be used.
2. **The best answer is D.** The simple past-tense verb "rewarded" best fits the context of this sentence.

3. **The best answer is A.** This sentence is best as it is written. It effectively uses "high-powered" as an adjective to describe "snow blower" and is free from ambiguity. The other answer choices are somewhat awkward.

4. **The best answer is D.** The phrase "the highest price ever paid for one of his paintings" is not essential to the meaning of the sentence. Therefore, it should be set off with the relative pronoun "which." Answer choice B incorrectly uses the participle "being." The other answer choices are wordy and awkward.

5. **The best answer is D.** "Amount" is used to denote a quantity of something that cannot be divided into separate units. Because the sentence refers to students, who can be individually counted, "number" is the best word to use. Likewise, "less" refers to a quantity or degree of something, not to a number of something, making "smaller" the best choice.

6. **The best answer is C.** The word "good" is an adjective used to describe a noun, but in this sentence, "good" is improperly used as an adverb. "Well" can be used as both an adjective and an adverb. In this sentence, "well" would be used as an adverb. "Well" adds meaning to the verb "feeling." Answer choice B is grammatically correct, but it is wordy and awkward.

7. **The best answer is A.** The sentence is correct because "lie" means "to recline, rest, or stay," or "to take a position of rest," as Melanie would be doing during a nap.

8. **The best answer is C.** "Ensure" means "to make certain," which best fits the context of the sentence.

9. **The best answer is D.** The sentence is incorrect because "already" means "before a specified time," which doesn't fit the context of the sentence. "All ready" means "completely ready," which best fits the sentence. Although C uses "all ready," the inclusion of "completely" makes the phrase redundant.

10. **The best answer is A.** The sentence is correct as written. "Between" is used with two subjects, whereas "among" is used with more than two subjects.

Redundant Language

1. **The best answer is D.** Answer choices A, B, and C are incorrect because it is redundant to state that an "escalating rate" is also "rising," "has risen," or "is rising." Answer choice D fixes the sentence's redundancy problems, and the progressive verb "keeping" is appropriate to describe an ongoing action.

2. **The best answer is C.** The sentence as it is written uses the passive voice and includes redundancy, which makes it awkward. Answer choice C clearly and effectively indicates who reached the finish line by using the pronoun "they" to replace the antecedent "runners," and also clearly conveys the proper sense of time by using "when." Likewise, the finish line is the end of the race, so it is not necessary to include both sentiments in the same sentence.

3. **The best answer is D.** As it is written, the sentence is awkward. To make the sentence more clear and concise, the phrase "that is" should be omitted. Only answer choice D clearly and effectively conveys the intended meaning of the sentence and avoids redundancy.

4. **The best answer is C.** As it is written, the sentence is redundant. The most clear and concise way to phrase the underlined portion is the

simplest, answer choice C. The remaining answer choices are awkward and redundant.

5. **The best answer is D.** Answer choices A and B are incorrect, because it is redundant to say that variations "could be endless for an eternity" or "could go on endlessly for an eternity." Answer choice C makes the sentence awkward. Answer choice D is best because it is concise and fixes the sentence's redundancy problem.

6. **The best answer is B.** The sentence as it is written is redundant, because "first time" and "initially" express the same idea. Answer choice B eliminates all existing issues of redundancy, and clearly and simply expresses the idea.

7. **The best answer is D.** The sentence as it is written is redundant because you can assume that "*each* member" has "*individual* political power." Answer choice D effectively eliminates this redundancy.

8. **The best answer is D.** It is redundant to say that the thief was "surrounded on all sides"; to be surrounded by something means to be "covered on all sides." Answer choices B and C are also incorrect because they introduce new problems of redundancy by saying that a robber is "completely surrounded" or "enclosed in totality."

9. **The best answer is A.** The sentence is correct as written. A summary of a book is also a recap, and it is brief. Therefore, answer choices B, C, and D all introduce new issues of redundancy.

10. **The best answer is D.** The only answer choice that avoids redundancy in this sentence is "decades." Stating that forty years is four decades is not required in the sentence and serves to overcomplicate the language.

Parallelism

1. **The best answer is B.** Because the action taking place in the sentence took place in the past, you must use the simple past-tense verb "consisted."

2. **The best answer is C.** In order to maintain parallelism in this sentence, the verbs in a series at the end of the sentence must be parallel. Only answer choice C includes verb forms that are consistent and appropriately follow the article "the."

3. **The best answer is A.** The verb phrases listed in the sentence must be parallel in form. The underlined portion is a complete verb phrase that begins with the participle "sorting," making it parallel to the other verb phrases that begin with "deciding," "preparing," and "creating." Answer choice D correctly includes "sorting," but it is awkward and otherwise grammatically incorrect.

4. **The best answer is C.** The correct verb to use in this sentence is the transitive verb "enact." Answer choice D is incorrect because, although it uses the correct verb, it is awkwardly constructed.

5. **The best answer is D.** Answer choice D is correct because it clearly and concisely states the comparisons between one species and most other species. In addition, this choice correctly uses the simple present-tense verb "lays" to match the simple present-tense verb "is restricted."

6. **The best answer is D.** Answer choice D is clear and concise, and correctly uses the singular verbs "revolves" and "is" to refer to the singular subject of the sentence, "speed."

7. **The best answer is A.** This sentence is best as written. It effectively expresses the idea and matches the previous verb phrase "as being" with the verb phrase "as having."

8. **The best answer is D.** This sentence is intended to describe how the state's board of tourism subsidizes the museum and that the museum consists of hundreds of exhibits from the medieval time period. The phrase "consisting of hundreds of exhibits from the medieval time period" is parenthetical and should be set off with commas. If this extra information is removed, the rest of the sentence should be complete and able to stand alone. The only answer choice that meets this requirement is answer choice D.

9. **The best answer is D.** The auxiliary verb "have" can be implied with [have] "ridden," and should also be implied for [have] "thrown." Only answer choice D allows for this construction.

10. **The best answer is A.** The sentence is correct as written because the nouns included in the parenthetical are all in the same form. The other answer choices break the parallel construction of the article "a" followed by a noun.

Misplaced Modifiers

1. **The best answer is C.** A modifier should be placed directly before or after the word or phrase it modifies. The intended meaning of the sentence is that the debate quickly fell apart when the speaker lost her place; only answer choice C allows for the modifier to convey this meaning.

2. **The best answer is B.** The phrase "on a designer plate" is meant to modify the salmon dish. As the sentence is currently written, it appears as though the critic was sitting atop a designer plate. Place the modifier directly before or after the word or phrase that it is modifying to avoid this confusing construction.

3. **The best answer is C.** A modifier should be placed directly before or after the word or phrase it modifies. As it is written, the sentence implies that the speaker is "stretching across the horizon," when in fact the speaker is referring to clouds that are "stretching across the horizon."

4. **The best answer is A.** The sentence is correct as it is written. Moving the underlined clause anywhere else within the sentence would dilute the meaning of the sentence and create confusion as to why swing dancing was making a comeback on college campuses.

5. **The best answer is D.** The clearest, most logical statement is made when the prepositional phrase "during the Civil War" modifies "a black regiment." A modifier should be placed directly before or after the word or phrase it modifies, so the phrase "during the Civil War" is best placed at the end of the sentence.

Dangling Modifiers

Please note that these sentences are examples. You might have come up with something different that is also correct.

1. The sentence as it is written implies that the mystery itself kept an oath of secrecy. To make the sentence better, include a subject that performs the action, as follows:

> "After keeping an oath of secrecy for twenty years, Mr. Jones revealed the mystery."

2. This sentence is correct as written. It contains a clear subject, "I," performing an action, "entered the building." The modifying clause "a strange feeling came upon me" is correctly placed within the sentence.

3. The sentence as it is written implies that the "sandbar" was "windsurfing on Lake Michigan." To make the sentence better, include a subject that performs the action, as follows:

> "As Jeff was windsurfing on Lake Michigan, he spotted a sandbar."

4. The sentence as it is written implies that the "toilet" was "cleaning the bathroom." To make the sentence better, include a subject that performs the action, as follows:

> "After I cleaned the bathroom, the toilet overflowed."

5. The sentence as it is written implies that Elizabeth was barking. Rewrite the sentence as follows:

> "Elizabeth could tell how strong the dog's impulses were based on its barking."

This sentence clearly indicates who was doing what.

Active/Passive Voice

Please note that these sentences are examples of active voice. You might have come up with something different that is also correct.

1. **Active voice:** "While Garvey performed some imprudent actions during his career, remember that he devoted his life to a cause in which he believed."
2. **Active voice:** "Compared to his siblings, Fairfield Porter showed a lack of artistic talent."
3. This sentence is correctly written in active voice.
4. **Active voice:** "A final count determined that Dennis won the contest."
5. **Active voice:** "Rembrandt differed from many of his fellow painters because he painted people in a realistic and humble manner."
6. **Active voice:** "Because applicants have failed the entrance exam for five consecutive years, school officials think it's time to make a change."
7. **Active voice:** "A recent study found that senior surgeons use intuition significantly more often than do most residents or mid-level doctors."
8. This sentence is correctly written in active voice.
9. **Active voice:** "Eli Whitney's cotton gin changed the face of the agricultural industry."
10. **Active voice:** "Many students believed that Mrs. Mauro was the best reading teacher."

Improving Paragraphs

1. **The best answer is C.** The sentence in answer choice C clearly and effectively combines the two ideas presented in Sentences 1 and 2. Sometimes you should eliminate unnecessary words to simplify your sentences and best express the intended idea.
2. **The best answer is B.** The sentence as it is written includes the phrase "influencing of producing," which is awkward and nonsensical. Answer choice B is written in the active voice, is clear and concise, and is punctuated correctly.

3. **The best answer is B.** When talking about speed, it is more appropriate to use the word "increased" than to use the word "arisen," or the phrases "gone up," "jumped up," or "taken off." The past tense of "speed" is not "speeded," so answer choice C is incorrect.

4. **The best answer is D.** The "greenhouse effect" is not discussed until the third paragraph, so it is not appropriate to mention it in the second paragraph, which focuses on a discussion of ocean currents.

5. **The best answer is B.** The pronoun "its" in the sentence does not have a clear antecedent. Therefore, it is best to restate the possessive noun "man's" for the sake of clarity. Answer choice B is more succinct and less awkward than answer choice D.

6. **The best answer is C.** The paragraph would make the most logical sense if the sentences were ordered as follows:

> (15) Weather patterns may also be influenced by manmade objects such as vehicles and buildings. (11) Much controversy has developed in determining its degrees of impact on the weather. (13) Studies show that the heat that radiates from a major city changes the air around it. (14) These urban heat islands emit warm air during the day, which reduces the rainfall in those areas. (12) The ultimate hope is that man and nature begin to develop a more symbiotic relationship.

Other combinations of sentences do not clearly and concisely relate the ideas within the paragraph to one another.

7. **The best answer is B.** The revision in answer choice B simply and clearly combines the two sentences using the active voice. There is no ambiguity or awkwardness.

8. **The best answer is A.** The sentence is best as it is written, and requires no revision. The other answer choices are awkward and do not clearly express the intended idea.

9. **The best answer is B.** The phrase "started the beginning" is redundant and not idiomatic. It is better to say "marked the beginning" to clearly indicate that the publication of Frost's book of poetry initiated his success as a writer. Answer choice A is incorrect because it is redundant and includes the plural noun "beginnings." Answer choice C is incorrect primarily because it is in the present tense, and answer choice D is incorrect because it is not idiomatic.

10. **The best answer is D.** The primary focus of the second paragraph is Frost's literary beginnings and his acceptance as a legitimate author. Sentence 10 has nothing to do with the topic of the paragraph, and so should be deleted.

11. **The best answer is A.** The sentence is best as it is written, and requires no revision. The adjective "literary" effectively describes Frost's "talent." Answer choice B is incorrect because it replaces "literary" with "literally." Both answer choices C and D create incomplete sentences.

12. **The best answer is A.** This paragraph is correct as it is written. The sentences are already ordered in the clearest, most direct way to convey the meaning and ideas of the paragraph.

13. **The best answer is B.** The context of the passage indicates that Rhyolite, Nevada, is the ghost town, so it is best to place the modifying phrase (the ghost town) directly before the noun that it modifies Rhyolite, Nevada). Only answer choice B creates a sentence that correctly places the modifier and is free from grammatical errors.

14. **The best answer is A.** The sentence is correct as written and needs no revision. The other answer choices are either grammatically incorrect or awkward.

15. **The best answer is D.** The word "imbedded" means "layed in surrounding matter." Based on the context and style of the passage, the phrase "imbedded in clay" is a better way of saying "mashed into the clay."

16. **The best answer is D.** Since the second paragraph deals with the appearance of the ghost town, the image of the curator is important; however, the actions of the cat in her lap do not add to the paragraph. Because Sentence 12 only talks about the cat, it distracts from the paragraph and removing it would improve the unity of the paragraph.

17. **The best answer is A.** The sentence as it is written is clear and concise, and effectively expresses the author's intended meaning while maintaining the proper verb tense. The remaining answer choices are unnecessarily awkward and wordy.

18. **The best answer is B.** The clearest, most logical order for the sentences of this paragraph is as follows:

> (15) I take my tiny new digital camera out of the backpack, longing to capture Rhyolite's quaintness forever, only to discover the camera's battery pack is dead. (17) This angers my father, who is looking forward to a bit of Rhyolite on his computer desktop. (14) Unfortunately, driving the two miles into Beatty to purchase new batteries is not a solution; this camera is outfitted with a battery *pack* that requires recharging with its special charger. (19) My father is further incensed. (16) We spend only a few more minutes exploring the other Rhyolite foundations and then silently get back into the car. (18) We will return to this ghost town another time, and you can be sure we will be carrying two cameras, both freshly charged!

The other answer choices create a paragraph that is disjointed and lacks logical transitions from one idea to the next.

▪ WHAT'S NEXT?

Chapters 19 and 20 present simulated ACT Writing Tests. Apply the strategies and techniques you learned in the previous chapters to write essays based on the prompts provided.

CHAPTER 19

ACT WRITING PRACTICE TESTS—SET 1

This chapter includes two ACT Writing practice tests. Follow the directions printed below for each test.

DIRECTIONS: This test is designed to assess your writing skills. You have forty minutes to plan and write an essay based on the given perspectives. Read and carefully consider these perspectives. Each suggests a particular way of thinking about the issue. Organize your ideas in a focused and logical way, and use the English language to clearly and effectively express your position.

Write your essay on separate sheets of paper. On the actual ACT you will receive approximately two and a half pages of scratch paper on which to develop your essay, and approximately four pages of notebook paper on which to write your essay. We recommend that you limit yourself to this number of pages when you write your practice essays.

When you have finished writing, refer to the Scoring Rubrics discussed in Chapter 15 to estimate your score. We have also included sample essays to which you can compare your essays. Read the scoring explanation for each sample essay to see why a particular score was awarded—this will help you to improve your writing.

ACT WRITING PRACTICE TEST 1

Student Breakfasts

Some schools in the United States have considered spending a portion of their limited funding on breakfast service for students. Educators fear that some students are not getting nutritious meals at home and that the school system needs to step in. Is this a proper use of resources? Given funding and fairness considerations, it is worth considering whether such programs are viable and useful.

Perspective One	Perspective Two	Perspective Three
Nutrition is vital to learning. Students who are hungry cannot pay attention in class, and their brains are not functioning at their best. From a purely practical point of view, breakfast service will contribute to learning.	Schools have already taken on too much responsibility for students' lives. It is difficult to learn self-reliance and responsibility when institutions are providing for all of an individual's needs.	Most schools already have food service and dining facilities that are unused early in the day. It is not unreasonable to make use of the space and equipment earlier in the day if it benefits students and their families.

Essay Task

Write a unified, coherent essay in which you evaluate multiple perspectives on the implications of schools' providing breakfast for students. In your essay, be sure to:

- analyze and evaluate the perspectives given
- state and develop your own perspective on the issue
- explain the relationship between your perspective and those given

Your perspective may be in full agreement with any of the others, in partial agreement, or wholly different. Whatever the case, support your ideas with logical reasoning and detailed, persuasive examples.

ACT WRITING PRACTICE TEST 2

Personal Financial Management

Some high schools in the United States require a personal financial management course as a graduation requirement. Many educators believe that fiscal responsibility is a necessary basic life skill. Is this a good use of resources for the students and the schools? Given the ever-changing nature of economic life, it is worth considering the question of whether personal finance education should be required.

Perspective One	Perspective Two	Perspective Three
Many adults currently lack the knowledge and skills to manage their money in the best way possible. This ignorance contributes to larger societal problems and affects everyone.	Schools are not well-situated to provide adequate specific advice for each student's personal financial circumstances. Moving forward, the economy in general and each person's individual situation are likely to change.	Basic financial literacy is a vital survival skill. Schools are shirking their responsibility to their students and to society by ignoring it. There are certainly less important courses that could be cut to make room for financial education.

Essay Task

Write a unified, coherent essay in which you evaluate multiple perspectives on the implications of requiring a personal financial management course. In your essay, be sure to:

- analyze and evaluate the perspectives given
- state and develop your own perspective on the issue
- explain the relationship between your perspective and those given

Your perspective may be in full agreement with any of the others, in partial agreement, or wholly different. Whatever the case, support your ideas with logical reasoning and detailed, persuasive examples.

SAMPLE ESSAYS WITH SCORING EXPLANATIONS

■■■■ **PRACTICE ACT WRITING TEST 1**

Essay: Score of 6

The pace of American life seems only to be quickening. There are only so many hours in a teenager's day, and the status quo seems to prefer that we try as hard as we can to use them all up. In doing so, we wake up before dawn only to rush in and out of the shower, then dress, and finally fly down the road toward school for hours and hours of mental gymnastics. For some, the final school bell means welcome relief, but for many students, it signals the start of an afternoon filled with music lessons, sports practice, work, or any of a myriad of opportunities afforded teenagers. High school students must step back from their furious lives for a moment, inhale deeply, and examine their routines for the crucial elements that are missing. The most common of these is good nutrition, which begins in the home in the early morning hours. Parents often forget that their children's minds cannot be enriched without first nourishing their bodies. Because many families cannot provide enough nutrition to their children, and because other families just don't make time, schools must intervene to ensure that all students come to their first class physically prepared to learn. Providing breakfast to students would be valuable to high schools by paying dividends in increased academic performance.

Students who eat breakfast are less likely to be distracted from their school-work by their grumbling stomachs. Satiated people are more cheerful, energetic, and attentive than those who haven't eaten since the night before. Teachers can better meet their lesson goals and respond to student problems and questions when the teachers don't have to be disciplinarians, continually telling students to regain focus or stop gossiping. A morning breakfast period would also be a welcome buffer between the hectic morning at home and the pressure-filled day ahead of students. Students would eat and chat, becoming relaxed and ready to learn.

High schools' primary objection to a breakfast service would be cost; however, breakfast foods are not very expensive. Moreover, school cafeterias could serve them at very low cost, especially considering their institutional buying power. Fresh fruit and lean sources of protein could replace expensive processed foods such as toaster pastries and sweetened cereals that students often have at home. At my local farmers market, grapefruits were selling for thirty cents per pound in ten-pound increments. Many shoppers couldn't see eating so many grapefruits, but for a high school, that's a piece of cake! Breakfast meats like ham and bacon are also much cheaper than many people realize when bought in bulk packages. My school already has a slicer, so buying unsliced hams and slabs of bacon could save them even more money. Finally, milk and eggs are inexpensive yet valuable breakfast commodities. As a Boy Scout, my food budget for camping was seven dollars per person per day.

For high school breakfast, I would encourage schools to set their breakfast budget at two dollars per person per day. With a concerted effort, food service professionals could no doubt achieve a nutritious breakfast service cheaply, improving student achievement, nutrition, and behavior simultaneously.

Scoring Explanation

This essay demonstrates effective skill in responding to the writing task.

The essay takes a position on the issue *Providing breakfast to students would be valuable to high schools by paying dividends in increased academic performance*) and offers a critical context for discussion (*Because many families cannot provide enough nutrition to their children, and because other families just don't make time, schools must intervene to ensure that all students come to their first class physically prepared to learn*). Complexity is addressed as the writer anticipates and responds to a counterargument (*High schools' primary objection to a breakfast service would be cost; however, breakfast foods are not very expensive*). Development is ample and logical, and contains specific evidence in support of ideas (*Satiated people are more cheerful, energetic, and attentive than those who haven't eaten since the night before. Teachers can better meet their lesson goals and respond to student problems and questions when the teachers don't have to be disciplinarians, continually telling students to regain focus or stop gossiping ... At my local farmers market, grapefruits were selling for thirty cents per pound in ten-pound increments*). Clear focus on the specific issue in the prompt is maintained.

Organization of the essay is clear though predictable (introduction with thesis, pro, con/counterargument). Most of the essay demonstrates a logical sequencing of ideas (*For high school breakfast, I would encourage schools to set their breakfast budget at two dollars per person per day. With a concerted effort, food service professionals could no doubt achieve a nutritious breakfast service cheaply, improving student achievement, nutrition, and behavior simultaneously*). Transitions are used throughout the essay (*For some ... But for many, ... however ... so*) and are often integrated into the essay (*Because many families cannot provide enough nutrition to their children, and because other families just don't make time, schools must intervene to ensure that all students come to their first class physically prepared to learn*). The introduction is well developed and effective. The conclusion is integrated into the counterargument paragraph. Despite being only one sentence, it succeeds in tying up the points raised in the essay while reiterating the thesis.

The essay shows a good command of language, with precise and varied sentences and word choice (*For some, the final school bell means welcome relief, but for many students, it signals the start of an afternoon filled with music lessons, sports practice, work, or any of a myriad of opportunities afforded teenagers. ... A morning breakfast period would also be a welcome buffer between the hectic morning at home and the pressure-filled day ahead of students. ... High schools' primary objection to a breakfast service would be cost; however, breakfast foods are not very expensive*).

There are few, if any, errors to distract the reader.

Essay: Score of 5

Humans are creatures, too, just like my dog, my friend Joes' ferret, and the squirrels in the park. And when creatures get hungry, they get cranky and very unreasonable. In the school setting, cranky, unreasonable people destroy the cool and collected classroom vibe that keeps everyone on track to learn the material being taught. Because so many students hurry to high school in the morning unfed, schools should offer at least some nutritional foods in the morning. Limited funding would not warrant a full hot breakfast, but some simpler offerings could make a great difference in high schools by increasing overall classroom performance and alertness.

Beginning this year in my high school, cafeteria workers tour the hallways of the building with cooler carts filled with prepacked nutritious snacks. The offerings change frequently, and students are becoming hooked on most of them. My favorite is the baby carrots with lowfat ranch dressing. Many people love the apple slices and caramel, grapes, dried apricots, and banana chips. While this snack does not constitute a full-size breakfast, it provides valuable complex carbohydrates important for brain function. Some students eat their baggies of food immediately, while others save them for between hours. Either way, few people find themselves starving at lunchtime. Personally, I love not being distracted by grumbling or pain in my stomach. I am often rushing to class in the morning, so I never have eaten breakfast before hand. With the packaged fruit and vegetable snacks, I can get some nutrition without having to break up my hectic lifestyle. A simple snack service in the morning would be very beneficial to student performance yet not cost very much money, since nothing is being cooked or cleaned.

Contrary to the common notion that three meals a day is the right way to eat, new evidence suggests that the human body benefits more from perhaps as many as six meals a day. This is because there is a delay between chewing and swallowing food and feeling satisfied from it. This means that when you are feeling starved, you will end up eating a lot more than you need to satisfy yourself. Greater calorie intake than necessary means you gain weight. By having a small breakfast, you let your body "catch up" in satisfaction; therefore, you eat a smaller lunch. The last few hours of the day could benefit from an afternoon snack, too. Then, by dinner time, you're not completely starved, and you eat more balance portions.

Whether or not a small school breakfast takes away all your hunger, it has the incidental benefit of forming a habit of eating nutritious foods in the morning. The way people eat and what they eat are products of a lifetime of habit-forming. If you had four years of high school eating a sound breakfast, then you are more likely to continue that healthy trend into your college years and adult life.

Being simple to implement and cheap to fund, a small, nutritious morning snack should be a part of every high school's food service program. Students need the energy for all the hard work ahead of them, and because high schools are so influential over students, they can help instill healthy eating habits and curb the obesity problem in this country.

Scoring Explanation

This essay demonstrates competent skill in responding to the task.

The essay shows a clear understanding of the task, which is supporting one side of the issue of school-sponsored student breakfast. The essay takes a position on the issue (*Because so many students hurry to high school in the morning unfed, schools should offer at least some nutritional foods in the morning*) and places it in the broader context of maintaining a positive learning environment (*increasing overall classroom performance and alertness*).

While the essay's counterargument (*Contrary to the common notion that three meals a day is the right way to eat, new evidence suggests that the human body benefits more from perhaps as many as six meals a day*) does not flow logically—there are no transitions to place it relative to the main idea—it does show an awareness of other positions (*why can't students just eat at home?*). It also answers an implied counterargument that overweight students don't need to be offered more food in school (*Greater calorie intake than necessary means you gain weight*).

Other than the introduction of the counterargument, the development of ideas in the essay is specific and logical. Most ideas are elaborated, with clear movement between general statements (*A simple snack service in the morning would be very beneficial to student performance*) and specific reasons, examples, and details (*Personally, I love not being distracted by grumbling or pain in my stomach*). Focus on the specific issue in the prompt is generally maintained, though the writer tends to get bogged down in details in the early part of the essay and to be overly general towards the end.

The organization of the essay is clear. Ideas are logically sequenced, although simple and obvious transitions are used (*Personally, Contrary to, Whether or not*). The introduction and conclusion are clear and generally well developed.

Language is competent. Sentences are somewhat varied and sophisticated (*While this snack does not constitute a full-size breakfast, it provides valuable complex carbohydrates important for brain function*). Word choice is usually varied and precise (*prepacked nutritious snacks, Greater calorie intake*). There are a few errors, but they are rarely distracting (*balance portions*).

Essay: Score of 4

As high schools struggle to boost student performance, they consider many ideas, some are bound to fail. One such bad idea is providing a breakfast service for students. People are very picky about their food, so schools would end up wasting a lot of money for very little nutrition given to students. The typical American breakfast isn't that good for you anyway. Therefore, high schools should not use any of thier limited funds to give breakfast to students.

Very few people would eat the breakfast made by thier school. Some students just don't trust the cafeteria staff to cook well. Others just aren't used to eating in the morning and would never be persuaded to start. The third group is the picky eaters, the people who have never bought a school lunch and never will. Although I am a huge fan of things the cafeteria serves for lunch like mac and cheese and rolls, some people refuse to even try stuff that they or thier mom didn't make just for them. More than they are annoying, picky eaters are stubborn. If they won't eat such innocent foods as pizza, spaghetti, or salad for lunch, how can school expect that they would eat more mystery breakfast foods like eggs and precooked sausage? Running a cafeteria is expensive. They'd have to sell a whole lot of pancakes and such to make *thier* money back, but they won't.

School cafeterias have so little funding that they cut as many corners as possible on ingredients. In the case of lunch, this means that almost everything comes out of a sealed package. All the processed fats and sugars are making people overweight, and this is specifically not helpful to learning. If high schools started making breakfast, it would probably be a bunch of fatty bacon and sausage and sugary cereals and hot cocoa and a bunch of junk like that. Students and *thier* parents can do a better job of selecting nutritious breakfast foods if they so choose.

Students can survive until lunch even if they are starving. Your still able to pay attention in class a little bit if your stomach is growling. Besides, lots of people have snacks with them to tide them over until lunch. The government says that schools only have to provide a lunch service. That means that the other meals are up to students and families. In conclusion, schools should spend thier money on educational needs instead of breakfast.

Scoring Explanation

The essay demonstrates adequate skill in responding to the task.

The writer takes a position (*high schools should not use any of thier limited funds to give breakfast to students*) and offers some context for the discussion (*People are very picky about thier food, so schools would end up wasting a lot of money for very little nutrition given to students*). The essay also shows some recognition of complexity by providing some response to an implied counterargument to the writer's position (*Students can survive until lunch even if they are starving. Your still able to pay attention in class a little bit if your stomach is growling*).

Development of ideas is adequate with two main points to the argument. There is some movement between general statements (*School cafeterias have so little funding that they cut as many corners as possible on ingredients*) and specific examples and details (*If high schools started making breakfast, it would probably be a bunch of fatty bacon and sausage and sugary cereals and hot cocoa and a bunch of junk like that*). Focus on the specific issue in the prompt is maintained.

The organization of the essay is apparent, though somewhat predictable, with few transitions (*Therefore, In conclusion*). Some evidence of logical sequencing is apparent (*If high schools started making breakfast, it would probably be a bunch of fatty bacon and sausage and sugary cereals and hot cocoa and a bunch of junk like that. Students and thier parents can do a better job of selecting nutritious breakfast foods if they so choose*). The introduction and conclusion are both clear and somewhat developed.

The writer demonstrates adequate ability with language, using a variety of sentence types (*The third group is the picky eaters, the people who have never bought a school lunch and never will ... They'd have to sell a whole lot of pancakes and such to make their money back, but they won't*) and some appropriate word choice (*persuaded, nutritious breakfast foods*). However, the writer includes several instances of inaccurate and distracting word choice (*mystery, thier*). Most sentences are simple, and syntax is occasionally awkward and distracting (*More than they are annoying, picky eaters are stubborn*). Other errors may distract the reader, but they do not impede understanding.

Essay: Score of 3

Schools have limited resourses, and it would not be a wise decision to use these on a free breakfast service for students. I know that breakfast is considered the most important meal of the day but I don't think providing a free breakfast service is the best way that schools can use their limited funds. If students aren't eating breakfast now, it's a good chance that a lot of them won't eat the breakfast at school, either.

I have another idea, instead. I think that it's a good idea for schools to offer breakfast, but not for free. If schools are really concerned about students eating breakfast, then they could offer a discounted breakfast in the morning. That way, students still have the chance to eat an afordable breakfast and schools can feel better about their students without spending too much. Then schools can use the left over money for other problems.

There are a lot of places that schools could spend their limited resourses. I just don't think it's very smart to spend all of the money on a free breakfast service that probably a lot of students won't even eat. A compramise is the best thing for schools to do. With a discounted breakfast, schools, students, and the budget wins.

Scoring Explanation

The writer takes a position on the issue given in the prompt, (*Schools have limited resourses, and it would not be a wise decision to use these on a free breakfast service for students*) but does little to recognize the opposing viewpoint, which decreases the validity of the writer's argument. Through the essay, the writer maintains focus on the general topic (*If schools are really concerned about students eating breakfast, then they could offer a discounted breakfast in the morning*), but does not quite stay focused on the specific issue in the prompt, which shows a slight misunderstanding of the task. Ideas are grouped together in a logical manner, but they are not properly sequenced together and many are not quite developed enough (*schools can use the left over money for other problems … There are a lot of places that schools could spend their limited resourses*). The essay is organized into an introduction, a body, and a conclusion, but all sections are minimal and could use some more substance. In addition, several spelling errors (*resourses, afordable, compramise*) may be distracting to the reader.

Essay: Score of 2

I disagree that schools should spend it's money on breakfast for students. There are lots of other things that school should spend its money on anyways. It is parents that should have to be making there kids eat breakfast not the school. They should cook breakfast in the morning and not have to make the school spend their money on it instead.

The school should spend money on stuff that is more important to the students then breakfast. I like lunch more then breakfast and I now tons of other kids thinks the same way as me. Breakfast is good for you I know but I never feel like eating so early during the morning. If the school spend tons of money on making breakfast every mornings for kids they wouldn't have enough money for more important stuff like for knew helmets for the football team and they really need those I now because I play football. All students would rather gets something like this instead of breakfast.

This is just some of the reasons why my school shouldn't spend tons of money on having too make us breakfast for the morning. The parents should be the ones who is doing that not the school because them are to take care of kids before and after school.

Scoring Explanation

This essay demonstrates a weak understanding of the task.

While the essay takes a position on the issue (*I disagree that schools should spend it's money on breakfast for students*) and provides some reasons for this stance (*There are lots of other things that school should spend its money on anyways … If the school spend tons of money on making breakfast every mornings for kids they wouldn't have enough money for more important stuff … The parents should be the ones who is doing that not the school*), the essay fails to develop these reasons. There is no recognition of the counterargument in the essay. Examples are used but are not relevant to the topic (*I like lunch more then breakfast … I now because I play football*). There is some indication of organizational structure, but ideas are underdeveloped and transitions are not used. Grammar and spelling errors (*they really need those I now because I play football … my school shouldn't spend tons of money on having too make us breakfast for the morning*) are frequent and distracting.

Essay: Score of 1

Always I am hungry at school. We has to be at school for too many hurs that it always makes me hungry in class and not wanting to learn. In this essay I think that our school should give us breakfast in the first class than students wouldn't be always hungry. My first class is boaring anyways and so we should just be able to eat for some parts of it. I think the school should fed us cereal and maybe some apples or some juice or some granola bars. I know that apples are tasting more better then oranges so that's why their should be apples in my first class. Also they are helthy for kids to eat so that does help to make us helthy and learning better for class. My favorite food to eat is hamburgers but not for breakfast I like them for lunch. I know the school have lots of extra money anyway so instead of buying more junk that not anybody cares about there should have to buy breakfasts food for kids so that I won't be so hungry in class and then I can learn better in class.

Scoring Explanation

This essay shows little skill in responding to the task.

   While it does take a position (*I think that our school should give us breakfast in the first class*), the essay doesn't adequately support this position. In the instances that the essay does offer support (*they are helthy for kids to eat so that does help to make us helthy and learning better for class*), it's clouded with an excess of irrelevant information (*I know that apples are tasting more better then oranges … My favorite food to eat is hamburgers but not for breakfast I like them for lunch*). Sentences are incomplete and grammatically incorrect (*Always I am hungry at school … I know the school have lots of extra money anyway*). The essay lacks organization and contains multiple and distracting spelling errors (*hurs, boaring, helthy*).

▉ PRACTICE ACT WRITING TEST 2

Essay: Score of 6

One of the most important hats we wear in society is as a consumer. Money comes into a family through work, and that money can be exchanged for things a family wants and needs to consume. Therefore, it is vital that as high school students become independent adults they have the knowledge and skills required to make smart decisions with their money. If the true mission of high school is to prepare us for the "real world," then high school students should be required to learn sound financial practices.

People say that money is the root of all evil, but I assert that it is mostly the main root of joylessness. Poverty destroys families, neighborhoods, and even whole countries. It leads to property crime, violence, and the break-up of relationships between people. High school students should be taught that smart spending and investing for the future can eventually bring people out of poverty and into safer, happier circumstances. Personal financial management classes would promote quality of life, which, after all, is everyone's ultimate goal.

Although students come from many different financial backgrounds, there are universal concepts that a personal financial management class could teach. Money makes all the institutions of the United States tick, so learning about money matters in high school would give students the knowledge they need to be more engaged citizens. Students could learn how to file their taxes, how to get a loan, and how to pay for college. There could be lessons about the stock market and mutual funds. This would prevent kids from taking too great of risks with their money or being deceived by a dishonest broker. Even if you don't have any money to allocate to different things, a personal financial management class would teach you how to build wealth and how to make it work for you and your future family.

High schools should try harder to give students a practical education. The complexities of math, science, and English are useful to learn, but we must be careful not to overlook the basic skills of life. Among the most important of these is the knowing what to do with our money. It is crucial that everyone learns financial management, and there is no better time to teach it than during high school, before people have a career and great responsibilities. Therefore, high schools should make a personal financial management class part of the mandatory curriculum.

Scoring Explanation

This essay demonstrates effective skill in responding to the writing task.

The essay takes a position on the issue (*high school students should be required to learn sound financial practices*) and offers a critical context for discussion (*it is vital that as high school students become independent adults they have the knowledge and skills required to make smart decisions with their money*). Complexity is addressed by examining different perspectives on the issue (*Poverty destroys families, neighborhoods, and even whole countries. ... Although students come from many different financial backgrounds, there are universal concepts that a personal financial management class could teach*). Development is ample, specific, and logical, and most ideas are elaborated in terms of their implications (*Even if you don't have any money to allocate to different things, a personal financial management class would teach you how to build wealth and how to make it work for you and your future family*). A clear focus on the specific issue in the prompt is maintained.

Organization of the essay is clear (*poverty is bad, but financial management classes will help students avoid poverty*). Most of the essay demonstrates a logical sequencing of ideas (*Poverty destroys families, neighborhoods, and even whole countries. … High school students should be taught that smart spending and investing for the future can eventually bring people out of poverty … Personal financial management classes would promote quality of life*). Transitions are used throughout (*Therefore, Although, Even if*) and are integrated into the essay (*The complexities of math, science, and English are useful to learn, but we must be careful not to overlook the basic skills of life*). The introduction and conclusion are effective, clear, and well developed.

The essay shows a good command of language, with precise and varied sentences and word choice (*Although students come from many different financial backgrounds, there are universal concepts that a personal financial management class could teach. … This would prevent kids from taking too great of risks with their money or being deceived by a dishonest broker*).

There are few, if any, errors to distract the reader.

Essay: Score of 5

Finance is not as intimidating as some people believe. Nevertheless, that intimidation factor is probably what prevents lots of people from having much of a clue about what's going on with their bank accounts and investments. Personal financial management classes would be a great idea for high school, not to give specific advice about how to use your money, but to explain the basics that everyone needs to have. I think there are several reasons that high schools should require students to pass a personal financial management class in order to graduate.

For example, people can be really careless with their money. They rack up huge debts because they can't control their spending. Television ads and internet articles indicate that credit card debt is through the roof across the country. Few people understand how to make a budget or even how to balance a checkbook. Personal finance operates on a very basic principle: don't spend more than you earn. Schools could do a great job reinforcing that message with specific advice. For example, a student could be warned not to fall into the sorts of traps that their parents might have fallen into. Finance classes could teach the basics of car and home financing and all the other kinds of loans a bank offers. If students knew about loans, they could better figure out what payments they could afford. This would keep students from adding a bunch of options they can't afford to a new car or buying a home with a few too many rooms for their needs. The class could teach how taxes work, which would help students prevent screwing up their paperwork for the IRS, which can lead to costly fines. Finance class could also teach about how to manage risk with investing, and how not to get ripped off by stock scams. Overall, personal financial management classes would help the economic health of the community, and schools are probably a better place to learn such skills than home.

Some might argue that discussing personal finances is an invasion of a student's privacy. There's plenty to say about personal finance without making specific recommendations about what each student should do with his or her money. There are things everyone should do regardless of how rich or poor you are. For example, the class should include how to fill out your W-2's right. Also, many high school students do not know how to balance money during college, when most people take at least a year off from working. You can learn about making a budget, balancing your checking account, and how to use credit wisely. Life is expensive, so learning how to manage your money earlier as opposed to later is a good thing.

By requiring passing a personal financial management class, high schools would be doing a great service to the community. No one can deny that such a class would be a better use of a student's time than gym or computer applications (since we're already experts anyway) or being a student assistant mindlessly grading papers.

Scoring Explanation

The essay demonstrates competent skill in responding to the task.

The writer takes a position (*high schools should require students to pass a personal financial management class in order to graduate*) and offers some context for the discussion (*Personal financial management classes would be a great idea for high school, not to give specific advice about how to use your money, but to explain the basics that everyone needs to have*). The essay also shows some recognition of complexity by acknowledging multiple perspectives and providing some response to a counterargument to the writer's position (*Finance is not as intimidating as some people believe*).

Development of ideas is adequate, with clear movement between general statements (*Finance classes could teach the basics of car and home financing and all the other kinds of loans a bank offers*) and specific examples and details (*This would keep students from adding a bunch of options they can't afford to a new car or buying a home with a few too many rooms for their needs*). Focus on the specific issue in the prompt is maintained throughout the essay.

The organization of the essay is clear, with transitions to guide the reader (*For example, Overall, Also*). Logical grouping and sequencing is more apparent in the second paragraph (*Finance classes could teach the basics of car and home financing and all the other kinds of loans a bank offers. If students knew about loans, they could better figure out what payments they could afford. This would keep students from adding a bunch of options they can't afford to a new car or buying a home with a few too many rooms for their needs*) than the third. The introduction and conclusion are both clear and somewhat developed.

The writer demonstrates competent ability with language, using a variety of sentence types and appropriate word choice (*a very basic principle, manage risk with investing, specific recommendations*). Other minor errors (*a student* [singular noun], *their* [plural pronoun]) may distract the reader but do not impede understanding.

Essay: Score of 4

Right up there with religion, a person's money situation is a highly taboo topic for public discussion. In a high school classroom setting, although valuable personal financial information could be learned, too many personal financial figures and stories would be exchanged during class discussions, thereby breaking the important privacy factor about which most people are at least somewhat sensitive. So financial classes should not be required in high school because high schools are too great of gossip machines to allow students' families financial circumstances stay secret.

Generally speaking, high school students have big mouths that get themselves and others in trouble. Sure, students can control which secrets they tell and which they save for only themselves or a few close friends. Many times during high school, though, we are forced to endure the incredibly awkward "too much information" moments created by some classroom discussion gone too far. I remember my health class teacher's discussion of human skin and various common skin problems. The class hour was moving along without a hitch until a student in the back lifted up the back of his shirt and asked, "Is this the kind of rash you're talking about?" His back had a wide swath of red bumps running from his left shoulder down to the small of his back. Everyone in the class let out a gasp. Even the teacher took several seconds before responding: "Yes, I suppose. You should probably have that looked at." All of a sudden, a perfectly nutral discussion on skin problems crossed the privacy line. For the rest of the school year, rumors bounced around the building about what could possibly be wrong with Rash Kid's back. He new he should have just kept his mouth shut.

In a personal finance class, I invision many more "too much information" moments. What if in a discussion of debt some student mentions how his parents can't pay their credit card bills? Will they earn a poor-kid reputation? On the flip side, what if a student brings up points about his dad's finances and the stocks he owns? I can keep classroom talk in the classroom, but I know for a fact that some students can't resist blabbing everything to their parents. If parents catch wind of other parent's financial status, the community gossip machine just gets uglier.

Financial education can wait until students end up in college or become employed and have to make decisions about taxes and retirement plans and other money matters. High schools already struggle to get results in subjects such as math and writing. Until American high schools' academic issues can be solved, nonacademic classes such as personal finance should not be part of the standard classes.

Scoring Explanation

This essay demonstrates adequate skill in responding to the task.

The essay shows a clear understanding of the task of arguing for or against financial education in high schools, but is too conversational at times (*Sure, students can control which secrets they tell*). The essay takes a position on the issue (*Financial classes should not be required in high school*) and places it in the broader context of a right to personal financial privacy (*high schools are too great of gossip machines to allow students' families financial circumstances stay secret*).

The essay shows some recognition of complexity by partially evaluating the implications of the issue, especially the individual and communitywide complications of students sharing too much personal information in a finance class. In fact, most of the essay is devoted to developing this one argument. Greater sophistication could be gained by introducing a counterargument to the writer's position.

Development of ideas is specific and logical, with some movement between general statements (*In a personal finance class, I invision many more "too much information" moments*) and specific reasons, examples, and details (*What if in a discussion of debt some student mentions how his parents can't pay their credit card bills? Will they forever earn a poor-kid reputation?*). Focus on the specific issue in the prompt is maintained.

The organization of the essay is clear, although it sticks closely to developing the one point ("*too much information*"). Ideas are logically sequenced, although simple and obvious transitions are used (*thereby, All of a sudden*). The introduction and conclusion are clear and generally well developed.

Language is adequate. Sentences are varied and somewhat sophisticated in structure (*In a high school classroom setting, although valuable personal financial information could be learned, too many personal financial figures and stories would be exchanged during class discussions, thereby breaking the important privacy factor about which most people are at least somewhat sensitive. ... Will they earn a poor-kid reputation?*) and word choice is frequently varied and precise (*valuable personal financial information*). There are a few distracting errors (*invision, new, nutral*).

Essay: Score of 3

It is true that schools should require students to pass a personal financial management class in order to graduate. After graduation, a lot of students have to take on more responsibilit for their finances. I think a lot of students would find a finacial management class helpful.

Although the personal finacial management class couldn't necessarily help student with the personal details of their finances, it would help them to make good decisions. Because some knowledge is better than no knowledge. Some students may be upset that they will have to pass the class in order to graduate, but I really don't see how anything bad could come out of learning how to manage your finances. Plus, the class is good for all students, whether they are going to go to college after graduation or get a job. I have a job right now and I think a class on managing my money would help me to save more than I spend.

A personal finacial management class will encourage students to think about their financial futures. I also think that schools would do a good job in teaching such classes. If students are going to be able to build good credit and be debt free, they have to know how to do it. Its' true that parents and peers can help students learn, but a class is an added bonus. Schools should require all students to pass a personal financial management class in order to graduate.

Scoring Explanation

This essay demonstrates a partial understanding of the task given.

The writer takes a position on the issue (*schools should require students to pass a personal finacial management class in order to graduate*), and maintains focus on the general topic (*Although the personal financial management class couldn't necessarily help student with the personal details of their finances, it would help them to make good decisions*), but does not quite stay on the specific topic in the prompt (*Some students may be upset that they will have to pass the class in order to graduate*). There is no mention of a counterargument to the writer's position. Development of ideas is rather limited (*I have a job right now and I think a class on managing my money would help me to save more than I spend*), and there is little evidence of a logical sequencing of these ideas. The essay is organized into an introduction, a body, and a conclusion, but all sections are lacking and could use more examples and support. A few, simple transitions are used throughout the essay (*Although, Plus*), and word choice is simple. There are some distracting errors, including incomplete sentences (*Because some knowledge is better than no knowledge*) and spelling errors (*finacial, Its'*).

Essay: Score of 2

A class about managing finances would be very good for students to have, it would help lots of kids learn lessons about life on there own. Some people say that high school kids are to young for this stuff, but it should help us to learn it anyways so that we can learn more about it as we get older. Also I think this class could give kids a good start to trying to manage the money that they make at there jobs.

High school students learn a lot of useful subjects like history, math, science, and social studies but they don't really learn a lot about how to live life without help from parents. Students go out to college and onto real jobs and are not sure how that they can manage the money that they make at there job in the best way and they end up wasting lots of it and end up in tough times. Maybe having this class at are school would help lots of students later on in there live.

Most students are spoiled by there parents who never make them manage finances, a class like this would be a great idea. And anyways, if somebody doesn't want to take the class they can just sign up for something else so we should have this class for people who do want to learn about it.

Scoring Explanation

This essay demonstrates weak skill in responding to the prompt task.

Although it does take a position on the issue (*A class about managing finances would be very good for students to have*), the examples offered by the essay to support its thesis are general and assuming (*Students go out to college and onto real jobs and are not sure how they can manage the money that they make at there job in the best way and they end up wasting lots of it and end up in tough times … Because most student are spoiled by there parents who never make them manage finances*). The essay fails to acknowledge the counterargument. The essay is somewhat organized, but the body section is minimal, transitions are absent, and the essay ends abruptly. Punctuation and grammar errors (*A class about managing finances would be very good for students to have, it would help lots of kids learn lessons about life on there own … Maybe having this class at are school would help lots of students later on in there live*) are frequent and distracting.

Essay: Score of 1

Well I don't think that they should have to make kids take a class about how to take care of money because, not everybody who is at school have the same kind of family life and same number of money. I think that some people might be poor and hate this class because it makes them feel bad that there family doesn't have so much money as do someone else family. If the school starts to teach this class. Than lots of kids maybe will be upset from it. I now that it is important to have saving money instead of just always spending it all so then I think this class would be no point because that is all it would talking about anyway. Some day I am going to work for job were I make lots and lots of money and so than I won't be having to worry about my money. My favorate kind of classes are jym class because I like to go outside and playing games and this class would be boring and many student would hate to go to it.

Scoring Explanation

This essay shows a very limited understanding of the essay task.

While the essay does take a position (*I don't think that they should have to make kids take a class about money*) and supports it with a few statements (*not everybody who is at school have the same kind of family life and same number of money*), punctuation, spelling, and grammar errors both confuse and distract the reader (*If the school starts to teach this class. Than lots of kids maybe will be upset from it … favorate … jym*), therefore weakening the argument. The essay lacks organization; there is no breakdown of ideas into paragraphs, and transition phrases are minimal. The essay moves from one idea to the next without warning, and by the end of the essay, the focus is completely off task (*Some day I am going to work for job were I make lots and lots of money*).

CHAPTER 20

ACT WRITING PRACTICE TESTS—SET 2

This chapter includes two ACT Writing practice tests. Follow the directions printed below for each test.

DIRECTIONS: This test is designed to assess your writing skills. You have forty minutes to plan and write an essay based on the given perspectives. Read and carefully consider these perspectives. Each suggests a particular way of thinking about the issue. Organize your ideas in a focused and logical way, and use the English language to clearly and effectively express your position.

Write your essay on separate sheets of paper. On the actual ACT you will receive approximately two and a half pages of scratch paper on which to develop your essay, and approximately four pages of notebook paper on which to write your essay. We recommend that you limit yourself to this number of pages when you write your practice essays.

When you have finished writing, refer to the Scoring Rubrics discussed in Chapter 15 to estimate your score. We have also included sample essays to which you can compare your essay. Read the scoring explanation for each sample essay to see why a particular score was awarded—this will help you to improve your writing.

ACT WRITING PRACTICE TEST 3

School Start Time

In some school districts, community members and the school board have debated whether to schedule the start of the high school day one to two hours later. Many educators believe that students will be more productive if they get more sleep. Given the various implications for the lives of students, their families, and the community at large, it is worth considering the merits of such a proposal.

Perspective One	Perspective Two	Perspective Three
Research is clear: Teenagers do not get enough sleep. Whether the primary cause is electronic devices or simple biology is irrelevant. Steps must be taken to create an environment where students can get more sleep, which is vital to health and learning.	Most high school students are members of families that include adults with daily responsibilities. Families count on the current schedule, and a delayed start time will negatively impact transportation and other aspects of family life.	High school students are young adults and, as such, should be learning valuable skills, including time management and responsibility. The current schedules are manageable. Teenagers simply need to learn to adapt and get to sleep earlier in the evenings so that they are fresh for school the next day.

Essay Task

Write a unified, coherent essay in which you evaluate multiple perspectives on the implications of starting the school day later. In your essay, be sure to:

- analyze and evaluate the perspectives given
- state and develop your own perspective on the issue
- explain the relationship between your perspective and those given

Your perspective may be in full agreement with any of the others, in partial agreement, or wholly different. Whatever the case, support your ideas with logical reasoning and detailed, persuasive examples.

ACT WRITING PRACTICE TEST 4

Violence in Video Games

Many people debate whether video game makers should be required to limit the violent content included in their products. There is concern over whether exposure to violence causes violent behavior. Given the prevalence and reach of video games and societal concerns about violent behavior in the real world, it is worth considering the implications of such a requirement.

Perspective One	Perspective Two	Perspective Three
All people should be free to decide what media they are exposed to. Attempts to limit access to information tread on the liberty of individuals to make their own choices. Censorship of video games is a dangerous threat to intellectual self-determination.	Game players are well aware that they are merely simulating violence. Violent play was common long before video games were invented. Gamers and their families should be free to decide what is appropriate for them.	Human beings are creatures of habit. Exposing one's mind to intense, repeated, simulated violence creates a stronger likelihood of actual violence. Desensitization through immersion in lifelike virtual worlds makes actual violence more acceptable to game players.

Essay Task

Write a unified, coherent essay in which you evaluate multiple perspectives on the implications of violence in video games. In your essay, be sure to:

- analyze and evaluate the perspectives given
- state and develop your own perspective on the issue
- explain the relationship between your perspective and those given

Your perspective may be in full agreement with any of the others, in partial agreement, or wholly different. Whatever the case, support your ideas with logical reasoning and detailed, persuasive examples.

SAMPLE ESSAYS WITH SCORING EXPLANATIONS

Essay: Score of 6

Considering all the ways a high school can be held accountable for the performance of its students, it comes as no surprise that school districts take serious looks at any proposal that promises instant improvement in student performance. Many of these proposals involve simple changes to the way classes are taught, tests given, and grades awarded. Others, however, involve drastic changes to the way the entire high school is run. One such proposal is to accommodate teens' sleep needs by pushing the school day back a few hours. Such a change should not be made without careful assessment of the costs and benefits. In my opinion, the foreseeable negative effects of delaying the school day significantly outweigh any potential benefits.

Regardless of when it might start, most students are not thrilled to wake up for high school. In my experience, the ease of getting out of bed is directly related to how excited I am about the events of the day ahead of me. Be it at 7 A.M., 9 A.M., or even later, neither any of my friends nor I would be more or less eager to file into the first class of the day. The real problem with student performance is how interesting the teachers make the material. Occasionally over the last three years, I have enjoyed my experience in class. If the subject matter is interesting and students are given work they don't perceive as trivial, then attentiveness, personal conduct, and academic performance skyrocket. This is just as likely to happen at 8 o'clock in the morning as it is when everyone is fully awake after lunch. Unfortunately, many teachers fail to engage students by convincing them that the material being taught is both relevant and worthy of their attention. Time of day has nothing to do with teacher quality.

Secondly, it is important to remember that although high school is the most important part of teens' lives, it is not the only worthy use of their time. Besides in class, I spend my time playing hockey, camping, and practicing with my heavy metal band. All these activities take hours of my time, and I need the afternoons free in order to fit it all in. In the case of my friend Sara, she already has to hurry at the sounding of the 2:30 P.M. dismissal bell in order to make it to diving practice on time. For my coworker Brad, he has to leave school right on time, too, to pick up his younger sister from the middle school on the other side of town. Pushing the school day back would ruin all these activities.

Instead of considering a delay to the school day, community members and school boards should think about resolving to plan their family lives better and insist that their teenage sons and daughters go to bed at a reasonable hour. This costs no money and upsets no one's carefully arranged routines.

Scoring Explanation

This essay demonstrates effective skill in responding to the writing task.

The essay takes a position on the issue (*In my opinion, the foreseeable negative effects of delaying the school day significantly outweigh any potential benefits*) and offers a critical context for discussion (*Such a change should not be made without careful assessment of the costs and benefits*). The essay addresses complexity by examining different perspectives on the issue (*The real problem with student performance is how interesting the teachers make the material. ... although high school is the most important part of teens' lives, it is not the only worthy use of their time*), while a counterargument is implied and addressed in the second paragraph (*Regardless of when it might start, most students are not thrilled to wake up for high school*). Development of ideas is ample, specific, and logical, with ideas discussed in terms of their implications (*Be it at 7 A.M., 9 A.M., or even later, neither any of my friends nor I would be more or less eager to file into the first class of the day. The real problem with student performance is how interesting the teachers make the material*). A clear focus on the specific issue in the prompt is maintained.

The organization of the essay is clear and appears to grow from the writer's purpose, with a logical and persuasive sequencing of ideas (*it comes as no surprise that school districts take serious looks at any proposal that promises instant improvement in student performance. Many of these proposals involve simple changes to the way classes are taught, tests given, and grades awarded. Others, however, involve drastic changes to the way the entire high school is run*). Transitions are plentiful (*however, In my opinion, Unfortunately*) and are well integrated into the essay (*Secondly, it is important to remember that although high school is the most important part of teens' lives, it is not the only worthy use of their time*). The introduction and conclusion are effective and well developed. They restate the writer's thesis without being repetitive.

The essay shows a good command of the language, with varied sentence structure and precise word choice (*In my opinion, the foreseeable negative effects of delaying the school day significantly outweigh any potential benefits. If the subject matter is interesting and students are given work they don't perceive as trivial, then attentiveness, personal conduct, and academic performance skyrocket*). There are few, if any, errors to distract the reader.

Essay: Score of 5

I have never been able to figure out why the school day is scheduled to completely contradict the common understanding of how sleep needs change over our lifetime. As a young child, you can't stand sleep. You wake up as early as you can to catch as many morning cartoons as possible before going to elementary school. In middle school, you like sleep a little more, but you still wake up early to watch TV or play video games. The middle school day starts a little bit later, but you still make it school with many minutes to spare. High school, though, is an entirely different story. Teenagers never seem to get enough sleep and hate waking up in the morning. But for some reason, high school's day is the earliest of them all, 7:45 A.M. for me and 6:00 for those poor marching band or swim team members at my school! The high school day's start time is out of control. Most workplaces don't open until 9, and their workers aren't nearly as physically, emotionally, and intellectually exhausted as teens are. For the sake of student health and learning, the start of the high school day should be pushed back to a more reasonable hour.

In general, teenagers do not go to bed early enough to justify coming to school for a dawn first hour. It would be impossible to get teens to shut down their cars, cell phones, computers, and televisions in order to relax and finally fall asleep in the late evening hours. These days, 11 P.M., midnight, or even 1 A.M. are typical bedtimes, and these are beyond schools' control. In fact, given the early school day, a student can only reasonably expect to get at most eight hours of sleep a night. Child development experts frequently cite eight hours as the bare minimum sleep amount for teens to prevent daily fatigue, which is always joined by irritableness and loss of focus. Parents and school administrators should also be more concerned about the effect lack of sleep has on growth stunting. Sleep cycles play an important role in hormone managment, so who knows what weird things are happening with our body chemistry when we don't sleep enough? Certainly, a very early school start time has no benefit except allowing for an early dismissal time.

Tired students can't accomplish much in the classroom. When I'm tired, I lay my head down, think about what I'm going to eat for lunch, or how much I'd rather be outside throwing the football. Other people fall asleep in the chair or sneakily tap away a text message to one of their friends elsewhere in the building. It is proven that fatigue depresses critical thinking skills. With the exception of perhaps gym and keyboarding class, critical thinking skills are about the most important things to have on a school day. It is ridiculous that high schools ignore the impact of reduced sleep on overall student achievement. Instead of pumping all kinds of money into before and after school programs, tutors, and fancy Internet-based learning systems, high schools should just let their students get more sleep. Performance would go up almost instantly, and best of all, shifting the school schedule is free—what a no-brainer!

Scoring Explanation

This essay demonstrates competent skill in responding to the task.

The essay shows a clear understanding of the task of arguing for or against a later start to the school day. The essay takes a position on the issue (*the start of the high school day should be pushed back to a more reasonable hour*) and places it in a broader context of the physical needs of high school students (*For the sake of student health and learning ...*).

The essay shows recognition of complexity by partially evaluating the implications of the issue (*preventing daily fatigue, regulating hormones, encouraging normal growth, etc.*). However, the writer does not introduce a counterargument, and he assumes without support that a later start time will result in more sleep for students.

Development of ideas is specific and logical. Most ideas are elaborated, with clear movement between general statements (*Tired students can't accomplish much in the classroom*) and specific reasons, examples, and details (*When I'm tired, I lay my head down, think about what I'm going to eat for lunch. ... It is proven that fatigue depresses critical thinking skills*). Focus on the specific issue in the prompt is maintained.

The organization of the essay is clear. However, with only three relatively short paragraphs, the writer does not explore a lot of ground. Ideas are logically sequenced, although simple and obvious transitions are used (*In general, In fact*). The introduction and conclusion are clear and generally well developed.

Language is competent. Sentences show rhetorical variety and sophistication (*Sleep cycles play an important role in hormone management, so who knows what weird things are happening with our body chemistry when we don't sleep enough?*), and word choice is sometimes varied and precise (*Child development experts, depresses critical thinking skills*). There are a few errors and infelicitous phrases (*irritableness, weird things*), but they are rarely distracting.

Essay: Score of 4

Most people have hard times getting out of bed for things they don't like to do. In my experience, most people don't like high school, so it will always be hard to get out of bed for it. Regardless of when the school day is scheduled, students will continue to push their bed time later and later and, therefore, continue to fail to get out of bed quickly and in a cheerful mood. Changing the school day would not only be ineffective in increasing student performance but also be disruptive to all the other scheduled activities that people have every day of the week.

If teenagers truely got all the sleep they needed they would probably be bored and boring individuals. Most of the best things of the day come in the evening and at night, so going to bed earlier to get more sleep is obviously an undesirable idea. If you weren't a part of nighttime activities, you would feel like you are missing out and you would gain the reputation of being a boring person. No student wants that. If the school day were scheduled later, students would have to get a later start on the after school activities, so students would start staying up much later. Add the fact that school is incredibly boring already and you have a recipe for tired kids at school, perhaps even more tired than they are already.

My second reason not to delay the school day is that it would be difficult to change all the other things students and their parents do before and after the school day. For example, my dad drops me off in the morning and races to work, normally arriving with only minutes to spare. If the school day started later, I'd have to get someone else to drive me. At the end of the day, I'd arrive home right about dinner time. I wouldn't even have time to relax before eating and beginning homework.

I can appreciate that administrators might want to simulate what the adult work day is like, but they don't understand that teenagers are tired every morning anyway and that we have lots to do after school. Everyone can appreciate having daylight hours after school, even in the middle of winter. In general, delaying the school day would be a bad idea.

Scoring Explanation

The essay demonstrates adequate skill in responding to the task.

The writer takes a position (*Changing the school day would not only be ineffective in increasing student performance but also be disruptive to all the other scheduled activities that people have every day of the week*) and offers some context for the discussion (*In my experience, most people don't like high school, so it will always be hard to get out of bed for it*). The essay also shows some recognition of complexity by acknowledging multiple perspectives and providing some response to counterarguments to the writer's position (*Regardless of when the school day is scheduled, students will continue to push their bed time later and later and, therefore, continue to fail to get out of bed quickly and in a cheerful mood*).

Development of ideas is adequate if threadbare, with two main ideas and some movement between general statements (*My second reason not to delay the school day is that it would be difficult to change all the other things students and their parents do before and after the school day*) and specific examples and details (*If the school day started later, I'd have to get someone else to drive me*). The writer could do more to flesh out the ideas given in the prompt. Focus on the specific issue in the prompt is maintained throughout the essay.

The organization of the essay is apparent but predictable, with few transitions to guide the reader (*My second reason, In general*). Logical sequencing is better in the third paragraph than in the second (*At the end of the day, I'd arrive home right about dinner time. I wouldn't even have time to relax before eating and beginning homework*). The introduction and conclusion are both clear and somewhat developed.

The writer demonstrates good command of the language, using a variety of sentence types (*No student wants that. ... Add the fact that school is incredibly boring already and you have a recipe for tired kids at school, perhaps even more tired than they are already*) and appropriate word choice (*ineffective, simulate*). There are few errors to distract the reader.

Essay: Score of 3

Many high schools around the country are considering a change that would set the start of the school day back by a couple of hours. I disagree with this proposed change, I feel that the school day is just fine the way that it is. I know that high school students need a lot of sleep in order to do their best, but I don't think their lack of sleep has to do with an early high school start time. I think it has to do with students not going to bed at a time that garantees them enough sleep.

If high schools delayed the start of the school day by a couple of hours, it would effect more than the start of the school day. It would also delay the start of everything after school, like sports, the arts, and driver's education. If these activities are delayed, it means that students are getting home later in the day, eating dinner later than before, and starting homework later, too. Plus the later students get home the less time they have with their families. Delaying the start of the school day only delays everything that follows, and results in students getting to bed even later then before. At the end, one isn't getting any more sleep than they did before.

I understand why school officials want to delay the start of the high school day, but I don't think they realize that it will effect more than just the school day. I don't think this idea will really solve the bigger problem. Instead of delaying the start of the school day, they should reinforce the idea of a decent bedtime to their students.

Scoring Explanation

This essay shows some understanding of the task.

In the first paragraph, the writer clearly takes a stance on the issue (*I disagree with this proposed change, I feel that the school day is just fine the way that it is*) but the supporting argument is limited (*If high schools delayed the start of the school day by a couple of hours, it would effect more than the start of the school day … Plus the later students get home the less time they have with their families*). There is no recognition of the counterargument, which, if used, would help to strengthen the writer's argument. The writer highlights the negative sides of starting the school day later in the essay but does not discuss the positive aspects of the current start time. There is a simple organizational structure to the essay that helps tie the ideas together, but transitions are lacking and the body section could use more substance. There are a handful of errors (*effect* instead of *affect*, *garantees*, ambiguous pronouns *one, they*) that are somewhat distracting.

Essay: Score of 2

I do not believe that high schools should start the school day later. We have had to start school this early for our whole live so it wouldn't make a lot of sents to start later now. Starting the day later would mean that one would be stuck in school until its almost dark out and this would cause problems with sports practices and other activities, it would be hard for parents to give rides to kids to because they would have to be going to work before we have to be going to school. This would be a undesirable morning routine for parents.

Since we started school we have had to be up early to get there. If we started school later all of a suddenly it would be hard to get use to that kind of day. Waking up early gets us kids ready for our career that some day we will be having to wake up for anyways. It would be hard for teams who practice outside to have their practice because school would got out so late that their would already be no sunlight outside. They would have too practice early before school and than kids would have to shower and change and this would be to much to do before class. I would rather wake up early in the morning and be finished with my day while there is still hours of sunlight then sleep in and get out of school when it is dark.

Because of the conflicts because of this schedule change we should keep the school day the way that it is. It would not make sents to make such a big change to the day at this point, if some kids are to tired at school they should just try and get to sleep earlier so that they feel better at school. We have had early days since we started going to school and there is no need to change that now.

Scoring Explanation

This essay demonstrates weak skill in responding to the task.

While the essay does take a position on the issue (*I do not believe that high schools should start the school day later*) and offer support for its thesis (*We have had to start school this early for our whole live, it would be hard for parents to give rides to kids, this would cause problems with sports practices*), the support is general and redundant. The counterargument to the essay's position is not recognized. The essay is organized into an introduction, a body, and a conclusion, but the paragraphs lack cohesiveness. Punctuation and grammar errors are frequent (*They would have too practice early before school and than kids would have to shower and change and this would be to much to do before class ... It would not make sents to make such a big change to the day at this point, if some kids are to tired at school they should just try and get to sleep earlier so that they feel better at school*).

Essay: Score of 1

I think that high school should be starting lots later then it is now. I am always tired at school because I can't get enough sleep because we had to be at school so early every morning. I think that sleeping in is a lot funner then waking up real early. By going to school real tired is a bad thing because lots of kids don't paying lots of attention and maybe even sometimes they fall back to sleep because they had to wake up that early. I like to stay up late and I know that much other kids think the same way and nobody really goes to sleep that early enough to wake up at such an early hour that we have to for school. I think that kids would learn much more good at school if they get to sleep in a little bit and start a later day. Teachers should like to sleep a little more to. They have to wake up more early then us kids so they would be happy to start school late. I know that I learn lots better when I'm not real tired from having to be waking up so early and I can get better grades in my classes. I like to watch sports highlights in the morning but I never get to see them because I am up so early and have to run to get to school but if we started late then I could watch sports and maybe have breakfast to which is good for a start to the day. I think that every students at my school should like to sleep in for a few hours and that would make school a lot better for us all.

Scoring Explanation

This essay demonstrates a lack of engagement with the task.

Although the essay does take a position (*high school should be starting lots later then it is now*), it fails to adequately develop the evidence needed to support the position. The essay makes unsupported assumptions (*nobody really goes to sleep that early, teachers should like to sleep a little more*), which weakens the argument. Run-on sentences occur throughout the essay, making it difficult to follow. Off-topic statements (*I like to watch sports highlights*) distract the reader from the essay's original purpose. Spelling errors are frequent, along with misuse of verb forms (*don't paying lots of attention, having to be waking up so early*). Also, the essay as a whole lacks organization.

PRACTICE ACT WRITING TEST 4

Essay: Score of 6

Every generation thinks the one that comes after is corrupted in some way. The baby boomers who had children during the 40s and 50s were horrified at the free love, mind expansion philosophy of the 60s. Children of the 50s, 60s, and 70s grew up and had our current generation, which is stigmatized for our hectic pace of life, unrelenting narcissism, and dependence on electronic devices. People naturally long for the good old days, and in doing so, they reject much of the new, especially what they are not familiar with. Society must learn to analyze the greater culture and its values instead of placing the blame on fads and material things that come and go. Lately, video games have been the subject of controversy for their depictions of violence. It is clear that although children have perpetually committed violent acts throughout history, there is now an easy scapegoat for explaining the bad deeds—and it's one that can't defend itself. Some people who have never picked up a controller may be pacified knowing that video games are finally in the moral crosshairs, but it is all a charade. Restricting violent content in video games would do nothing to curb youth violence but instead push more creative works onto the dangerous slippery slope of censorship.

Young adults are violent because of their natural constitution, the circumstances of their upbringing, and the influence of their peers. Playing video games containing violence has no apparent effect on how violent someone can be. For example, I know that my good friends Roger and Justin, my classmate Joe, and I have all completed all the missions of <u>Grand Theft Auto: Vice City</u> for Microsoft's Xbox video game system. This particular title made headlines in the first months after its release because the dialog contains swearing and racist language, and the plot relies on the player pulling off violent crimes involving drugs, guns, and prostitution. Congress even heard testimony about how it might be poisoning the nation's children! <u>Vice City</u> is indeed an extreme example of objectionable content in video games; nevertheless, it has had no effect on me or my peers' propensity for violence. Roger and Justin are still cool as cucumbers, just as they have always been. Joe is an excitable, passionate kid occasionally involved in a schoolyard tussle, but that has been his way since elementary school, long before video game violence was such a big deal. As for me, I don't even like killing flies in my house; there's not a violent bone in my body. For young people, video games with lewd and violent subject matter are not influences but rather escapes. By simulating bad behavior on a TV screen, we don't feel drawn to experience it in the real world. After all, people have always needed to satisfy their appetite for destruction, be it by rubbernecking at traffic accidents, watching the (depressing) local news, gossiping about other people's misfortunes, or shooting gangsters in a video game. People should be able to feed their dark side in a peaceful, victimless way.

Certainly many people will continue to insist that violence on a video screen leads to violence on the street, and therefore, the best course of action is to limit the violence in video games. These people must realize that any restriction on video game content would be difficult to define and dangerous for future creativity. What constitutes unacceptable violence? Is a soldier shooting a terrorist in battle more acceptable for children than a vigilante shooting a mob kingpin? Is it acceptable to imply violence or talk about violence, but not to show it? These questions have no certain answers, so regulators should not attempt to find any. In the past, such censorship almost killed comic books. Today, it should be strongly avoided with video games for fear that it continue to chip away at free-speech rights. Hopefully, a future generation will take power and realize that young people are too sophisticated to be ruined by the contents of fiction, whatever its form.

Scoring Explanation

This essay demonstrates effective skill in responding to the writing task.

The essay takes a position on the issue (*Restricting violent content in video games would do nothing to curb youth violence but instead push more creative works onto the dangerous slippery slope of censorship*) and offers a critical context for discussion (*Society must learn to analyze the greater culture and its values instead of placing the blame on fads and material things that come and go*). The essay addresses complexity by evaluating the implications and complications of the issue (*What constitutes unacceptable violence? Is a soldier shooting a terrorist in battle more acceptable for children than a vigilante shooting a mob kingpin? Is it acceptable to imply violence or talk about violence, but not to show it?*). Development of ideas is ample, specific, and logical. Ideas are discussed in terms of their implications. A clear focus on the issue in the prompt is maintained because lengthy examples are placed in the context of their significance (*For young people, video games with lewd and violent subject matter are not influences but rather escapes. By simulating bad behavior on a TV screen, we don't feel drawn to experience it in the real world*).

The organization of the essay is clear and follows logically from the thesis statement. Ideas within each paragraph are also logically sequenced (*Roger and Justin are still cool as cucumbers, just as they have always been. Joe is an excitable, passionate kid occasionally involved in a schoolyard tussle, but that has been his way since elementary school, long before video game violence was such a big deal. As for me, I don't even like killing flies in my house*). The essay makes good use of transitions (*Lately, As for me, For example, therefore*) with most of them reflecting and supporting the writer's logic (*In the past, such censorship almost killed comic books. Today, it should be strongly avoided with video games for fear that it continue to chip away at free-speech rights*). The introduction is effective and extremely well developed. The conclusion is folded in with the argument against restricting creativity and so furthers the writer's argument beyond simply restating a thesis.

The essay shows a good command of the language, with varied sentence structure, rhetorical devices, and precise word usage (*Vice City is indeed an extreme example of objectionable content in video games; nevertheless, it has had no effect on my or my peers' propensity for violence. … What constitutes unacceptable violence?*). There are few, if any, errors to distract the reader.

Essay: Score of 5

Young people today have so many things to cram into the day: school, sports, music lessons, dance, clubs, church groups, homework, housework, etc. There's barely enough time to relax in between any two committments. For this reason, young people seem to have less and less opportunities to unwind, vent their stress, and make a careful assessment of their life in order to make good decisions. Video games take advantage of this vulnerability. When young people, especially boys, could be relaxing, they are instead keeping their adrenaline up playing violent video games. What results is a large population of boys with short attention spans and bundles of energy. Unfortunately, from among this group, some boys will end up cracking, substituting their video game reality for the true one, committing acts of violence against their families, peers, and perhaps even perfect strangers. It is high time that government and the public force video game manufacturers to tone down the violence in their products.

While it is true that video games are fantasy, they are almost never totally made up. For example, zombies from outer space do not exist, but shotguns do. When a child blasts a zombie in the face, it is not unrealistic to believe that the child thinks a human could be just as well defeated in the same way. In a typical shooting game, the main character controlled by the player gets to move all over, shooting things at will with a variety of extravagant weapons. A shot or two wastes the enemy, but your character gets to take all kinds of hits and keep going. By the end of the game, you've probably shot a thousand baddies. This idea of the invincible hero is dangerous to implant in young boys' minds, since they already feel invincible in the first place. The last things we need are boys with guns and delusions of immortality.

Besides glorifying violence, violent video games also suggest that life is cheap. In video games, anyone can die for any reason: innocent bystanders, common criminals, soldiers, evil geniuses, and your own character. Constantly reminding young people of the impermanence of life has the effect of making young people believe that each day is but one day closer to death. Self-esteem drops and the result is a whole generation juiced up on medications their psychiatrists gave them, overweight and unhealthy, and poorly adjusted to dealing with other people. Video game makers must admit now that they have a responsibility to limit this general feeling of hopelessness found in their products.

Some may argue that violent tendencies in youth have more to do with their upbringing than whether they play violent video games. While I admit that family life is the most important factor in young people's development, video games cannot be excluded as one too. A long time ago, move theatres used to insert subliminal messages in between frames. Brief flashes of pop and popcorn would cause tons of people to scurry out to the concession stand. Eventually, the government ruled that it was unjust to mess with people's subconscious like that, so they put a stop to it. With video games, the messages aren't subliminal, but they are subconscious. The violence amounts to brain-washing, which is the method of convincing someone of something by repeating it over and over and over again. If a child blows away zombies over and over and over again, why is it so hard to believe that the child won't have a hankering for blowing something away in real life? Clearly, for the benefit of players and nonplayers alike, violence must no longer have a place in video games.

Scoring Explanation

This essay demonstrates competent skill in responding to the task.

The essay shows a clear understanding of the task, which is to argue for or against imposed limitations on violence in video games. The essay takes a position on the issue (*It is high time that government and the public force video game manufacturers to tone down the violence in their products*) and places it in the broader context of how young men respond to the general stresses of their lives (*For this reason, young people seem to have less and less opportunities to unwind, vent their stress, and make a careful assessment of their life in order to make good decisions*).

The essay shows recognition of complexity by directly responding to a counterargument to the writer's position (*Some may argue that violent tendencies in youth have more to do with their upbringing than whether they play violent video games. While I admit that family life is the most important factor in young people's development, video games cannot be excluded as one too*). The writer also does a good job throughout the essay of exploring the possible complications of subconscious manipulation (*The violence amounts to brain-washing, which is the method of convincing someone of something by repeating it over and over and over again*).

Development of ideas is specific and logical within paragraphs. Most ideas are elaborated, with clear movement between general statements (*Besides glorifying violence, violent video games also suggest that life is cheap*) and specific reasons, examples, and details (*Self-esteem drops and the result is a whole generation juiced up on medications their psychiatrists gave them, overweight and unhealthy, and poorly adjusted to dealing with other people*). Unfortunately, the second and third paragraphs seem to contradict each other, with the second claiming violent video games enforce players' "*delusions of immortality*" while the third states the opposite (players feel "*each day is but one day closer to death*"). The writer needs to reconcile the apparent contradiction. Despite this flaw, focus on the specific issue in the prompt is consistently maintained.

The organization of the essay is clear, although it is hampered by the flaw mentioned above. Ideas are logically sequenced (e.g., the introduction of the idea that anyone can die at any time leading to a general feeling of hopelessness), with smooth transitions to guide the reader (*While it is true, Eventually, Some may argue, For this reason*). The introduction and conclusion are clear and generally well developed.

Language is competent. Sentences are somewhat varied and occasionally complex (*For example, zombies from outer space do not exist, but shotguns do*) and word choice is sometimes varied and precise (*extravagant, invincible, subliminal*). There are a few errors of usage (*less and less opportunities*) and mechanical errors, but they are rarely distracting.

Essay: Score of 4

Ever since graphics became very realistic and 3D, violence in video games has started getting out of control. Many times, the violence depicted is crime like murder or assault with a motor vehicle. High schools students are impressionable and must be protected from criminal influences, so video game companies must have their violence limited.

Life can be tough at times, but teenagers must be reminded as often as possible that hard work and a positive attitude are powerful forces. Violence and crime don't serve you well in the long run. Unfortunately, video games promote violence because after shooting, blowing up, and running over a bunch of gangsters, zombies, etc., you win the game and all is well for you. Combined with all the cool music and cinematic effects, video game violence is romantic. I can definitely see middle or high school boys admiring violent video game characters, even if they aren't real. People get involved in the same way with characters from TV or a novel.

Every once in a while the news has a story about the death or paralisys of a kid because he was doing backyard wrestling. All kinds of people wanted to place the blame on pro wrestling on TV and in video games, but each time wrestling was able to convince the world that they believe and want to convey that they are professionals doing things that shouldn't be done at home. Regardless, some kids want to experience it themselves. The same goes for video games. Whose to say that kids wouldn't graduate from playing at violence to participating in it? Lots of people haven't totally formed their idea of right and wrong by the age that they might be able to pull of crimes. Video game companies, and indeed all companies, should make sure that their products aren't a bad influence on young people.

In conclusion, everyone must realize that the world is a much more complicated place now than it ever has been. Young people are pulled in some many directions that it is easy to see how they could get pulled in the wrong direction. People should make sure that although there is nothing to do about the hecktic pace and technological complication of modern life, they can still try to make it a nurturing life, in part by restricting the realistic violence in kid's video games.

Scoring Explanation

The essay demonstrates adequate skill in responding to the task.

The writer takes a position (*High schools students are impressionable and must be protected from criminal influences, so video game companies must have their violence limited*) and offers some context for the discussion (*Ever since graphics became very realistic and 3-D, violence in video games has started getting out of control*). The essay also shows some recognition of complexity by acknowledging multiple perspectives and providing some response to counterarguments to the writer's position (*All kinds of people wanted to place the blame on pro wrestling on TV and in video games, but each time wrestling was able to convince the world that they believe and want to convey that they are professionals doing things that shouldn't be done at home*).

Development of ideas is adequate, with some movement between general statements (*Violence and crime don't serve you well in the long run*) and specific examples and details (*Unfortunately, video games promote violence because after shooting, blowing up, and running over a bunch of gangsters, zombies, etc., you win the game and all is well for you*). Focus on the specific issue in the prompt is maintained throughout the essay.

The organization of the essay is apparent, with a few transitions to guide the reader (*Unfortunately, Regardless, In conclusion*). There is some evidence of logical sequencing within the essay, especially the third paragraph (*Every once in a while the news has a story about the death or paralisys of a kid because he was doing backyard wrestling. … The same goes for video games. Whose to say that kids wouldn't graduate from playing at violence to participating in it?*). The introduction and conclusion are both clear and somewhat developed.

The writer demonstrates adequate ability with language, using a variety of sentence types (*Whose to say that kids wouldn't graduate from playing at violence to participating in it?*) and appropriate word choice (*impressionable, criminal influences, cinematic effects*), as well as some awkward and distracting sentence structure (*but each time wrestling was able to convince the world that they believe and want to convey that they are professionals doing things that shouldn't be done at home*). Other errors (*hecktic*) also distract the reader but do not impede understanding.

Essay: Score of 3

Some video games can be violent but this does not mean that people who play them will become violent. Therefore, the content of video games doesn't have to be limited. Parents must be aware of what their children are doing at all times and make sure they are not getting into trouble.

There are a lot of different video game manufacturers and they should all be responsible for what goes into their games. They should not have to change their games but they should be aware of what's going on in the world. I think that violent people will be violent regardless of whether they play video games or not. The games do not make them violent. My brother plays video games all the time before and after school. He wastes a lot of time but can still get his homework and chores done. Plus, he is not a violent person. He often helps my mom and dad around the house and has many friends (who he plays video games with!) I mean, he's a really good kid. So playing violent video games isn't going to make him violent.

In conclusion, video-game makers should not be required to limit the content of their games only be careful that they don't mimic what's going on in the world because some people might be offended. Video games do not lead to violence and I disagree with those people who think the content should be limited. Come on parents, its your job to monitor your kids.

Scoring Explanation

This essay shows a limited understanding of the task.

The writer takes a position on the issue (*Therefore, the content of video games doesn't have to be limited*), but fails to adequately respond to the question (*There are a lot of different video game manufacturers and they should all be responsible for what goes into their games. They should not have to change their games but they should be aware of what's going on in the world*). The essay remains on the general topic of violence in video games (*I think that violent people will be violent regardless of whether they play video games or not. The games do not make them violent*), but does not maintain focus on the specific issue of whether video-game makers should limit the content of violent video games. Examples are used but are very general and are not relevant to the prompt (*My brother plays video games all the time before and after school. He wastes a lot of time but can still get his homework and chores done*). The counterargument to the writer's position is not recognized. The writer also writes a few sentences in colloquial (informal) language (*I mean, he's a really good kid … Come on parents, its your job to monitor your kids*), which is not appropriate for a formal essay. Transitions are rare and simple. The essay is organized into an introduction, a body, and a conclusion, but all sections are underdeveloped and vague. Sentence structure and word choice are simple.

Essay: Score of 2

I think that it is up to parents to have to regulate what kind of violence there child sees on video games. It is not the game maker's dillema. All they have to do is make a fun game. Lots of people can play violent video games and know it's just a game and just for fun and not go out and do violent things like kill people just because they saw it in a game.

A lot of video games are violent and this is the way it has been for a long time and it probably won't change. People just have to except. Some games are more violent then others and it is a person's decision what they play. If a game is too vilent than parents should just not buy it or let them play it. Plenty of people can play these games and be responsible about it and they shouldn't have that taken away from them just because of some crazy kids that couldn't see that it is just a game they is playing.

Parents are supposed to watch there kids and what kinda stuff they are playing and watching. Its not the gamers job. If a game is too violence for there kids, then parents have to not buy or rent that game and then the kid is not playing it at home. There's all ready lots of vilence in movies and TV and that is not going to change so why have to change video games.

Scoring Explanation

This essay shows a limited understanding of the task.

While the essay does take a position (*I think it is up to parents to have to regulate what kind of violence there child sees on video games*) and offer some support for this position (*If a game is too vilent than parents should just not buy it or let them play it … Parents are supposed to watch there kids and what kinda stuff they are playing and watching*), the support is general and underdeveloped. There is no recognition of a counterargument to the essay's position. Run-on sentences (*Lots of people can play violent video games and know it's just a game and just for fun and not go out and do violent things like kill people just because they saw it in a game*) and spelling errors (*dillema, vilent, vilence*) are distracting. The essay employs colloquialisms (*kinda*), which are inappropriate for formal writing. While there is evidence of organizational structure in the essay, the body does not offer enough support, transitions are not used, and the conclusion (*There's all ready lots of vilence in movies and TV and that is not going to change so why have to change video games*) is awkward and abrupt.

Essay: Score of 1

I have decide to write my essay that violence in video games should be limited. If kids play these video games lots and they see this violence than they might do something stupid and violent like what they are seeing on the game. The little kids who see this violent acts might take it the wrong way and go and act violent to there friends or something because they think it is ok to do thanks to a game. I think the people who made the video game coulda just cut down some of the violence and probably still had a good game just less blood and guts. My favorite game to play is Super Speed Baseball and that game has no violence it is just a holesome fun game without all of that stuff. I know lots and lots of kids really like when they playing games with lots of violence because maybe they think it looks cool or something but they should also play games that aren't so violent some times. We don't need a bunch of little kids runnin around and beatin the heck out of each other just because they seen it in video games. I think the people who made these games should be a lot responsible and do something to change all the violence of games.

Scoring Explanation

This essay demonstrates a lack of engagement with the task. While the essay offers a clear position on the issue (*violence in videogames should be limited*) and attempts to support it (*If kids play these video games lots and they see this violence than they might do something stupid and violent like what they are seeing on the game*), the essay fails to flesh out any of this support. For example, the essay states that "*the people who made the video game coulda just cut down some of the violence,*" but it does not specify which game or add any supporting details. The extensive use of colloquial phrases (*coulda, runnin, beatin*) throughout the essay is both distracting and inappropriate for formal writing. The inclusion of the personal anecdote (*My favorite game to play is Super Speed Baseball*) distracts the reader from the issue at hand. Punctuation errors and misuse of verbs (*decide, playing, seen*) are frequent. The essay lacks transitions and organizational structure, and fails to adequately address the prompt task.

PART IV

APPENDICES

APPENDIX A

ACT VOCABULARY LIST

While this is by no means a comprehensive list, it does contain words that have appeared on actual ACT tests, each followed by a sentence or sentences appropriately using the word or a derivation of the word. The words are included here because they have been selected by experienced ACT instructors as representative of the vocabulary level that is expected on the ACT.

A

Absence: state of being away or lacking; inattentiveness

My mom is taking a medical leave of <u>absence</u> from work in order to recuperate from her upcoming surgery.

Absurd: extremely ridiculous or completely lacking reason

The idea that Samantha would fail her test was <u>absurd</u>; she had studied for hours and was completely prepared.

Abundance: great amount

The farmer rejoiced at the <u>abundance</u> of fruit the sunny weather had helped grow that season.

Accommodate: become adapted; make room for; give shelter, lodging, etc., to

The Johnsons built a nursery to <u>accommodate</u> the baby they are expecting.

Accusation: statement of blame

Police hesitate to make direct <u>accusations</u> when there is no evidence that a person has committed a crime.

Acrid: harsh or bitter (as of the taste or smell of something)

Sean immediately turned the engine off when he smelled <u>acrid</u> smoke billowing from beneath the hood of his car.

Acute: quick; precise, intense; sharp; keen

The <u>acute</u> pain in Sarah's wrist kept her from performing even the simplest activity.

Henry is an <u>acute</u> observer who quickly learns the rules of new games.

Adapt: change or modify to suit a particular purpose; change in response to change(s) in the environment

Successful business leaders understand that when markets change for better or worse, companies must <u>adapt</u> to the new conditions.

Adjacent: in the nearest position; next to

Chase took a new job in downtown Chicago but purchased a house in an adjacent suburb.

Aesthetic: (*n.*) visual qualities; (*adj.*) appealing to the senses, especially with beauty

The florist demonstrated an interesting aesthetic in her use of color and texture.

The aesthetic quality of the painting was more appealing than its historical significance.

Affiliation: relationship or association

Many people think Jimmy Hoffa's mysterious abduction and disappearance are evidence of his affiliation with the Detroit mafia.

Agility: the quality of being quick and nimble

Sarah's agility was apparent as she performed her dance routine.

Alienate: to isolate oneself from others or another person from oneself

Gregg often felt alienated from his classmates because of his illness.

Allegiance: loyalty (as to a person, group, country, cause, etc.)

Before being accepted into the exclusive club, inductees must swear their allegiance to the group.

Ambiguous: unclear or capable of having more than one meaning

The student's ambiguous answer left the professor wondering whether the student had studied the assigned material.

Amiable: friendly and pleasant

Joe was very amiable; as a result, he made friends easily at his new school.

Ample: more than sufficient; roomy

The three-bedroom apartment provided ample space for the two room-mates.

Anomaly: something different from the norm or what is expected

Botanists question whether the newly discovered orchid is indeed a new species or just a genetic anomaly with no other examples existing in nature.

Analogous: similar or correspondent in function

The wing of a bat is analogous to the arm of a human, as both species are mammals.

Ancestry: heritage; bloodline; a series of ancestors; developmental history

My aunt has taken it upon herself to uncover the many mysteries of our ancestry.

Anticipate: look forward to; expect

In light of the difficult subject matter, Mr. Mauro anticipated many questions and concerns from his students.

Apathy: lack of any emotion or concern

Mary's apathy showed on her face at sentencing; she looked almost bored as her guilty verdict was read.

Appealing: (*adj.*) attractive or inviting; gerund of (*v.*) *appeal*: request (as of help, a decision, mercy, justice) with earnest; apply for review of a case in a higher court

Although the doctor's invitation to dinner was <u>appealing</u>, Christa had to decline because of prior commitments.

As we speak, mediators are <u>appealing</u> to both sides of the labor dispute to return to the bargaining table before any more profit is lost.

Aristocratic: belonging to or characteristic of the elite, ruling class

Clothing herself in fine lace and diamonds, Marie Antoinette was symbolic of <u>aristocratic</u> privilege.

Articulate: (*v.*) clearly explain; (*adj.*) able to speak clearly; expressed clearly and skillfully

Young children often find it difficult to <u>articulate</u> exactly what they are thinking.

The defense attorney was soft-spoken and <u>articulate</u>.

Assert: demonstrate (as of power, influence, etc.); state with confidence

Parents must <u>assert</u> their authority in matters of their child's health and safety.

Although lightning is a frequent cause of local forest fires, I <u>assert</u> that this one started from a poorly supervised campfire.

Assiduous: constant; characteristic of careful and persistent effort

Only the most <u>assiduous</u> students can expect to become valedictorians.

Assumption: something believed to be true without proof; unstated evidence

The <u>assumption</u> that Sue wore contact lenses was proven false when she told us about how effective her laser eye surgery was in correcting her vision.

Astonishing: amazing or bewildering

The leader's <u>astonishing</u> decision to flee the country threw the country into great turmoil.

Aversion: strong dislike

Kelly has such an <u>aversion</u> to strenuous exercise that she never goes to the gym.

B

Banished: forced to leave

The deposed dictator was <u>banished</u> from his native country.

Beneficiary: recipient of benefits (as of funds, property, insurance payments, etc.)

Carol named her children as the <u>beneficiaries</u> of her life insurance policy so that they would remain financially secure in the event of her death.

Benign: kind, mild, harmless; not cancerous

At the prison, only the most <u>benign</u>, well-mannered prisoners are allowed to bunk in the large recreation hall, complete with cable television, exercise equipment, and reading materials.

Bereave: deprive, especially by death

A car accident bereaved John of his best friend, whose funeral is later today.

Burgeon: sprout (as of new leaves, buds, etc.); grow in size or intensity

Once a vast, empty field, the land now burgeons with high-rent housing, boutique restaurants, and an expansive mall.

C

Capacity: maximum amount that an object or area can hold, contain, endure, etc.; mental ability; function or role

The Italian restaurant had a capacity of 200 people.

Studies have shown that chimpanzees have the capacity to learn bits of human language.

Required always to act in the capacity of a medical professional, each physician in America is bound by oath and law to render aid to victims in any emergency situation he or she may encounter.

Capricious: impulsive; prone to sudden change

Jill's sudden move to Hollywood was considered capricious by the rest of her family.

Catalyst: agent that induces or speeds up a reaction

The catalyst of the statewide manhunt was the expertly crafted rumor that Bob had run away to join the circus.

Chaos: state of complete disarray

Leah lost control of her kindergarten class, and total chaos ensued.

Characteristics: distinguishing attributes or qualities

She had many positive underline(characteristics): a calm temper, kind smile, and sense of humor.

Chronicle: (*n.*) detailed narrative; (*v.*) document or record

The dancer wrote a chronicle of her illness and ultimate recovery.

Several biographers have chronicled the auspicious life of Albert Einstein.

Chronology: list of events arranged by time of occurrence

To fill in the final gap in their chronology of the night's events, investigators had to ask Martha where she was between 9 and 10 P.M.

Coherent: quality of being logical or clear, especially in speech or writing

The patient will become more coherent as the anesthesia wears off.

Cohesiveness: quality of being unified; stickiness

A roster of individually talented players cannot win unless they develop cohesiveness and learn to play as one.

Coincidental: occurring by chance; occurring at the same time

The coincidental meeting of the two old friends was a pleasant surprise for them both.

The two phone calls were coincidental; Patrick could not have made them both.

Commendable: worthy of praise

Hank saved three people in the Los Angeles apartment fire; everyone agrees that his actions were <u>commendable</u>.

Comparison: description or examination of similarities or differences

Anyone who doubts the team's management should look at the statistical <u>comparison</u> between this year's team and last year's.

Competence: the quality of having adequate skill, knowledge, and experience

Margaret's experience and knowledge of the product increased her <u>competence</u> as a salesperson.

Compose: form by placing parts or elements together; create (as of music, writing, etc.); bring (as of oneself, one's mind, one's wits) to a state of calm

This machine <u>composes</u> the toy trucks from all these binfuls of various parts.

Mozart <u>composed</u> many timeless pieces of music.

The emotional advocate had to pause and <u>compose</u> herself before continuing the speech.

Comprehensive: complete; thorough (as of an examination); all-inclusive

In order to complete her science report, Francos prepared a <u>comprehensive</u> list of astronomy books to check out from the library.

Concede: admit or reluctantly yield; to surrender

The presidential candidate decided to <u>concede</u> defeat based on the latest poll results, which had him trailing far behind the leader.

Conducive: favorable or tending to produce (usually used with the prep. *to*)

Limiting fat and cholesterol intake is <u>conducive</u> to good heart health.

Congruence: state of agreeing or corresponding

To prevent anyone from backing out of the arrangement, all three parties must establish in writing their <u>congruence</u> to the terms.

Conjure: bring to mind; produce as if by magic

The poem's vivid language <u>conjured</u> up pictures of turbulent winds and thrashing waves.

The three witches in Macbeth <u>conjured</u> evil spells.

Conscience: the mental sense that guides moral decisions

While all of Christy's friends wanted her to attend the party, her <u>conscience</u> told her otherwise.

Consecutive: occurring in sequence

A victory tonight would make six <u>consecutive</u> wins for the red-hot Cougars!

Consent: (*n.*) permission; (*v.*) authorize (usually used with the prep. *to*)

Medical studies require the informed <u>consent</u> of human test subjects.

After much deliberation, Angela <u>consented</u> to the psychological exam.

Consequence: result of an action

The <u>consequence</u> for cheating was immediate expulsion from school.

Contemplate: consider carefully

Practical people contemplate the potential outcomes of all their actions.

Contemporary: current, modern

Jon used only contemporary resources in his essay, referring to statistics he discovered in recent newspapers and journals.

Context: text or speech that influences the meaning of nearby words or speech

When taken out of context, Sam's statement appeared to be insensitive.

Contradict: assert the opposite

Some members of the community believe the mayor is a hypocrite because his actions contradict his promises.

Contrive: invent; bring about by a plan or scheme; plot (as of evil, crimes, etc.)

Alaskan horticulturists have contrived a greenhouse system for growing delicious tomatoes in the season of nearly constant sunlight.

Converge: meet or come together at a common point

Ambulances, police cars, and fire trucks quickly converged on the scene of the accident.

Cordial: sincere; courteous

The doorman at the luxury hotel offers each visitor a cordial "Good day!"

Correlate: have a mutual relation; establish a mutual relation

Researchers attempted to correlate the length of time a student studies and the grades that he or she receives.

Corroborate: confirm, substantiate with evidence

Further laboratory tests corroborated the scientist's theory that certain trace minerals help maintain good health.

Credulity: tendency to trust too easily

Although Amber's credulity gives her a delightful air of innocence, it also leaves her open to manipulation.

Criterion (pl. *criteria*):   requirements on which judgment is based

Near-perfect vision is just one criterion of commercial pilot certification.

Crucial: extremely important

To be accepted at the university of his choice, it was crucial that David maximize his ACT score.

■ **D**

Decipher: interpret meaning, usually of a code

Jessica could not decipher her father's messy handwriting.

Decry: denounce or criticize

A loyal fan of classical music, Megan decried the trend toward rap and hip-hop.

Delve: search thoroughly; dig (usually used with the prep. *into*)

Humans have not yet developed a submarine sturdy enough to delve into the deepest regions of the oceans.

Derive: infer certain knowledge; originate (usually used with the prep. *from*)

Many new scientific hypotheses derive from existing, proven theories.

Delegate: (*v.*) transfer responsibilities; (*n.*) official representative

Sara knew that the school dance would be most successful if she tried to delegate the various preparation tasks.

The Irish delegate did his best to convey his country's concerns to the French president.

Deliberate: (*adj.*) carefully planned out or executed; (*v.*) consider carefully, especially evidence in a court proceeding

Rana was known for making deliberate attempts to reconcile her friends' broken relationships.

The jury deliberated for only one hour before reaching a verdict.

Demean: lower in worth or dignity

The role of the coach is to express his or her frustrations without demeaning the players.

Demise: end of existence

The demise of the Roman Empire in 476 can be attributed to a combination of social, economic, and governmental factors.

Demur: (*v.*) object

The C.E.O. wanted to fund a massive new headquarters building, but the frugal board of directions demurred.

Descend: to come from a particular origin; to move down from a higher point

Both my maternal and paternal grandfathers descend from British nobility.

The airplane quickly descended for its arrival into sunny Acapulco.

Descendant: a person, animal, or plant that can be traced back to a certain origin; future or subsequent generations

Kerri learned that she is a descendant of English royalty.

Deterrent: hindrance or restraint

Alarm systems have a questionable record as deterrents to car theft.

Devise: (*v.*) design or create (usage note: often confused with the *n.* "device," meaning "tool that fulfills a certain purpose")

I will buy you dinner if you can devise a way to get us out of this predicament.

Diligent: exhibiting great and steadfast effort

Ben trained diligently for the marathon, running at least forty miles per week.

Diminished: made smaller, decreased, or lessened

The prognosis diminished any chances she had of walking again.

Disavow: to deny knowledge of, responsibility for, or association with

I made it a point to disavow the irresponsible actions of my younger brother.

Discern: to differentiate or distinguish; to perceive

The moon's distance from the earth makes it difficult to <u>discern</u> most of the features on the surface of the moon with the naked eye.

Disconcerting: unsettling

Linda found the movie <u>disconcerting</u>; there were too many strange similarities between the plotline and her own life.

Disdainful: scornful

The beauty queen cast a <u>disdainful</u> glance toward the younger girl with messy hair and clothes.

Dispel: alleviate; drive out; disperse

To <u>dispel</u> any rumors that they had broken up, the celebrity couple began a barrage of public appearances together.

Disperse: scatter; spread out

The crowd began to <u>disperse</u> as the concert came to an end.

Disquieting: unsettling

Murder scenes in horror movies are <u>disquieting</u> for Richard.

Dissolution: the process of dissolving; disintegration

The military overthrow of the government was complete after the <u>dissolution</u> of the freely elected legislature.

Distinct: easily distinguishable from others

The boys knew the object could not be a star because it was composed of two <u>distinct</u> points of light that moved across the sky together.

Docile: easy to train, manage, or teach

The normally <u>docile</u> students became very antsy as spring break was approaching.

Drastic: severe; extensive; violent

Unforeseen budget limitations require <u>drastic</u> job cuts in all the company's departments.

Dubious: of questionable character; inclined to doubt

Few Germans foresaw Adolf Hitler's <u>dubious</u> intentions when he first burst onto the political landscape.

E

Egregious: noticeably bad or offensive

William committed an <u>egregious</u> error when he failed to mention his wife during his acceptance speech.

Elaborate: (*adj.*) rich with detail; well developed; (*v.*) expand (as of an idea or argument)

The antique armoire exhibited both <u>elaborate</u> woodworking and sturdy construction.

After handing us the assignment, Professor Albers <u>elaborated</u> on the grading criteria.

Eloquent: very clear and precise; quality of being skilled in clear and precise speech

Ronald Reagan's acting background helped solidify his reputation as an eloquent public speaker.

Embittered: possessing bitter feelings

A harsh life left the widow embittered and friendless.

Emigration: leaving one place and traveling to live in another

Michigan's emigration rate is the second highest in the nation, partly because of increasing unemployment.

Emit: release

Environmentalists protested against construction of the new factory because they feared that the factory would emit too many pollutants into the air.

Empirical: based on or able to be proven by observation and experiment

Conclusions based on experiments need the support of empirical evidence to be accepted in the scientific community.

Emulate: follow an example; imitate

As Lisa entered law school, she hoped to emulate her older sister, who had already become a partner in a prominent law firm.

Endorse: approve; support; sign one's name on

The sports superstar was paid more than $10 million to endorse a new athletic shoe.

Endow: provide (as by donation to a school, church, charity, etc.) a permanent source of income; furnish (as of a talent, skill, power, etc.)

The benefactor endowed the hospital with the funds needed to open a pediatric clinic.

Rachel's mother endowed all her daughters with good looks and personality.

Enigmatic: unexplainable; mysterious

The Mona Lisa is famous for the subject's enigmatic smile.

Enrich: supply with money, riches, etc.; add value; add nutrients (as to soil or processed foods)

The goal of education is to enrich minds and promote positive relationships.

Entangle: twist and tie up in a complicated manner

Climbing roses often become entangled in the fence along which they are permitted to grow.

Enumerate: state things as if counting

At his performance review, the employee listened to his boss enumerate several ways he could improve his performance in the workplace.

Envision: picture mentally

Guidance counselors attempt to have students envision themselves later in life in the working world.

Ephemeral: temporary; short-lived

Considered a one-hit wonder, the pop star experienced ephemeral fame.

Epic: (*n.*) long narrative in verse, usually centered around a hero, as in Greek poet Homer's *Iliad*; (*adj.*) very impressive, heroic, or extraordinary

Beowulf *is an epic comprising about ten percent of all Old English poetry.*

Hundreds of miles from civilization, the downed pilot continued his epic struggle to survive the punishing cold and wind.

Essential: indispensable; necessary

It is essential for college students to develop good study habits in order to succeed.

Establish: create; prove; bring about

Josh hoped his television appearance would help establish his reputation in the music industry.

Ethical: in agreement with the principles of right and wrong

The attorney's ethical guidelines prevented him from defending a client with whom he had prior contact in a related case.

Exacerbate: intensify severity or violence

The terrorist attacks exacerbated the already strained relations between the two countries.

Exceptional: having uncommon qualities

Kevin was an exceptional basketball player and received many offers to play at the collegiate level.

Exhibit: (*v.*) display; (*n.*) something that is displayed; piece of evidence submitted to a court during a trail

The cadet I just interviewed exhibits many of the qualities we desire of new recruits.

The museum's pottery exhibit revealed similarities in the works of ancient potters and modern ceramicists.

Exhort: urge, advise, or caution strongly

After graduating from college, Diana exhorted her parents to lend her the money to start her own business.

Expertise: skill or knowledge in a certain area

The chef's expertise was evident in the succulent flavors and the beautiful presentation of the dish.

Expunge: eliminate or erase

Traffic court will expunge the speeding violation from John's driving record after he pays a $600 fine and does not receive any more tickets for one year.

Exquisite: characterized by great beauty and intricacy

The crown jewels were even more exquisite in real life than they appeared to be in photographs.

Extensive: detailed; far-reaching; long

Paris's underground is snaked with extensive networks of burial tunnels known as catacombs.

Exultant: triumphant

The exultant fans cheered louder than ever when their team captain was handed the championship trophy.

F

Fabricate: fake in order to deceive; make using labor and materials

Much to the surprise of detectives, forensic evidence suggests that the suspect fabricated his claim that he fabricated the weapon.

Facilitate: assist; make easier

To facilitate good relations between the groups, a meeting was held during which all members had an opportunity to speak.

Feign: fake or pretend

Having already heard about the surprise party, the birthday girl knew she should feign astonishment anyway for the sake of the guests.

Fickle: unpredictable and inconsistent

Bob is going to replace that fickle coffee maker, which never seems to brew the same way twice.

Figurative: using symbolic language or illustrations

Sometimes I long for the bare facts without analogies, metaphors, and other figurative language politicians like to use to make government business seem more interesting.

Flourish: (v.) thrive; (n.) dramatic gesture; written embellishment

Orange trees flourish in areas with warm weather.

With a flourish of his baton, the conductor signaled the bold trumpet fanfare.

Forage: (v.) search for food or provisions; (n.) food for horses or cattle

During the cold winter months, many wild animals are forced to forage for scarce food.

The cattle roamed many miles in search of forage.

Foresee: anticipate

Many automotive engineers foresee a world with automated freeways filled with electric cars.

Forgo: refrain from doing something previously planned

A conflict of interest caused the journalist to forgo the original story idea.

Formidable: capable of arousing fear or awe; powerful

The reigning championship team would be a formidable opponent for any team.

Frivolous: unnecessary and silly

Dave's mother lectured him constantly about curtailing his frivolous spending habits in order to begin saving for college.

Frugal: thrifty, not wasteful

My mother was always very frugal, spending less money on food for a month than I spend on food for a week.

G

Garrulous: very talkative

The normally garrulous teenager was very subdued at the party; contrary to her nature, she barely spoke to anyone.

Gaudy: tastelessly flashy

The 1980s are best represented by the bright and gaudy clothing of the decade.

Glib: with ease and slickness, but lacking sincerity

The president's glib remarks about the state of the company's finances resulted in a general sense of unease among shareholders.

Grandiose: of great size or magnitude; pompous

The grandiose palace that the dictator had built for himself mirrored his massive ego.

Gratuitous: for no reason; at no cost

Her gratuitous acts of kindness earned her fondness and respect within the community.

Gullible: easily tricked

Internet scams can easily fool gullible people into giving away valuable personal information.

H

Hackneyed: unoriginal, overused

The hackneyed plot of the television show led to its cancellation after only three episodes.

Haggle: bargain; harass

Stephen haggled with the street vendor to get a better price on a shirt.

Hamper: impede

The lack of a solid business plan often hampers a company's ability to succeed.

Harbinger: sign or omen that foreshadows upcoming events; person who travels ahead to detect the approach of others (such as enemy soldiers)

Cellular phones and the Internet are harbingers of the wholly interconnected world of the future, where privacy is a cherished memory.

Hierarchy: systemic ranking or placement of things in order

The strict social hierarchy prevented even the most talented members of the lower classes from finding high-paying jobs.

Hostile: unfriendly; adversarial

The hostile crowd booed as the opposing team ran out onto the field.

Hypothetical: based on an assumption or a theory

The teacher described the hypothetical situation of a person bouncing a ball on a moving train rather than providing an actual example to illustrate Einstein's theory of relativity.

I

Ideological: relating to the fundamental ideas of an individual or group

Many Americans are disillusioned by the apparent unwillingness of political opponents to reconcile their <u>ideological</u> differences.

Idiosyncrasy: peculiar characteristic

One of the most annoying <u>idiosyncrasies</u> of my computer is that it occasionally restarts without warning.

Immerse: submerge; involve deeply

If not for the prospect of a painful sunburn, I would <u>immerse</u> myself in a book all day at the beach.

Imminent: close to happening; impending

The struggling business is in <u>imminent</u> danger of declaring bankruptcy if sales don't increase soon.

Impartiality: fairness, lack of bias

The court must be satisfied of the <u>impartiality</u> of any potential jurors with regard to specific legal questions.

Implicit: implied, not directly expressed

Although she never had to voice her disappointment, it was <u>implicit</u> in her physical reactions.

Imply: suggest indirectly

High standardized-test scores are viewed to <u>imply</u> excellent potential of a student for further study.

Improvise: do or perform without preparation

Convinced that she was a long shot, Karen had to <u>improvise</u> an acceptance speech when it was announced that she had won.

Inalienable: impossible to take away

Life, liberty, and the pursuit of happiness are some <u>inalienable</u> rights granted by the Constitution to every American.

Inauguration: formal initiation or induction

The President prepared a speech for his official <u>inauguration</u>.

Incarcerate: put in jail or prison

Mark was <u>incarcerated</u> in a maximum-security prison after being convicted of embezzling over $250,000 from the restaurant he managed.

Inclined: disposed to a certain path of thought; sloping

Many people are <u>inclined</u> to stop at yield signs even when there is no traffic on the road.

The new <u>inclined</u> sidewalk allows patrons in wheelchairs to enter the building.

Incorporate: to make a part of

I tried to <u>incorporate</u> both a sense of nostalgia and a sense of a new beginning in the speech I gave to my high school's graduating class.

Incorrigible: impossible to change or reform

The child was <u>incorrigible</u>; he refused to listen when his parents repeatedly told him to stop teasing the dog.

Indifference: total lack of concern or interest

The students' indifference frustrated the teacher, who wanted them to be as excited about history as he was.

Indigenous: native; innate

The Maori are the indigenous people of New Zealand.

Indignant: angry due to unfairness

Leslie became indignant when her professor refused to change the grading error.

Inevitable: impossible to avoid; predictable

After spending the weekend doing everything but studying, it was inevitable that she would fail her exam.

Inexhaustible: plentiful; impossible to use up completely

Physicists hope that one day nuclear fusion will provide an inexhaustible energy source, unlike fossil fuels, which are quickly running out.

Inexplicable: impossible to give the reason for; unexplainable

Inexplicably, although he parked in a no-parking zone all day, he did not get a parking ticket.

Infer: conclude from evidence

Mr. Mauro was able to infer from his employee's attitude that she was not satisfied with her job.

Infuse: soak in a liquid to extract certain substances (as with tea); cause to penetrate; inspire

To provide a more delicate flavor, the chef infused the sauce with whole garlic cloves but then removed them prior to serving.

Ingenious: brilliant and clever

The prisoner's escape plan was quite ingenious, allowing his absence to go unnoticed for several days.

Inherent: naturally occurring; permanent

The inherent risks of driving in a car are surprisingly more severe than those of riding in an airplane.

Inscribe: write or engrave on a surface; write one's name

As I ponder the cemetery, I wonder how many of the dead actually chose what epitaph to inscribe on their headstone.

Insinuate: subtly imply; insert

I can't tell if by buying lots of salad ingredients my husband is insinuating that I'm overweight.

Interpret: translate; explain; derive meaning from

Roger found it difficult to interpret the new engineer's broken English.

Intricate: highly involved or elaborate

The design team understands that even the smallest changes can have major effects on so intricate a plan.

Invaluable: priceless

An *invaluable* collection of ancient artifacts was destroyed when one wing of the museum flooded during the storm.

Involuntary: done without one's consent or against one's free will

Josh shuddered *involuntarily* when the door suddenly creaked open and no one was there.

Irony: outcome of events contrary to what was expected; use of words to convey meaning opposite to the words' literal meaning (similar to and often confused with *sarcasm*, which means the use of irony to insult or scorn)

Watching the cold rain pour down on the beach, Noelle reflected on the *irony* of the situation: "I'm so glad we left sunny North Dakota for this tropical paradise!"

Irreconcilable: impossible to adjust or compromise

After years of trying to solve their problems, the couple decided that their differences were simply *irreconcilable*, and the only solution was divorce.

Irrelevant: not pertinent; outside the scope of a discussion or argument

We are discussing your work schedule in this meeting, so any points you make about your office's location in the building are *irrelevant*.

Irrevocable: impossible to reverse

The destruction of Victorian-era homes to make room for high-rises was an *irrevocable* change to our charming community.

J

Jeopardize: threaten; endanger

Eliza knew that letting her grades slip would *jeopardize* her chances of getting into college.

Judicious: sensible, having good judgment

Kate's decision not to take the advertising job appeared quite *judicious* considering that she had no previous marketing experience.

Juxtapose: place (usually two things) next to each other in order to compare or contrast

The exhibition *juxtaposed* some of the painter's early sketches with some of his later works to show how much his style has changed over time.

K

Keen: quick-witted, sharp

His *keen* sense of smell allowed him to guess what was for dinner long before he reached the kitchen.

L

Languish: exist in a dreadful or gloomy situation; become weak

The convict had been *languishing* in prison for nearly 20 years before new evidence proved his innocence.

Lavish: (*adj*.) elaborate and luxurious; (*v*.) bestow freely and boundlessly

The wedding reception was a <u>lavish</u> affair of fine dining and dancing to a masterful swing band.

My brother advised me to "play it cool" by avoiding <u>lavishing</u> my new girlfriend with compliments.

Lenient: easy-going, tolerant, permissive

Sarah's parents were not <u>lenient</u> at all when it came to grades; she was expected to earn straight A's.

Listless: characterized by a lack of energy and interest

Mr. Roloson thought an activity involving moving around the classroom might awaken his group of <u>listless</u> math students.

Lithe: gracefully slender

Her <u>lithe</u>, athletic figure helped her to excel as a dancer.

Loathsome: causing nausea; disgusting; repulsive

The most junior employee has always undertaken the <u>loathsome</u> task of shoveling solids out of the drainpipe.

Loquacious: very talkative; rambling

Sometimes I have to lie about how busy I am to end telephone conversations with my <u>loquacious</u> sister.

M

Magnanimous: courageous, generous, or noble

Coach Davis was <u>magnanimous</u> in defeat, congratulating the winning team on a game well played.

Malevolent: evil; malicious; wishing harm to others

The villain in the movie was a <u>malevolent</u> old man who would stop at nothing to gain power over the citizens in his community.

Manifest: (*adj*.) clearly recognizable; (*v*.) make clear; (*n*.) list of transported goods or passengers used for record keeping

The workers' displeasure was <u>manifest</u> in the scathing slogans printed on picketing signs.

The illness <u>manifested</u> in the patient's gait and facial expressions.

A thorough review of the ferry's <u>manifest</u> proved that all passengers had made it aboard the life rafts.

Mediocre: lacking any special qualities (usually meaning inferior in quality)

A thorough audition process assures that no <u>mediocre</u> acts are part of the talent show.

Melancholy: (*n*.) glumness; deep contemplative thought; (*adj*.) characterized by or showing melancholy or sadness

Neither Joe nor his psychiatrist could pinpoint the source of his <u>melancholy</u>, but both agree that an exercise regime or an engrossing hobby could help Joe keep his mind from dwelling on his misfortunes.

The demolition of the old stadium was a <u>melancholy</u> affair for those fans who remember all the championships that were won and lost there.

Melodramatic: overly emotional or sentimental

I am tired of all these <u>melodramatic</u> people clouding our negotiations with their fears and regrets.

Mere: small; nothing more

Oh, but he's a <u>mere</u> boy; he shouldn't be expected to know any better at his young age.

Metamorphosis: transformation or change

Upon completing its <u>metamorphosis</u>, the caterpillar emerges from the chrysalis as a butterfly.

Meticulous: devoting a high amount of attention to detail

Janine was <u>meticulous</u> about her appearance and refused to be seen in public without makeup.

Minuscule: extremely small; unimportant

My broken finger seemed a <u>minuscule</u> problem compared to what some people were in the emergency room for.

Mollify: calm or alleviate; soften

The experienced referees attempted to <u>mollify</u> the angry players before a fight broke out.

Monotony: repetition; lack of variety

The <u>monotony</u> of the professor's lecture quickly put many of her students to sleep.

Moral: (*adj.*) based on standards of good and bad; (*n.*) a rule of proper behavior

Many people blame objectionable content in television and video games for the <u>moral</u> decline of America's youth.

Morale: mental well-being; mood

It seemed that boosting the team's <u>morale</u> would be crucial in increasing their chances of winning.

Mundane: common, ordinary; pertaining to this world or the universe as opposed to heaven

Although <u>mundane</u> tasks such as cleaning the house and cooking meals are boring, they are necessary for quality of life.

Munificence: great generosity

The soup kitchen is able to feed over 1,000 homeless people every day thanks to the <u>munificence</u> of its donors.

Mutability: fickleness; liability to change or transform

Soon you will appreciate the <u>mutability</u> of the weather here and remember to keep an umbrella in your car at all times.

N

Naive: lacking experience; exhibiting simplicity of nature and understanding

She was very <u>naive</u> to believe that everything she read in the tabloids was true.

Narcissism: conceit; admiration of oneself

Carrie cringes at her boyfriend's <u>narcissism</u> when he stands and smiles at himself flexing his muscles in a mirror.

Negligent: characterized by carelessness and neglectfulness

The humane society is empowered to seize animals from <u>negligent</u> owners.

Negligible: so small or insignificant that it may be disregarded

Inserting a warm thermometer into a pool of cold water has only a <u>negligible</u> effect on the water's temperature.

Nonchalant: indifferent or unconcerned

Libby's <u>nonchalant</u> manner infuriated the judge, who felt she did not fully understand the gravity of the charges against her.

Nostalgia: sentimental yearning for the past

High school reunions are often marked with feelings of <u>nostalgia</u>.

Noxious: harmful, especially to physical health

Mixing ammonia and bleach would create <u>noxious</u> gases that demand evacuation of the building.

Numerous: existing in great numbers

Admiral Wells called his fleet to retreat after learning just how <u>numerous</u> the opposition force would be.

Nurture: support or help in development

The young parents tried to <u>nurture</u> their toddler's intellectual development by reading five books to him every day.

O

Onerous: very troublesome or oppressive

The police had the <u>onerous</u> task of convincing the kidnapper to set his hostages free.

Onus: burden of responsibility

The <u>onus</u> is on the prosecutor to prove your guilt with evidence.

Ostracize: eliminate from a group

Rachel's friends <u>ostracized</u> her when they found out that she had been gossiping about them behind their backs.

Overt: not concealed

Mark could detect the group's <u>overt</u> hostility from the moment he entered the room.

P

Paradox: self-contradictory statement; something that appears to be self-contradictory, but is nonetheless true

It is a strange <u>paradox</u> that although my university encourages people to ride the bus instead of park on campus, the bus system is entirely funded by parking fees.

Peculiar:	unusual; distinctive of a person or thing
	Red is a <u>peculiar</u> color of shirt to wear with orange pants.
	"Y'all" is a second-person plural pronoun <u>peculiar</u> to the southern United States.
Penchant:	taste (for something); fondness
	Michelle's <u>penchant</u> for designer clothes was something that her meager income could simply not support.
Perceive:	become aware, usually through the senses
	<u>Perceiving</u> the sadness in his voice, I asked him if anything was wrong.
Perfunctorily:	in a manner that suggests little interest or attention
	Staring blankly ahead, Matt <u>perfunctorily</u> tied his shoes, grabbed his backpack, and headed out the door.
Periphery:	outermost boundary of an area
	Paul jogged daily along the <u>periphery</u> of the lake, enjoying the view of the water as he exercised.
Peruse:	examine or review in detail
	Each day Liz <u>perused</u> the classified advertisements in the newspaper, desperately trying to find a job.
Pervasive:	spreading or spread throughout
	Living on a farm, it was impossible to avoid the <u>pervasive</u> smell of cow manure on hot days.
Phenomenon (pl. *phenomena*):	observable fact or event; unusual, significant, or outstanding occurrence
	For centuries, inquiring minds have agonized over the cause of the atmospheric <u>phenomenon</u> known as the Northern Lights.
Plagiarize:	copy another's work representing it as original
	Today, a quick Internet search can identify when a student has <u>plagiarized</u> portions of a research paper.
Plausible:	reasonable, likely
	The detectives dismissed Anne as a suspect because all the facts of her alibi seemed <u>plausible</u>.
Pragmatic:	practical
	She was <u>pragmatic</u> in her approach to applying for the job, thoroughly researching each company prior to an interview.
Preceding:	coming before
	The <u>preceding</u> glossary entry is "pragmatic."
Precipitate:	(*v.*) cause to happen very suddenly; fall (as of a solid) out of liquid solution; rain, sleet, snow, or hail; (*n.*) solid having fallen out of a solution
	Small fractures in the concrete <u>precipitated</u> the collapse of the bridge.
	The chemical reaction resulted in a bright red liquid and a hot-pink <u>precipitate</u>.

Predominant: more noticeable, important, or powerful; most common or prominent

The predominant reason for the huge jump in sales was the millions of dollars pumped into the product's advertising campaign.

Preliminary: preceding or coming prior to

Preliminary election polls predict that Grant will win the election, but we'll have to wait until Election Day to know for sure.

Prerequisite: required beforehand

As a prerequisite for U.S. citizenship, applicants must not have a felony conviction in another country.

Prestigious: honored; reputed

Joey won the prestigious "Associate of the Year" award for posting higher sales than anyone in his region.

Prevail: triumph; overcome adversity

Amy prevailed over fierce competition to become the spelling bee champion for the second year in a row.

Prevalent: widely or commonly occurring or accepted

Poverty is prevalent in societies with unstable economies.

Primordial: happening first or very early; original; constituting the beginning of development

Evolution holds that all creatures descended from one or more ancient, single-celled, primordial organisms.

Procure: acquire

Phoebe managed somehow to procure two tickets to the sold-out concert.

Promulgate: publicize; declare publicly

At the township meeting, the mayor promulgated his beliefs that the new governor was unfit for the job.

Protagonist: main character in a plot

It is difficult to say whether the primary protagonist in the play is the disobedient son or the overbearing mother.

Prototype: original form or model; typical example

Automotive designers create prototypes of car bodies out of clay before fabricating the actual metal panels.

Protracted: lengthy

Mr. Miller took a protracted leave of absence from school to research and write his masterpiece novel.

Prowess: great skill or ability in something

Chandler's athletic prowess was overshadowed by that of his legendary older brother, who was named MVP all four years of his high school football career.

Q

Quasi- (prefix): resembling to some degree

The United States Postal Service is a quasi-governmental agency, which is run like a private company but overseen by Congress.

Quintessential: considered the most typical

The Smiths, having two children, one dog, and a clean house surrounded by a white picket fence, are certainly the quintessential suburban family.

Quixotic: unrealistic, impractical; having extremely romantic views

Heaven knows how these protestors develop their quixotic notions that the war will end simply because they rant and rave about it.

R

Rapid: quick

I found the rapid growth of my mom's plant to be quite surprising considering its little exposure to light and poor soil conditions.

Rapt: completely occupied by or focused on something

The children watched the magician with rapt attention, enchanted by his illusions.

Reciprocate: give and take in equal amounts

After I purchased all of Rachel's groceries for her, it was only fair that she reciprocated by cooking me dinner.

Recount: describe the facts or details of a past event; retell

Mr. Meyer is everyone's favorite science teacher, because no matter what he's teaching, he always manages to recount some of his African safari stories.

Recurrent: taking place over and over

While I enjoy her company, Susanna's recurrent idiosyncrasies get on my nerves.

Redeem: exchange for money or goods; pay off; make amends for

After four hours in the arcade, Max redeemed his 2,000 tickets for a remote-control truck.

Alex's only hope of winning his girlfriend back is by redeeming himself through sweet letters and boxes of chocolate.

Reluctant: unwilling; resistant

The student was reluctant to reveal his poor grades to his mother.

Remedial: intending to correct or remedy

Josh will have to take remedial math courses until he can pass the basic college algebra test.

Reproach: express disapproval

Zach's wife reproached him for spending all of his time watching sports on TV instead of working on the landscaping.

Resolute: definite, determined

Kelly is resolute in her decision to run a marathon this year, despite her current inability to run more than one mile without a break.

Resonant: strong and deep; lasting; echoing

The _resonant_ voices of the choir could be heard several blocks from the church.

Respectively: in the order given

The first, second, and third place titles go to: Sam, Jesse, and Amy, _respectively_.

Rife: prevalent; abundant

As soon as the leak is made, you can be sure that news coverage will be _rife_ with speculation about the identity of the source.

Rifle: (_v._) search through, especially as if looking for something to steal

From the disorder of the apartment, it was clear that whoever went _rifling_ through my drawers and cupboards was looking for hidden valuables.

Rift: split or break

I'm afraid that the fact that Dad didn't leave a will is going to create a _rift_ between my side of the family and our in-laws.

Rudimentary: relating to basic facts; elementary

The child's painting was very _rudimentary_; it did not display the skill of a more accomplished artist.

S

Scrutinize: examine closely

Jenna _scrutinized_ her face in the mirror every morning, hoping that she wouldn't find any new wrinkles.

Seminal: forming the basis for future development; at the beginning; original

Many describe Picasso's Les Demoiselles d'Avignon as a _seminal_ work of Cubism.

Shrouded: covered, concealed

Staci's wedding plans were _shrouded_ in secrecy; she refused to share even the smallest detail.

Simultaneously: happening or existing at the same time

When Jane was hired, she felt _simultaneously_ happy and concerned.

Skepticism: attitude of doubt or disbelief

Miranda's claim of being a psychic was met with _skepticism_ from her friends and family.

Solace: comfort, safety

Paul sought _solace_ from the cold near the roaring fireplace in his living room.

Span: distance, especially between two things, or time, especially between two moments

Bridge engineers take weather, traffic, construction materials, and other factors into account when computing the roadway's _span_ between pylons.

Stagnant: not moving or changing; stale

The water in the pond was <u>stagnant</u> and choked with weeds.

Stoic: indifferent or unaffected

Kevin's <u>stoic</u> expression gave no clue as to what his thoughts were.

Strident: offensively harsh and loud

Few people had the courage to interrupt and object to the speaker's <u>strident</u> commentary.

Subjective: depending or based on a person's attitudes or opinions

I think that my best friend is the greatest actress in the world, although I realize my opinion of her is <u>subjective</u>.

Subsequent: coming next or later

The <u>subsequent</u> glossary entry is "suppress."

Suppress: restrain; reduce

Maria couldn't <u>suppress</u> an excited yelp when the recruiter called to inform her that she had gotten the job.

Sustenance: things that provide nourishment for survival

Meals from fast-food restaurants are high in calories yet provide little <u>sustenance</u>.

Synchronize: adjust to match or occur simultaneously

The lights in the show were <u>synchronized</u> with the pulsing rhythm of the music.

Synthesize: combine to form a new, more complex product

Ideas from all departments were <u>synthesized</u> to create the new operations manual.

T

Tacit: expressed using no words

With a smile, Rob's girlfriend gave <u>tacit</u> approval of his gift of roses.

Tenet: belief that is held to be true by a certain group

The idea of sola scriptura, or "word alone," is a crucial <u>tenet</u> of Protestant idealism.

Tenuous: very thin; consisting of little substance; lacking a logical basis

My sister has a <u>tenuous</u> grasp of physics; she still has many misconceptions of how the physical world works.

Transcend: rise above or beyond; exceed

His hard-earned financial success <u>transcended</u> his humble upbringing.

Transgress: violate (as a law); sin; exceed (as a limit, boundary, etc.)

Joel's edgy stand-up comedy occasionally <u>transgresses</u> the bounds of good taste.

Translucent: allowing light to pass through but clouded or frosted in such a way that objects on the other side are obscured (often confused with *transparent*, which means "clear")

Parishioners love multicolored light cast on the sanctuary floor by the <u>translucent</u> stained glass.

Trivialize: make to appear insignificant

She attempted to trivialize her failing grade by telling her parents that the class was not part of her required curriculum.

▬ U

Uniform: (*adj.*) continuing to be the same, consistent; (*n.*) identical clothing worn by members of a certain group

The teacher used a curve to score the papers, ensuring that the distribution of grades was uniform among the students.

The team's uniforms were blue and white with a red star on the left breast pocket.

Unparalleled: without an equal or comparison

The NBA has produced many gifted players, but I assert that Michael Jordan's talent remains unparalleled.

Unprecedented: having no previous example

The coffee shop franchise was opening new locations at an unprecedented rate, with an average of eight new stores opening per week across the country.

Unsolicited: not requested

Lisa kept walking, trying to ignore the man's unsolicited comments.

Utilitarian: useful or practical

Teenagers love the clothing company's utilitarian designs, which feature durable fabrics and lots of pockets.

▬ V

Variegated: having a variety of colors or marks

Calico cats have variegated coats of many shades of brown, tan, black, and white.

Versatile: having many uses or a variety of abilities

She is a very versatile singer, and is equally as comfortable singing operatic arias as she is singing country-western ballads.

Vindication: act of clearing someone or something from blame

The suspect was vindicated when the person who actually committed the robbery turned himself in.

Virtually: almost completely; in almost all instances; simulated, as by a computer

The scar from my car accident has virtually disappeared over the past few months.

▬ W

Wane: decrease gradually

Randy's interest in his baseball card collection began to wane as he got older.

Wary: cautious and untrusting

Emily shot a <u>wary</u> glance at the man who had been following her for nearly five blocks.

Wily: very sly; deceptive

The <u>wily</u> politician convinced many voters that he had their best interests at heart, when really he only wanted power for personal gain.

Z

Zealous: very passionate or enthusiastic

As a dedicated and honest attorney, Kara remains a <u>zealous</u> seeker of the truth.

APPENDIX B

QUICK REVIEW SHEET

These pages contain useful information about preparing for the ACT English, Reading, and Writing tests. Be sure to read the book and take the practice tests before referring to this sheet. You should tear these pages out of the book and review the information included here prior to entering the testing center. This sheet should not be used as a substitute for actual preparation; it is simply a review of important information presented in detail elsewhere in this book.

GENERAL TEST-TAKING STRATEGIES

1. **Relax.**
   - Don't panic if you are having a hard time answering the questions! You do not have to answer all the questions correctly to get a good score.
   - Take a few moments to relax if you get stressed during the test. Put your pencil down, close your eyes, take some deep breaths, and stop testing. When you get back to the test, you will feel better.

2. **Do the easy stuff first.**
   - You don't have to do the questions from each section in order. Skip the hard ones and come back to them later.
   - Keep moving so that you don't waste valuable time. If you get stuck on a question, move on!

3. **Manage the grid.**
   - Do not go to your answer sheet after each question. Mark your answers in the book, and then transfer them every one to two pages. Pay attention to question numbers, especially if you skip a question. Your score depends on what is filled in on your answer sheet.

4. **Use the test booklet.**
   - Circle your answer choices, cross out answers you eliminate, and mark questions that you

will need to come back to later. If you cannot eliminate an answer choice but think that it might work, underline it.
   - Make notes and marks in the margins on the reading passages as needed.

5. **Be aware of time.**
   - Pace yourself. You learned in practice which questions you should focus on and which questions you should skip and come back to later if you have the time.
   - Time yourself with a watch. Do not rely on the proctor's official time announcements.
   - You have only a limited amount of time. Read and work actively through the test.
   - Stay focused. Ignore the things going on around you that you cannot control.
   - Check over your answers if you have time remaining.

6. **Make educated guesses.**
   - Eliminate answer choices that you know are wrong. The more you can eliminate, the better your chance of getting the question right.
   - Never leave any questions blank on your answer sheet!

7. **Don't change your mind.**
   - Do not second-guess yourself. Your first answer choice is more likely to be correct. If you're not completely comfortable with your first choice, place a mark next to your answer and come back to it later if you have time.
   - Only change your answer when you are sure your first answer is wrong.

ENGLISH TEST STRATEGIES

Apply these strategies to approach the ACT English Test with confidence.

1. You do not have to do the questions in order. Skip the hard ones (often the lengthy ones), circle them in your test booklet, and come back to them later if you have time.

2. The underlined portion of the sentence might need to be revised. Apply the rules of standard written English to determine whether a revision is necessary.

3. If the underlined portion seems correct as it is within the sentence, mark NO CHANGE on your answer sheet.

4. If the underlined portion does not seem correct, try to predict the correct answer. If an answer choice matches your prediction, it is most likely correct.

5. If your predicted answer does not match any of the answer choices, determine which of the selections is the clearest and simplest.

6. Your linguistic intuition is your best asset. Never force yourself to like an answer choice; if it "sounds" funny in your mind, it is almost certainly wrong.

7. The ACT English Test does not reward wordiness. The shortest answer is usually the best answer.

8. No edit that is required on the ACT English Test is optional or stylistic. All edits are necessary ones based on the rules of standard written (American) English.

READING TEST STRATEGIES

Apply these strategies to approach the ACT Reading Test with confidence.

1. Read the question stems (but not the answer choices) first, making notes on the passage when the questions refer to specific lines or words. Do not try to memorize—just get an idea of what you should be looking for in the passage.

2. Read each passage for topic, scope, and purpose (the main idea). Then skim for structure. Try to isolate one topic word or sentence for each paragraph. The details will still be there when you need them. Don't spend precious time trying to "learn" them.

3. Do not stop on unfamiliar words the first time through. You may not need to know the meaning of a word to answer the questions. Remember that you will be rereading most of the passage as you work on the questions.

4. Read the question (again) and the answer choices before making a selection. Answer the questions carefully, referring back to the passage as needed.

5. Try to predict an answer in your own words before looking at the answer choices. If an answer choice matches your prediction, it is most likely correct.

6. Paraphrase when you need to. Putting the question into your own words makes it easier to answer.

7. You do not have to do the questions in order. Skip the hard ones, circle them in your test booklet, and come back to them later if you have time. You may prefer to begin with the questions referencing specific line numbers.

WRITING TEST STRATEGIES

Apply these strategies to approach the ACT essay with confidence.

1. You will have forty minutes to complete this section. Use your time wisely.

2. Carefully read the prompt. Reread as necessary to understand it precisely. Remember that an essay written off the topic will receive a score of zero.

3. Spend about ten minutes planning your essay. Create an outline to keep you on track.

4. Remember that there is no correct position on the topic, so choose the position that you can most strongly support.

5. No matter which position you take, make sure you have compelling reasons and examples to support it. Prioritize your arguments and examples so the best ones make it into your essay. Because of time constraints, be prepared to leave some of your low-priority arguments and examples out of the essay.

6. Leave no holes in your argument. Consider how someone might challenge or question your position.

7. Do not worry about the number of examples included in your essay or the length of your essay. Focus on the quality and cohesiveness of your ideas.

8. With any time remaining after you've finished writing, scan your essay for critical errors of logic, grammar, and word choice. Fix these before turning your attention to less important spelling and punctuation errors.

9. With major edits, you can save time and keep your essay neat by striking out with a single line instead of erasing or making heavy scribbles. Essay graders will disregard any word you strike out.

APPENDIX C

ADDITIONAL RESOURCES

The purpose of this book is to help you prepare for the ACT Verbal Tests—English, Reading, and Writing. While this book provides you with helpful information about the tests and realistic practice materials to get you ready for the real thing, the following additional resources might be useful in your preparation:

ACT, INC.

The ACT website at http://www.act.org offers a wealth of up-to-date information about the ACT.

The Real ACT Prep Guide, published by ACT, is a great source of practice material. This book is usually available at all the major bookstores.

ADVANTAGE EDUCATION

Advantage Education offers many programs for college-bound students, including programs that prepare students for the PSAT, SAT, and ACT, as well as Admissions Counseling and College Preparation. To learn about individual tutoring, workshops, courses, and other programs for college-bound students, visit http://AdvantageEd.com.

Advantage Education has also written *McGraw-Hill Education ACT* and *McGraw-Hill Education 10 ACT Practice Tests*, both available in bookstores. These books include many additional simulated full-length practice tests.

HUMAN RESOURCES

Middle school and high school textbooks are extremely valuable resources. The content areas tested on the ACT are the same content areas that you've been studying in school. Hence, textbooks cover many of the relevant skills and subjects you will need for success on the ACT. If you do not have your textbooks, your school library should have copies that you can use.

Don't forget to talk to teachers and older students who have some experience with the ACT. They might be able to shed some additional light on getting ready for the test. It is in your best interest to be as well prepared as possible on test day.